Prentice Hall **Realidades 2**

Teacher's Resource Book

Temas 5–9

PEARSON

Boston, Massachusetts Chandler, Arizona Glenview, Illinois Upper Saddle River, New Jersey

PEARSON

ISBN-13: 978-0-13-320379-0
ISBN-10: 0-13-320379-4
5 6 7 8 9 10 V056 16 15 14

Table of Contents

Welcome to *Realidades!*

Realidades is based upon the belief that the purpose of learning Spanish is to communicate with people who speak it and to understand their cultures. Across the different levels, ***Realidades*** offers you and your students a variety of print and digital tools that get them communicating from the first day!

Overview of the *Teacher's Resource Book*

This *Teacher's Resource Book* provides detailed support for teaching with ***Realidades.*** The introductory section gives an overview of different program components and teaching tips for using many of them in your classroom. The remaining section provides chapter-by-chapter support including answer keys, scripts, and blackline masters. All pages in this book are available digitally in the Interactive Teacher's Edition and Resource Library DVD and in **realidades.com** in the Teacher eText. For additional teaching support, we invite you to read the front matter articles in the Teacher's Edition and to visit MyPearsonTraining.com for training on using the digital components.

Program Components

The following charts highlight the program components. They provide a brief description of the component and indicate the different formats and locations of each component across our print and digital resources.

Legend:
Audio: Audio Program
EV: ExamView® Assessment Suite CD-ROM
IWB: Activities and Tools for Interactive Whiteboards DVD
PE: PresentationExpress™ Premium DVD
PV: *¡Pura vida!* DVD
TE: Interactive Teacher's Edition and Resource Library DVD
TRB: Teacher's Resource Book
VC: *Videocultura* DVD
VM: *Videomodelos* DVD
VP: Video Program DVD

Student Editions
The ***Realidades*** Student Editions are available in three formats: online, DVD, and print. The eText (on DVD and online within **realidades.com**) contains all the content from the print Student Edition plus embedded audio and video files, flashcards, and study tools. Individual eText activities are also available as assignable assets within the Course Content on **realidades.com**. For details on using the ***Realidades*** eText, visit the training modules on MyPearsonTraining.com.

In addition to the ***Realidades*** eText, **realidades.com** contains the eText edition of the highly acclaimed DK Spanish-English Bilingual Visual Dictionary. This resource gives students access to over 6,000 vocabulary words with audio support. The eText and individual visuals are also available on the Spanish Activities and Tools for Interactive Whiteboards DVD. For schools wanting the print edition of the DK dictionary, it can be purchased separately through PearsonSchool.com or your Pearson representative.

Component	realidades.com	DVD	Print
Student Edition Core instructional tool organized around thematic chapters	eText Course Content	eText	✓
DK Spanish-English Bilingual Visual Dictionary 6,000+ vocabulary words organized by topics	eText	IWB	✓

Workbooks

Realidades provides a variety of differentiated workbooks available in three formats: online, DVD, and print. The workbook activities available within the Course Content on **realidades.com** can be assigned and graded online. For details on assigning and grading within **realidades.com**, visit the training modules on MyPearsonTraining.com.

Component	realidades.com	DVD	Print
Leveled Vocabulary and Grammar Workbook Guided and core practice for new vocabulary and grammar plus puzzles and organizers	Course Content	TE	✓
Communication Workbook with Test Preparation Worksheets for audio and video activities plus reading skills worksheets, reading tests, and Integrated Performance Assessments	Course Content	TE	✓
Realidades para hispanohablantes All-Spanish companion worktext for heritage learners	Teacher eText Lesson Plans	TE	✓

Video, Multimedia, Audio, and Transparencies

Realidades features an outstanding selection of video, multimedia, and audio files accessible to both teachers and students. Resources available in the **realidades.com** Course Content can be assigned to students. Students can also access these resources through their Home Page.

Component	realidades.com	DVD/CD	Print
Video Program Contains the following video segments: • *Videohistoria* • *GramActiva* • *¿Eres tú, María?* (Levels A/B-1) • *En busca de la verdad* (Level 2)	eText Course Content	VP	n/a
Tutorial Videos Detailed grammar explanations; often include comparison of English and Spanish grammar	eText Course Content Tools	n/a	n/a
Videocultura Culture videos per theme in English or Spanish; activities online (Levels A/B-1 and 2)	Course Content	VC	n/a
Videomodelos Short videos of chapter speaking tasks modeled by teens from the Spanish-speaking world	eText Course Content	VM	n/a
¡Pura vida! Storyline video filmed in Costa Rica (Level 3); activities online	Course Content	PV	n/a
Animated Grammar Animations of verb conjugations	Course Content	PE	n/a
Canciones de hip hop Songs to teach new vocabulary and grammar	Course Content	n/a	n/a
Audio Program Audio for Student Edition, *Communication Workbook*, and Assessment Program	eText Course Content	AP	n/a
Transparencies All transparencies are online and on DVD; for vocabulary, grammar, fine art, maps, graphic organizers, and answers	Teacher eText	TE PE	n/a

Geography and Global Positioning

Realidades offers interactive KMZ files that transport students to locations in the Spanish-speaking world using global positioning technology. For details on using KMZ files, visit the training module on MyPearsonTraining.com.

Component	realidades.com	DVD/CD	Print
Mapa global interactivo Downloadable KMZ files with links to locations in Spanish-speaking world and accompanying culture notes and activities	eText Content Library	n/a	n/a
DK Reference Atlas Links to information on the various Spanish-speaking countries	Tools	n/a	n/a

Reading and Common Core

Realidades provides extensive support for helping students learn and apply reading skills and strategies. In addition to the reading support within the Student Edition, the program offers additional resources. For a correlation between ***Realidades*** and the Common Core English Language Arts Standards, visit PearsonSchool.com/Realidades2014.

Component	realidades.com	DVD/CD	Print
Lecturas Sixteen selections with comprehension questions	Teacher eText	TE	✓
Lecturas Teacher's Guide Answers and discussion questions	Teacher eText	TE	✓
Reading Skills Worksheets that practice essential reading strategies; found in the *Communication Workbook with Test Preparation*	Course Content	TE	✓

Grammar

The Grammar Study Guides are a popular "grammar at a glance" study tool. The three-ring punched laminated guides are ideal for placing in binders.

Component	realidades.com	DVD/CD	Print
Grammar Study Guides • Levels 1–2 • Levels 3–4	n/a	n/a	✓

Assessment

The program provides a variety of leveled assessment options available in multiple formats: online, DVD, and print. Assessments available in Course Content can be assigned to students and graded online.

Component	realidades.com	DVD/CD	Print
Instant Checks Auto-graded activities that quickly check for comprehension of new vocabulary and grammar	Course Content	n/a	n/a
Self-test End-of-chapter multiple-choice test	Course Content	n/a	n/a
Pruebas Assignable, auto-graded vocabulary recognition quizzes	Course Content	n/a	✓
Pruebas **with Study Plans** Assignable vocabulary production quizzes and all grammar quizzes; includes auto-assigned remediation and retesting	Course Content	n/a	✓
Examen del capítulo, Examen cumulativo, **Placement Test** Chapter, cumulative, and placement tests (online includes RealTalk!)	Course Content	TE	✓
Assessment Program Front matter, quizzes, tests, rubrics, answer keys, scripts	Teacher eText	TE	✓
Alternate Assessment Program Adapted chapter tests based upon core assessment; ideal for students needing extra help	Lesson Plans Teacher eText	TE	✓
Assessment Program: *Realidades para hispanohablantes* All-Spanish assessment for heritage learners	Lesson Plans Teacher eText	TE	✓
Integrated Performance Assessments Integrated assessments in the test practice section of the *Communication Workbook*	Course Content	TE	✓
Practice Tests Spanish or English readings with multiple-choice responses in the test practice section of the *Communication Workbook*	Course Content	TE	✓

ExamView® Assessment Suite Differentiated test banks per chapter with powerful editing and customization tools	Custom Content (test banks only)	EV	n/a

Planning and Presentation

With ***Realidades***, you have variety of planning and presentation tools in multiple formats: online, DVD, and print. For details on using many of these planning and presentation tools, visit the training modules on MyPearsonTraining.com.

Component	realidades.com	DVD/CD	Print
Interactive Teacher's Edition and Resource Library Teacher's Edition with embedded links to resources; PDF files of program print resources and transparencies	Teacher eText	TE	n/a
PresentationExpress™ Premium Presentational tool for vocabulary, grammar, and review: audio, video, clip art, photo gallery, maps, self-tests, transparencies	n/a	PE	n/a
Activities and Tools for Interactive Whiteboards Activities written in SMART Notebook Express software for practicing new vocabulary and grammar; includes DK Bilingual Visual Dictionary eText, visuals with embedded audio in Image Gallery	Teacher Resources Folder	IWB	n/a
Teacher's Resource Book Provides program overview and key resources in print format	Teacher eText	TE	✓
Transparencies All transparencies are online and on DVD	Teacher eText	TE PE	n/a
Pre-AP* Resource Book Suggestions and activities for preparing students for the AP® Spanish Language and Culture Exam	Teacher eText	TE	✓
TPR Stories Suggestions and activities for integrating TPRS; written by Karen Rowan	Teacher eText	TE	✓

Integrating Technology in the *Realidades* Classroom

Realidades offers teachers and students a wide range of technology tools to plan, teach, practice, explore, assess, and remediate.

Student Technology on realidades.com

realidades.com

Students using *Realidades* have access to a wide range of digital tools on **realidades.com**. These tools include:

- ***Realidades*** eText with embedded audio and video
- ***Realidades*** eText for mobile devices
- *DK Spanish-English Bilingual Visual Dictionary* eText with embedded audio
- Course Content (assignable content)
  - eText activities with embedded audio and video*
  - RealTalk! activities*
  - Leveled Vocabulary and Grammar Workbook*
  - Communication Workbook with Test Preparation*
  - *Mapa global interactivo**
  - *Canciones de hip hop*
  - Animated Grammar
  - Videos: *Videocultura, Videohistoria, Videomodelos, GramActiva, Videomisterio, Videodocumentario, Pura vida,* Tutorial
  - Flashcards
  - Instant Checks*
  - Culture reading tasks*
  - Games and puzzles*
  - Self-test
  - *Pruebas* (with and without Study Plans)*
  - Integrated Performance Assessments*
  - *Examen del capítulo**

* Indicates activities that require computer or teacher grading and must be assigned by the teacher. The scoring feeds into the Gradebook.

For details on using **realidades.com** with students, visit MyPearsonTraining.com under the SuccessNet Plus tab.You will also find important information for using **realidades.com** on home computers and mobile devices.

Teacher Technology on realidades.com

realidades.com

Getting Started on realidades.com

To get started, teachers need to create an account on SuccessNet Plus, the learning management system that serves as the platform for **realidades.com**. Use the following self-registration process to accomplish this:

1. Go to **realidades.com** and register as a new user.
2. Request and/or enter the School Code.
3. Continue self-registration by providing the requested information. Create a unique username and a password.
4. Once your account has been set up, log in using the username and password.
5. Use the provided link to check your computer for compatible browsers, software, etc.
6. Go to MyPearsonTraining.com to learn more details on how to add products, create classes and calendars, and enroll students. You will find extensive resources for teachers, students, and parents related to using **realidades.com** and the many digital tools that come with ***Realidades.***

Management and Instructional Tools

SuccessNet Plus and **realidades.com** offer teachers powerful management, reporting, and customization tools. In **realidades.com**, teachers can:

- Register and create a Home Page
- Add product, create classes, set up calendars, and enroll students
- Assign activities with or without Due Dates
- Personalize and differentiate assignments to individual or groups of students

- Set Preferences such as customizing the grade schema, determining when assignments are due, and setting the number of attempts for an activity
- Assess vocabulary and grammar as well as listening, speaking (using RealTalk!), reading, and writing
- Communicate with students
- Create a wide range of Reports
- Add, Customize, and Create Content

For in-depth training on how to get started and use the many teacher tools on **realidades.com**, visit MyPearsonTraining.com to view the many SuccessNet Plus and *Realidades* Video Modules.

Using realidades.com for Assessment

There are a variety of ways to use the content and tools on **realidades.com** for assessment. The assessments listed below are all assignable through the Course Content. For details, see the information in Program Components. In addition, **realidades.com** offers a variety of assessment templates in the Custom Content: Add Content section.

Formative assessment

- Instant Checks
- *Pruebas* (vocabulary recognition)
- *Pruebas* with Study Plans (vocabulary production and grammar)

Summative assessment

- *Examen del capítulo* (vocabulary, grammar, listening, speaking, reading, writing, and culture)
- *Examen cumulativo* (vocabulary, grammar, listening, speaking, reading, writing, and culture)
- Placement Tests (listening, speaking, reading, writing)

Performance assessment

- Integrated Performance Assessment
- *Presentación escrita*
- RealTalk! *Presentación oral*
- RealTalk! Communicative Pair Activities
- RealTalk! Situation Cards

Teacher Resources Within Pearson Content

Teachers using **realidades.com** have access to same Course Content listed previously in the Student Technology section. Teachers can preview, assign, and customize any of the Pearson Content.

From the teacher Home Page within **realidades.com**, teachers have additional teaching resources in the Pearson Content link. These resources include:

- Teacher eText: includes Student Edition plus all the PDF files found on the Interactive Teacher's Edition and Resource Library DVD. Teachers can link to program resources.
- Teacher Resources Folder that contains:
  - Lesson Plans
  - Teacher's Resource Book
  - Answer Keys: Student Textbook, Core Workbook, Guided Practice Workbook, Assessment Program
  - Vocabulary and Grammar Transparencies
  - Pre-AP* Resource Book
  - *Videomisterio* Teacher's Guide (Levels 1 and 2)
  - Spanish Interactive Whiteboard Teaching Tools
  - *Mapa global interactivo*

Using the *Mapa global interactivo* Files

The *Mapa global interactivo* files uses global positioning technology that enables students to zoom in on the places they are studying across the Spanish-speaking world. To access these files, you need to download them to your computer from the Teacher Resources Folder and use them with third-party global positioning software. For in-depth training on using this technology, visit MyPearsonTraining.com to see the module under *Realidades* ©2014.

Using Activities and Tools for Interactive Whiteboards

The Activities and Tools for Interactive Whiteboards component is available both as downloadable files within **realidades.com** and on a separate DVD. You will find a variety of activities per chapter that provide practice for the new vocabulary and grammar. The activities are written in SMART Notebook Express but can be used on most interactive whiteboards. For detailed information on how to use these activities, please read the information provided within the **realidades.com** folder or on the DVD.

Teaching Support in the *Teacher's Resource Book*

This *Teacher's Resource Book* is divided into two volumes. Volume I contains the teaching resources to supplement the preliminary chapter, called *Para empezar*, and *Temas* 1–4. Volume 2 includes the resources needed for *Temas* 5–9. For your convenience, both volumes are also provided digitally on the Interactive Teacher's Edition and Resource Library DVD and within **realidades.com** in the Teacher eText.

The following resources are provided for each chapter in ***Realidades.***

Theme Project

Each *Tema* has a classroom theme project. These projects span the two chapters within the *Tema* and encourage students to prepare products and presentations directly related to the *Tema* subject matter. These projects help students internalize both vocabulary and grammar, and allow them to apply the language in a performance-based task. The blackline masters in this section introduce students to the theme project and contain instructions for preparing the project. A rubric is also provided for students so that they will understand how the project and presentation will be evaluated. Each project is accompanied by suggestions for integrating 21st Century Skills, including digital tools, into the project. A second rubric has been provided to assess 21st Century Skills. Feel free to integrate these skills into the project as appropriate.

School-to-Home Connection Letter

Parental involvement plays an integral part in student success and in supporting language learning at home. To that end, we provide a model letter for each chapter that you can either photocopy or personalize and send home to parents or guardians.

Videocultura Scripts

This section contains the complete video script in English and Spanish for the *Videocultura* segments. Use these scripts to complement the accompanying video program or as a student comprehension aid in class. You might want to use them to familiarize yourself with the videos before using them in class.

A primera vista Input Scripts

Each chapter of ***Realidades*** has a language input section called *A primera vista: Vocabulario en contexto* that introduces vocabulary and lexical uses of grammatical structures to students. The Input Scripts offer a step-by-step approach to presenting the new terms in a contextualized manner that engages students, yet requires minimal production on the learner's part. They can be followed in their entirety or they can be used as a resource for ideas to supplement the suggestions found in the Teacher's Edition. The Input Scripts are based on the theory of comprehensible input as a teaching tool. (For more information on how to use the Input Scripts, see the discussion under Teaching with Input Scripts on p. xvi.)

Audio Scripts

This section contains the complete script for Student Edition audio including vocabulary, activities, pronunciation, end-of-chapter vocabulary, and *Preparación para el examen*. It also includes the script for the audio activities in the *Communication Workbook with Test Preparation*. The scripts for the listening associated with the chapter tests can be found in the Assessment Program.

Video Scripts

The ***Realidades*** program has a comprehensive video component to support each chapter. The captivating input video for the *A primera vista: Vocabulario en contexto* section, corresponding to the *Videohistoria*, was shot on location in Spain, Mexico, Costa Rica, and Texas, and integrates culture and vocabulary with real-life, often humorous, situational interactions. In addition, ***Realidades*** offers the unique *GramActiva* Videos that explain and practice grammar structures in high-energy, entertaining segments that complement the *Gramática* sections within each chapter. Finally, in Temas 3 to 7, a third video component further engages student interest by means of a suspense-filled mystery story called *En busca de la verdad*. In some cases, you may want to provide copies of the video scripts to students as an aid to comprehension when they view the videos. You may also want to use them to identify specific vocabulary and grammar structures that you want to focus on in the videos before you show videos in class.

Communicative Pair Activities

These Communicative Pair Activities blackline masters focus on student-to-student involvement where students have some control over the communicative elements. They allow for personalization and individualization, and often allow students to share real information. They practice communication and help students become comfortable interacting in a second language. Although a given activity may focus on particular vocabulary or structures, the emphasis is always on using language to give or obtain information. These activities have been designed to complement the ones found within ***Realidades*** and are meant to help students develop better communicative skills. (For more information on these blackline masters and how to use them, see Teaching with Communicative Pair Activities on p. xvi.)

You also have the option to record the Communicative Pair Activities within **realidades.com** using RealTalk! Each Communicative Pair Activity can be assigned from the Course Content (located in the *¡Adelante!* folder). Students can open the activity and print off the PDF for *Estudiante A* and *Estudiante B*. The PDF is identical to the copy in this *Teacher's Resource Book*. This gives you the option of printing it yourself for students, or having them print it in preparation for completing the activity. Students record their conversation and send it to you for evaluation. For details on using RealTalk!, visit MyPearsonTraining.com and view the video module.

Situation Cards

The Situation Cards blackline masters are designed to help students build confidence and develop skills as they work toward the goal of communicative proficiency. These guided conversations will provide your students with the opportunity to complete real-life tasks in Spanish. They will build confidence in even the most uncertain or reluctant students, and will enable more talented students to be truly creative with the language. There are a total of 38 pairs of Situation Cards, two per chapter. (For more information on these blackline masters and how to use them, see the section Teaching with Situation Cards on p. xvii.)

You also have the option to record the Situation Cards within **realidades.com** using RealTalk! The activity can be assigned from the Course Content (located in the *¡Adelante!* folder). Students can open the activity and print off the PDF for *Estudiante A* and

Estudiante B. The PDF is identical to the copy in this *Teacher's Resource Book*. This gives you the option of printing it yourself for students, or having them print it in preparation for completing the activity. Students record their conversation and send it to you for evaluation. For details on using RealTalk!, visit MyPearsonTraining.com and view the video module.

GramActiva Blackline Masters

The *GramActiva* reproducible masters are templates and graphic organizers to be used in conjunction with specific hands-on activities in the Student Edition. These blackline masters require students to create products or to use charts, graphs, and other visual aids such as Venn diagrams, word webs, and surveys. They are referenced at point of use in the Teacher's Edition. Depending on the activity, you may want to pass these out the day before so students can fill them in or otherwise prepare for using them.

Vocabulary Clip Art

The Vocabulary Clip Art offers reproducible images of the visualized vocabulary in each chapter of ***Realidades***. These visuals can be used in a variety of ways to provide students with a hands-on opportunity to work with the new vocabulary. Engaging students in activities in which they "see, hear, say, and do" will help more students learn the new words and phrases. The Clip Art is available online. You can also access digital images of this vocabulary through the Interactive Teacher's Edition and Resource Library DVD. You will find this visualized vocabulary used through the program:

- PresentationExpress™ Premium DVD
- Flashcards (eText)
- Leveled Vocabulary and Grammar Workbook: Guided Practice

Leveled Vocabulary and Grammar Workbook

Answer Key: Core Practice

The Answer Key for the *Core Practice* activities allows you to quickly check the answers so students can have quick feedback. You may wish to reproduce these as a classroom set that you keep in a resource center or hand out so students can check their own work. You can also access pages with the answers displayed on the PresentationExpress™ Premium DVD.

Answer Key: Guided Practice

These are reduced pages of the *Leveled Vocabulary and Grammar Workbook: Guided Practice*. You can use them yourself to check work, or reproduce them in booklet form or on overheads so that students can check their own work. You can also access these pages on the PresentationExpress™ Premium DVD.

Communication Workbook with Test Preparation

Answer Key: Writing, Audio & Video Activities

These are reduced pages of the Writing, Audio & Video Activities with the answers printed on them. You can use them yourself to check work, or reproduce them in booklet form or on overheads so that students can check their own work. You can also access pages with the answers displayed on the PresentationExpress™ Premium DVD.

Answer Key: Test Preparation

This page provides answers for the Reading Skills worksheets and the Practice Test. Please note that answers to the Integrated Performance Assessments will always vary. The rubrics that you can use to assess student performance are given right on the student's page so that the students can see how they are to be evaluated.

Teaching Tips for the *Teacher's Resource Book*

Teaching with Input Scripts

The Input Scripts are based on the notion of comprehensible input. Rather than putting pressure on students to produce complex sentences with their newly acquired vocabulary and structures, they are given opportunities to show their comprehension through minimal responses. These responses range from physical responses (such as pointing to images in their textbook or manipulating the Vocabulary Clip Art images found in this *Teacher's Resource Book*) to short verbal responses (such as answering yes-no questions or questions with a choice of two answers) to short, structured conversations.

Input Vocabulary: This section provides a script for presenting the vocabulary in *Vocabulario en contexto*. The vocabulary from both pages may be presented at once, or it may be broken up into two presentations. For example, in the *A primera vista* for *Capítulo 2A*, a boy's daily routine is presented on one page, while a girl's daily routine is presented on the facing page. In this case, the Input Scripts present the two sets of vocabulary separately. The emphasis in this section is on presenting the new terms in a creative fashion.

Input Dialogue/Monologue: In the *A primera vista*, grammatical structures are presented in context through dialogues and monologues. Although they are quite short, many key concepts are embedded in the dialogues. The goal of this section of the Input Scripts is to help you present the dialogues in manageable sections that allow you to stop and ask students minimal-response questions that target the key grammatical concepts.

Comprehension Check: This section provides additional activities to help you gauge how well students understand the vocabulary and grammatical structures presented. Additionally, this section reinforces learning through high-interest games and other activities.

Teaching with Communicative Pair Activities

Learning a foreign language does involve learning important linguistic skills, such as grammar, syntax, and spelling, but also involves developing communicative skills, such as the ability to carry on a conversation in the target language, the ability to make a brief oral presentation, and the ability to communicate through written language.

These communicative activities focus primarily on listening and speaking skills—those skills that are more difficult to acquire outside of the classroom. Most of the activities are completed in pairs. One type of activity *(Actividades en grupo)* is intended for small groups of students. Students must communicate with each other to complete the activities. They ask and answer questions, role-play different scenes, share opinions on a variety of topics, and exchange real, but limited, information. In short, they use language in realistic situations that do not involve the teacher or a recording.

Activity Types: There are nine basic types of communicative activities included in this book: *Con otro(a) estudiante* (Partner Practice), *Descubrir ...* (Discovery), *Diagramas* (Diagrams), *Entrevista* (Interview), *Hacer un papel* (Role-Play), *Opiniones* (Opinions), *Opiniones y reacciones* (Opinions and Reactions), and *Tres en raya* (Tic-Tac-Toe).

General Guidelines: Because most true communication takes place between two people or in small groups, most of the activities are to be used by pairs of students. You will want to determine the assignment of partners for the activities to be completed by student pairs. Also, you will want to have partners for a week or more, but partners should change at least once a month. Working together for several activities helps students get to know each other and learn to work together; changing partners at least once a month prevents students from getting too comfortable and wasting time. Reassign partners if a partnership simply doesn't work out, for whatever reason. Before students begin an activity, check to make sure that everyone understands the directions. As students complete these activities, keep in mind that most conversation, even in one's native language, involves hesitation, mispronunciation, and errors. These will occur more frequently while learning a second language. Remember that these activities are not intended as grammar practice, but are designed as conversational activities to practice communication. If you notice consistent errors while students are working, make brief notes and review the relevant structures after the activity has been completed. Although difficult, it is best not to comment on errors while students are completing the activities. Students should be focusing on communication, not on structure.

Teaching with Situation Cards

The Situation Cards are designed to focus on the chapter's communicative objectives while integrating the vocabulary and grammar. In addition, they guide an exchange between two students, in which Student A initiates the conversation and Student B responds (both students know what the general topic is, but neither knows exactly what the other one's instructions are). Finally, they provide a structured role-play with opportunities for personalization and open-ended conversation.

Using the Situation Cards: The Situation Cards are most successful when students have already worked with the vocabulary and grammar. You will see the cards referenced in the *Repaso del capítulo* section of the *Teacher's Edition*. There are a variety of ways to use the Situation Cards. You can photocopy them, cut them out, and paste them on 3 x 5 cards. Some teachers copy them directly onto colored paper and use a different color for each level. Other teachers laminate them for use as class sets. Use the cards for extended oral practice at the beginning of the class, as a warm-up, as practice for the speaking section of the *Examen del capítulo* (found in the Assessment Program book that is also part of the ***Realidades*** ancillary program), as informal speaking practice, or as the chapter's formal assessment for speaking proficiency. The Situation Cards also work well as a review for an end-of-quarter or final exam or at the beginning of the following year.

Directions:

1. Organize the students in pairs.
2. Distribute the cards. You can give each pair both situations to work on or you can give one situation to a pair of students and then have them exchange with another pair when completed.
3. Quickly brainstorm vocabulary and expressions that might be helpful in completing the tasks on the Situation Cards.
4. Start the activity. Remember that Student A will always initiate the conversation. Keep the activity within reasonable time limits. Three to seven minutes is ideal.
5. Circulate to verify that students are on task. This is also a good moment to informally assess students' level of comfort with the vocabulary and the speaking task, and to decide whether any reteaching is necessary. Do not correct errors at this point.
6. Signal when students should stop. You may ask them to reverse roles. Or you may devise a "traffic pattern" in which each pair of students puts their two cards together and exchanges them with another pair of students.

Assessment for Situation Cards: The Situation Cards can be used as a tool for informal or formal assessment. Students can act out the conversation with the partner with whom they practiced, with an assigned partner, or with the teacher.

Assessment can be based on a single criterion or on several different ones. For informal assessment, you might want to choose from any of the following criteria: completion of the task, appropriateness, comprehensibility, originality, quality above and beyond base expectations, individual improvement, group improvement, accuracy, or fluency. For a more formal assessment tool, see the *Scale for Evaluating Writing/Speaking Proficiency*, found in the *To the Teacher* section, pp. T1–T9, of the Assessment Program book. Whatever system you use, be sure to share it with your students before the assessment begins so that they will understand how they are to be graded.

Finally, once students have become accustomed to the Situation Cards, you might encourage them to write their own.

The use of these Situation Cards is a motivating and effective tool for guiding students to a level of increased comfort and confidence, and to a quality performance in the very challenging process of developing speaking proficiency.

Teaching with the Vocabulary Clip Art

The following ideas for using the Vocabulary Clip Art are only a sample of the many ways in which it can be used. You will probably devise additional ways to get students physically involved with learning and practicing new vocabulary. You will need to make copies of the art for each student to participate in these activities. You may wish to laminate one or two complete sets for permanent classroom use.

Homework Assignment: Have students use the visuals to create flashcards. They can cut and paste the visuals on cards and write the Spanish word on the back of the card.

Picture Dictionary: Have students write the Spanish word for each picture on photocopies of pages as art of a "picture dictionary." These pages can be kept in a notebook that can be used as a valuable reference or review tool for students.

Assess Listening Comprehension: Begin by simply identifying a word on a page and by having students identify objects. Describe an object and have students point to it. Tell a story using the visual and have students point to vocabulary words in the story or indicate the sequencing through drawing lines or arrows. You might want to make an overhead transparency so that you (or a student) can be at the overhead doing both activities at the same time.

Additional Assessment of Listening Comprehension: Have students work in pairs to use the ideas in the prior bullet item. Circulate to keep the students on task and assess pronunciation and comprehension. Do not correct errors at this point; rather, use this time to determine areas needing further work.

Individual Images: Have students cut out the individual pictures and keep them in their notebook in a large zippered freezer bag that is three-hole punched. Here are some ideas for using the individual images:

1. Repeat the activities in the "Assess Listening Comprehension" section, and have students sort through the individual images to indicate comprehension. For example: If you say the word *lápiz*, students should place the picture for "pencil" in the center of their desks and then continue to add the pictures for objects you call out. Cut up the overhead transparency of the vocabulary art so that you (or a student) are at the overhead manipulating the image simultaneously with the students.
2. Have students work with each other saying the vocabulary words, telling stories, and

asking questions. For example, a student might say, *"Dame el libro."* The partner should use the visuals to perform the action. Getting each student to manipulate the vocabulary images is an excellent way to assist learning.

3. Have students draw a background for the visuals, such as a classroom. Have them sit back-to-back, and have one student arrange objects in a certain order. He or she then tells the partner where each item is located. For example, one student can tell the partner, *La silla está delante de la mesa*. The other student can ask questions, but should not see the layout of the objects until he or she thinks the placement is correct. Students can then compare layouts.
4. Encourage students to color in the pictures or personalize them and use them to decorate their compositions.
5. Have students create their own Bingo cards using the visuals. Have each student create a grid of five down and five across. Students then place 25 visuals in any order. Have one student be the "caller" and call out different vocabulary words. Students turn the words over on their grids until one has five down, across, or diagonally. The winning student names the vocabulary pieces he or she turned over and becomes the next "caller."
6. Use the individual pictures as an oral vocabulary quiz. Have students name each image as he or she lays them on the desk in front of you. Students who do not feel confident with all the chapter's vocabulary may select a handful of images and name those visuals for you.

Teaching Tips for the Test Preparation Section of the *Communication Workbook with Test Preparation*

The Test Preparation section reinforces the language arts skills and test-taking strategies needed for success on high-stakes exams. The activities in this section practice these key skills and strategies while building proficiency in Spanish.

Reading Skills Worksheets

For each chapter, you will find two worksheets that focus on core reading skills. Each activity allows students to practice the reading skill with existing activities from the corresponding ***Realidades*** chapter. These are important worksheets to use if you want to emphasize teaching students to read or if your school or district has an initiative to support reading across the curriculum or support for the Common Core. The Reading Skills worksheets can be completed in the print *Communication Workbook with Test Preparation*. In addition, all worksheets can be assigned to students within the Course Content in **realidades.com** and graded online.

Practice Tests

To further reinforce reading skills, the Test Preparation section of the *Communication Workbook* provides a reading passage for each chapter followed by three question types: multiple choice, short response, extended response. Each Practice Test can be completed in the print *Communication Workbook with Test Preparation*. In addition, all Practice Tests can be assigned to students within the Course Content in **realidades.com** and graded online.

Multiple Choice Multiple choice questions always have four answer choices. Students pick the one that is the best answer. Answers to the multiple choice questions are included in this *Teacher's Resource Book*.

Short Response This symbol appears next to questions that require short written answers:

This symbol appears next to questions requiring short written answers that are a creative extension based on the reading:

It is suggested that students take approximately 3 to 5 minutes to answer a Short Response question. These types of questions are called "performance tasks" and require that students read all parts of the question carefully, plan their answer, and then write the answer in their own words. A complete answer to a Short Response question is worth 2 points. A partial answer is worth 1 point or 0 points. The Short Response questions on the student test preparation pages are written in either English or Spanish. Students are instructed to respond in English when the question is in English and in Spanish when the question is in Spanish. Sample top-score Short Response answers are included in this *Teacher's Resource Book*.

Extended Response This symbol appears next to questions requiring longer written answers based on information that can be inferred from the reading:

This symbol appears next to questions requiring longer written answers that are a creative extension based on the reading:

It is suggested that students take about 5 to 15 minutes to answer an Extended Response question. These types of questions are also called "performance tasks" because they require that students read all parts of the question carefully, plan their answer, and then write the answer in their own words. A complete answer to an Extended Response question is worth 4 points. A partial answer is worth 3, 2, 1, or 0 points. The Extended Response questions on the student test preparation pages are written in either English or Spanish. Students are instructed to respond in English when the question is in English and in Spanish when the question is in Spanish. Sample top-score Extended Response answers are included in this *Teacher's Resource Book.*

How the Test Will Be Scored

Multiple Choice Questions

Multiple choice answers are either right or wrong. Students receive 1 point if the correct answer is selected.

Performance-Based Questions (Short Response and Extended Response)

Short Response and Extended Response questions, which are called "performance tasks," are often scored with rubrics. Sample rubrics follow. These rubrics describe a range of performance and students receive credit for how close their answers come to the anticipated response.

Rubric for Short Response Questions

READ THINK EXPLAIN

READ THINK CREATE

2 points The response indicates that the student has a complete understanding of the reading concept embodied in the task. The student has provided a response that is accurate, complete, and fulfills all the requirements of the task. Necessary support and/or examples are included, and the information given is clearly text-based. Any extensions beyond the text are relevant to the task.

1 point The response indicates that the student has a partial understanding of the reading concept embodied in the task. The student has provided a response that may include information that is essentially correct and text-based, but the information is too general or too simplistic. Some of the support and/or examples may be incomplete or omitted.

0 points The response is inaccurate, confused, and/or irrelevant, or the student has failed to respond to the task.

Rubric for Extended Response Questions

READ
THINK
EXPLAIN

READ
THINK
CREATE

4 points The response indicates that the student has a thorough understanding of the reading concept embodied in the task. The student has provided a response that is accurate, complete, and fulfills all the requirements of the task. Necessary support and/or examples are included, and the information given is clearly text-based. Any extensions beyond the text are relevant to the task.

3 points The response indicates that the student has an understanding of the reading concept embodied in the task. The student has provided a response that is accurate and fulfills all the requirements of the task, but the required support and/or details are not complete or clearly text-based.

2 points The response indicates that the student has a partial understanding of the reading concept embodied in the task. The student has provided a response that may include information that is essentially correct and text-based, but the information is too general or too simplistic. Some of the support and/or examples and requirements of the task may be incomplete or omitted.

1 point The response indicates that the student has very limited understanding of the reading concept embodied in the task. The response is incomplete, may exhibit many flaws, and may not address all the requirements of the task.

0 points The response is inaccurate, confused, and/or irrelevant, or the student has failed to respond to the task.

Using the Practice Tests

Practice Test and Answer Key Format

There is one Practice Test for each *tema* in Level 2. For each test, you will find three parts:

- reading selection
- questions
- response sheet

The student tests for *Communication Workbook with Test Preparation* are not reproduced in this *Teacher's Resource Book.* You will need to refer to the student workbook for copies of the tests. Answers to each test for *Temas* 5–9 appear in this *Teacher's Resource Book.*

Practice Tests

There is one reading per *tema.* This reading incorporates the themes and content of each *tema* (e.g., school, shopping, leisure activities).

The readings incorporate the chapter vocabulary and grammar and are most useful after completion of the *temas* for which they were written. Of course, these selections add the challenge of reading in Spanish to the other strategies used on reading tests. Encourage students to employ the same strategies used when reading in English (see "Tips for Improving Your Score" on pp. 204–207 of the Introduction to the *Communication Workbook with Test Preparation*). You will notice that the multiple choice questions are written in English. This practice is supported by research stating that students can demonstrate reading comprehension more effectively when the follow-up questions are in English and they are allowed to respond in English. The Short Response and Extended Response questions are generally written in English prompting an English response. Responses in English again allow students to demonstrate comprehension and allow them to practice reading skills, such as comparing and contrasting, recognizing cause and effect, and identifying author's purpose, required for success with standardized tests. This practice recognizes that beginning-level students do not have the proficiency in Spanish to respond to such in-depth questions.

Integrating the Practice Tests with Instruction

Decide when you want to use a practice test within your lesson plan. You can use the tests during class time or as homework assignments. Be sure to review with students how the test questions will be scored, including how the rubric is used. Students have a copy of the rubrics on pp. 207–208 of their workbook. Allow approximately 25 minutes for students to take the test. Grade the multiple choice questions as a whole-class activity and discuss the correct responses, or collect the papers and grade them on your own. The answers are provided in this *Teacher's Resource Book.* However, to grade the Short or Extended Response questions, it is suggested that you collect the papers and grade them using the rubrics and the sample top-score responses provided in this *Teacher's Resource Book.* When you return the tests to the students, you might want to share the sample top-score responses and discuss how they could best construct a response that earns the highest score on the rubric.

Preparing Students for Standardized Tests

Teaching Students to be Good Test-Takers

Many students are not successful on standardized tests because they lack the skills and strategies employed by good test-takers. You can use the strategies found on pp. 204–207 of the Introduction to the *Communication Workbook with Test Preparation* to review with students prior to administering the first practice test. It is helpful to remind students of these strategies each time that they take a practice test.

Success for ALL Students

Helping Students Raise Their Test Scores

The *Communication Workbook with Test Preparation* provides each teacher with complete support to prepare students for success on standardized tests. Students learn valuable test-taking tips, practice taking tests and responding to various types of questions, learn why a response was correct, and learn how to better shape their responses in the future. Over time, they will become more comfortable with taking standardized tests. In addition, the high-interest readings will enable students to expand their knowledge and understanding of the cultures of the Spanish-speaking world while building important reading and writing skills.

Table of Contents

Tema 5: En las noticias
Capítulo 5A: Un acto heroico

Capítulo 5B: Un accidente

Theme Project

En las noticias

En las noticias

Overview:

You will write and present a news brief about a fictitious accident, heroic act, or natural disaster. You must use the preterite and the imperfect and include information about:

- where, when, and how the event happened
- who was hurt and how
- who intervened to help

You must include a poster or other visual aid to help present your report.

Resources:

Digital or print photos, page layout/word processing software and/or poster board, markers, photos, glue or tape, scissors

Sequence:

STEP 1. Review instructions with your teacher.

STEP 2. Submit a rough draft of your news brief. Work with a partner and present your drafts to each other.

STEP 3. Create layouts, leaving room for photos and descriptions.

STEP 4. Submit a draft of your news brief.

STEP 5. Present your completed news brief to the class.

Assessment:

Your teacher will provide you with a rubric to assess this project.

Theme 5 Project: En las noticias

Project Assessment Rubric

RUBRIC	Score 1	Score 3	Score 5
Evidence of Planning	No written draft or sketch layout provided.	Draft was written and layout created, but not corrected.	Evidence of corrected draft and layout.
Use of Illustrations	No photos/ visuals included.	Very few photos/visuals included.	Several photos/ visuals included.
Presentation	Contains details that develop ideas about the event.	Gives two sentences about the event, the injuries, and the resolution.	Gives three or more sentences each about the event, the injuries, and the resolution.

21st Century Skills Rubric: Promote Communication

RUBRIC	Score 1	Score 3	Score 5
Eye contact	Neglects to engage the audience; rarely makes eye contact	Occasionally engages the audience by making eye contact	Actively engages the audience by making eye contact
Body language	Neglects to engage the audience; rarely uses movement to focus attention and interest	Occasionally engages the audience by movement to focus attention and interest	Actively engages the audience by using movement to focus attention and interest
Voice	Does not speak clearly/loudly	Usually speaks clearly/loudly	Always speaks clearly/loudly

Realidades 2

Capítulo 5A

School-to-Home Connection

Dear Parent or Guardian,

The theme of our current unit is *En las noticias* (In the news). This chapter is called *Un acto heroico* (A heroic act).

Upon completion of this chapter students will be able to:

- discuss emergencies, crises, rescues, and heroic acts
- discuss past situations and settings
- describe weather conditions
- understand cultural perspectives on natural disasters

Students will also explore:

- using accent marks to separate diphthongs

Our textbook, *Realidades,* helps with the development of reading, writing, and speaking skills through the use of strategies, process speaking, and process writing. In this chapter, students will:

- read about an earthquake in Chile
- speak about an accident scene

To reinforce and enhance learning, students can access a wide range of online resources on **realidades.com,** the personalized learning management system that accompanies the print and online Student Edition. Resources include the eText, textbook and workbook activities, audio files, videos, animations, songs, self-study tools, interactive maps, voice recording (RealTalk!), assessments, and other digital resources. Many learning tools can be accessed through the student Home Page on **realidades.com.** Other activities, specifically those that require grading, are assigned by the teacher and linked on the student Home Page within the calendar or the Assignments tab.

You will find specifications and guidelines for accessing **realidades.com** on home computers and mobile devices on MyPearsonTraining.com under the SuccessNet Plus tab.

realidades.com

For: Tips to Parents
Visit: www.realidades.com
Web Code: jce-0010

Check it out! At the end of the chapter, have your child tell you four things he or she would do in case of a fire. Then ask your child if he or she remembers the last natural disaster talked about in the news.

Sincerely,

Videocultura Script

Contra la contaminación

Spanish version:

Con más de 20 millones de habitantes, la Ciudad de México es una de las mega ciudades del mundo.

Hace casi 70 años, la Ciudad de México tenía un cielo despejado y un aire puro. Hoy día, las montañas y volcanes no se pueden ver, causa de la contaminación del aire que sufre la ciudad.

La mayor causa de contaminación en México es el tráfico. La emisión de gases contaminantes causa daño al medio ambiente y a la salud de la gente cada día.

Por suerte, al igual que otras ciudades del mundo, la Ciudad de México hace importantes esfuerzos por reducir la contaminación.

La principal estrategia para reducir el problema del transporte es el programa "Hoy no circula", que incentiva a las personas a no usar su auto durante un día de la semana. Otros esfuerzos incluyen la revisión del estado de los autos y la reducción de plomo y sulfuro en la gasolina.

El problema de la contaminación ha alcanzado niveles exorbitantes. Pero los mexicanos hacen un esfuerzo consciente y trabajan por estabilizar y mejorar la situación.

English version:

Mexico City is one of the largest urban areas in the world, with an estimated population of over 20 million people.

Before the 1940s, Mexico City was known for its clear air and spectacular views of snow-capped volcanoes. Today, due to air pollution, the city's mountains are rarely visible.

The biggest source of pollution in Mexico City is the exhausts from millions of cars, buses, taxis, and trucks. Emissions of pollutants from these vehicles take their toll on the environment and people's health.

But as in many other big cities of the world, Mexico City is making important efforts to reduce air pollution.

For example, the government has implemented a program called "Hoy no circula." One day every week, residents are not allowed to drive their personal automobile.

In addition, the government has increased inspection of vehicles' condition and emission levels. Lead and sulfur levels in fuel have been reduced, and catalytic converters are now mandatory.

Pollution levels have reached a crisis point, but Mexicans are determined to work together to stabilize and improve the situation.

Input Script

Presentation

Input Vocabulary 1 and Dialogue: Before the day of the presentation, enlist the help of friends to videotape you giving the news broadcast shown in *A primera vista.* Each natural disaster you describe will occur in the studio where you are filming your broadcast. Begin by reading the text about the hurricane. Have your friends turn a fan on high to scatter the papers on your desk. Gather your papers and regain your composure. Next read the text about flooding in Honduras. Have your friends squirt water from squirt guns in your direction. Have them throw torn up bits of white paper as you read about the snow in Chile. When you read about the earthquake, have your friend doing the videotape shake the camera. Dive under your desk for cover and then come back out nervously. Finally, read the news about the apartment fire. You might have a friend light an incense stick off camera so that the smoke wafts by you. Sniff the smoke with alarm and say: *¡Parece que hay un incendio en mi edificio de apartmentos que está al lado de la estación de noticias! ¡Me voy para ayudar a mi vecina que vive en el segundo piso! ¡Ella tiene 82 años y no va a poder escaparse! ¡Adiós!* Run off camera.

Play the video for students one time through. Then distribute copies of the Vocabulary Clip Art and have students tear the natural disasters into individual images. Replay the video and have students hold up the images of the disasters as they are mentioned.

Input Vocabulary 2: Place the transparency of the newspaper article on the screen. Open a real newspaper and pretend to read the article from the paper. As you read the article, act outraged because the man in the article, Carlos Arroyo Medina, is taking credit for saving a woman in an apartment building fire, when you were the one who really saved her! Distribute copies of the Vocabulary Clip Art showing terms from the article. Describe your version of the rescue story and have students hold up the appropriate Clip Art images as you mention them.

Comprehension Check

- Using a cell phone or play phone, pretend to make 911 phone calls to report the natural disasters from *A primera vista.* Describe them without saying the actual words for the disasters. Have students hold up the Clip Art image of each disaster.
- Prepare short news stories about people involved in natural disasters. Use the verbs and expressions from the news article about the apartment fire in your news stories. Give some of the stories happy endings and a few sad endings. Have students indicate with a "thumbs-up" or "thumbs-down" sign if each story has a happy or a sad ending.

Audio Script

Audio DVD, Capítulo 5A

Track 01: *A primera vista, Un acto heroico,* Student Book, p. 240, (3:25)

Vocabulario y gramática en contexto

Lee en tu libro mientras escuchas la narración.

Hoy hubo un incendio que destruyó unos apartamentos. No sabemos la causa del incendio, pero se cree que comenzó a causa de una explosión. Un vecino valiente ayudó a una señora a salir de su apartamento. Afortunadamente, no había más gente en el edificio. Llegaron los bomberos y apagaron el incendio después de unas horas. En otras noticias…

Hubo un terremoto en el sur de México. Dicen que más de cien personas se murieron en este desastre.

Ayer el huracán Gabriel llegó a la costa de Honduras cerca del pueblo de La Ceiba. Llovió por doce horas.

Hubo muchas inundaciones en Honduras a causa de las tormentas de lluvia, pero dicen que todos los habitantes están vivos.

En Chile, nevó durante tres días y las carreteras están cerradas.

Vas a escuchar cada palabra o frase dos veces. Después de la primera vez hay una pausa para que puedas pronunciar la palabra o frase. Luego vas a escuchar de nuevo la palabra o frase.

el edificio de apartamentos	los bomberos
quemarse	la locutora
el noticiero	la escalera
el incendio	el humo

Track 02: *A primera vista,* Student Book, p. 241, (2:28)

Vocabulario y gramática en contexto

Lee en tu libro mientras escuchas la narración.

La Prensa

Un héroe local

Carlos Arroyo Medina es un héroe según sus vecinos porque le salvó la vida a una señora de ochenta y dos años. Ayer ocurrió un incendio en su edificio de apartamentos. El señor Arroyo le cuenta a nuestra reportera lo que pasó:

Estaba delante del edificio y vi el humo. Pensé inmediatamente en la señora Hurtado que vive en el segundo piso. Tiene ochenta y dos años y yo sabía que no podía escaparse. Un vecino mío llamó por teléfono para pedir ayuda.

Entré corriendo y subí la escalera hasta llegar a su apartamento. Traté de abrir la puerta pero no pude. Creí que la señora Hurtado estaba dormida o, peor, muerta. Pero ella se escondía entre los muebles de su apartamento y gritaba "¡Socorro!" De repente pude abrir la puerta y entré en el apartamento.

Bajamos de prisa la escalera y nos escapamos del incendio. Lo que hice no fue un acto heroico. Ayudé a mi vecina, nada más. Ella también es heroína.

Vas a escuchar cada palabra o frase dos veces. Después de la primera vez hay una pausa para que puedas pronunciar la palabra o frase. Luego vas a escuchar de nuevo la palabra o frase.

Más vocabulario

a causa de	de repente
de prisa	el artículo

Track 03: *A primera vista,* Act. 1, Student Book, p. 241, (1:55)

¿Quién es?

Vas a escuchar las noticias. Señala con el dedo la noticia que se describe en la página anterior. Vas a escuchar las frases dos veces.

1. Hubo un terremoto en Nicaragua.
2. El incendio destruyó una casa en el centro de la ciudad.
3. Tres personas se murieron en el huracán que pasó por Cuba.
4. Un bombero le salvó la vida a un niño de tres años.
5. Muchas personas dicen que vieron humo detrás de la escuela.
6. Más de veinte personas se murieron en unas inundaciones en Venezuela.

Track 04: *A primera vista,* Act. 2, Student Book, p. 241, (4:20)

El noticiero de San José

Escucha las noticias y escoge la respuesta correcta.
Vas a escuchar las frases dos veces.

Noticia 1

Hoy hubo en terremoto muy cerca de la Ciudad de México. Nadie se murió pero el terremoto destruyó una escuela y unos edificios de apartamentos.

1. ¿Cuántas personas se murieron en el terremoto?
   a. muchas personas   b. nadie
2. ¿Qué destruyó el terremoto?
   a. una escuela   b. una tienda

Noticia 2

Un policía le salvó la vida a un señor de ochenta años. Hubo un incendio en su casa y el policía entró en la casa y le ayudó a salir.

1. ¿Quién le salvó la vida a un señor?
   a. un bombero   b. un policía
2. ¿Qué ocurrió en la casa del señor?
   a. un incendio   b. un terremoto

Noticia 3

Hoy el huracán Miguel llegó a la costa de la República Dominicana. Hubo inundaciones a causa de la lluvia y del viento. Se murieron más de cincuenta personas.

1. ¿Qué pasó en la costa de la República Dominicana?
   a. un incendio   b. un huracán
2. ¿Cuántas personas se murieron?
   a. más de cuarenta   b. más de cincuenta

Track 05: *Videohistoria,* Student Book, pp. 242–243, (2:14)

En el noticiero

Lee en tu libro mientras escuchas la *Videohistoria.*

See Student Book pages 242–243 for script.

Track 06: *Manos a la obra,* Act. 5, Student Book, p. 244, (2:30)

Escucha y escribe

Escucha las seis frases de un locutor que da las noticias del incendio que se describe en la Actividad 4. Escribe las frases. Después, con otro estudiante, pongan en orden estas frases siguiendo el orden de la Actividad 4 para contar lo que ocurrió. Vas a escuchar las frases dos veces.

1. Un paramédico ayudó al señor a bajar la escalera.
2. Afortunadamente el edificio de apartamentos no se quemó completamente.
3. Los vecinos oyeron la explosión y estaban asustados.
4. El incendio comenzó en el apartamento de una anciana.
5. Cuando entraron los bomberos, el señor se escondía en el baño.
6. A causa de la explosión, muchas personas gritaban "¡Socorro!"

Track 07: Audio Act. 5, Writing, Audio & Video Workbook, p. 91, (7:12)

Listen as these radio announcers break into regular programming to report emergency situations that have occurred. Match each radio report with one of the pictures below to indicate what type of emergency or crisis situation each was. Then, try to answer the bonus question in the last column for each news report. You will hear each report twice.

1. **Adult Male 1:** Estoy aquí en el centro de la ciudad a las dos y cinco de la tarde. Muchos edificios se quemaron completamente. Ah… Aquí tenemos al señor Morales… Señor Morales, todos sus vecinos dicen que usted es el héroe del día.
   Adult Male 2: ¿Un héroe? No. Solo ayudé a mi vecino, el señor Quiroga. Él estaba dormido cuando el incendio empezó. Cuando se despertó, no podía ver ni la puerta ni las ventanas a causa del humo. No podía escaparse. Yo corrí a su apartamento y lo bajé a la calle.
2. **Adult Male 3:** Jorge Ramos, informando desde la ciudad de Ponce. Hoy, en horas de la mañana, los vecinos de la ciudad sufrieron los efectos de un terremoto con resultados horribles. Un momento… el bombero López tiene más información para nosotros…
   Adult Male 4: Sí, el terremoto destruyó varios edificios en el centro de la ciudad, incluyendo un edificio de apartamentos. Afortunadamente, toda la gente de los apartamentos salió del edificio a tiempo.
3. **Adult Male 5:** Estamos en la ciudad de Vail, Colorado. Todas las carreteras a Vail están cerradas porque nevó por una semana sin parar. Los vecinos de Vail no tienen ni comida ni agua a causa de las condiciones de las carreteras. ¿Qué nos puede decir, sargento Pérez?
   Adult Male 6: La gente de Vail está muy asustada. Nos dicen que viene otra tormenta de nieve en dos días. Necesitamos ayuda inmediata para los vecinos de la ciudad. ¡Necesitamos su ayuda!
4. **Adult Male 7:** ¡La lluvia no para! Hay inundaciones en muchos pueblos de la costa de México. Sólo los botes pueden ir de un lugar a otro. Los voluntarios de la Cruz Roja Internacional están ayudando a los mexicanos afectados por la lluvia. Señor Hernández, ¿cuál es su trabajo?
   Adult Male 8: Soy voluntario de la Cruz Roja Internacional. Salvo las vidas de la gente que no puede escaparse de sus casas. Esta mañana, un niño pedía ayuda desde el tejado de su casa. Pude bajarlo al bote para llevarlo al hospital.
5. **Adult Male 9:** Tenemos más información sobre el desastre que ocurrió en Puerto Vallarta. El huracán Gabriel llegó a Puerto Vallarta ayer en la mañana. Llovió por casi veinticuatro horas. Hay muchas inundaciones a causa de la intensa lluvia. Todas las carreteras están cerradas. Muchas personas que vivían cerca de los ríos murieron porque no tenían a dónde ir.

Track 08: Audio Act. 6, Writing, Audio & Video Workbook, p. 92, (4:03)

As Ernesto is driving home from work, he turns on the radio and starts to scan for his favorite type of music. Each time he finds a station, a reporter is in the middle of the evening news report. As you listen, write the number of the excerpt under the corresponding picture. You will hear each report twice.

1. **Adult Male 1:** …y las últimas noticias de hoy. En la avenida Fúnebre hubo un incendio en la casa de Bernarda Alba. Los bomberos llegaron pronto así que pudieron salvar la casa, pero la mitad de la casa se quemó. Por suerte nadie se lastimó.
2. **Adult Female 1:** Ahora tenemos noticias acerca del huracán Felipe. Felipe ahora está pasando por la parte sur del estado, con una velocidad de ciento veinte kilómetros por hora.
3. **Adult Male 2:** Y ahora el pronóstico del tiempo. Mañana se espera un día lluvioso y frío, con una tormenta por la tarde.
4. **Adult Female 2:** En el norte del estado, la gente se está recuperando del terremoto de ayer, que destruyó más de doscientos edificios y casas.
5. **Adult Male 3:** La inundación en la parte oeste de la ciudad es la más grave que hayan visto los residentes de esa área en muchos años. Las fuertes lluvias pronosticadas para mañana…
6. **Adult Female 3:** Buenas noticias para los niños. Anoche nevó por seis horas sin parar. Todas las escuelas de la ciudad están cerradas hoy. Todas las carreteras alrededor de la ciudad están cerradas también. Es muy peligroso en las calles de los barrios…

Track 09: Audio Act. 7, Writing, Audio & Video Workbook, p. 92, (6:55)

A local jewelry store manager is holding a contest for young couples who purchase their wedding rings in his store. If there is bad weather on their wedding day, the manager promises to refund the couple the cost of their rings! Listen as each couple describes their wedding day. Which couples would qualify for a refund? Mark your answers in the grid below. You will hear each description twice.

1. **FEMALE VOICE 1:** Eran las cinco de la tarde cuando los invitados empezaron a llegar. Me sentía un poco nerviosa, pero todo parecía perfecto… las flores, mi vestido y, claro… mi novio, Javier.
   MALE VOICE 1: Pero de repente, hubo una explosión y mucho humo por todas partes.
   FEMALE VOICE 1: Sí. Fue horrible. Pero Javier me rescató y me llevó afuera.
2. **MALE VOICE 2:** La semana pasada el pronóstico del tiempo para nuestro día era perfecto: iba a hacer fresco con mucho sol. Era muy importante, porque nuestra boda iba a ser en el jardín de mi abuela.
   FEMALE VOICE 2: Pero durante la ceremonia, comenzó a llover. Era un desastre. Todos los invitados corrían hasta la casa y alguien se cayó encima del pastel de boda.
3. **FEMALE VOICE 3:** Ayer fue un día muy importante para nosotros. Eran las seis de la tarde cuando la ceremonia comenzó. Toda la gente estaba muy contenta por nosotros. La iglesia era la más elegante de la ciudad. ¡Qué lindo!
   MALE VOICE 3: Después de la ceremonia en la iglesia tuvimos nuestra fiesta. Muchos invitados querían un poco del pastel de boda, pero era muy pequeño. ¡Qué horrible!
4. **MALE VOICE 4:** Ayer llamé a mi hermano porque él trabaja para el Canal 4 y escribe el pronóstico del tiempo para la televisión. Me dijo que el tiempo era perfecto en mi día especial. Yo estaba muy contento porque quería un día inolvidable.
   FEMALE VOICE 4: ¡Qué horrible! Eran las ocho cuando comenzó a llover. Ninguno de los invitados pudo llegar a la iglesia a causa de la fuerte lluvia. Fue el peor día de mi vida.
5. **FEMALE VOICE 5:** Todo estaba listo para nuestra boda. Los invitados estaban en la iglesia. La ceremonia comenzaba cuando, de repente, vimos un pequeño incendio en la iglesia.
   MALE VOICE 5: Los invitados querían correr hacia la salida pero llovía muy fuerte. Una persona apagó el fuego. Todas las personas en la iglesia estaban asustadas.
6. **MALE VOICE 6:** Nuestra boda fue perfecta. El pronóstico del tiempo decía que no iba a llover el día de la boda. Toda la familia estaba muy contenta. ¡Ay!, pero yo tenía tanta hambre.
   FEMALE VOICE 6: Sí, mi novio estaba muy nervioso; por eso comía y comía sin parar. ¡Qué gracioso! Fue el mejor día de mi vida.

Track 10: *Manos a la obra,* Act. 15, Student Book, p. 250, (2:03)

Escucha y escribe

En una hoja de papel, escribe los números del 1 al 4. Vas a oír una conversación sobre un desastre. Mientras la escuchas, escribe las frases. Vas a oír la conversación dos veces.

ADULT MALE: Cristina, ¿oíste de la explosión en la escuela?
ADULT FEMALE: Sí, Pablo, oí algo en la radio pero no lo creí.
ADULT MALE: Pues yo leí un artículo en el periódico. ¡Es increíble!
ADULT FEMALE: Estoy de acuerdo. Dicen que destruyó el gimnasio y la cafetería.

Usa la conversación que escribiste en el Paso 1 y contesta las siguientes preguntas con frases completas.

1. ¿Dónde ocurrió la explosión? ¿Qué destruyó?
2. ¿Quién oyó de la explosión en la radio?
3. ¿Pablo leyó sobre la explosión en la Red o en el periódico?
4. ¿Los dos jóvenes creyeron la noticia fácilmente?

Track 11: *Pronunciación,* Accent marks to separate diphthongs, Student Book, p. 254, (1:44)

Remember that a single syllable called a diphthong occurs when *i* or *u* appear together or in combination with *a*, *e*, or *o*. Listen to and say these words:

causa	**muerto**
destruir	**oigo**
valiente	**hacia**

We use a written accent when the vowels that form what would otherwise be a diphthong need to be pronounced separately. Listen to and say these words:

oí	**creímos**
sabía	**país**
leíste	**envío**
país	

Refrán
Explica lo que quiere decir este refrán.
Consejo no pedido, consejo mal oído.

Track 12: Audio Act. 8, Writing, Audio & Video Workbook, p. 93, (4:40)

When it comes to the news, some people prefer to listen to the radio while others would rather read the newspaper. Listen to people talk about recent events. Determine whether they heard about it on the radio or if they read about it in the newspaper. Place a check mark in the appropriate row of the grid. You will hear each conversation twice.

1. **TEEN MALE 1:** Había muchos heridos, ¿no?
   TEEN MALE 2: Creo que sí. Mi hermano me llamó por teléfono y me dijo que lo oyó en las noticias. El huracán llegó a la costa de la Florida hace una hora, con un viento tan fuerte que algunos coches terminaron encima de unas casas.
2. **ADULT FEMALE 1:** ¿Murieron dos bomberos?
   ADULT FEMALE 2: Sí. Esos hombres valientes trataban de subir al quinto piso para salvar a una anciana. Leí en el artículo del periódico que el edificio de apartamentos se

destruyó en un instante y ellos murieron.

3. **Adult Male 1:** ¿Qué pasó en Guadalajara?
   Adult Male 2: Llovió por tres días. Hubo muchas inundaciones. Afortunadamente, todos los vecinos del lugar están bien. Leí que Guadalajara es una zona de desastre. La lluvia destruyó muchas casas y algunos edificios.
4. **Teen Male 3:** ¿Cómo? No puede ser. ¡Imposible!
   Teen Female 1: Sí. Un terremoto destruyó la casa de tu abuela. Los vecinos de tu abuela me dijeron que fue horrible. Luego oí que afortunadamente un bombero le salvó la vida. El bombero llegó a tiempo para sacarla de la casa.
5. **Adult Female 1:** ¿Las carreteras cerradas? ¡No!
   Adult Female 2: Todas las carreteras a la ciudad de Matamoros están cerradas. Hubo inundaciones a causa de un huracán. Llovió por una semana. Lo leí en el periódico de la mañana. No puedes ir a Matamoros.

Track 13: Audio Act. 9, Writing, Audio & Video Workbook, p. 93, (3:09)

Your teacher has asked you to listen to the news on a Spanish-speaking radio station. First, read the questions below. Then, listen to a news report of a hurricane that occurred yesterday in a small town near San Juan. As you listen to the story, circle the correct answers below. Your teacher might ask you to write a summary of the news story based on your answers. You will hear the report twice.

Adult Female: Carmen Dominó informando desde Dorado, Puerto Rico, para el noticiero del Canal 4. El huracán Felipe llegó a las costas de Puerto Rico ayer por la noche. ¡Qué sorpresa tan grande para los puertorriqueños! Muchas personas estaban dormidas cuando llegó el huracán. El huracán destruyó el pueblo de Dorado completamente. Los vecinos de Dorado perdieron sus casas y muebles a causa de las inundaciones. No tenían ni comida ni agua. Había basura por todas partes. Ciento cuarenta y cuatro personas murieron en las aguas de Felipe. Los vecinos de Dorado estaban muy asustados. Afortunadamente, los bomberos y la policía de Puerto Rico fueron los héroes en este desastre. Estos hombres y mujeres valientes les salvaron la vida a muchas personas que no podían escaparse de sus casas. El presidente de los Estados Unidos de América estaba muy triste cuando dijo que este fue el peor desastre en muchos años.

Vas a escuchar esta narración otra vez.

Track 14: *Repaso del capítulo*, Student Book, p. 262, (7:09)

Vocabulario y gramática

Escucha las palabras y expresiones que has aprendido en este capítulo.

See Student Book page 262 for vocabulary list.

Track 15: *Preparación para el examen*, Student Book, p. 263, (1:05)

Escuchar

Practice task

Listen as a talk-show host interviews a young woman who recently escaped from a dangerous situation. See if you can understand: a) what happened; b) what time it was; c) what she was doing at the time; and d) who she considered to be the hero of the day.

Female Voice: Era horrible. Tenía mucho miedo. Almorzaba en la cocina en mi edificio de apartamentos. Escuchaba la radio cuando, de repente, oí una explosión muy cerca. En este instante, miré el reloj. Eran las dos de la tarde. Afortunadamente, un bombero me vio y subió hasta mi ventana. Gracias a él, estoy viva hoy.

Video Script

A primera vista: *En el noticiero*, (4:13)

Raúl: ¡Espera! A ver, el canal con el noticiero. Creo que vi algo interesante.

Tomás: ¿En el noticiero?

Raúl: Sí, sí, mira. Anoche hubo un incendio en una casa. A ver… ¡Caramba!

Tomás: ¿Y ahora qué?

Raúl: ¡Esa casa está a dos calles de aquí!

Tomás: Qué interesante…

Raúl: Por supuesto que es interesante. ¡Tenemos que ir a verla!

Tomás: ¿Por qué? No quiero salir ahora…

Raúl: Vamos. Quiero saber lo que pasó.

Raúl: Increíble. Vamos, Tomás. De prisa. Mira, allí está la reportera.

Tomás: ¿Qué ocurrió?

Raúl: No sé. Vamos a investigar.

Firefighter: Buenos días, chicos.

Raúl: Acabamos de ver el noticiero y venimos a ver qué pasó.

Reporter: Les habla Laura Martínez, del Canal Cinco. Aquí con nosotros está el señor Roberto Sánchez, del servicio de bomberos. ¿A qué hora empezó el incendio?

Firefighter: No estamos seguros. Sobre las dos de la mañana.

Reporter: ¿Cómo comenzó?

Firefighter: Pensamos que hubo una explosión.

Reporter: ¿Una explosión de gas?

Firefighter: Ahora estamos investigando la causa. Es temprano para saber.

Reporter: ¿Había alguien en la casa?

Firefighter: Sí. Una familia de seis personas.

Reporter: ¿Hubo algún herido?

Firefighter: Afortunadamente, no. Estaban un poco asustados, pero nada más.

Reporter: ¡Increíble!

Firefighter: Sí. Un vecino vió el humo… También vinieron los paramédicos… Afortunadamente, pudimos rescatar a todos.

Reporter: Muchas gracias al señor Roberto Sánchez. Vamos a hablar ahora con dos vecinos.

Reporter: Y, Uds., ¿cómo se llaman?

Raúl: Pues, Raúl Padilla Salazar.

Reporter: ¿Y tú?

Tomás: Tomás.

Reporter: ¿Viven cerca de aquí?

Raúl: Más o menos.

Reporter: ¿Oyeron el incendio? ¿O vieron el humo?

Tomás: Pues, en la televisión…

Reporter: ¿Cómo?

Raúl: Estábamos viendo la televisión en casa, y cuando vimos el noticiero…

Reporter: Entonces, ¿no saben nada sobre el incendio?

Raúl: La verdad, no…

Reporter: Esto es todo por ahora. Laura Martínez, desde Calle 21, para el Canal Cinco.

***GramActiva* Videos, (6:45)**
The imperfect tense: other uses

Therapist: You are going deep, deep into your memory. Remember, the imperfect tense can describe an event when something happened.

Host V.O.: Yes, I remember…

Host V.O.: *Estaba en la ducha cuando comenzó a llover.*

Handyman: You can use the imperfect tense to talk about other things. It's very handy. We'll cover three of them—the time, the weather, and feelings.

Handyman: Time!

Host V.O.: *Eran las ocho cuando vi la explosión.*

V.O.: *Eran las seis cuando llegó mi esposo.*

Handyman: The weather!

Host V.O.: *Ayer llovía cuando fui al trabajo.*

Host V.O.: *Hacía frío en la Antártica.*

Handyman: Feelings!

V.O.: *La niña tenía miedo.*

Host V.O.: *Estaba cansado pero quería ayudar a la niña.*

Therapist: Three, two, one, and you are awake and feeling better now. So that's our three other uses for the imperfect tense: the time, the weather, and a whole bunch of feelings. Hmm…I'm getting another feeling. I feel like a quiz is coming up.

Quiz

V.O.: Complete the following sentences. Use the imperfect tense.

(ser) ______ las tres de la mañana.
Eran las tres de la mañana.
(hacer) ______ frío cuando ocurrió el incendio.
Hacía frío cuando ocurrió el incendio.
(estar) La bombera no ______ asustada.
La bombera no estaba asustada.

The preterite of *oír, leer,* and *creer*

Typewriter Host: *¡Oye!* Today, we're going to cover the preterite of three important verbs: *oír, leer,* and *creer*.

Newspaper Host: Good news, bad news. Bad news: *Oír, leer,* and *creer* all have spelling changes when they're in the preterite. Good news: The spelling changes are the same.

Guitar Guy : Why, why, why, do the *usted, él* and *ella* use a *y*?
Why, why, why do the *ustedes, ellos, ellas* use a *y*?

Gal: 'Cause they're irregular.

Old Man: What?

Crowd V.O.: *¡Oír!*

V.O.: *Oí. Oíste. Oyó. Oímos. Oísteis. Oyeron.*
Notice something? All forms but *oyeron* have an accent.

V.O.: *Oí la tormenta.*
¿Tú oíste la explosión?
La bombera oyó la sirena.
Oímos a alguien que gritó "¡Socorro!"
¿Qué oísteis?
Ellos oyeron el ruido.

Old Man: Next up, *leer*, "to read." Why won't the Martians leave us alone?

Crowd V.O.: *¡Leer!*

Alien V.O.: *Leí. Leíste. Leyó. Leímos. Leísteis. Leyeron.*

V.O.: *Leí el libro.*
Leíste la carta.
Leyó la tarjeta.
Leímos las revistas.
Leísteis el menú.
Leyeron los cuentos.

Old Man: You know what I think? I believe there's one more verb coming.

Crowd V.O.: *¡Creer!*

Lincoln V.O.: *Creí. Creíste.Creyó. Creímos. Creísteis. Creyeron.*

Old Man: Oh, I remember now. I think I've had enough of conjugating verbs. Let's listen to a young couple in love.

Guy: *¡Oí algo!*

Girl: *No oigo nada.*

Guy: *De verdad. Oí un ruido.*

Girl: *No oí ningún ruido.*

Guy: *Yo sé que oí algo.*

Girl: *Estaba aquí. No oíste nada.*

Guy: *Creo que tienes razón.*

Girl: *¡Espera! ¡Espera! ¿Oyes eso?*

Guy: *¡Sí! Es…*

Guy and Girl: *¡La prueba!*

Quiz

V.O.: Quiz time. Fill in the blank with the appropriate preterite form of the verb.
(leer) Usted ______ el artículo.
Usted leyó el artículo.
(oír) Ellos ______ la explosión.
Ellos oyeron la explosión.
(oír) Ayer nosotros ______ un programa musical.
Ayer nosotros oímos un programa musical.
(creer) Yo ______ que era inteligente.
Yo creí que era inteligente.

Videomisterio: *En busca de la verdad,* Episodio 5, (8:27)

Linda's V.O.: Al día siguiente recibí una llamada de Julio.

Julio: Buenos días, Señora Toledo.

Carmen: Bueno… Hola, Julio. Sí, un momento. Es para ti.

Linda: Bueno… Ah, Julio, claro que me acuerdo que vamos a comer juntos hoy. ¿Dónde?

Julio: Linda, ¿cómo estás? Pues, en la Plaza San Fernando hay un buen café, La oreja de Van Gogh. Al lado del Jardín Unión, muy cerca del hotel. Si quieres, puedo pasar por ti a las dos.

Linda: Bueno. Aunque yo puedo preguntar en la recepción. Hay un joven muy amable…

Julio: Sí, lo conozco… Oye, mejor paso por ti un poco antes… ¿A la una y media?

Linda: Está bien.

Linda: ¿Bueno?

Roberto: Hola, Linda. Habla Roberto.

Linda: Hola, ¿qué tal?

Roberto: Bien. Oye, ¿te gustaría dar una vuelta por Guanajuato? Puedo enseñarte algunas cosas de la ciudad.

Linda: Roberto, me encantaría, sólo que Julio me invitó a comer.

Roberto: Y después, ¿estás ocupada?

Linda: No sé qué planes tiene mi mamá… un momento.

Linda: Mamá, ¿qué vamos a hacer esta tarde?

Carmen: Quiero descansar hoy. Tengo que hacer varias llamadas.

Linda: Mi mamá quiere descansar. Puedo ir contigo.

Roberto: Bien. ¿Y dónde vas a comer con Julio?

Linda: En el café La oreja de Van Gogh. Si quieres, nos podemos ver allí a las dos.

Roberto: Umm, mejor a las tres. Así Uds. pueden terminar de comer.

Linda: Está bien.

Julio: La comida de aquí es muy buena. Aquí están los platos del día.

Linda: Crema de elote… Pozole… Ay, no sé qué pedir. Todo parece delicioso.

Julio: Pues yo te recomiendo las enchiladas mineras o las flautas de pollo, si quieres probarlas.

Linda: Bueno, voy a probar las enchiladas mineras.

Julio: Hola, Josefina, ¿qué tal?

Server: Bien, Julio.

Julio: Voy a pedir una sopa azteca, y para mi amiga, las enchiladas mineras.

Server: Muy bien. ¿Algo de tomar?

Linda: Para mí, una limonada, por favor.

Julio: Y para mí, agua de horchata.

Server: Bien. Voy a traerles sus bebidas enseguida.

Julio: ¡Amigo, qué coincidencia!

Linda: Julio, se me olvidó decirte. Roberto quiere enseñarme Guanajuato.

Roberto: Pues no hay prisa, puedo regresar más tarde.

Julio: No seas tonto, ya terminamos de comer. ¿Adónde piensan ir?

Roberto: A ver un poco de la ciudad.

Linda: Julio, ¿por qué no vienes con nosotros?

Julio: Hmm… Pues tengo la tarde libre. ¿Les molesta si los acompaño?

Linda: Mejor… así tengo dos guías.

Linda: ¿Adónde vamos?

Roberto: Hay mucho que ver. ¿Tienes alguna preferencia? Hay teatros, museos, hay de todo.

Julio: ¿Por qué no vamos al Callejón del Beso?

Linda: ¿Adónde? ¿Qué es un callejón?

Roberto: Un callejón es una calle pequeña.

Linda: Bueno, vamos.

Julio: El Callejón del Beso es muy famoso. Hay una leyenda muy popular entre los enamorados.

Linda: ¿Quién la sabe mejor?

Roberto and Julio: Todos aquí…

Roberto: Vamos a ver, Julio, tú.

Julio: A ver si recuerdo… es como Romeo y Julia.

Roberto: Julieta.

Roberto's V.O.: Había un joven que se enamoró de una señorita, que era muy guapa. Pero al padre de la señorita no le gustó la idea. Ella vivía en una casa con balcón que estaba tan cerca que podían besarse. ¿Y qué creen? Claro que Julio fue el joven que se enamoró y yo tuve que ser el papá…

Roberto's V.O.: Ahora, con la información que tenía de Chato Montesinos, empecé a investigar.

Roberto: …Sí, señorita. Chato Montesinos. Así es, en la ciudad de Dolores Hidalgo. Perfecto. ¿Cuál es la dirección? Muchas gracias.

Roberto: Hola, abuelita.

Abuela: Hola, Roberto. ¿Qué hay?

Roberto: Acabo de averiguar la dirección de Chato Montesinos en Dolores Hidalgo.

Abuela: ¿Chato Montesinos?

Roberto: Sí, el amigo de mi abuelo. Sin duda él podrá decirnos algo sobre Federico. Pienso ir a verlo lo antes posible.

Abuela: Muy bien, hijo.

Roberto: Adiós, Abuelita. Cuídate.

Nombre ______________________________

Fecha ______________________________

Communicative Pair Activity 5A-1
Estudiante A

Imagine you are a news reporter for a local television station and you want to know what happened in a town during a hurricane. Ask your partner, who is an emergency worker, the following questions. Record his or her answers in the spaces provided. Example: *Sólo se cayeron algunos de los árboles.*

1. ¿El viento era muy fuerte? ______________________________
2. ¿Llovía mucho? ______________________________
3. ¿Las calles estaban llenas de agua? ______________________________
4. ¿La gente tenía miedo? ______________________________
5. ¿Los árboles se cayeron? ______________________________

Now, imagine that your partner is the reporter writing about the hurricane. It is your turn to answer his or her questions by choosing any of the two options given for each question.

1. **a.** Sí, hacía mucho frío.
   b. No, hacía calor.
2. **a.** Algunas casas tenían luz.
   b. Ninguna casa tenía luz.
3. **a.** La gente se fue de la ciudad.
   b. La gente se escondió en el sótano de su casa.
4. **a.** Sí, todo estaba lleno de agua.
   b. Había mucha agua, pero no había una inundacíon.
5. **a.** Sí, el viento destruyó todos los árboles.
   b. Sólo se cayeron algunos de los árboles.

Realidades 2 Nombre ____________________

Capítulo 5A Communicative Pair Activity **5A-1**

Fecha ____________________ Estudiante **B**

Imagine you are an emergency worker during a hurricane. You are talking with a news reporter who wants to know what happened in that town during the hurricane. Answer the reporter's questions with the cues given in the pictures. Example: *La gente se escondió en el sótano de su casa.*

Now switch roles with your partner. You are the reporter and you want to find out more about the hurricane. Ask your partner the following questions and write the answers in the space provided.

1. ¿Hacía frío durante el huracán?

____

2. ¿Se fue la luz de las casas?

____

3. ¿Dónde se escondió la gente?

____

4. ¿Hubo inundación?

____

5. ¿Se cayeron todos los árboles o solo algunos?

____

Nombre ____________________

Fecha ____________________

Communicative Pair Activity **5A-2**
Estudiantes **A y B**

Which disasters are you most afraid of? Choose five natural disasters or accidents that you are most afraid of and write them on the lines under *JUEGO UNO. (Les tengo miedo a los tornados.)* Then, with a partner, take turns asking questions *(¿Les tienes miedo a los tornados?)* to see who is the first to guess the other person's five most feared disasters. Answer your partner's questions in complete sentences. Respond to your partner's answers with the conversational responses below *(Reacciones)*. For *JUEGO DOS,* choose five disasters that you are not so afraid of. *(No les tengo tanto miedo a las inundaciones.)*

1	2	
______	______	terremotos
______	______	inundaciones
______	______	erupciones volcánicas
______	______	accidentes de coche
______	______	incendios en casas y edificios
______	______	tornados
______	______	tormentas de nieve
______	______	huracanes
______	______	tormentas eléctricas
______	______	incendios forestales (*forest fires*)
______	______	explosiones

JUEGO UNO

____
____
____
____
____

JUEGO DOS

____
____
____
____
____

REACCIONES:

A mi también.
¿De verdad?
A mi tampoco.
Me dan mucho miedo.
¡Qué peligroso!

Realidades 2

Capítulo 5A

Situation Cards

Capítulo 5A Realidades 2 **1A**

Talking about natural emergencies

You are talking with a friend about natural emergencies.

— Ask your friend if he or she has lived through a natural emergency.

— Respond to your friend's question. If your answer is yes, explain the situation.

Capítulo 5A Realidades 2 **1B**

Talking about natural emergencies

You are talking with a friend about natural emergencies.

— Respond to your friend's question. Ask him or her if he or she has lived through a natural emergency.

— Respond to your friend's question and if the answer is yes, explain the situation.

Capítulo 5A Realidades 2 **2A**

Talking about the weather

You are talking with a friend about the weather.

— Ask your friend how the weather is today.

— Answer your friend's question and tell him or her the kind of weather you prefer.

— Ask him or her if she would like to go to the beach during the summer.

Capítulo 5A Realidades 2 **2B**

Talking about the weather

You are talking with a friend about the weather.

— Answer your friend's question.

— Then, ask him or her if he or she likes the weather today.

— Answer his or her question.

GramActiva

Un acto heroico

Los desastres naturales, p. 246

Desastre	Lugar	Destrucción	Cuándo ocurrió . . .

Vocabulary Clip Art

Vocabulary Clip Art

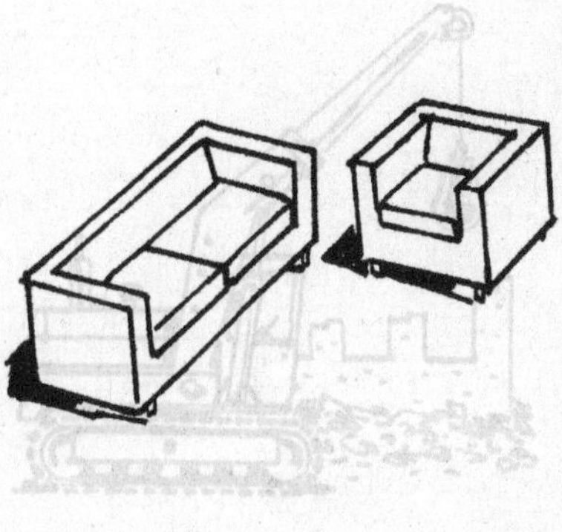

Capítulo 5A

Vocabulary Clip Art

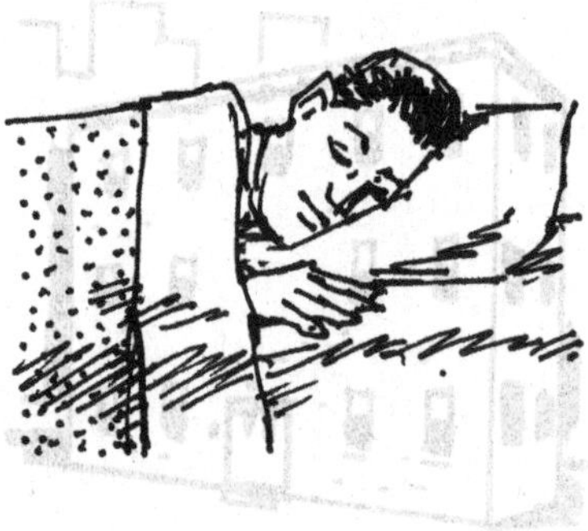

Vocabulary Clip Art

Realidades 2

Capítulo 5A

Core Practice Answers

5A-A

1. cuadros
2. lámpara
3. espejo
4. cortinas
5. equipo de sonido
6. cómoda
7. camas

5A-B

A.

1. tengo hambre
2. tiene miedo
3. tiene, años
4. tengo frío
5. tiene sed
6. tiene razón
7. tengo sueño
8. Tengo prisa

B.

1. ¡Qué bonita es la sala!
2. ¡Qué interesantes son los cuadros!
3. ¡Qué grande es el televisor!
4. ¡Qué moderna es la cocina!
5. ¡Qué altos son los árboles del jardín!
6. ¡Qué elegantes son las cortinas!

5A-1

1. un incendio
2. una explosión
3. un edificio de apartamentos
4. bomberos
5. la escalera
6. humo
7. los muebles
8. escapó
9. apagar

5A-2

A.

1. Ocurrieron
2. esconderse
3. llamaron
4. murieron
5. destruyó
6. nevó
7. quemaron
8. sube

B.

1. muertos
2. bajó
3. comenzar
4. apagar
5. salvar

5A-3

1. Oyeron
2. huracán
3. lluvia
4. tormentas
5. inundaciones
6. llovió
7. investigando
8. noticiero
9. escaparse
10. Sin duda
11. reporteros
12. artículos

5A-4

1. El terremoto ocurrió ayer.
2. Según la policía, el terremoto comenzó a las dos de la mañana.
3. No, la gente de la ciudad dormía cuando comenzó el terremoto.
4. Unas personas gritaron y otras llamaron a la policía.
5. Este desastre era uno de lospeores de todos en la historia de la ciudad.
6. Algunas son héroes porque trataron de rescatar a sus compañeros heridos del desastre.

5A-5

A.

<u>Paragraph 1</u>: P, I, P, I, I, I, P, P, P, I, I
<u>Paragraph 2</u>: I, P, I, I, P, P, P

B.

1. despertó
2. Eran
3. levantó
4. sentía
5. Parecía
6. estaba
7. durmió
8. quiso
9. Dijo
10. estaba
11. tenía
12. era
13. pudo
14. quería
15. estaba
16. Salió
17. acostó
18. llegó

5A-6

1. Nosotros oímos la noticia en la tele.
2. El incendio destruyó un apartamento en un edificio de apartamentos.
3. Los estudiantes leyeron el artículo en el periódico.
4. Yo leí mi libro en la biblioteca.
5. Gloria leyó las noticias en la Red (en la computadora).
6. Mis padres creyeron el noticiero en la tele.
7. El huracán destruyó unas casas en la playa.

5A-7

Answers will vary.

Crucigrama (5A-8)

Horizontal:

4. ocurrió
5. investigar
7. escalera
8. llamar
9. escondió
11. nieva
13. socorro
14. noticiero
16. dormidos
19. humo
20. salvó
22. artículo
23. bomberos
24. oyó

Vertical:

1. valiente
2. afortunadamente
3. heroína
6. incendio
7. explosión
8. lluvia
9. edificio
10. terremoto
12. inundaciones
15. asustados
17. muebles
18. vivos
21. héroe

Organizer (5A-9)

I. Vocabulary Answers will vary.

II. Grammar

1. the imperfect tense
2. **oír:**

oí	oímos
oíste	oísteis
oyó	oyeron
leer:	
leí	leímos
leíste	leísteis
leyó	leyeron
creer:	
creí	creímos
creíste	creísteis
creyó	creyeron
destruir:	
destruí	destruimos
destruiste	destruisteis
destruyó	destruyeron

Realidades 2 Nombre ____________ Hora ________

Capítulo 5A Fecha ____________ AVSR 5A-1

A ver si recuerdas: Expressions using *tener* (p. 237)

- Remember that **tener** is used in many expressions when English uses "to be."

Marta tiene prisa. *Marta is in a hurry.*
Luisito tiene ocho años. *Luisito is eight years old.*
Tenemos razón. *We are right.*
Ellos tienen miedo. *They are afraid.*
Los estudiantes tienen sueño. *The students are tired.*
Tengo hambre. *I am hungry.*
Tengo sed. *I am thirsty.*
Tienes cuidado. *You are careful.*
Tengo calor. *I am warm/hot.*
Tengo frío. *I am cold.*

A. Read each statement and choose the appropriate phrase within the parentheses. Follow the model.

Modelo Necesito beber algo. Yo (**tengo hambre / tengo sed**).

1. Juana quiere dormir ahora. Ella (**tiene sueño / tiene prisa**).
2. Nosotros sabemos mucho. Creemos que (**tenemos razón / tenemos miedo**).
3. Los niños miran en todas las direcciones antes de cruzar la calle. Ellos (**tienen frío / tienen cuidado**).
4. La temperatura está a ochenta y cinco grados. Tú (**tienes razón / tienes calor**).
5. Yo veo un oso en las montañas. Yo (**tengo miedo / tengo hambre**).

B. Write the correct **tener** expression according to each picture. Remember to conjugate **tener**. Follow the model.

Modelo  Ellos ***tienen*** ***hambre***.

1.  Jorge ***tiene*** ***sueño***.
2.  Yo ***tengo*** ***sed***.
3.  ¡Nosotros ***tenemos*** ***miedo***!
4.  Tú ***tienes*** ***frío***.

realidades.com
• Web Code: jdd-0501

Realidades 2 | Nombre ______ | Hora ______

Capítulo 5A | Fecha ______ | AVSR 5A-2

A ver si recuerdas: The use of *¡Qué...!* in exclamations (p. 237)

- As you know, **¡Qué...!** is used with adverbs and adjectives to exclaim "How . . . !"

  ¡Qué buenos son mis estudiantes! *How good my students are!*

  ¡Qué pronto llegaron! *How quickly they arrived!*

A. Read the following statements and circle the appropriate reaction. The first one is done for you.

1. El gato de Juan está enfermo. (**¡Qué triste!** / **¡Qué feo!**)
2. Llegamos a Boston en sólo cuarenta y cinco minutos. (**¡Qué rápido!** / **¡Qué sabroso!**)
3. Mmmmm. Me encantan las galletas de mi mamá. (**¡Qué graciosas!** / **¡Qué sabrosas!**)
4. Me gustan las flores de tu jardín. (**¡Qué lentas!** / **¡Qué bonitas!**)
5. Mi hijo saca buenas notas en todas sus clases. (**¡Qué inteligente!** / **¡Qué guapo!**)

- As you know **¡Qué ...!** is used with nouns to say "What (a) . . . !"

  ¡Qué bailarina es tu novia! *What a dancer your girlfriend is!*

B. Read the statements below and complete the exclamations with the appropriate nouns. Follow the model.

Modelo Tu hijo es un estudiante muy bueno. ¡Qué ***estudiante*** es tu hijo!

1. María es una cocinera fantástica. ¡Qué ***cocinera*** es María!
2. Los hermanos Rulfo son increíbles jugadores de fútbol. ¡Qué ***jugadores*** son los hermanos Rulfo!
3. Yo soy un buen músico. ¡Qué ***músico*** soy yo!
4. Nosotros somos doctores fantásticos. ¡Qué ***doctores*** somos nosotros!

realidades.com
• Web Code: jdd-0501

Realidades 2 | Nombre ______ | Hora ______

Capítulo 5A | Fecha ______ | **Vocabulary Flash Cards, Sheet 1**

Write the Spanish vocabulary word below each picture. Be sure to include the article for each noun.

el

incendio

la

lluvia

la

explosión

la

inundación

el

terremoto

el

huracán

llover

nevar

el

artículo

Realidades 2 Nombre ______ Hora ______

Capítulo 5A Fecha ______ **Vocabulary Flash Cards, Sheet 2**

Write the Spanish vocabulary word below each picture. Be sure to include the article for each noun.

la reportera

el reportero

la locutora

el locutor

el edificio de apartamentos

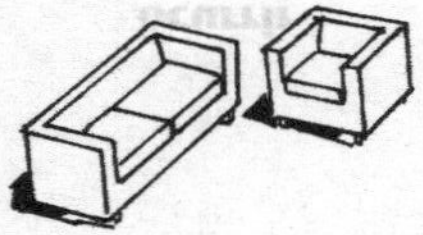

los muebles

el humo

el bombero

apagar

Realidades 2 Nombre ______ Hora ______

Capítulo 5A Fecha ______ **Vocabulary Flash Cards, Sheet 3**

Write the Spanish vocabulary word below each picture. Be sure to include the article for each noun.

el paramédico

la paramédica

destruir

dormido

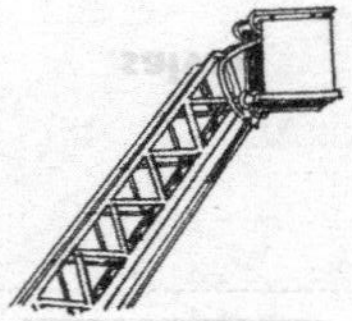

la escalera

bajar

subir

rescatar

esconder(se)

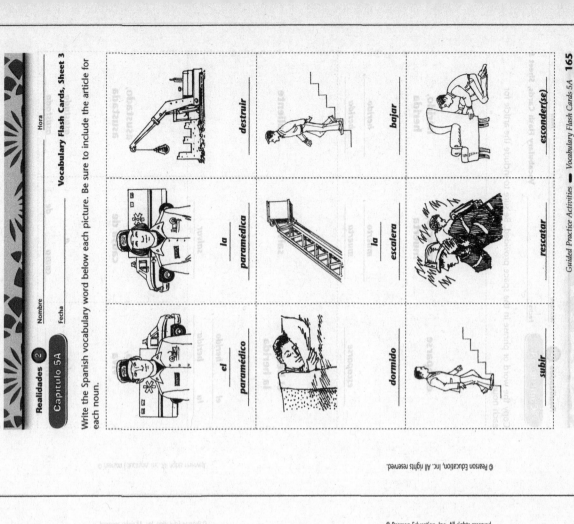

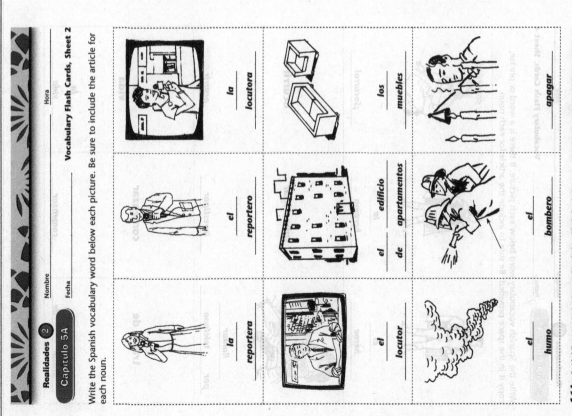

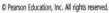

Realidades 2 Nombre ____________ Hora ________

Capítulo 5A Fecha ____________ **Vocabulary Flash Cards, Sheet 4**

Write the Spanish vocabulary word below each picture. If there is a word or phrase, copy it in the space provided. Be sure to include the article for each noun.

 *el* / *héroe*	 *la* / *heroína*	 *¡Socorro!*
 *llamar* / *por* *teléfono*	**investigar** / *investigar*	**ocurrir** / *ocurrir*
tratar de / *tratar* *de*	**comenzar** / *comenzar*	**la vida** / *la* / *vida*

Realidades 2 Nombre ____________ Hora ________

Capítulo 5A Fecha ____________ **Vocabulary Flash Cards, Sheet 5**

Copy the word or phrase in the space provided. Be sure to include the article for each noun.

escaparse / *escaparse*	**muerto, muerta** / *muerto*, *muerta*	**herido, herida** / *herido*, *herida*
el herido, la herida / *el* *herido*, *la* *herida*	**salvar** / *salvar*	**valiente** / *valiente*
vivo, viva / *vivo*, *viva*	**a causa de** / *a* / *causa* *de*	**asustado, asustada** / *asustado*, *asustada*

Realidades 2 Nombre ______ Hora ______

Capítulo 5A Fecha ______ **Vocabulary Flash Cards, Sheet 6**

Copy the word or phrase in the space provided. Be sure to include the article for each noun.

la causa	**de prisa**	**de repente**
la *causa*	*de* *prisa*	*de* *repente*
gritar	**hubo**	**se murieron**
gritar	*hubo*	*se* *murieron*
oír	**sin duda**	**el noticiero**
oír	*sin* *duda*	*el* *noticiero*

Realidades 2 Nombre ______ Hora ______

Capítulo 5A Fecha ______ **Vocabulary Flash Cards, Sheet 7**

Copy the word or phrase in the space provided. Be sure to include the article for each noun. The blank cards can be used to write and practice other Spanish vocabulary for the chapter.

afortunadamente	**la tormenta**	**quemar(se)**
afortunadamente	*la* *tormenta*	*quemar(se)*

Realidades 2 Nombre ______ Hora ______

Capítulo 5A Fecha ______

Vocabulary Flash Cards, Sheet 8

These blank cards can be used to write and practice other Spanish vocabulary for the chapter.

Realidades 2 Nombre ______ Hora ______

Capítulo 5A Fecha ______

Vocabulary Check, Sheet 1

Tear out this page. Write the English words on the lines. Fold the paper along the dotted line to see the correct answers so you can check your work.

llover	***to rain***
nevar	***to snow***
el terremoto	***earthquake***
la tormenta	***storm***
el artículo	***article***
el locutor, la locutora	***announcer***
el noticiero	***newscast***
ocurrir	***to occur***
el reportero, la reportera	***reporter***
apagar	***to put out (fire)***
el bombero, la bombera	***firefighter***
la escalera	***ladder***
escaparse	***to escape***
esconderse	***to hide (oneself)***

Fold In ←

Realidades 2 | Nombre | Hora

Capítulo 5A | Fecha

Vocabulary Check, Sheet 2

Tear out this page. Write the Spanish words on the lines. Fold the paper along the dotted line to see the correct answers so you can check your work.

to rain	***llover***
to snow	***nevar***
earthquake	***el terremoto***
storm	***la tormenta***
article	***el artículo***
announcer	***el locutor, la locutora***
newscast	***el noticiero***
to occur	***ocurrir***
reporter	***el reportero, la reportera***
to put out (fire)	***apagar***
firefighter	***el bombero, la bombera***
ladder	***la escalera***
to escape	***escaparse***
to hide (oneself)	***esconderse***

Fold In

Realidades 2 | Nombre | Hora

Capítulo 5A | Fecha

Vocabulary Check, Sheet 3

Tear out this page. Write the English words on the lines. Fold the paper along the dotted line to see the correct answers so you can check your work.

el humo	***smoke***
el incendio	***fire***
el paramédico, la paramédica	***paramedic***
quemar(se)	***to burn (oneself), to burn up***
el herido, la herida	***injured person***
rescatar	***to rescue***
salvar	***to save***
la vida	***life***
vivo, viva	***living, alive***
afortunadamente	***fortunately***
asustado, asustada	***frightened***
la causa	***cause***
gritar	***to scream***
¡Socorro!	***Help!***

Fold In

Tear out this page. Write the Spanish words on the lines. Fold the paper along the dotted line to see the correct answers so you can check your work.

smoke	***el humo***
fire	***el incendio***
paramedic	***el paramédico, la paramédica***
to burn (oneself), to burn up	***quemar(se)***
injured person	***el herido, la herida***
to rescue	***rescatar***
to save	***salvar***
life	***la vida***
living, alive	***vivo, viva***
fortunately	***afortunadamente***
frightened	***asustado, asustada***
cause	***la causa***
to scream	***gritar***
Help!	***¡Socorro!***

Fold In

To hear a complete list of the vocabulary for this chapter, go to www.realidades.com and type in the Web Code jdd-0589. Then click on **Repaso del capítulo.**

The imperfect tense: other uses (p. 248)

- You can use the imperfect tense to tell what time it was **(qué hora era)**, or what the weather was like **(qué tiempo hacía)** when something happened.

  ***Eran* las cinco de la mañana cuando el huracán comenzó.**

  It was five in the morning when the hurricane began.

A. Read the following statements and circle the verb that tells what time it was or what the weather was like (the imperfect tense). Then, underline the verb that gives the action (the preterite tense).

Modelo (**Eran** / **Fueron**) las diez de la noche cuando terminó el noticiero.

1. (**Llovía** / **Llovió**) mucho cuando me levanté.
2. (**Nevó** / **Nevaba**) cuando salí de casa.
3. (**Eran** / **Fueron**) las tres de la tarde cuando comenzó el huracán.
4. (**Hubo** / **Había**) una tormenta de lluvia cuando comenzó la inundación.
5. (**Era** / **Eran**) la una de la tarde cuando vi el incendio.
6. (**Eran** / **Era**) las nueve cuando me acosté.
7. (**Hacía** / **Hacían**) mal tiempo cuando llegué a casa.

B. Write the imperfect form of the verb in parentheses to complete the weather description or time expression in each sentence below. Follow the model.

Modelo (Ser) *Eran* las cuatro cuando la explosión ocurrió.

1. (Hacer) ***Hacía*** mucho viento cuando los paramédicos llegaron.
2. Cuando la locutora comenzó a hablar, (ser) ***eran*** las seis de la noche.
3. Cuando chocaron esos tres coches, (hacer) ***hacía*** mal tiempo.
4. (Llover) ***Llovía*** mucho cuando ocurrió el accidente.
5. (Ser) ***Eran*** las doce cuando mi hermano volvió a casa.

realidades.com
• Web Code: jdd-0504

The imperfect tense: other uses (*continued*)

- The imperfect tense is also used to tell how a person was feeling when something happened.
  Anoche me acosté temprano porque *tenía* sueño.
  Last night I went to bed early because I was sleepy.

C. In each sentence, underline the preterite verb, which tells what action took place. Then, complete the sentence with the imperfect form of the verb in parentheses to tell how the people were feeling. The first one is done for you.

1. Fuimos a comer algo porque nosotros ***teníamos*** hambre. (tener)
2. La reportera habló con muchas personas porque ella ***quería*** (querer) saber qué ocurrió.
3. Los paramédicos ***tenían*** (tener) prisa, y por eso salieron pronto.
4. Cuando apagaron el incendio, los bomberos ***querían*** (querer) descansar.
5. Cuando llegamos al edificio, nosotros ***estábamos*** (estar) nerviosos.
6. Juanita gritó porque ella ***estaba*** (estar) asustada.

D. You have learned three ways to tell about events in the past using the imperfect and preterite tenses in this chapter. Use the graphic below to create three sentences in the past. Remember to conjugate the verbs! Follow the model.

Modelo Telling Time: Ser las siete de la tarde → cuando → Action: nosotros ver el noticiero
Eran las siete de la tarde cuando nosotros vimos el noticiero.

1. How they feel: Los paramédicos estar cansados → porque → Action: subir las escaleras de prisa
Los paramédicos estaban cansados porque subieron las escaleras de prisa.

2. The weather: Hacer mucho viento → cuando → Action: el huracán llegar a la ciudad
Hacía mucho viento cuando el huracán llegó a la ciudad.

3. Telling time: Ser las cinco y media de la tarde → cuando → Action: los bomberos apagar el incendio
Eran las cinco y media de la tarde cuando los bomberos apagaron el incendio.

The imperfect tense: other uses (*continued*)

- Remember that **hubo** and **había** are forms of **haber.** Both words mean "there was" or "there were." Look at these rules:
- Use **hubo** to say that an event (such as a fire) took place.
  Hubo un incendio ayer. *There was a fire. = it took place*
- Use **había** to describe a situation in the past.
  Había mucho humo en el edificio. *There was smoke in the building. = the condition existed*

E. Below there are two sentences in the past for each drawing: one tells about an action and the other gives a description. If the sentence tells that an action took place, write **hubo**. If the sentence describes a situation or condition that existed, write **había**. Follow the models.

Modelos

Hubo una tormenta muy mala.
Había muchos árboles en la calle.

1. ***Hubo*** un terremoto en esta ciudad.
2. ***Había*** poca gente en las calles.

3. ***Había*** muchos heridos.
4. ***Hubo*** un incendio a las siete de la mañana.

5. ***Hubo*** una inundación en la ciudad.
6. ***Había*** muchas casas destruidas.

The preterite of the verbs *oír, creer, leer,* and *destruir* (p. 250)

- The verbs **oír, creer, leer,** and **destruir** are irregular in the preterite.
- These verbs are irregular in the **Ud./él/ella** and **Uds./ellos/ellas** forms. Instead of an "i" on the endings there is a "y".
- The verbs **oír, leer,** and **creer** have accent marks on the **tú, nosotros/nosotras** and **vosotros/vosotras** forms, whereas **destruir** does not.

yo	**oí**	**leí**	**creí**	**destruí**
tú	**oíste**	**leíste**	**creíste**	**destruiste**
usted/él/ella	**oyó**	**leyó**	**creyó**	**destruyó**
nosotros/nosotras	**oímos**	**leímos**	**creímos**	**destruimos**
vosotros/vosotras	**oísteis**	**leísteis**	**creísteis**	**destruisteis**
ustedes/ellos/ellas	**oyeron**	**leyeron**	**creyeron**	**destruyeron**

A. Read the sentences below and look at the underlined verbs. Write an **X** in either the **Present** or the **Preterite** column, according to the tense of the underlined verb. The first one is done for you.

	Present	Preterite
1. Anoche oí un grito en la casa.		X
2. Ella oye al locutor por la radio.	***X***	
3. ¿Tú crees que la gente se escapó?	***X***	
4. Nosotros creímos al reportero.		***X***
5. El incendio destruyó el edificio de apartamentos.		***X***
6. Anoche Amalia leyó el artículo del terremoto.		***X***

B. Complete the following sentences with the correct form of the verb in parentheses.

1. Ayer tú ***oíste*** (oír) el noticiero en la radio.
2. Mis padres ***creyeron*** (creer) las noticias.
3. El huracán ***destruyó*** (destruir) las casas.
4. Los bomberos ***oyeron*** (oír) la explosión.
5. El incendio ***destruyó*** (destruir) los muebles.
6. Los estudiantes ***leyeron*** (leer) las noticias en la biblioteca.

realidades.com
• Web Code: jdd-0505

Lectura: Desastre en Valdivia, Chile (pp. 256–257)

A. The reading in your textbook is about natural disasters that occurred in Valdivia, Chile. Think of four things that you already know about earthquakes and tsunamis, and write them below.

1. ______ 3. ______
2. ______ 4. ______

B. Cognates are words that are similar in spelling and pronunciation. Here are some sentences from your textbook reading, in which some of the Spanish words have been circled. Write the English cognates beneath each set of sentences.

1. A las seis y dos minutos de la mañana, el 21 de mayo 1960, una gran parte del país sintió el primer terremoto.

   a. ***minutes*** b. ***May*** c. ***part***

2. Unos minutos después del desastroso terremoto, llegó un tsunami que destruyó lo poco que quedaba en la ciudad y en las pequeñas comunidades.

   a. ***disastrous*** b. ***tsunami*** c. ***communities***

3. La gran ola de agua se levantó destruyendo a su paso casas, animales, botes y, por supuesto, muchas vidas humanas.

   a. ***destroying*** b. ***animals*** c. ***humans***

C. Read the following rules from your textbook reading about what to do and what not to do during an earthquake. Place an **X** next to the things you should do in the **Sí** column, and should not do in the **No** column.

Si estás en un edificio durante un terremoto:	Sí	No
1. Debes mantener la calma.	***X***	
2. Debes mantenerte cerca de las ventanas.		***X***
3. Debes utilizar los elevadores.		***X***
Si estás fuera de un edificio durante un terremoto:		
4. Debes estar lejos de los postes de energía eléctrica.	***X***	
5. Debes ir a un edificio alto.		***X***

realidades.com
• Web Code: jdd-0506

Realidades 2 | Nombre ______ | Hora ______

Capítulo 5A | Fecha ______ | **Guided Practice Activities 5A-6**

Presentación oral (p. 259)

Task: You and a partner will role-play an interview about an imaginary fire that happened in your town or city. You will need to create a list of questions and answers for the interview. Use your lists during the interview.

A. Read the following phrases. Write **dónde** if the phrase describes *where* the fire happened. Write **cuándo** if it describes *when* it happened. Write **quién** if it names people *who* were involved. Write **por qué** if it describes *why* it happened. Follow the model.

Modelo problema eléctrico ***por qué***

1. en una escuela	***dónde***	5. a las cinco de la mañana	***cuándo***
2. ayer por la noche	***cuándo***	6. un cable eléctrico	***por qué***
3. una explosión	***por qué***	7. en un edificio	***dónde***
4. muchos niños	***quién***	8. algunas personas	***quién***

B. Use the information from **part A** or make up your own to answer the following questions about the fire. The first one is done for you.

1. ¿Dónde fue el incendio? *El incendio fue en un edificio.*
2. ¿Cuándo ocurrió? ***Answers will vary.***
3. ¿Quiénes estaban allí? ______
4. ¿Por qué ocurrió? ______

C. Use the questions and your answers from **part B** to practice for the interview.

D. Your teacher will tell you which role to play. Listen to your partner's questions or answers and keep the interview going. Remember that you should ask or tell "when," "where," and "why" the imaginary fire occurred, and "who" was involved. Complete the paragraph below to start the interview.

Anoche hubo un incendio en ***Answers will vary.*** Los bomberos estuvieron allí ______. ______ se salvaron.

El incendio ocurrió porque ______

Antes de ver el video

Actividad 1

In this video, you are going to see part of a television newscast. Fill out the survey below about the news program that you normally watch at home.

Nombre del noticiero **Answers will vary.**

Canal ______

Horario ______

¿Recuerdas el nombre de algún reportero (alguna reportera)? ______

¿Te gusta más ver los deportes? ¿las noticias? ¿el pronóstico del tiempo (*weather forecast*)?

¿Por qué te gusta esa sección más? ______

¿Comprendes?

Actividad 2

Read the following parts of the plot. Then, put them in the order in which they occurred. Write **1** for the first thing that happened and **7** for the last thing that happened.

5 Raúl y Tomás ven el noticiero en la tele.
7 Raúl y Tomás hablan con la reportera.
2 Comienza el incendio.
1 Ocurre la explosión.
6 El bombero habla con la reportera.
3 Un vecino ve el humo.
4 Vienen los paramédicos.

Actividad 3

In the video, Raúl and Tomás are watching TV when they hear the news about a fire. What happens afterwards? Answer the following questions in order to better understand the plot.

1. ¿En dónde ocurre el incendio?
   Ocurre cerca de la casa de Raúl.

2. ¿Quién es Laura Martínez? ¿Por qué está en el sitio del incendio?
   Ella es la reportera del canal cinco. Está entrevistando al bombero.

3. ¿Cómo comenzó el incendio?
   Piensan que hubo una explosión alrededor de las dos de la mañana.

4. ¿Quién estaba en la casa cuando ocurrió el incendio?
   Una familia de seis personas estaba en la casa.

5. ¿Quiénes vinieron para ayudar a rescatarlos?
   Vinieron los paramédicos.

6. ¿Por qué la reportera termina rápido la entrevista con Raúl y Tomás?
   Termina rápido porque ellos no saben nada del incendio. Ellos lo vieron por la tele.

Realidades 2 **Nombre** ____ **Hora** ____

Capítulo 5A **Fecha** ____ **VIDEO**

Y, ¿qué más?

Actividad 4

Imagine that you are a reporter for a television newscast and you have to report on something that happened in your high school. Write a reporting script about a real or imaginary event at your high school. Follow the model.

Modelo *Les habla Lucía Pacheco, del canal 8. Estamos en el colegio Spring, donde un grupo de estudiantes de noveno grado está lavando coches. El dinero que reciben es para pagar un viaje a San Antonio, organizado por la profesora de historia, la Sra. Martínez. El viaje está planeado para el próximo mes de marzo. Esto es todo por ahora. Lucía Pacheco, desde el colegio Spring, para el canal 8.*

Answers will vary.

Realidades 2 **Nombre** ____ **Hora** ____

Capítulo 5A **Fecha** ____ **AUDIO**

Actividad 5

Listen as these radio announcers break into regular programming to report emergency situations that have occurred. Match each radio report with one of the pictures below to indicate what type of emergency or crisis situation each was. Then, try to answer the bonus question in the last column for each news report. You will hear each report twice.

						**Answers may vary slightly.** **Bonus Question**
1				X		Según sus vecinos, ¿qué es el Sr. Morales? **un héroe**
2		X				¿Qué fue(ron) destruido(s)? **unos edificios**
3					X	¿Qué necesita la gente? **ayuda**
4			X			¿Cómo puede ir la gente de un lugar a otro? **en bote**
5	X					¿Quién es Gabriel? **el huracán**

Actividad 6

As Ernesto is driving home from work, he turns on the radio and starts to scan for his favorite type of music. Each time he finds a station, a reporter is in the middle of the evening news report. As you listen, write the number of the excerpt under the corresponding picture. You will hear each report twice.

1

2

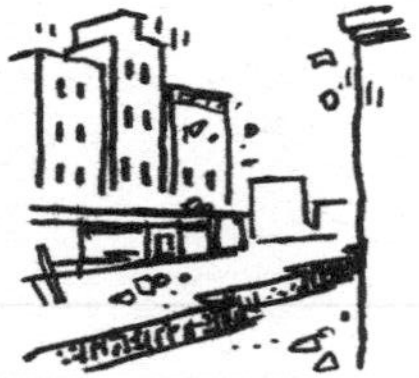
4

3

6

5

Actividad 7

A local jewelry store manager is holding a contest for young couples who purchase their wedding rings in his store. If there is bad weather on their wedding day, the manager promises to refund the couple the cost of their rings! Listen as each couple describes their wedding day. Which couples would qualify for a refund? Mark your answers in the grid below. You will hear each description twice.

	1	2	3	4	5	6
Qualify		X		X	X	
Do not qualify	X		X			X

Actividad 8

When it comes to the news, some people prefer to listen to the radio while others would rather read the newspaper. Listen to people talk about recent events. Determine whether they HEARD about it on the radio or if they READ about it in the newspaper. Place a check mark in the appropriate row of the grid. You will hear each conversation twice.

	1	2	3	4	5
	X			X	
		X	X		X

Actividad 9

Your teacher has asked you to listen to the news on a Spanish-speaking radio station. First, read the questions below. Then, listen to a news report of a hurricane that occurred yesterday in a small town near San Juan. As you listen to the story, circle the correct answers below. Your teacher might ask you to write a summary of the news story based on your answers. You will hear the report twice.

1. ¿Quién es Carmen Dominó?
   a. Una reportera. b. Una bombera. c. Una heroína.
2. ¿Qué es Felipe?
   a. Un noticiero. **b. Un huracán.** c. Un pueblo.
3. ¿Qué hacían muchas personas cuando el huracán llegó?
   a. Escuchaban la radio. b. Leían. **c. Dormían.**
4. ¿Qué pasó en Dorado a causa del huracán?
   a. Había mucha comida. **b. Muchos vecinos perdieron sus casas.**
   c. Había muchos muebles.
5. ¿Quiénes fueron los héroes de Dorado?
   a. Los médicos. b. Los reporteros. **c. Los bomberos.**

Actividad 10

You just finished watching the evening news. Under each news category below, write a short summary of the stories of the day by looking at each picture and using appropriate vocabulary. The first one has been started for you.

1. El tiempo

Hoy pasó un gran huracán por las islas de Venezuela.

Answers will vary.

2. La ciudad

Answers will vary.

3. Una ocurrencia heroica

Answers will vary.

Actividad 11

You are working as a reporter for the school newspaper and are trying to get the facts about several different stories. Read the headlines below and write the questions you need to ask in order to round out your reports. Follow the model.

Modelo EL EQUIPO DE BÁSQUETBOL GANÓ AYER

¿Qué hora era cuando empezó el partido?

¿Quién y cómo era el otro equipo?

¿Cómo se sentía el equipo de nuestra escuela cuando ganó?

1. NUESTRA ESCUELA #2 EN EL CONCURSO DE MATEMÁTICAS

Answers will vary.

2. EL PRINCIPAL DECLARÓ: ¡NO SE PERMITE LLEVAR PANTALONES CORTOS!

3. ¡EL BAILE DE LA ESCUELA UN ÉXITO!

4. JONES Y RULFO GANARON LAS ELECCIONES

5. ¡INCENDIO EN LA CAFETERÍA!

Actividad 12

Your local television station's news reporters are investigating two stories from last night and want to talk to people who witnessed the events. Using the pictures provided, write what a witness would say to a reporter about each scene. Follow the model.

Modelo La señora Alfonso *oyó los perros ladrando (barking)*.

Possible answers:

1. Enrique y Roberto **leyeron una novela de horror**.
2. El incendio **destruyó un edificio de apartamentos**.
3. Tú **oíste los coches de la policía**.
4. Ignacio **oyó cuando rompieron la ventana**.
5. El ladrón (*robber*) **entró por la ventana**.
6. Marisol y yo **oímos el teléfono**.
7. Yo **leí la historia en el periódico**.

Actividad 13

A. You want to write a mystery story about a crime that took place in a small town. In order to start developing the plot, answer the questions below using your imagination.

1. ¿Qué hora era y dónde estabas? **Answers will vary.**
2. ¿Qué era el ruido (*noise*) que oíste?
3. ¿Cómo era el hombre que viste? ¿Qué hizo?
4. ¿Qué tenía en su mochila?
5. ¿Qué hora era cuando empezó el incendio?
6. ¿A qué hora llegaron los bomberos?
7. ¿Qué hiciste después?

B. Now, organize your answers into a short description of the plot of your story. You may wish to add details or connecting words to make it flow well. Be creative!

Answers will vary.

Realidades 2

Capítulo 5A

Test Preparation Answers

Reading Skills
p. 247 2. **C**
p. 248 2. **A**

Integrated Performance Assessment
p. 249
Answers will vary.

School-to-Home Connection

Dear Parent or Guardian,

The theme of our current unit is *En las noticias* (In the news). This chapter is called *Un accidente* (An accident).

Upon completion of this chapter students will be able to:

- describe an accident scene
- talk about injuries and treatments
- talk about what they were doing when an accident occurred
- understand cultural perspectives on healthcare

Students will also explore:

- false cognates (words that look alike in Spanish and English, but that have different meanings)

Our textbook, *Realidades,* helps with the development of reading, writing, and speaking skills through the use of strategies, process speaking, and process writing. In this chapter, students will:

- read about a health campaign
- write about an accident scene

To reinforce and enhance learning, students can access a wide range of online resources on **realidades.com,** the personalized learning management system that accompanies the print and online Student Edition. Resources include the eText, textbook and workbook activities, audio files, videos, animations, songs, self-study tools, interactive maps, voice recording (RealTalk!), assessments, and other digital resources. Many learning tools can be accessed through the student Home Page on **realidades.com.** Other activities, specifically those that require grading, are assigned by the teacher and linked on the student Home Page within the calendar or the Assignments tab.

You will find specifications and guidelines for accessing **realidades.com** on home computers and mobile devices on MyPearsonTraining.com under the SuccessNet Plus tab.

realidades.com

For: Tips to Parents
Visit: www.realidades.com
Web Code: jce-0010

Check it out! At the end of the chapter, have your child name eight parts of the body. Then ask him or her to explain what the medical treatment would be if one were to fall and break an arm.

Sincerely,

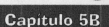

Videocultura Script

Contra la contaminación

Spanish version:

Con más de 20 millones de habitantes, la Ciudad de México es una de las mega ciudades del mundo.

Hace casi 70 años, la Ciudad de México tenía un cielo despejado y un aire puro. Hoy día, las montañas y volcanes no se pueden ver, causa de la contaminación del aire que sufre la ciudad.

La mayor causa de contaminación en México es el tráfico. La emisión de gases contaminantes causa daño al medio ambiente y a la salud de la gente cada día.

Por suerte, al igual que otras ciudades del mundo, la Ciudad de México hace importantes esfuerzos por reducir la contaminación.

La principal estrategia para reducir el problema del transporte es el programa "Hoy no circula", que incentiva a las personas a no usar su auto durante un día de la semana. Otros esfuerzos incluyen la revisión del estado de los autos y la reducción de plomo y sulfuro en la gasolina.

El problema de la contaminación ha alcanzado niveles exorbitantes. Pero los mexicanos hacen un esfuerzo consciente y trabajan por estabilizar y mejorar la situación.

English version:

Mexico City is one of the largest urban areas in the world, with an estimated population of over 20 million people.

Before the 1940s, Mexico City was known for its clear air and spectacular views of snow-capped volcanoes. Today, due to air pollution, the city's mountains are rarely visible.

The biggest source of pollution in Mexico City is the exhausts from millions of cars, buses, taxis, and trucks. Emissions of pollutants from these vehicles take their toll on the environment and people's health.

But as in many other big cities of the world, Mexico City is making important efforts to reduce air pollution.

For example, the government has implemented a program called "Hoy no circula." One day every week, residents are not allowed to drive their personal automobile.

In addition, the government has increased inspection of vehicles' condition and emission levels. Lead and sulfur levels in fuel have been reduced, and catalytic converters are now mandatory.

Pollution levels have reached a crisis point, but Mexicans are determined to work together to stabilize and improve the situation.

Input Script

Presentation

Input Vocabulary 1 and Dialogue 1: Come to class with your arm in a sling, bandages everywhere, and limping along on crutches to reflect all of the injuries sustained by the boy in *A primera vista*. Distribute copies of the Vocabulary Clip Art and have students cut them into individual images. Place the transparency showing the boy's accident on the screen. Tell students you saw the boy laying at the bottom of the stairs and you went over to see if he needed help. Point to the images and tell students what the boy told you by reading the text under the images. Then tell them that when the ambulance came, they got confused and took you to the hospital instead of the boy! You tried to assure them that you were fine, but they assumed that you had bumped your head and were not thinking well. Turn off the projector and tell students what you told the paramedics about the boy's accident. Have students hold up the Clip Art images of the vocabulary words you mention.

Input Vocabulary 2 and Dialogue 2: Next, place the transparency showing the hospital activities on the screen and read the text below each image to tell what they did to tend to the injuries that you did not sustain. Then say that it was a good thing that you went though, because they took an X-ray and discovered something very interesting. Place a transparency on the screen of a brain X-ray showing a hamster running on a wheel, or a similarly comical X-ray. Tell students: *¡Explica mucho!*

Next, tell students that you almost became a doctor instead of a teacher, but you discovered that you were afraid of needles. You could do everything else, put casts on people's arms, take X-rays, write prescriptions, stitch up wounds, but you fainted whenever you had to give a shot. Have students hold up the Vocabulary Clip Art images of the hospital terms you mention in your story.

Comprehension Check

- Describe actions you cannot do *(No puedo lavar nada sin dolor.)* and have students diagnose your problems by holding up the Clip Art image of the body part you most likely injured.
- Call out the different vocabulary words and have students arrange their Clip Art images into three rows: body parts, hospital personnel, and medical treatments.
- Bring a large stuffed animal or doll to class along with bandages, a needle and thread, and a syringe (with no needle). First, call out body parts and have students come up and point to the part you mention on the stuffed animal. Then call out medical treatments and have students perform the treatments on the toy.

Audio Script

Audio DVD, Capítulo 5B

Track 01: ***A primera vista, Un accidente,*** **Student Book, p. 266, (3:32)**

Vocabulario y gramática en contexto

Vas a escuchar cada palabra o frase dos veces. Después de la primera vez hay una pausa para que puedas pronunciar la palabra o frase. Luego vas a escuchar de nuevo la palabra o frase.

tropezar con	el codo
caerse	la sangre
el cuello	el tobillo
el hombro	la ambulancia
la muñeca	la venda
la espalda	el hueso
la rodilla	

Lee en tu libro mientras escuchas la narración.

Teen Male: Estaba bajando, caminando al lado de la escalera y hablando con Marta. De repente tropecé con una estatua. ¡Ay! Me caí delante de la escuela. ¡Qué accidente tan absurdo!

Me dolían todos los músculos en el cuello y la espalda. Me corté la rodilla y había sangre en mis pantalones. ¡Y mi muñeca! ¿Me rompí un hueso? ¡Qué dolor!

Vinieron los paramédicos y me llevaron al hospital en una ambulancia.

Track 02: ***A primera vista,*** **Student Book, p. 267, (3:25)**

Vocabulario y gramática en contexto

Vas a escuchar cada palabra o frase dos veces. Después de la primera vez hay una pausa para que puedas pronunciar la palabra o frase. Luego vas a escuchar de nuevo la palabra o frase.

la inyección	la enfermera
las puntadas	poner una inyección
las pastillas	dar puntadas
examinar	el yeso
el enfermero	la receta
la radiografía	las muletas
sacar una radiografía	la silla de ruedas

Lee en tu libro mientras escuchas la narración.

Teen Male: Cuando entré en la sala de emergencia, el enfermero sacó una radiografía de mi muñeca. La enfermera me puso una inyección y el médico me dio puntadas.

Cuando estaba listo para salir, el médico me recetó medicina. Sí, me rompí un hueso en la muñeca y ahora necesito llevar yeso por unas seis semanas. Si me siento muy mal, el médico me dijo que puedo tomar una pastilla cada ocho horas. ¡Qué día horrible!

Track 03: ***A primera vista,*** **Act. 1, Student Book, p. 267, (2:10)**

¡Acción!

Escucha estas frases sobre varias partes del cuerpo y problemas medicos. Representa la acción para indicar que comprendiste la frase. Vas a escuchar las frases dos veces.

1. ¡Ay! Creo que me rompí la muñeca.
2. Siento mucho dolor en el cuello.
3. Ayer me torcí el tobillo.
4. Doctora, me duele la espalda.
5. Me caí y me lastimé el codo.
6. La enfermera me puso una inyección.
7. Tuve que usar muletas por una semana.
8. Tomé unas pastillas para el dolor.

Track 04: ***A primera vista,*** **Act. 2, Student Book, p. 267, (2:24)**

La sala de emergencia

Escucha las frases. Si la frase que escuchas es lógica, señala con el pulgar hacia arriba. Si la frase no es lógica, señala con el pulgar hacia abajo. Vas a escuchar las frases dos veces.

1. Necesito muletas si me rompo la muñeca.
2. El médico me dio una inyección en la cabeza.
3. Si me rompo el tobillo, necesito un yeso.
4. Si no puedo caminar, necesito una silla de ruedas.
5. Voy en ambulancia a la escuela.
6. El codo es parte del brazo.
7. El cuello está al lado del tobillo.
8. Cuando hay un accidente viene una ambulancia.

Track 05: ***A primera vista, Videohistoria,*** **Student Book, pp. 268–269, (2:01)**

¡El pobrecito soy yo!

Lee en tu libro mientras escuchas la *Videohistoria.*

See Student Book pages 268–269 for script.

Track 06: ***Manos a la obra,*** **Act. 5, Student Book, p. 270, (2:18)**

Escucha y escribe

Escucha lo que dicen unas personas que fueron a la sala de emergencia ayer. En una hoja de papel, escribe los números del 1 al 6. Escribe lo que escuchas. Vas a usar las frases para la Actividad 6. Vas a escuchar las frases dos veces.

1. Me corté el codo y me pusieron una venda.
2. Me caí y me lastimé la espalda. Ahora me duele mucho.
3. Me pusieron una inyección y me dieron doce puntadas en la rodilla.
4. El médico me recetó una medicina porque me sentía muy mal.
5. Cuando choqué con el árbol, me rompí la muñeca.
6. Me trajeron una silla de ruedas porque no podía mover la pierna.

Track 07: Audio Act. 5, Writing, Audio & Video Workbook, p. 100, (5:28)

Your friend Juan Luis just spent his first day as a volunteer in the local hospital's emergency room. Listen as he tells his parents what happened. Write the number of the description in the corresponding circle in the picture below. You will hear each description twice.

1. Eran las dos de la tarde cuando un paramédico vino a la sala de emergencia con una joven en una silla de ruedas. Fue mi primera "paciente." Me parecía que le dolía el hombro. Tenía una venda en la muñeca también. Creo que estuvo en un accidente de auto.
2. Había un pobrecito de cinco años que se cortó la rodilla. Lloraba y lloraba cuando el médico le dio las puntadas. Y cuando la enfermera le puso una inyección, él gritó llamando a su mamá. Yo creo que se cayó de una bicicleta.
3. Una señora llegó a la sala de emergencia con mucho dolor de espalda. Un enfermero la llevó a sacar una radiografía. La señora tenía tanto dolor en la espalda que pensaron que la tenía rota, pero todo estaba bien en la radiografía.
4. Una muchacha se sentía muy mal cuando llegó a la sala de emergencia. Ella estaba muy cansada y triste. El médico la examinó y le recetó unas pastillas. La muchacha fue a la farmacia y allí una enfermera le dio pastillas para el dolor.
5. Dos paramédicos entraron con una joven de quince años a la sala de emergencia. Parecía que había tenido un accidente muy malo porque estaba como dormida y los paramédicos corrían con ella. Vi que la ropa de la joven tenía mucha sangre también.
6. Un hombre caminaba con mucho dolor al lado de una silla de ruedas. Su camisa estaba rota y tenía mucha sangre en el codo. El hombre se cortó el codo. El médico le puso unas vendas y le dio una receta.

Track 08: Audio Act. 6, Writing, Audio & Video Workbook, p. 101, (4:05)

Listen as several teenagers talk about what happened when they were injured recently. Match what each describes to one of the pictures below. Write the corresponding letter in the blanks below. You will hear each description twice.

TEEN FEMALE 1: Me sentía muy mal cuando llamé a la enfermera en el consultorio. Le dije que me torcí el tobillo cuando jugaba al vóleibol. El médico me recetó una medicina y ahora estoy tomándome una pastilla cada cuatro horas para el dolor.

TEEN MALE 1: Durante el almuerzo ayer, tropecé con unas mochilas que estaban en el suelo. ¡Qué asco! Todos me miraban cuando la enfermera de la escuela vino con unas muletas. Pero había una cosa buena… ¡la enfermera era muuuuyy bonita!

TEEN FEMALE 2: Me corté el dedo con un cuchillo cuando estaba preparando una ensalada. Había mucha sangre y decidí ir a la sala de emergencia. Cuando el médico lo vio, me dio puntadas. ¡Voy a tener más cuidado en la cocina!

TEEN FEMALE 3: Un perro me cortó en el brazo con sus dientes. El perro parecía muy enojado. Le salía mucha agua blanca por la boca. El médico examinó mi brazo y me dijo que tenía que ponerme una inyección.

TEEN MALE 2: Tenía mucho dolor en la pierna después de caerme de la bicicleta. Me salía mucha sangre de la pierna. Estaba muy asustado y comencé a llorar. El médico dijo que no era nada malo, pero tuvo que ponerme una venda en la pierna.

Track 09: *Manos a la obra*, Act. 12, Student Book, p. 274, (2:14)

Escucha y escribe

Javier fue a esquiar en las montañas. El primer día tuvo un accidente. Escucha su descipción de lo que pasó y escribe las seis frases, pero ten cuidado. Javier no está contando en orden lo que pasó.

1. Fui al hospital donde otro médico me puso un yeso.
2. Estuve esperando en la silla de ruedas por más de una hora.
3. Dijo que el hueso estaba roto.
4. Una enfermera me trajo una silla de ruedas.
5. Tuve que llevarlo por dos meses y no pude esquiar durante todo el invierno.
6. Por fin el médico vino y me examinó el tobillo.

Track 10: Audio Act. 7, Writing, Audio & Video Workbook, p. 101, (3:51)

A popular *telenovela* added a new character to the cast of people who work at the fictitious hospital in the show. The character, Lola Loca, was added to give humor to the show. Many of the things she does are illogical and silly. Just listen to the things she did last week on the show! Fill in the grid below to show how you would categorize her actions. You will hear each statement twice.

1. Cuando una joven vino al hospital después de un accidente de esquí, Lola Loca le trajo a ella una revista de deportes para leer.
2. Cuando un niño estuvo en la sala de emergencia y necesitaba ayuda, Lola Loca empezó a bailar y cantar.
3. Cuando una anciana lloraba porque el médico le dijo que tenía cáncer, ella la abrazó.
4. Cuando Lola Loca vio una radiografía, le dijo a otra enfermera que era una decoración muy buena para Halloween.
5. Cuando un hombre tenía dolor de cabeza, Lola le trajo agua y una aspirina.
6. Cuando Lola Loca vio a una joven con un brazo roto, le trajo unas muletas para caminar.
7. Cuando un niño no podía caminar porque tenía mucho dolor en las piernas, ella lo puso en una silla de ruedas.
8. Cuando el médico pidió una inyección para una señora muy enferma, Lola Loca le hizo un pastel.

Track 11: Audio Act. 8, Writing, Audio & Video Workbook, p. 102, (2:27)

A group of friends was recalling what each was doing when the police arrived at the scene of an accident. Write the number of the statement in the corresponding circle in the picture below. You will hear each statement twice.

1. **ADULT MALE 1:** Cuando la policía vino, yo estaba buscando mi licencia de manejar porque yo estaba manejando el coche.
2. **ADULT MALE 2:** Yo pensé que era importante tener los nombres de todos los que vieron el accidente. Por eso estaba escribiendo la información de la señora cuando llegó la policía.
3. **ADULT FEMALE 1:** Cuando vino la policía, yo estaba hablando con la víctima en el coche. Ella se sentía mal.
4. **ADULT FEMALE 2:** No me lastimé, pero tenía mucho miedo después del choque. Cuando la policía llegó, estaba llorando.
5. **ADULT MALE 3:** Yo estaba corriendo hacia el teléfono para llamar a los padres de la víctima cuando vino la policía.

Track 12: Audio Act. 9, Writing, Audio & Video Workbook, p. 102, (3:15)

As a counselor at a boy's summer camp, Jorge is the person to whom the children report any accidents or injuries. Listen as children run to Jorge and tell him what campers were doing when a recent injury occurred. Take notes in the grid below about what happened to each child. You will hear each set of statements twice.

1. **GIRL 1:** ¡Jorge! ¡Jorge! Algo pasó con Jaime. Él estaba saltando a la cuerda y de repente se cayó. Creo que se torció el tobillo.
2. **BOY 1:** ¡Ay! Luis se cortó la rodilla. Estaba corriendo muy rápido y chocó con un árbol. Él tiene mucho miedo porque le duele la rodilla y hay mucha sangre.
3. **GIRL 2:** ¡Qué horrible! Cristóbal estaba subiendo a un árbol muy alto cuando de repente se cayó. Él gritó mucho porque le dolía la pierna rota.
4. **BOY 2:** ¡Jorge, Jorge, ven rápidamente! Óscar se lastimó la espalda cuando estaba corriendo en su bicicleta. Le duele mucho y no puede caminar.
5. **GIRL 3:** El pobrecito de Félix estaba caminando en el parque del campamento cuando tropezó y se cayó. Parece que se rompió el brazo. ¡Qué lástima!

Track 13: *Repaso del capítulo,* Student Book, p. 288, (6:07)

Vocabulario y gramática

Escucha las palabras y expresiones que has aprendido en este capítulo.

See Student Book page 288 for vocabulary list.

Track 14: *Preparación para el examen,* Student Book, p. 289, (0:49)

Escuchar

Practice task

Listen as a 911 operator takes a call from someone who is at the scene of an accident. See if you can understand: a) what the victim was doing before the accident occured; b) what happened to cause the accident; and c) what the injury appears to be.

TEEN FEMALE: Mi hermano tuvo un accidente. Él estaba corriendo con sus amigos cuando, de repente, tropezó con una bicicleta. Creo que se torció la rodilla.

Video Script

A primera vista: *¡El pobrecito soy yo!*, (5:57)

ROSA: De verdad, Raúl, no entiendo. Deberías tener más cuidado.

LORENZO: Ya, ya. Vamos. Todos al coche. Ya es tarde.

LORENZO: Eso es. Con cuidado.

ROSA: ¡Tomás! ¡Tomás!

GLORIA: Tomás está durmiendo. ¡Raúl! ¿Qué te pasó?

RAÚL: Pues, tuve un accidente. Fue increíble… todo comenzó a las tres de la mañana. Yo estaba durmiendo… y, cuando de repente, oí el despertador.

GLORIA: ¿A las tres de la mañana? ¿Por qué?

RAÚL: No sé…

GLORIA: Y Tomás?

RAÚL: Tomás, Tomás…

RAÚL: Traté de despertar a Tomás, pero él no se despertó. No se movió. Si no hay un terremoto él no se despierta…

GLORIA: ¿Qué pasó entonces?

RAÚL: Pues, yo tenía que apagar el despertador. Me levanté y empecé a caminar, pero todo estaba tan oscuro que tropecé.

RAÚL: Ay, Ay…

GLORIA: ¿Te caíste?

RAÚL: Pues, sí… Me torcí el tobillo y me caí al suelo. Choqué con la mesa y me lastimé el brazo. Me corté la muñeca…

GLORIA: ¡Qué lástima!… ¿Y Tomás?

RAÚL: Nada… ¡estaba durmiendo!

GLORIA: ¿Qué pasó entonces?

RAÚL: ¡Me sentí muy mal!

ROSA: ¡Raúl! ¿Qué pasó?

RAÚL: Me siento mal. Creo que me lastimé.

ROSA: ¡Oh! ¡Ay, Dios mío!

RAÚL'S V.O.: Bueno, mamá y papá me pusieron una venda en la muñeca, y me llevaron al hospital.

GLORIA: ¿En una ambulancia?

RAÚL: No, no, no, en coche. Entramos en la sala de emergencia. Y me pusieron en una silla de ruedas…

GLORIA: No te pusieron yeso.

RAÚL: No, no. Sólo me lastimé un poco.

GLORIA: ¿Te dieron puntadas?

RAÚL: Sí, aquí, cinco puntadas. ¿Quieres verlas?

GLORIA: No, no, te creo.

RAÚL: …Y me dieron estas pastillas para el dolor.

GLORIA: ¿Ves, Raúl? ¡No debes despertarte a las tres de la mañana!

RAÚL: Gracias.

ROSA: ¡Pobre Tomás! ¡Nos fuimos tan de prisa que lo dejamos aquí, sólo! Ahora mismo te preparo el desayuno.

RAÚL: ¿Tomás? ¡El pobrecito soy yo!

TOMÁS: Raúl, ¿qué te pasó? ¿Cuándo…?

RAÚL: Anoche.

TOMÁS: ¿Por qué no me dijeron nada?

***GramActiva* Videos, (6:03)**

Irregular Preterites: *venir, poner, decir,* and *traer*

TYPEWRITER HOST: Oh, hello, I'm just dashing off another chapter of the Preterite Papers. Today we'll cover *venir, poner, decir,* and *traer.*

NEWSPAPER HOST: Good news, bad news. Bad news: The verbs *venir, poner, decir,* and *traer* are really irregular in the preterite. Good news: They have the same preterite endings as *hacer, tener, estar,* and *poder,* which you've already seen.

COWBOY: Why do they all share the same endings? Because irregular verbs travel in herds.

COWBOY V.O.: *¡Venir!*

V.O.: *Vine. Viniste. Vino. Vinimos. Vinisteis. Vinieron.*

V.O.: *Vine a la casa para hablar con mi amiga. ¡No eres mi amiga!*

COWBOY V.O.: *¡Poner!*

V.O.: *Puse. Pusiste. Puso. Pusimos. Pusisteis. Pusieron.*

V.O.: *Pusimos el mapa en la mesa. ¡No es mi mapa!*

COWBOY V.O.: *¡Decir!*

V.O.: *Dije. Dijiste. Dijo. Dijimos. Dijisteis. Dijeron.*

V.O.: *Dijo "Me estás volviendo loca." Dije "¿De verdad?"*

COWBOY V.O.: *¡Traer!*

V.O.: *Traje. Trajiste. Trajo. Trajimos. Trajisteis. Trajeron.*

V.O.: *Ella trajo mi chaqueta. Yo traje su libro.*

Quiz

V.O.: Complete the sentence with the correct preterite form of the verb.

(venir) Tú ______ a la escuela el sábado.
Tú viniste a la escuela el sábado.

(traer) Ellos ______ el helado a la mesa.
Ellos trajeron el helado a la mesa.

(poner) Los bomberos ______ al señor en la ambulancia.
Los bomberos pusieron al señor en la ambulancia.

(decir) Ella ______ que estaba bien.
Ella dijo que estaba bien.

Imperfect progressive

HOST: If you want to talk about an action that is happening right now, you use the present progressive: *Estoy hablando con mi amigo.*

HOST: And if you want to talk about an action that was happening in the past, then you use the imperfect progressive: *Estaba hablando con mi amigo.*

GUY: We need two things to form the imperfect progressive. The imperfect tense of *estar*…

SINGING V.O.: *Estaba. Estabas. Estaba. Estábamos. Estabais. Estaban.*

GUY: …and the present participle.

SINGING V.O.: Participles!
-ar verbs, stem plus *-ando!*
-er verbs, stem plus *-iendo!*
-ir verbs, stem plus *-iendo!*
Yeah! Participles!

GUY: Uh, thanks. So, if I want to say, "I was singing," I'd say, *Estaba cantando.* Or to say "They were writing," I'd say, *Estaban escribiendo.*

V.O.: Ah, but there is more. The imperfect progressive describes what was taking place and the preterite tells what happened at a specific time in the past.
Estaba mirando la tele cuando me caí.
Estaba caminando a la puerta cuando me caí otra vez.
Me estaba levantando cuando choqué con la silla.
Estaba buscando la medicina cuando me rompí el dedo.

GAL: ¿Qué te pasó?

Quiz

V.O.: Complete the sentence with the correct imperfect progressive form.
(hablar) Ustedes ______ con la enfermera.
Ustedes estaban hablando con la enfermera.
(comer) Nosotros ______ en el restaurante
Nosotros estábamos comiendo en el restaurante.
(leer) Yo ______ el libro.
Yo estaba leyendo el libro.

Videomisterio: *En busca de la verdad,* Episodio 6, (11:35)

ROBERTO'S V.O.: Como ya tenía la dirección de Chato Montesinos en Dolores Hidalgo, llamé a Linda para invitarla a ir conmigo.

ROBERTO: Con la habitación número 16, por favor. ¿Linda? Habla Roberto. Oye, mañana voy a ir a Dolores Hidalgo para hablar con un señor que fue amigo de mi abuelo. ¿Quieres ir conmigo?

LINDA: Y este hombre en Dolores Hidalgo, ¿qué conexión tiene con tu abuelo?

ROBERTO: No sé. Se llama Chato Montesinos. Creo que podrá decirnos algo.

LINDA: Tu abuelo… Y Uds. saben poco de él. ¡Qué lastima!

ROBERTO: Pues sí; él desapareció. ¿Y el tuyo, digo, tu abuelo Federico?

LINDA: Mi abuelo tampoco habló mucho de su familia. Todo lo que sabemos es que llegó de México.

ROBERTO'S V.O.: Así, Linda y yo llegamos a Dolores Hidalgo. Paseamos por el centro, tomamos un helado y hablamos de muchas cosas. Dolores Hidalgo es una ciudad con mucha cultura e historia. Yo he estado varias veces allí y sabía más o menos dónde estaba la casa de Chato Montesinos.

ROBERTO: Tú estudias historia, ¿verdad?

LINDA: Sí.

ROBERTO: A ver… ¿Sabes quién era el padre Hidalgo?

LINDA: Era el líder de un pequeño grupo que empezó el movimiento de la independencia mexicana de España.

LINDA: Impresionante.

ROBERTO: Mira, la casa de Chato está al final de esa calle.

ROBERTO: ¿Señor Montesinos?

CHATO: ¿Sí…?

ROBERTO: Me llamo Roberto Toledo. Soy nieto de Federico Zúñiga.

CHATO: Federico Zúñiga…

ROBERTO: Sí, mi abuelo Federico. Se casó con Nela, mi abuela.

CHATO: Ah, sí, Federico. Claro, claro. Hace tanto tiempo… Pero, por favor, pasen.

ROBERTO: Y ésta es mi amiga Linda, de los Estados Unidos.

CHATO: Qué bien. Por aquí. ¿Les puedo ofrecer un café?

ROBERTO: Muchas gracias, Señor.

CHATO: Y bien, ¿qué los trae por aquí? ¿Y cómo está Federico?

ROBERTO: Es lo que no sabemos. Nadie ha visto a mi abuelo desde que se fue a los Estados Unidos con Ud. Por eso pensamos que tal vez Ud. podría decirnos algo.

CHATO: Hmm. Pues sí, Federico y yo nos fuimos juntos. Nuestros padres eran compañeros de Zapata, hombres de honor. Llegamos a Tejas, a San Antonio, y entramos al ejército de los Estados Unidos. Luego él desapareció… Federico quería hacerse ciudadano y tener dinero, para traer a su esposa. ¿Cómo está ella… Nela?

ROBERTO: Está bien. Vive en San Miguel de Allende. ¿Y Ud. no ha oído algo de mi abuelo: una carta, un mensaje?

CHATO: No, no sé nada. Esperen. Tengo algo que tal vez pueda ayudarles. Cuando Federico y yo entramos en el ejército, abrimos cuentas en este banco, el Banco de la Frontera, en San Antonio. Tal vez allí puedan darles más información.

ROBERTO: Buena idea.

LINDA: Y Ud., ¿cuándo regresó a México?

CHATO: Uy… Es una larga historia… Después de salir del ejército…

ROBERTO'S V.O.: Al día siguiente llamé al Banco de la Frontera en San Antonio. Hablé con el departamento de cuentas cerradas.

DE LEÓN: Cuentas cerradas. Habla De León. ¿En qué puedo servirle?

ROBERTO: Buenos días, Señor. Busco información sobre mi abuelo, Federico Zúñiga.

DE LEÓN: Otra vez: ¿el apellido?

ROBERTO: Zeta, u, eñe, i, ge, a. Zúñiga.

DE LEÓN: Um… no lo encuentro en la computadora. Tengo que buscar en los archivos. Pero antes, ¿de parte de quién?

ROBERTO: Me llamo Roberto Toledo.

DE LEÓN: ¿Cuál es su relación con este señor?

ROBERTO: Como le dije, es mi abuelo y desapareció hace muchos años. Soy su nieto; mi padre, el doctor Tomás Toledo, es su hijo.

DE LEÓN: Pero Ud. dice que su apellido es Toledo. Y su abuelo se llama Federico Zúñiga. Hay un error.

ROBERTO: No, no, lo que le digo es correcto. Él es Zúñiga.

DE LEÓN: No puedo darle esa información por teléfono. Alguien de la familia del Sr. Zúñiga tiene que presentarse aquí en San Antonio… con documentos, y tiene que ser una persona mayor, un adulto…

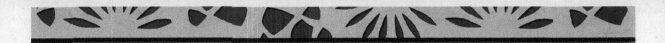

Roberto: ¡Yo soy un adulto!

De León: Con documentos, entiende, o no se puede hacer nada.

De León: ¿Turrón? Aquí De León… sí, eso es. Mire, un joven de Guanajuato, México, acaba de llamar. Pregunta por Federico Zúñiga… sí, exactamente, ése… una cuenta antigua, pero bastante dinero.

Turrón: ¿Está seguro?

De León: Sí, pero no entiendo lo de "Toledo." Se llama Roberto Toledo, el joven.

Turrón: Déjelo en mis manos. Y no hable con nadie, ¿eh?

De León: Entendido.

Turrón: Aquí Turrón. Sí, necesito un boleto para Guanajuato. El próximo vuelo, hoy si es posible.

Nombre ______________________________

Fecha ______________________________

You are interested in learning about people and things in a hospital and you ask your partner to answer some questions. Record his or her answers on the lines provided.

1. ¿Con qué camina Ernesto? ______________________________
2. ¿Qué toma la señora Gómez para mejorarse? ______________________________
3. ¿Qué hace la doctora Pérez con el enfermo? ______________________________
4. ¿Cómo le examinan los huesos a Juan? ______________________________
5. ¿Qué le pusieron a Luisa en el brazo roto? ______________________________
6. ¿Qué le hicieron a la señora Martínez para cerrarle la herida?

   ____

7. ¿Cómo transportan a los enfermos de emergencia?

   ____

8. ¿Cómo se mueve don Pablo si no puede caminar?

   ____

Use the following information to answer your partner's questions.

Antonio

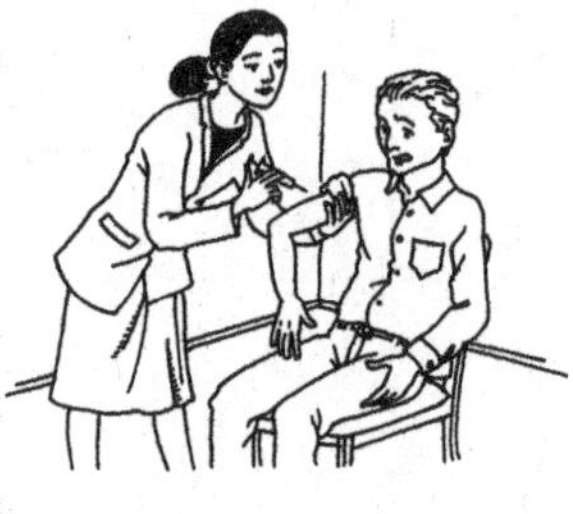

Juana

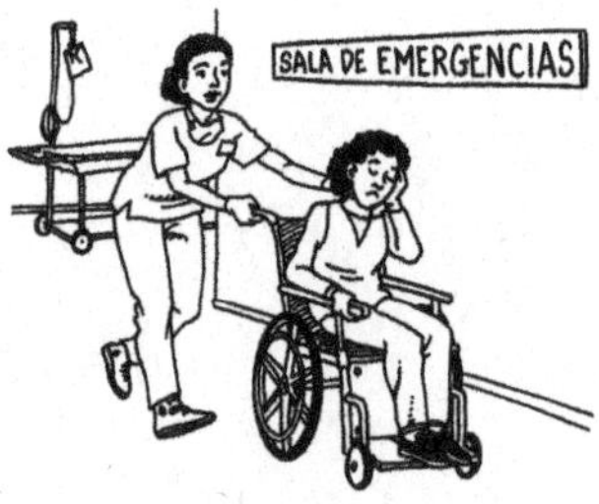

María

Alberto y Francisco

Harold

Victoria

Ana

Realidades 2

Capítulo 5B

Nombre ______________________

Fecha ______________________

Communicative Pair Activity **5B-1**

Estudiante **B**

Use the following information to answer your partner's questions.

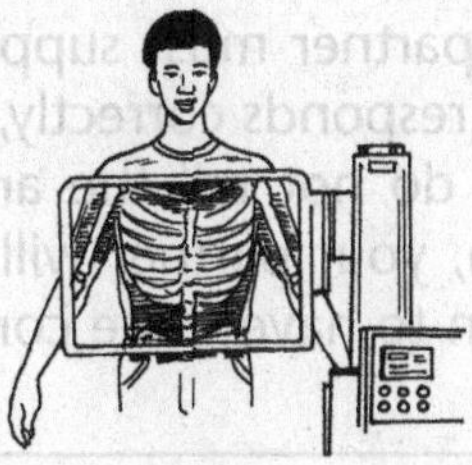
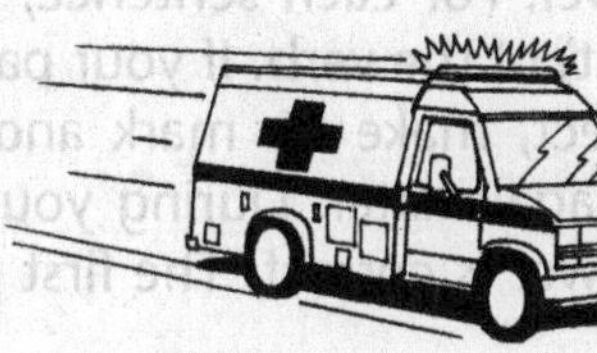

Ernesto	**Juan**	**¡Emergencia!**

la señora Gómez	**Luisa**	**don Pablo**

la Dra. Pérez	**la señora Martínez**

Ask your partner the following questions to find out if he or she can figure what each person is or doing by looking at the cue. Record your partner's answers on the lines provided.

1. ¿Cuál es el trabajo de Antonio? ______________________
2. ¿Qué hace Victoria en el hospital? ______________________
3. ¿Qué trabajo hacen Alberto y Francisco? ______________________
4. ¿Qué va a hacer Juana con esa jeringa? ______________________
5. ¿Cuál es el trabajo que hace Harold? ______________________
6. ¿Dónde está Ana con la receta? ______________________
7. ¿Adónde llevan a María en la silla de ruedas?
____

Nombre

Fecha

Communicative Pair Activity **5B-2**
Estudiante **A**

In this activity, you and your partner take turns. You are **O** and your partner is **X.** Your partner will begin the activity by choosing a number. Read the sentence in that box and wait for his or her answer. For each sentence, your partner must supply the correct past tense (preterite or imperfect) of the verb. If your partner responds correctly, mark an **X** in the box. If the response is incorrect, make no mark and and do not tell the answer. Your partner may choose that number again later. During your turn, your partner will mark an **O** in the appropriate box if your answer is correct. The first person to have three correct answers in a row is the winner.

1 Andrés se *(romper)* la pierna jugando al fútbol americano. (rompió)	**2** El médico le *(dar)* unas puntadas a Helena. (dio)	**3** Este hospital *(ser)* el más grande de la ciudad. (era)
4 Mi habitación en el hospital *(tener)* televisión. (tenía)	**5** Los paramédicos *(llegar)* muy rápido al lugar del accidente. (llegaron)	**6** El doctor me *(recomendar)* comer un buen desayuno. (recomendó)
7 La enfermera *(sugerir)* descansar por una semana. (sugirió)	**8** Mi mamá *(querer)* llegar de prisa al hospital. (quería)	**9** A Lucía le *(poner)* una inyección. (pusieron)

Realidades 2

Capítulo 5B

Nombre ___

Fecha ___

Communicative Pair Activity **5B-2**

Estudiante **B**

In this activity, you and your partner take turns. You are **X** and your partner is **O.** You begin by choosing a number. Listen to the sentence in that box and give the correct past tense (preterite or imperfect) form of the verb. If you respond correctly, your partner will mark an **X** in that box. If the response is incorrect, the box will be left with no marks. You may choose that number again later. During your partner's turn, you will read the sentence that he or she chooses and will mark an **O** in the appropriate box if the answer is correct. The first person to get three correct answers in a row is the winner!

1 Amalia se *(caer)* jugando básquetbol. (cayó)	**2** La patrulla aérea *(rescatar)* a las personas en la montaña. (rescató)	**3** Ronaldo se *(lastimar)* la rodilla derecha jugando al fútbol. (lastimó)
4 El camión grande se *(salir)* de la carretera y se estrelló. (salió)	**5** Pepe se *(comer)* un helado en el hospital. (comió)	**6** Laura *(tener)* que ir a la sala de emergencia cuando se rompío el brazo. (tenía)
7 Lorena *(trabajar)* como voluntaria en la clínica del barrio. (trabajó)	**8** Las enfermeras me *(cuidar)* mucho. (cuidaron)	**9** A Francisco le *(dar)* dolor del cuello. (dio)

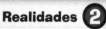

Situation Cards

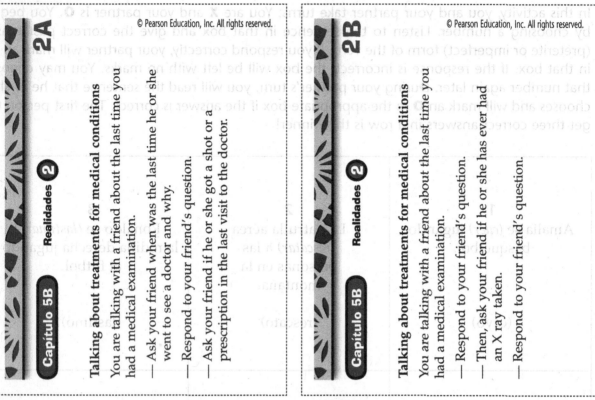

1A

Capítulo 5B Realidades 2

Describing the scene of an accident

You are talking with a friend about accidents.

— Ask your friend if he or she has hit his or her toe against a chair.

— Respond to your friend's question. Then, ask your friend if he or she has ever seen a car accident.

1B

Capítulo 5B Realidades 2

Describing the scene of an accident

You are talking with a friend about accidents.

— Respond to your friend's question about how you hurt your toe. Then, ask your friend if he or she has ever hit his or her head against something hard.

— Respond to your friend's question.

2A

Capítulo 5B Realidades 2

Talking about treatments for medical conditions

You are talking with a friend about the last time you had a medical examination.

— Ask your friend when was the last time he or she went to see a doctor and why.

— Respond to your friend's question.

— Ask your friend if he or she got a shot or a prescription in the last visit to the doctor.

2B

Capítulo 5B Realidades 2

Talking about treatments for medical conditions

You are talking with a friend about the last time you had a medical examination.

— Respond to your friend's question.

— Then, ask your friend if he or she has ever had an X ray taken.

— Respond to your friend's question.

GramActiva

Un accidente

Documentar el accidente, p. 285

Nombre(s)	
Descripción del accidente	
¿Cuándo y dónde ocurrió?	
Descripción de los heridos	
Tipo de ayuda ofrecida	
Otra información	

Vocabulary Clip Art

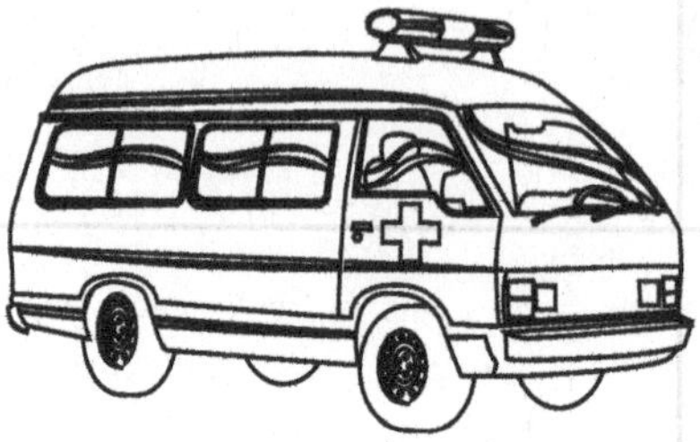

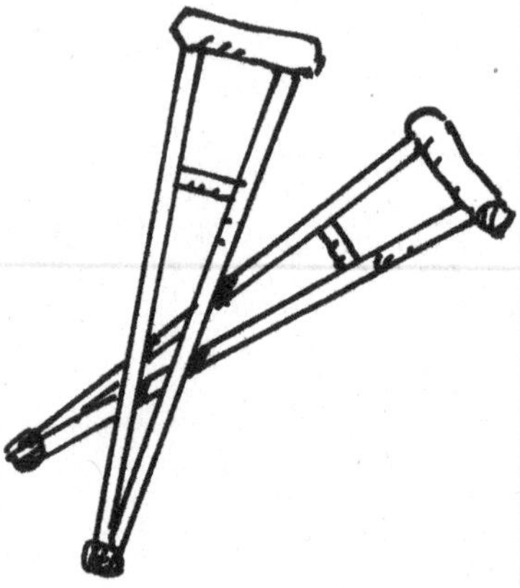
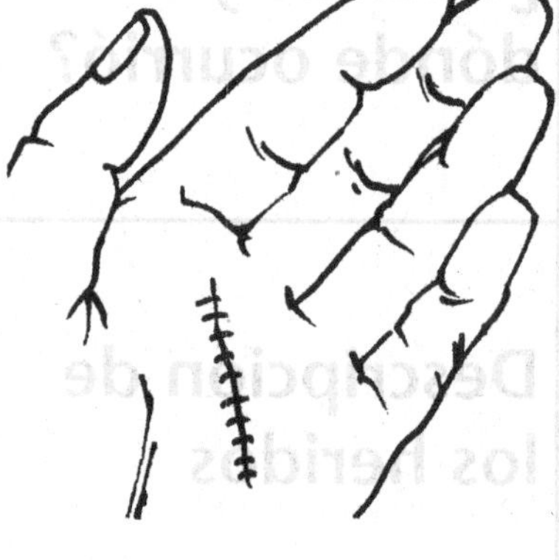
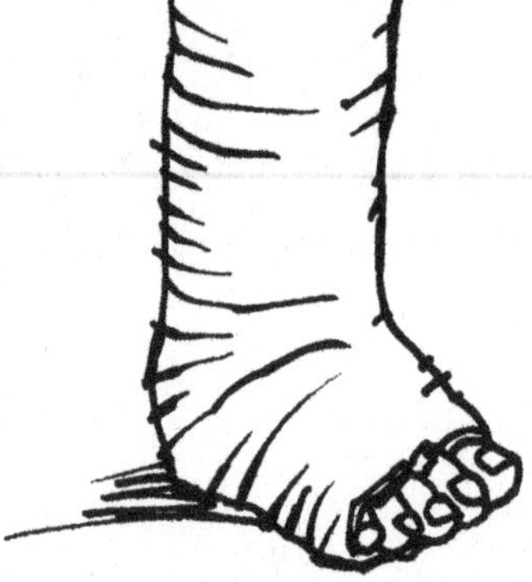
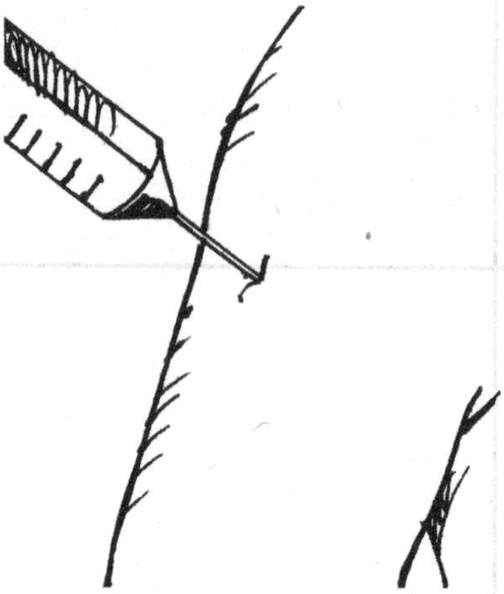
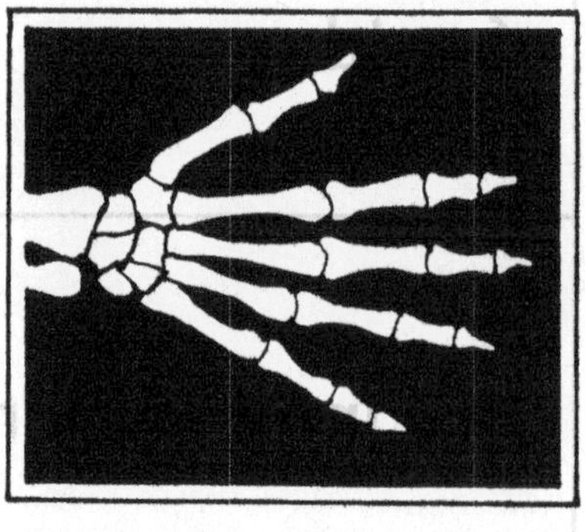

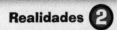

Vocabulary Clip Art

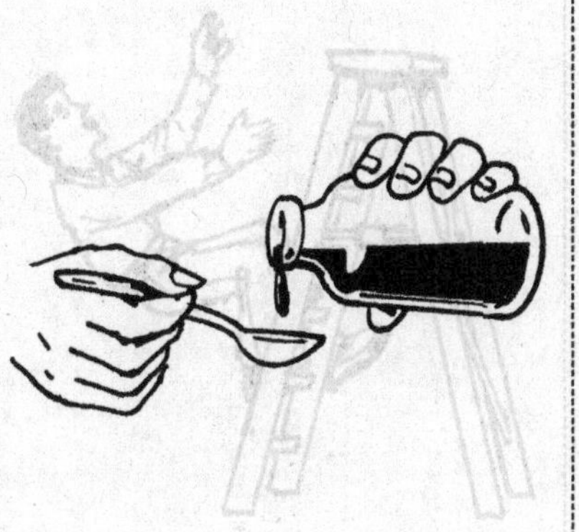

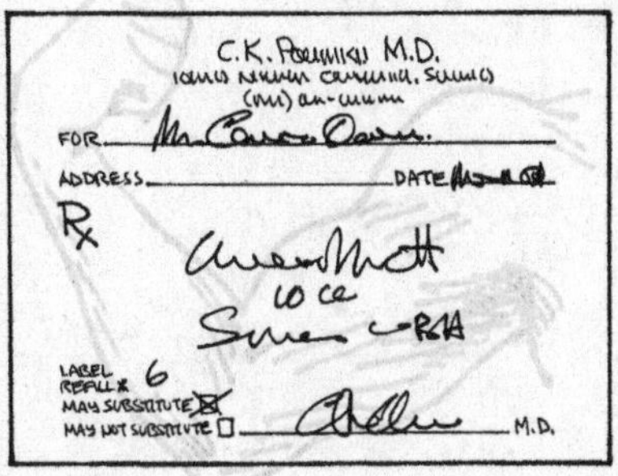

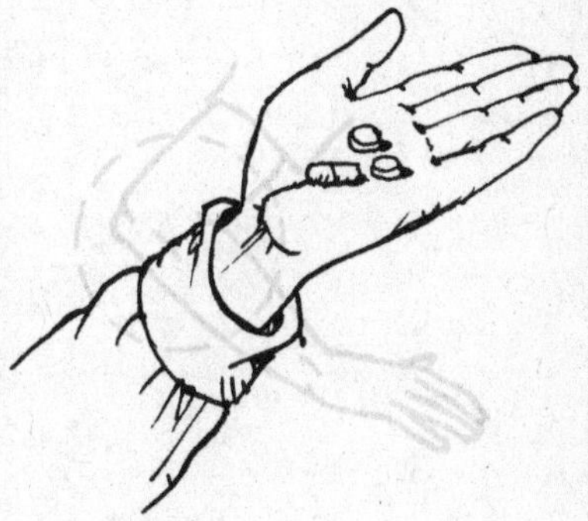

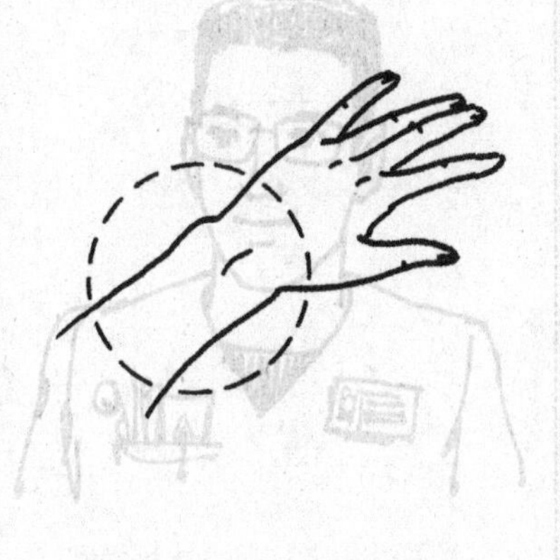

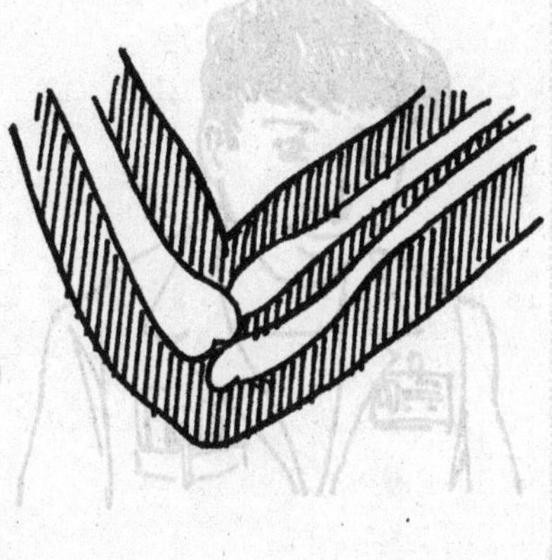

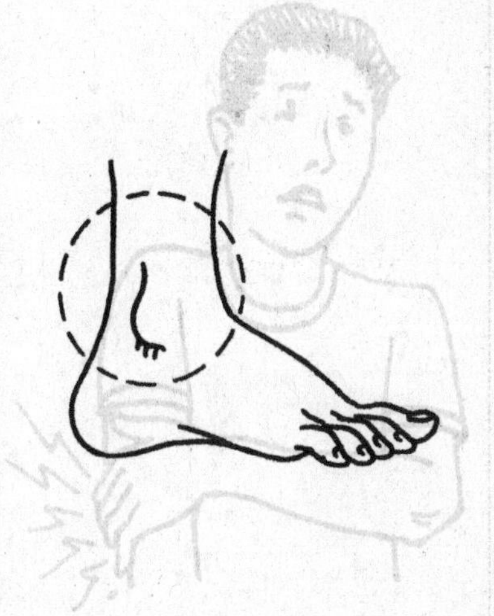

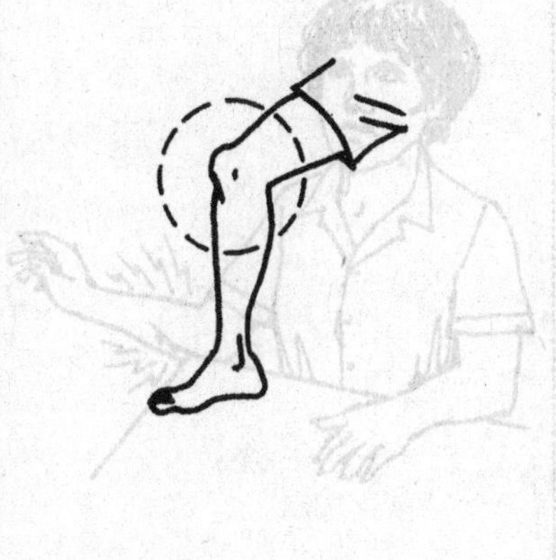

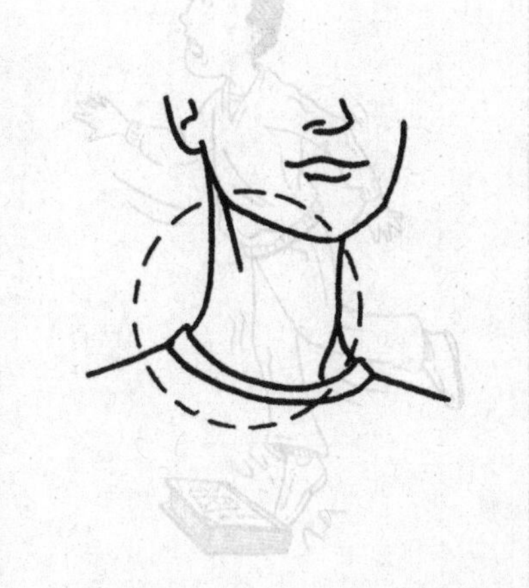

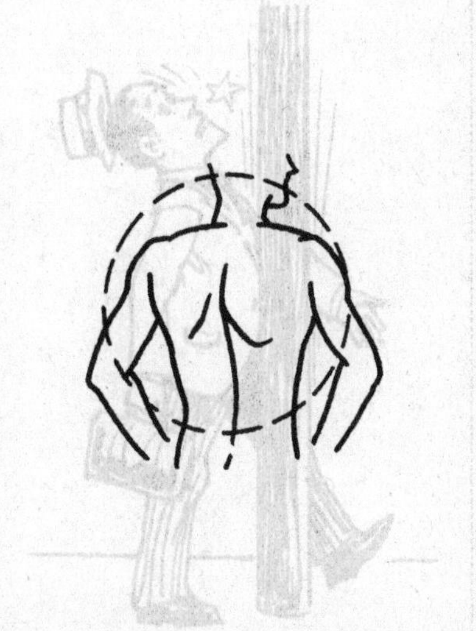

Vocabulary Clip Art

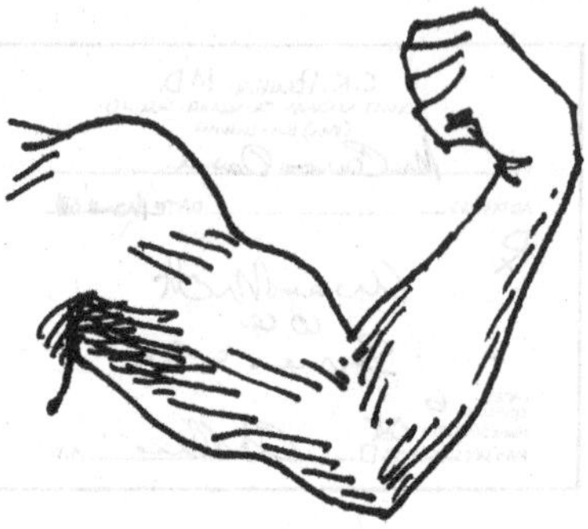

Realidades 2

Capítulo 5B

Vocabulary Clip Art

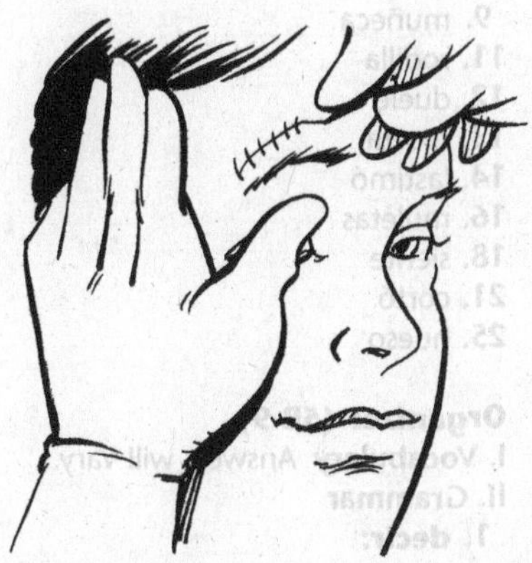

Realidades 2

Capítulo 5B

Core Practice Answers

5B-1

A.
1. examinó
2. dolían
3. hueso
4. recetó
5. inyección
6. yeso
7. radiografías
8. dio puntadas

B.
1. La muñeca
2. El codo
3. El tobillo
4. La ambulancia
5. La sangre
6. La medicina

5B-2
1. la espalda
2. la rodilla
3. muletas
4. venda
5. enfermeros
6. silla de ruedas
7. receta
8. sala de emergencia

5B-3
1. pasó
2. Tropezó
3. se cayó
4. lastimó
5. dolía
6. cortó
7. rota
8. muletas
9. yeso
10. lástima

5B-4
1. La familia Suárez trabajaba en casa.
2. Paquito chocó con la escalera y el papá se cayó al suelo.
3. Paquito se cayó y se lastimó la cabeza.
4. Al papá le dolía mucho el tobillo y la espalda porque se lastimaron los dos.
5. Mamá tropezó con Paquito y se cayó sobre el papá.
6. Los tres estaban en el suelo cuando entró Sarita.

5B-5
1. Tuve
2. caí
3. pude
4. Vino
5. llevó
6. trajeron
7. examinaron
8. puso
9. dijeron
10. pusieron
11. enseñaron
12. recetaron
13. Estuve

5B-6
1. se estaba afeitando (estaba afeitándose)
2. se estaba vistiendo (estaba vistiéndose)
3. estaban jugando
4. estábamos pidiendo
5. estaba escribiendo
6. estaba sirviendo
7. estaba leyendo

5B-7

Paragraph 1: P, I, P, I, P, P, P
Paragraph 2: P, P, I, P, p, P, P,
Paragraph 3: I, P

B.
1. ocurrió
2. estábamos caminando
3. vimos
4. estaba corriendo
5. me caí
6. oí
7. me lastimé
8. hablé
9. dijeron
10. estaban leyendo
11. oyeron
12. dijo
13. se lastimaron
14. murieron
15. estaba cruzando
16. se chocó

Crucigrama (5B-8)

Horizontal:
2. emergencia
4. radiografía
5. ambulancia
8. espalda
10. recetó
15. enfermera
17. pastillas
19. venda
20. medicina
22. puntadas
23. torció
24. chocó
26. yeso
27. puso

Vertical:
1. inyección
3. ruedas
6. músculos
7. tropezó
9. muñeca
11. rodilla
12. duele
13. receta
14. lastimó
16. muletas
18. siente
21. cortó
25. hueso

Organizer (5B-9)

I. Vocabulary Answers will vary.

II. Grammar

1. **decir:**

dije	dijimos
dijiste	dijisteis
dijo	dijeron

venir:

vine	vinimos
viniste	vinisteis
vino	vinieron

traer:

traje	trajimos
trajiste	trajisteis
trajo	trajeron

poner:

puse	pusimos
pusiste	pusisteis
puso	pusieron

2. diciendo, pidiendo, siguiendo, durmiendo, vistiendo, creyendo

Realidades 2 — Capítulo 5B

Nombre ______________________ Hora ______

Fecha ______________________

Vocabulary Flash Cards, Sheet 1

Write the Spanish vocabulary word or phrase below each picture. Be sure to include the article for each noun.

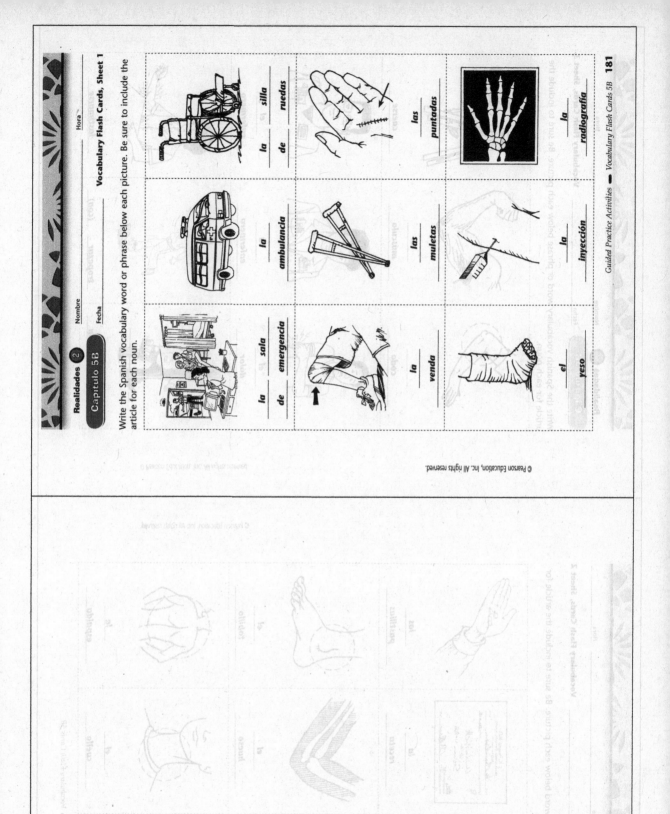

la sala de emergencia

la ambulancia

la silla de ruedas

la venda

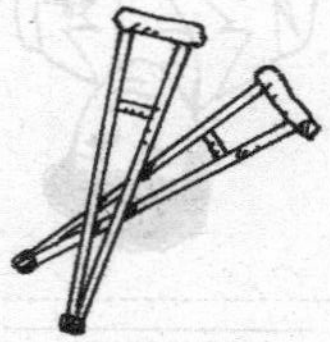

las muletas

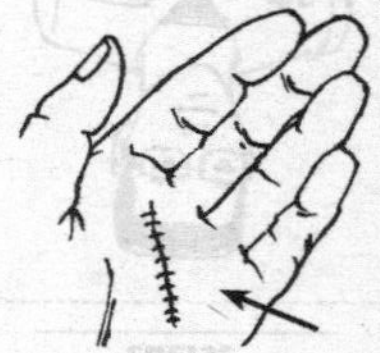

las puntadas

el yeso

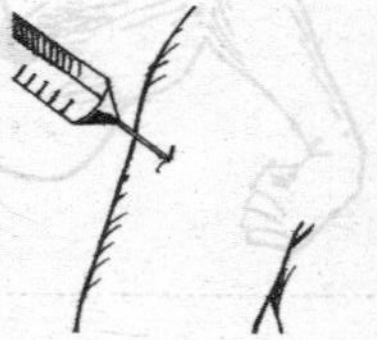

la inyección

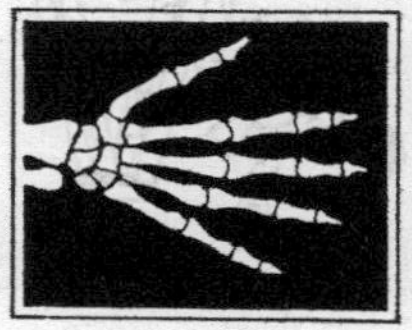

la radiografía

Realidades 2 Nombre ______ Hora ______

Capítulo 5B Fecha ______ **Vocabulary Flash Cards, Sheet 2**

Write the Spanish vocabulary word below each picture. Be sure to include the article for each noun.

la

medicina

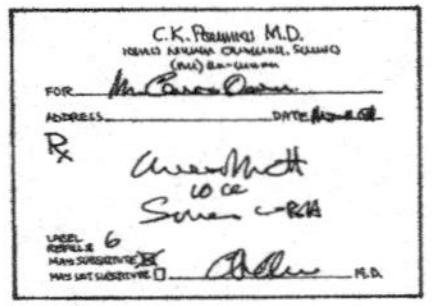

la

receta

las

pastillas

la

muñeca

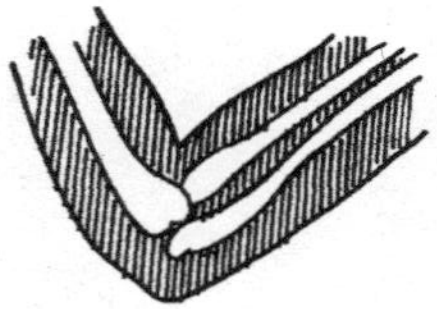

el

hueso

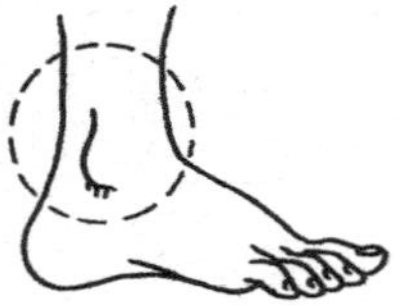

el

tobillo

la

rodilla

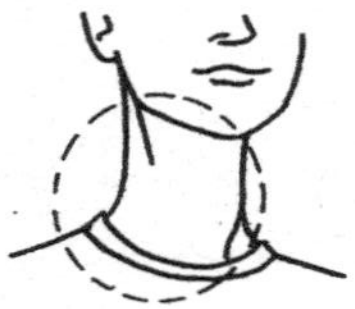

el

cuello

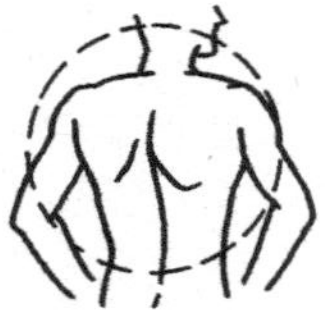

la

espalda

Realidades 2 Nombre ______ Hora ______

Capítulo 5B Fecha ______ **Vocabulary Flash Cards, Sheet 3**

Write the Spanish vocabulary word or phrase below each picture. Be sure to include the article for each noun.

el

codo

el

músculo

caerse

el

dolor

la

enfermera

el

enfermero

chocar **con**

tropezar **(con)**

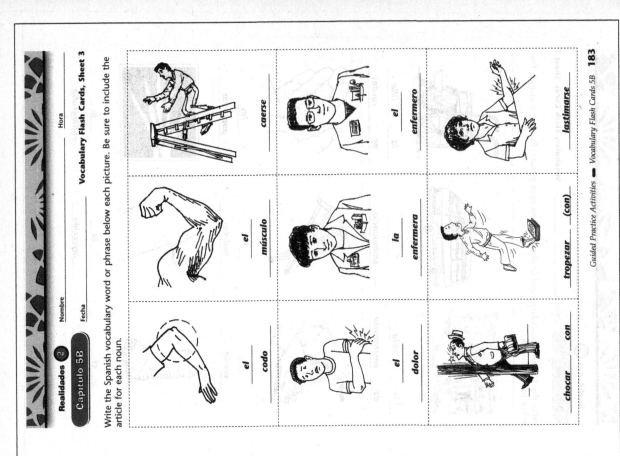

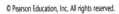

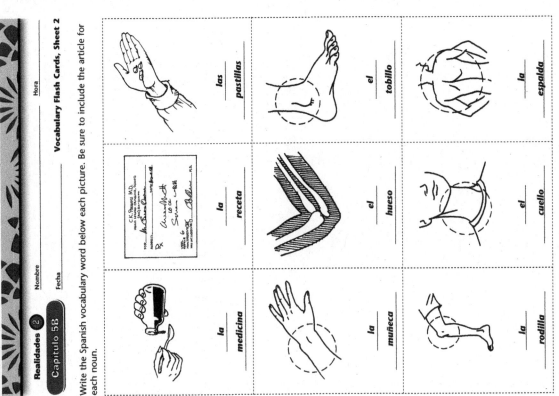

lastimarse

Realidades 2 | Nombre ______ Hora ______

Capítulo 5B | Fecha ______

Vocabulary Flash Cards, Sheet 4

Write the Spanish vocabulary word below each picture. If there is a word or phrase, copy it in the space provided. Be sure to include the article for each noun.

 romperse	 sacar una radiografía	 poner una inyección
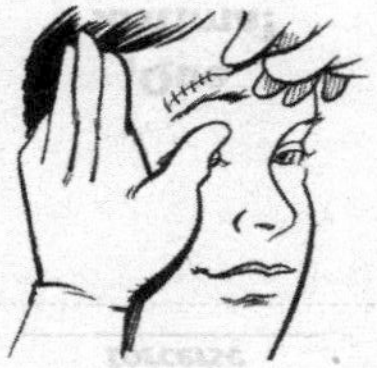 dar puntadas	 el hombro	 examinar
 se cayó	**doler** — doler	**pobrecito, pobrecita** — pobrecito, pobrecita

Realidades 2 | Nombre ______ Hora ______

Capítulo 5B | Fecha ______

Vocabulary Flash Cards, Sheet 5

Copy the word or phrase in the space provided. Be sure to include the article for each noun.

la sangre — la sangre	**recetar** — recetar	**roto, rota** — roto, rota
me caigo — me caigo	**el accidente** — el accidente	**te caes** — te caes
se cayeron — se cayeron	**cortarse** — cortarse	**¿Qué te pasó?** — ¿Qué te pasó?

Realidades 2 | Nombre ____ | Hora ____

Capítulo 5B | Fecha ____ | **Vocabulary Flash Cards, Sheet 6**

Copy the word or phrase in the space provided. The blank cards can be used to write and practice other Spanish vocabulary for the chapter.

torcerse ***torcerse***	**sentirse** ***sentirse***	**moverse** ***moverse***
¡Qué lástima! ***¡Qué lástima!***	____	____
____	____	____

Realidades 2 | Nombre ____ | Hora ____

Capítulo 5B | Fecha ____ | **Vocabulary Check, Sheet 1**

Tear out this page. Write the English words on the lines. Fold the paper along the dotted line to see the correct answers so you can check your work.

el enfermero, la enfermera	***nurse***
la inyección	***injection, shot***
la medicina	***medicine***
las pastillas	***pills***
las puntadas	***stitches***
la radiografía	***X-ray***
la receta	***prescription***
la sala de emergencia	***emergency room***
la sangre	***blood***
la venda	***bandage***
el yeso	***cast***
el accidente	***accident***
la ambulancia	***ambulance***
cortarse	***to cut oneself***
lastimarse	***to hurt oneself***

Fold In

Realidades 2 Nombre Hora

Capítulo 5B Fecha **Vocabulary Check, Sheet 2**

Tear out this page. Write the Spanish words on the lines. Fold the paper along the dotted line to see the correct answers so you can check your work.

nurse	***el enfermero, la enfermera***
injection, shot	***la inyección***
medicine	***la medicina***
pills	***las pastillas***
stitches	***las puntadas***
X-ray	***la radiografía***
prescription	***la receta***
emergency room	***la sala de emergencia***
blood	***la sangre***
bandage	***la venda***
cast	***el yeso***
accident	***el accidente***
ambulance	***la ambulancia***
to cut oneself	***cortarse***
to hurt oneself	***lastimarse***

Fold In

Realidades 2 Nombre Hora

Capítulo 5B Fecha **Vocabulary Check, Sheet 3**

Tear out this page. Write the English words on the lines. Fold the paper along the dotted line to see the correct answers so you can check your work.

romperse	***to break, to tear***
torcerse	***to twist, to sprain***
tropezar (con)	***to trip (over)***
el codo	***elbow***
el cuello	***neck***
la espalda	***back***
el hombro	***shoulder***
el hueso	***bone***
la muñeca	***wrist***
el músculo	***muscle***
la rodilla	***knee***
el tobillo	***ankle***
pobrecito, pobrecita	***poor thing***

Fold In

Realidades 2 Nombre ______ Hora ______

Capítulo 5B Fecha ______ **Vocabulary Check, Sheet 4**

Tear out this page. Write the Spanish words on the lines. Fold the paper along the dotted line to see the correct answers so you can check your work.

to break, to tear	***romperse***
to twist, to sprain	***torcerse***
to trip (over)	***tropezar (con)***
elbow	***el codo***
neck	***el cuello***
back	***la espalda***
shoulder	***el hombro***
bone	***el hueso***
wrist	***la muñeca***
muscle	***el músculo***
knee	***la rodilla***
ankle	***el tobillo***
poor thing	***pobrecito, pobrecita***

Fold In

To hear a complete list of the vocabulary for this chapter, go to www.realidades.com and type in the Web Code jdd-0599. Then click on **Repaso del capítulo.**

Realidades 2 Nombre ______ Hora ______

Capítulo 5B Fecha ______ **Guided Practice Activities 5B-1**

Irregular preterites: *venir, poner, decir,* and *traer* (p. 274)

- The verbs **venir, poner, decir,** and **traer** have a similar pattern in the preterite as that of **estar, poder,** and **tener.** They have irregular stems. Remember that the endings do not have any accent marks.

Infinitive	Stem
decir	dij-
estar	estuv-
poder	pud-
poner	pus-
tener	tuv-
traer	traj-
venir	vin-

Irregular Preterite Endings	
-e	-imos
-iste	-isteis
-o	-ieron, -eron

Preterite of *venir*	
vine	vinimos
viniste	vinisteis
vino	vinieron

A. Look at the drawings showing what happened to Diego. Then, read the paragraph and circle the correct irregular preterite form of the verb in parentheses. The first one has been done for you.

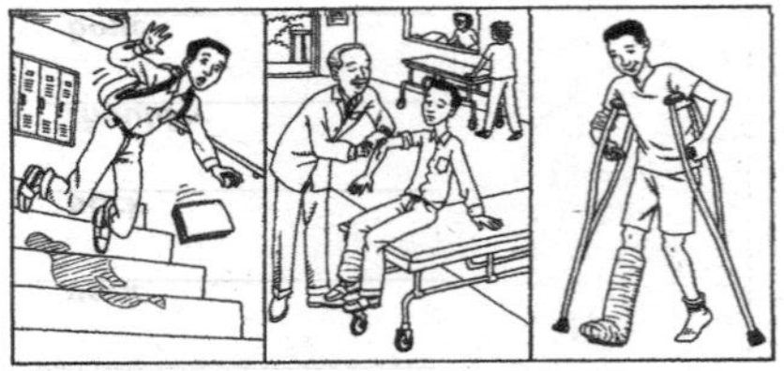

Ayer Diego **(tuve / tuvo)** un accidente. Sus padres **(vino / vinieron)** a la escuela porque Diego **(tuvo / tuve)** que ir a la sala de emergencia. Yo fui con ellos. Nosotros **(estuvieron / estuvimos)** con él en el hospital por seis horas. Diego no **(pudo / pudiste)** moverse por dos horas. Después, el enfermero le **(trajo / trajimos)** una venda y le **(puso / pusieron)** la venda en el brazo.

El enfermero **(dije / dijo)** que su brazo no estaba roto pero ellos le **(pusimos / pusieron)** un yeso en el tobillo. Luego, Diego **(tuvo / tuvieron)** que caminar con muletas. Yo le **(dijiste / dije)** a Diego que quería escribir mi nombre en el yeso.

realidades.com • Web Code: jdd-0513

Irregular preterites: *venir, poner, decir,* and *traer* (*continued*)

B. Look at the sentences below and fill in the missing stem of the verb in parentheses for each ending that is given. Follow the model.

Modelo (traer) La enfermera me *traj* o una silla de ruedas.

1. (venir) Todos ***vin*** ieron a la sala de emergencia conmigo.
2. (decir) Tú ***dij*** iste "¡Ay!" cuando te lastimaste.
3. (traer) Nosotros le ***traj*** imos una venda y medicina.
4. (poner) La enfermera me ***pus*** o una inyección.
5. (estar) La familia ***estuv*** o en el hospital por cuatro horas.
6. (tener) El coche ***tuv*** o un accidente anoche.
7. (poder) Yo no ***pud*** e ver lo que pasó.

C. The following actions happened in the past. Write in the correct form of the verb in parentheses to complete each sentence. Follow the model.

Modelo Los enfermeros me *pusieron* una inyección. (poner)

1. Mi mamá y papá me ***trajeron*** una silla de ruedas. (traer)
2. El enfermero me ***dijo*** que debo tomar una pastilla para el dolor. (decir)
3. Mi hermano ***vino*** a la sala de emergencia. (venir)
4. ¡Qué lástima que tú no ***pudiste*** venir con mi hermano! (poder)
5. Yo no ***estuve*** en la sala de emergencia anoche. (estar)
6. Nosotros ***tuvimos*** que salir del edificio porque un incendio comenzó. (tener)
7. Por desgracia, nadie ***trajo*** botellas de agua. (traer)

Imperfect progressive and preterite (p. 277)

- Remember that the present progressive is used to tell what someone is doing. It is formed by the present tense of the verb **estar** + present participle (**-ando** or **-iendo**):

  La doctora está hablando. *The doctor is talking.*
  Laura y Juan están corriendo. *Laura and Juan are running.*

- As shown above, the present progressive is used to tell what *is* happening. The imperfect progressive is used to tell what *was* happening. It uses the imperfect tense of **estar** + present participle:

  La doctora estaba hablando. *The doctor was talking.*
  Laura y Juan estaban corriendo. *Laura and Juan were running.*

A. First, circle the present progressive in each sentence. Then, change each sentence from the present progressive to the *imperfect* progressive. Follow the model.

Modelo Eliana está caminando con muletas. *estaba* *caminando*

1. Juana está hablando con el doctor. ***estaba*** ***hablando***
2. Nosotros estamos bebiendo bastante agua. ***estábamos*** ***bebiendo***
3. Yo estoy examinando las puntadas. ***estaba*** ***examinando***
4. Tú estás sacando una radiografía. ***estabas*** ***sacando***
5. La enfermera está poniendo una inyección. ***estaba*** ***poniendo***
6. El doctor me está dando puntadas. ***estaba*** ***dando***
7. Los paramédicos le están moviendo a otro piso. ***estaban*** ***moviendo***

- You can use the imperfect progressive tense to describe something that was happening over a period of time. The imperfect progressive uses the imperfect tense of **estar** + the present participle:

  Teresa estaba escribiendo un cuento. *Teresa was writing a story.*

B. The following sentences tell what people were doing yesterday in the hospital when the storm began. Complete each sentence by writing in the correct form of **estar** and the participle of the verb in parentheses. Follow the model.

Cuando la tormenta comenzó...

Modelo Mario *estaba* *caminando* con muletas. (caminar)

1. mi hermano ***estaba*** ***sacando*** una radiografía. (sacar)
2. mis amigos y yo ***estábamos*** ***esperando*** la ambulancia. (esperar)

Imperfect progressive and preterite (*continued*)

3. la Dra. Carrillo ***estaba*** ***escribiendo*** una receta. (escribir)
4. usted ***estaba*** ***ayudando*** a Javier. (ayudar)
5. tú ***estabas*** ***poniendo*** una inyección. (poner)

- Remember that some present participles have changes in their spelling.
- -ir stem-changing verbs have a vowel change to "i" or "u":
  pedir → pidiendo   vestir → vistiendo   dormir → durmiendo
- **leer, caer, creer,** and **traer** have a "y":
  leer → leyendo   caer → cayendo   creer → creyendo   traer → trayendo

C. A paramedic has to report to his boss about what different patients were doing when they got hurt. Complete his statements. Follow the model.

Modelo Los niños / seguir / a sus hermanos mayores
Los niños estaban siguiendo a sus hermanos mayores .

1. Los camareros / servir / sopa muy caliente
   Los camareros estaban sirviendo sopa muy caliente .
2. Felipe Sánchez / leer / una novela muy interesante
   Felipe Sánchez estaba leyendo una novela muy interesante .
3. Adelita Romero / vestir / a su perro
   Adelita Romero estaba vistiendo a su perro .
4. Nosotros / subir / las escaleras
   Nosotros estábamos subiendo las escaleras .
5. El señor Peña / dormir / en el sofá
   El señor Peña estaba durmiendo en el sofá .

realidades.com • Web Code: jdd-0514

Imperfect progressive and preterite (*continued*)

- The imperfect progressive and the preterite tenses can be used in the same sentence. The imperfect progressive describes what was happening while the preterite tells about something specific that happened or that interrupted an action.

  Ella estaba corriendo cuando se lastimó el tobillo.
  She was running when she hurt her ankle.

D. For each sentence below, draw a line beneath the verb in the imperfect progressive tense that identifies what was happening. Then, identify the interrupted action by circling the verb in the preterite tense. The first one is done for you.

1. Yo estaba corriendo cuando tropecé.
2. Cuando Miguel se lastimó, él estaba jugando al fútbol.
3. Tú estabas sirviendo la comida cuando te lastimaste.
4. Las hermanas Paulatino estaban usando la silla de ruedas cuando tuvieron el accidente.
5. Cuando Teresa llegó a la sala de emergencia le estaba doliendo mucho el brazo.

E. The sentences below describe what different people were doing when something bad happened to them. Read the sentences and circle the verb that completes each sentence in the most logical way. Follow the model.

Modelo Antonio (**estaba jugando** / **jugó**) al tenis cuando se lastimó la rodilla.

1. María y Fernando estaban esquiando cuando (**se estaban cayendo** / **se cayeron**).
2. Nosotros estábamos peleándonos cuando yo (**me estaba rompiendo** / **me rompí**) el dedo.
3. MaríaTeresa (**estaba caminando** / **caminó**) a casa sin chaqueta cuando comenzó a nevar.
4. Cuando yo me lastimé, (**estaba corriendo** / **corrí**) un maratón.

F. Look at the information in the boxes below. Use the imperfect progressive and the preterite to fill in the blanks with the phrases contained in the boxes. Follow the model.

Modelo

What was happening	Specific occurrence that took place
levantar pesas	lastimarse

Marcos *estaba levantando pesas* cuando *se lastimó* el hombro.

1.

What was happening	Specific occurrence that took place
usar tijeras	cortarse

Tú ***estabas usando tijeras*** cuando ***te cortaste*** el dedo.

realidades.com • Web Code: jdd-0514

Imperfect progressive and preterite (*continued*)

2.

What was happening	Specific occurrence that took place
leer el periódico	ver

Maricarmen ***estaba leyendo el periódico*** cuando ***vio*** del accidente.

3.

What was happening	Specific occurrence that took place
pedir una silla de ruedas	caerse

Yo ***estaba pidiendo una silla de ruedas*** cuando ***me caí***.

4.

What was happening	Specific occurrence that took place
vestirse	sentir dolor

Tú ***te estabas vistiendo*** cuando ***sentiste dolor*** en la espalda.

- When you use pronouns with the imperfect progressive, you can put them before **estar** or attach them to the participle. Remember to add an accent over the "e" or "a" of the participle ending.
  Yo me estaba sirviendo. *or:* **Yo estaba sirviéndome.**

G. Rewrite the sentences below by putting the underlined object pronoun after the conjugated present partciple. Follow the model.

Modelo Javier se estaba cepillando los dientes.
Javier estaba cepillándose los dientes

1. Tía Luisa me estaba trayendo un sándwich.
   Tía Luisa estaba trayéndome un sándwich
2. Cristina y Julia nos estaban pidiendo ayuda.
   Cristina y Julia estaban pidiéndonos ayuda
3. Tú te estabas duchando.
   Tú estabas duchándote
4. Nosotros nos estábamos levantando.
   Nosotros estamos levantándonos

Lectura: Mejorar la salud para todos (pp. 282–283)

A. The articles in your textbook reading are about health campaigns. A good strategy for understanding these articles is to look for cognates. The following words are cognates from the reading. Say each word in Spanish aloud and then write the letter of the English word that matches it.

1. ***a*** internacional — **a.** international **b.** internal
2. ***a*** institución — **a.** institution **b.** inspiration
3. ***b*** promover — **a.** protect **b.** promote
4. ***a*** prevención — **a.** prevention **b.** preview
5. ***b*** voluntarios — **a.** volume **b.** volunteers

B. Look at this title from one of the health articles in your textbook. Then, read the sentences that follow and write **L** (for **Lectura**) if it's something you read in the title. Write **N** (for **No**) if it's something you didn't read in the title.

> *Cuerpo de la Paz* (Peace Corps) *y Medical Aid for Children of Latin America (MACLA) ayudan a niños que requieren cirugía plástica* (plastic surgery).

1. MACLA significa *Medical Aid for Children of Latin America.* ***L***
2. Cuerpo de la Paz y MACLA ayudan a niños que requieren cirugía plástica. ***L***
3. Los niños son de Europa. ***N***

C. The following are quotes from the reading in your textbook. Read what was said by the singers Luis Enrique and Mercedes Sosa. Then, circle the option that best completes each sentence.

> *"La vida nos pone a prueba* (test) *día a día, con momentos buenos y malos. Es nuestra responsabilidad tomar las decisiones correctas. ¡Dile no a las drogas y dile sí a la vida, siempre!" –Luis Enrique*
>
> *"No les falles* (fail) *a tus chicos, llévalos a vacunar* (to be vaccinated). *Así pueden estar completamente protegidos y darle ¡gracias a la vida!" –Mercedes Sosa*

1. Luis Enrique speaks about
   ⓐ the prevention of drug abuse.
   b. vaccinations.
2. Mercedes Sosa speaks about
   a. donating blood.
   ⓑ vaccinations.

Presentación escrita (p. 285) *Answers will vary.*

Task: Imagine you have to report an accident you saw near school. Organize your ideas before you write the report for your school.

A. First, you need to describe what you were doing when the accident occurred. Choose an activity from the list below. Then, circle the activity.

¿Qué estabas haciendo?

1. Estaba saliendo de la escuela.
2. Estaba jugando con mis amigos.
3. Estaba hablando con la profesora.
4. Estaba entrando en la escuela.
5. Estaba caminando con mi hermano.

B. Next, the chart below can help you organize information about the accident. You need to determine: What happened? When did it happen? Who was hurt? Who helped? Circle one option in each column.

¿Qué pasó?	¿Cuándo ocurrió?	¿Quién se lastimó?	¿Quiénes ayudaron?
un árbol se cayó	por la mañana	un estudiante una estudiante	los estudiantes
un coche chocó con algo	por la tarde	un profesor una profesora	los bomberos
una ventana se rompió	por la noche	una señora un hombre	una enfermera la policía

C. Now, use your answers from **parts A and B** to complete a report of the accident. You can follow the model below.

Yo ____________ cuando vi un accidente. ____________

____________ y ____________ se lastimó.

____________ lo/la ayudó.

D. Read through your accident report to check for spelling, correct verb usage, vocabulary, and clarity.

E. Share the report with a partner who should check the following:

_____ Is the report easy to understand?

_____ Is the information in a clear, logical order?

_____ Is there anything to add to give more information?

_____ Are there any errors?

Realidades 2 Nombre Hora

Capítulo 5B Fecha **VIDEO**

Antes de ver el video

Actividad 1

When do you need to stay in bed because you are sick, and when do you need to go to the hospital? Write three examples for each. The first ones have been done for you.

¿Cuándo me quedo en cama?	¿Cuándo voy al hospital?
Cuando tengo un dolor de cabeza muy fuerte	*Cuando me lastimo el brazo*
Answers will vary.	Answers will vary.

¿Comprendes?

Actividad 2

Identify the speaker of each of the following quotes from the video.

1. "Si no hay un terremoto él no se despierta ..." **Raúl**
2. "¡Qué lástima! ... ¿Y Tomás?" **Gloria**
3. "¡Ay, Dios mío!" **Rosa**
4. "¿Qué pasó entonces?" **Gloria**
5. "¡Pobre Tomás!" **Rosa**
6. "¡El pobrecito soy yo!" **Raúl**
7. "¡No debes despertarte a las tres de la mañana!" **Gloria**
8. "¿Por qué no me dijeron nada?" **Tomás**

Actividad 3

Look at each video scene and write one or two complete sentences to tell what is happening.

1. Answers may vary.
Raúl estaba durmiendo cuando oyó el despertador a las tres de la mañana.

Realidades 2 Nombre Hora

Capítulo 5B Fecha **VIDEO**

2. Raúl tenía que apagar el despertador.

3. Raúl chocó con la mesa y se lastimó el brazo. También se cortó la muñeca.

4. La mamá dice: "¡Raúl! ¿Qué paso? ¡Ay, Dios mío!"

5. Su mamá y su papá le pusieron una venda en la muñeca y lo llevaron al hospital.

6. Entraron en la sala de emergencia y lo pusieron en una silla de ruedas.

Y, ¿qué más?

Actividad 4

Have you ever had a silly accident? What happened? Answer the questions about your accident or the accident of someone you know.

1. ¿Qué hacías cuando ocurrió el accidente?
Answers will vary.
2. ¿Te lastimaste algo?
3. ¿Fuiste a la sala de emergencia? ¿Qué pasó?

Realidades 2 Nombre ____ Hora ____

Capítulo 5B Fecha ____ **AUDIO**

Actividad 5

Your friend Juan Luis just spent his first day as a volunteer in the local hospital's emergency room. Listen as he tells his parents what happened. Write the number of the description in the corresponding circle in the picture below. You will hear each description twice.

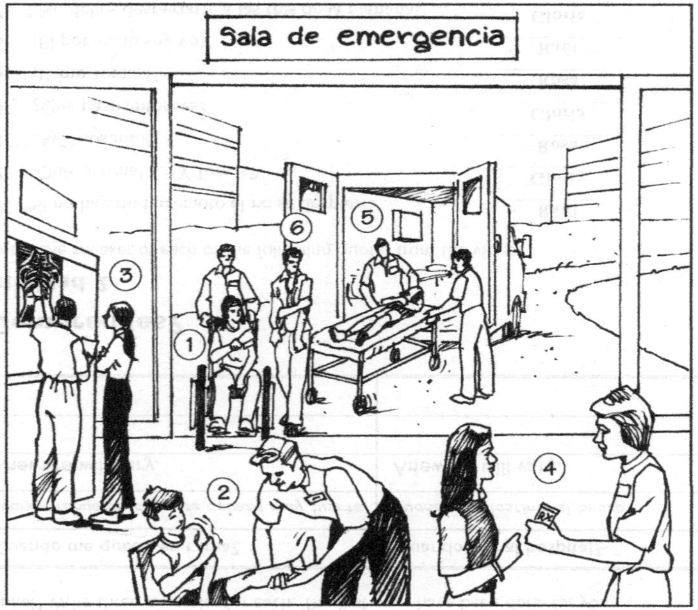

Realidades 2 Nombre ____ Hora ____

Capítulo 5B Fecha ____ **AUDIO**

Actividad 6

Listen as several teenagers talk about what happened when they were injured recently. Match what each describes to one of the pictures below. Write the corresponding letter in the blanks below. You will hear each description twice.

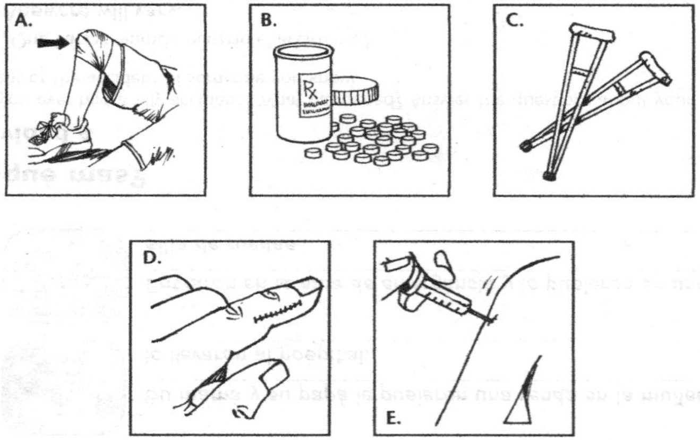

1. B 2. C 3. D 4. E 5. A

Actividad 7

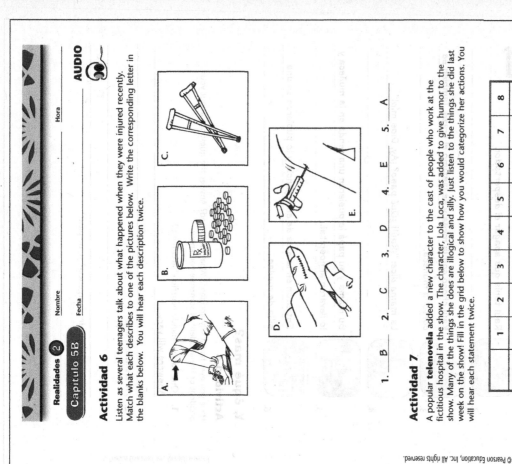

A popular **telenovela** added a new character to the cast of people who work at the fictitious hospital in the show. The character, Lola Loca, was added to give humor to the show. Many of the things she does are illogical and silly. Just listen to the things she did last week on the show! Fill in the grid below to show how you would categorize her actions. You will hear each statement twice.

	1	2	3	4	5	6	7	8
Lógico			X		X		X	
Ilógico	X	X		X		X		X

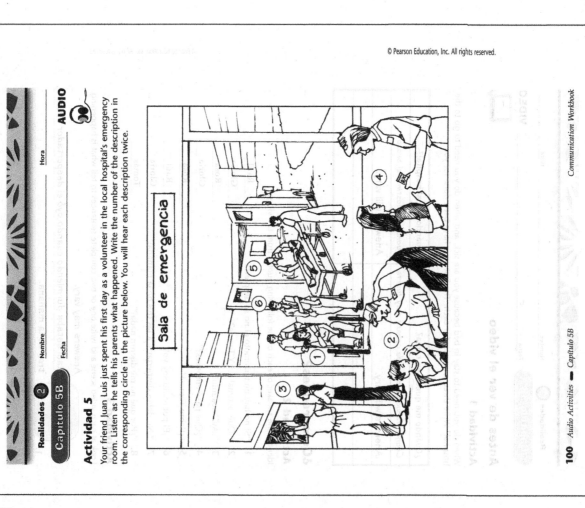

Actividad 8

A group of friends was recalling what each was doing when the police arrived at the scene of an accident. Write the number of the statement in the corresponding circle in the picture below. You will hear each statement twice.

Actividad 9

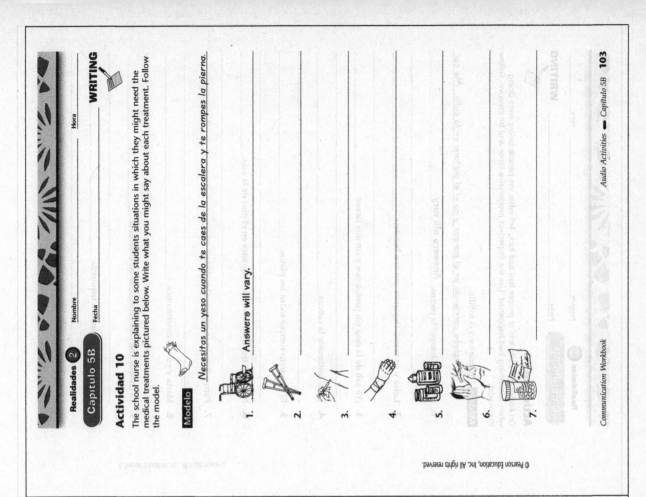

As a counselor at a boy's summer camp, Jorge is the person to whom the children report any accidents or injuries. Listen as children run to Jorge and tell him what campers were doing when a recent injury occurred. Take notes in the grid below about what happened to each child. You will hear each set of statements twice.

Nombre del niño	¿Qué estaba haciendo el niño?	¿Qué se lastimó?
Jaime	estaba saltando la cuerda	el tobillo
Luis	estaba corriendo	la rodilla
Cristóbal	estaba subiendo un árbol	la pierna
Óscar	estaba corriendo en su bicicleta	la espalda
Félix	estaba caminando	el brazo

Actividad 10

The school nurse is explaining to some students situations in which they might need the medical treatments pictured below. Write what you might say about each treatment. Follow the model.

Modelo *Necesitas un yeso cuando te caes de la escalera y te rompes la pierna.*

1. **Answers will vary.**

2. ______

3. ______

4. ______

5. ______

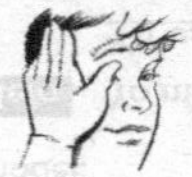

6. ______

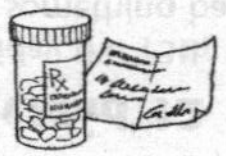

7. ______

Realidades 2 | Nombre ____ Hora ____

Capítulo 5B | Fecha ____ **WRITING**

Actividad 11

Carmela is writing in her diary after a busy day. Look at the pictures below of what she and her friends did, and write short diary entries based on each one. Follow the model.

Answers may vary.

Modelo Javier *le dijo la verdad a su padre. No pudo mentirle a su papá.*

1. Mariel **vino a mi casa. Me trajo un pastel.**

2. Elena y yo **le trajimos flores a nuestro vecino. Las pusimos enfrente de la casa.**

3. Mis hermanos **hicieron la tarea de...**

4. Ayer yo **tuve que dar de comer al perro.**

5. El cartero **me trajo un paquete interesante.**

6. A las nueve los estudiantes **estuvieron en la clase.**

Realidades 2 | Nombre ____ Hora ____

Capítulo 5B | Fecha ____ **WRITING**

Actividad 12

On Friday the 13th, lots of people had bad luck. Tell what the people below were doing when something bad happened. Use the imperfect progressive tense and be creative. Follow the model.

Modelo Yo me torcí el tobillo.
Yo estaba corriendo en el parque y no vi el plátano en la calle. Me caí.

1. Marcos se rompió la pierna. **Answers will vary.**
2. Luisa y su mamá chocaron con una bicicleta. ____
3. ¡Yo salí de la casa sin pantalones y sin mis llaves! ____
4. Tú te lastimaste la cabeza. ____
5. El camarero rompió todos los platos. ____
6. Nosotros tropezamos con los juguetes en el piso de la sala. ____
7. Paco y Ramón se cortaron los dedos. ____
8. Marta y yo nos enfermamos. ____
9. Yo choqué con otro estudiante en la escuela. ____
10. Tú te torciste la muñeca izquierda. ____

Realidades 2 Nombre ____ Hora ____

Capítulo 5B Fecha ____ **WRITING**

Actividad 13

Julieta is a girl who likes to do too many things at once. Last week, her hectic lifestyle finally caught up with her.

A. Look at the picture below and describe at least four activities Julieta was doing at the same time. Follow the model.

Modelo *Julieta estaba leyendo.*

1. estaba escuchando la música
2. estaba hablando por teléfono
3. estaba preparando una ensalada
4. estaba cocinando
5. estaba mezclando la salsa

B. Now, think about a hectic day you or someone you know had recently. Write five sentences to tell what happened. Follow the model.

Modelo *Mi hermana Julia estaba caminando y comiendo cuando se cayó y se lastimó la cabeza.*

1. Answers will vary.
2. ____
3. ____
4. ____
5. ____

Test Preparation Answers

Reading Skills
p. 250 2. **B**
p. 251 2. **D**

Integrated Performance Assessment
p. 252
Answers will vary.

Practice Test: Las rosas de Casilda
p. 254

1. D
2. J
3. A
4. H
5. Answers will vary, but may include: When Casilda saw the prisoners for the first time, she might have felt confused, but later she felt empathy for them, and wanted to help them. She might have felt helpless and afraid to help, but later gained courage and tried to ease their suffering. She risked her father's anger because she put the prisoners' suffering before her own well-being and safety.
6. Las respuestas variarán, pero los estudiantes pueden decir que generalmente es necesario obedecer a los padres y las reglas de la familia, la escuela y la comunidad, pero no es necesario obedecer a las personas que no respetan a los demás.

Table of Contents

Tema 6: La televisión y el cine

Capítulo 6A: ¿Viste el partido en la televisión?

Capítulo 6B: ¿Qué película has visto?

Theme Project

La televisión y el cine
Las películas y la televisión: un juego

Overview:

You will create a game in which you ask questions in Spanish about your favorite movies and television shows. You can choose the type of game you would like to create. You must ask and answer questions about:

- actors, actresses, directors, celebrities, sports figures
- kinds of television programs and movies
- plots and characters

On a board or poster, you should include photos or drawings of the movies or shows you ask questions about.

Resources:

Digital or print photos, page layout/word processing software and/or poster board, markers, photos, glue or tape, scissors, game pieces (buttons, pennies etc.)

Sequence:

STEP 1. Review instructions with your teacher.

STEP 2. Submit a rough draft of your questions. Work with a partner and present your drafts to each other.

STEP 3. Create layouts of your game, leaving room for photos or drawings.

STEP 4. Submit a draft of the instructions to your game.

STEP 5. Play your game in a small group.

Assessment:

Your teacher will provide you with a rubric to assess this project.

Theme 6 Project: Las películas y la televisión: un juego

Project Assessment Rubric

RUBRIC	Score 1	Score 3	Score 5
Evidence of Planning	No written draft or gameboard layout provided.	Draft was written and layout created, but not corrected.	Evidence of corrected draft and layout.
Use of Illustrations	No photos/ visuals included.	Very few photos/visuals included.	Several photos/ visuals included.
Presentation	Contains details that develop ideas about shows and movies.	Includes a gameboard and some questions.	Includes a gameboard and enough questions to play the game.

21st Century Skills Rubric: Promote Collaboration

RUBRIC	Score 1	Score 3	Score 5
Research and gather information	Does not collect any information that relates to the project	Collects some basic information: some related to the topic	Collects a great deal of information: all relates to the topic
Fulfillment of team role	Does not perform any duties of assigned team role	Performs some of the duties of assigned team role	Performs all of the duties of assigned team role
Listen to others in group	Is always talking; never allows others to speak	Listens but sometimes talks too much	Listens and speaks a fair amount

School-to-Home Connection

Dear Parent or Guardian,

The theme of our current unit is *La televisión y el cine* (Television and movies). This chapter is called *¿Viste el partido en la televisión?* (Did you watch the game on TV?).

Upon completion of this chapter students will be able to:

- talk about what they saw on television
- explain how they feel about watching television
- understand cultural perspectives about television programs

Students will also explore:

- regional pronunciation variations of *ll* and *y*, and of *c* and *z*

Our textbook, *Realidades*, helps with the development of reading, writing, and speaking skills through the use of strategies, process speaking, and process writing. In this chapter, students will:

- read about the Pan American games
- speak about their favorite TV program

To reinforce and enhance learning, students can access a wide range of online resources on **realidades.com,** the personalized learning management system that accompanies the print and online Student Edition. Resources include the eText, textbook and workbook activities, audio files, videos, animations, songs, self-study tools, interactive maps, voice recording (RealTalk!), assessments, and other digital resources. Many learning tools can be accessed through the student Home Page on **realidades.com.** Other activities, specifically those that require grading, are assigned by the teacher and linked on the student Home Page within the calendar or the Assignments tab.

You will find specifications and guidelines for accessing **realidades.com** on home computers and mobile devices on MyPearsonTraining.com under the SuccessNet Plus tab.

realidades.com

For: Tips to Parents
Visit: www.realidades.com
Web Code: jce-0010

Check it out! At the end of the chapter, have your child use the new vocabulary from this chapter to tell you about the different emotions he or she might feel at sporting events, and why.

Sincerely,

Realidades 2

Capítulo 6A Videocultura Script

Cine y televisión

Spanish version:

En la actualidad, la industria del cine y la televisión de América Latina y España goza de un gran éxito internacional.

Actores como Benicio del Toro, Javier Bardem y Penélope Cruz son ya estrellas reconocidas en el mundo entero.

Los directores de cine Alfonso Cuarón y Pedro Almodóvar han dirigido películas que cautivaron a una gran audiencia.

No importa de que país o lengua se trate, las películas son el resultado de un intenso proceso creativo y de una gran colaboración.

Además del cine, la televisión es una forma de entretenimiento muy popular en los países hispanos.

Uno de los tipos de programas de televisión más vistos en América Latina es la telenovela.

Estas series de telenovela entrelazan el romance, la aventura, el misterio y la historia en tramas que en algunos casos captan la atención de un país entero.

Las telenovelas se emiten diariamente, de cinco a seis veces por semana y duran varios meses.

Hoy en día, algunas de las telenovelas populares se emiten en los Estados Unidos a una creciente audiencia latina que sintoniza diferentes canales de televisión para hispanohablantes.

English version:

In Latin America and Spain, the television and movie industries are enjoying international success.

Movie actors such as Benicio del Toro, Javier Bardem, and Penélope Cruz are recognized around the world.

Talented film directors such as Alfonso Cuarón and Pedro Almodóvar create movies that appeal to a wide audience.

No matter the country or language, movies are the result of a collaborative, creative process.

In addition to going to the movies, watching television is a popular form of entertainment across the Spanish-speaking world.

One of the highest-rated television shows in Latin America is the *telenovela*.

These soap opera miniseries weave together romance, adventure, mystery, and history in storylines that often capture the attention of an entire country.

They generally appear five or six nights a week and end after a run of several months.

Today in the United States, popular *telenovelas* are broadcast to the growing Latino audience on the different Spanish television networks.

Realidades 2

Capítulo 6A

Input Script

Presentation

Input Vocabulary 1 and Dialogue: Present the *A primera vista* athlete and sports fan vocabulary by staging a paper football game. Make a paper football, or ask a student to make one for you. Explain the rules or have a student explain them: one team at a time tries to shove the football across the table so that part of the football is hanging over the edge of the table. This is a touchdown, worth six points. The team scoring the touchdown gets to attempt a field goal for an extra point by "kicking" the football with an index finger through uprights formed by the opponent's hands. Place the transparency on the screen and use it to explain to students their roles during the football game. You will be the sports announcer. There will be four players on each team and one trainer per team. The rest of the class will be the sports fans. Divide them into fans for one team or the other. Teach the fans the emotions in *A primera vista* that they will display during the game. Begin the game. Announce the score each time a team makes a touchdown or field goal. Point out when the game is tied. Describe the reactions of the fans and coach them into showing the appropriate reactions. After the game, have students listen as you read about the game described in *A primera vista*. Have them hold up the Clip Art image representing the words mentioned.

Input Vocabulary 2: Place the transparency of the newspaper articles on the screen. Read the beauty contest article and shake your head in disbelief. Explain that your cousin was also in the contest and you cannot believe she didn't win. Describe her exquisite beauty and remarkable talents. Then ask students if they would like to see a photo of your cousin. Show them a very unattractive composite photo you made from the facial features of several magazine photos. Then distribute copies of the Vocabulary Clip Art related to beauty contests and have students tear them into individual images. Describe the contest as your cousin described it to you. Have students hold up the Clip Art of the words you mention.

Next, read the quiz show article and ask students if they believe they could win on a game show. Distribute the Vocabulary Clip Art images related to quiz shows. Then call for a volunteer to be a contestant. Introduce yourself as the host and describe to the class the prizes he or she could win. Have students hold up the Clip Art images of the host and the prize whenever you mention these terms. Conduct the game by asking the student two easy questions (*¿Cuál es la fecha? ¿Dos y dos son ___?*) then say: *Y ahora, por un millón de pesos: ¿Cómo se llama la abuela del presidente de México?* (or an equally tough question). Discuss with students any game shows they know that operate this way.

Comprehension Check

- Call out different emotions and have students draw pictures of people expressing each emotion.
- Make statements that an athlete, a coach, a sports fan, or a sports commentator might make. Have students hold up the Clip Art image that shows the person who would make the statement.
- Name different celebrities and have students hold up the Clip Art image of a beauty contest or a game show to indicate on which type of program each celebrity would do best on. Have them hold up both images if they believe the celebrity has both beauty and intelligence.

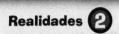

Audio DVD, Capítulo 6A

Track 01: *A primera vista, ¿Viste el partido en la televisión?*, Student Book, p. 294, (4:04)

Vocabulario y gramática en contexto

Vas a escuchar cada palabra o frase dos veces. Después de la primera vez hay una pausa para que puedas pronunciar la palabra o frase. Luego vas a escuchar de nuevo la palabra o frase.

los aficionados	el público
el jugador	enojada
el campeón	furioso
el tanteo	el entrenador
alegre	aburrirse
los campeones	los atletas
el empate	el comentario

Lee en tu libro mientras escuchas la narración.

Los aficionados del equipo Toluca se pusieron alegres y muy emocionados cuando su equipo ganó el campeonato de la Liga Mexicana por tercera vez. El equipo de Puebla perdió el partido final con un tanteo de 3 a 2. La competencia entre estos dos equipos siempre resulta muy intensa.

El partido entre Monterrey y Pachuca terminó en un empate, 1 a 1. Al final del partido el entrenador de Monterrey dijo: "Pareció que nos aburrimos y nos dormimos mientras jugábamos. Tenemos que competir con más emoción. También hubo problemas entre el público. Los aficionados se pusieron muy agitados. Se enojaron y empezaron a pelearse. En mi opinión, pueden aplaudir y gritar, pero nunca deben volverse locos."

Track 02: *A primera vista*, Student Book, p. 295, (2:22)

Vocabulario y gramática en contexto

Vas a escuchar cada palabra o frase dos veces. Después de la primera vez hay una pausa para que puedas pronunciar la palabra o frase. Luego vas a escuchar de nuevo la palabra o frase.

la reina	el presentador
la presentadora	el premio

Lee en tu libro mientras escuchas la narración.

Noticias

Concurso del Carnaval ayer

Felicidades a Rosalinda Pérez Urcillo. Anoche en el Auditorio Nacional fue escogida Reina del Carnaval. En el concurso de belleza participaron treinta jóvenes talentosas, pero Rosalinda fascinó al público con su presentación de guitarra. La presentadora le entregó un cheque para pagar por su primer año de estudios en la universidad.

¡Número uno!

Nuestra comunidad tiene una ganadora en la profesora Cecilia Mendoza. La semana pasada participó y ganó en el programa de concursos *¿Quién lo sabe?* Cecilia es profesora de historia en el Colegio Andrés Bello. Como premio, Cecilia recibió un coche nuevo y el presentador del programa le entregó un cheque por un millón de pesos.

Track 03: *A primera vista*, Act. 1, Student Book, p. 295, (2:36)

¿Cierta o falsa?

Escucha las siguientes frases sobre las noticias deportivas de la página 294 y escribe *C* si la frase es cierta o *F* si es falsa. Vas a escuchar las frases dos veces.

1. El equipo de Toluca ganó el partido contra el equipo de Puebla.
2. El tanteo del partido entre Toluca y Puebla fue 3 a 1.
3. El partido de Monterrey y Pachuca terminó con un tanteo de 2 a 1.
4. Pareció que los atletas del equipo de Monterrey se durmieron durante el partido.
5. Para competir el equipo de Monterrey necesita un nuevo entrenador.
6. Hubo problemas con los aficionados de los dos equipos.
7. Según la locutora, es mejor aplaudir y gritar que pelearse.

Track 04: *A primera vista*, Act. 2, Student Book, p. 295, (2:19)

¿Cuál es el concurso?

Vas a escuchar seis frases. Si la frase describe un concurso de belleza, levanta una mano. Si describe programa de concursos, levanta dos manos. Vas a escuchar las frases dos veces.

1. ¡Si puedes decirme el precio de esta caja de cereal, vas a ganar el coche nuevo!
2. Marta, ¿por qué quieres ser Miss Carnaval?
3. ¡Pablo, quiero comprar dos letras, por favor!
4. ¡Lo siento! No es la respuesta correcta. Pierdes el turno.
5. ¡Aquí está la señorita más talentosa de toda la ciudad! ¡Felicidades!
6. ¡Bienvenidos amigos al programa donde pueden ganar un millón de pesos!

Track 05: *A primera vista, Videohistoria*, Student Book, pp. 296–297, (2:47)

El partido final

Lee en tu libro mientras escuchas la *Videohistoria*.

See Student Book pages 296–297 for script.

Track 06: *Manos a la obra*, Act. 8, Student Book, p. 300, (1:57)

Escucha y escribe

Unos jóvenes hablan de cómo se sienten cuando ven diferentes programas de televisión. Escribe las cinco frases que escuchas. Vas a escuchar las frases dos veces.

1. **Teen Male:** Me pongo enojado cuando mi equipo favorito pierde el campeonato.
2. **Teen Female:** Me aburro cuando tengo que ver una competencia de golf en la tele.
3. **Teen Male:** Me enojo cuando no puedo ver una entrevista con mi cantante favorita.
4. **Teen Female:** Me vuelvo loca cuando anuncian el nombre de la reina del concurso de belleza.
5. **Teen Male:** Me duermo durante los comentarios sobre los desastres naturales.

Track 07: Audio Act. 5, Writing, Audio & Video Workbook, p. 109, (4:54)

The popular radio program *Nuestra comunidad* is highlighting three successful young women from the local Spanish-speaking community. As you listen to parts of their interviews, use the pictures below to decide whether the young woman speaking is Laura, Flor, or Isabel. Then write the name of the young woman in the corresponding space. You will hear each set of statements twice.

1. **Teen Female 1:** Mi entrenador se enojó mucho mientras jugábamos. Nos dijo que perdimos porque creíamos que éramos ya campeones.
2. **Teen Female 2:** En el momento en que me escogieron como la reina, no pude creerlo. Había tantas jóvenes talentosas y bonitas.
3. **Teen Female 3:** La última pregunta fue muy difícil. Hacía muchos años que no estudiaba sobre los exploradores españoles en las clases de historia.
4. **Teen Female 1:** Yo metí el último gol en el partido del campeonato y nuestro equipo ganó el premio de la Liga Central. Fue la primera vez que lo ganó y nos volvimos locos.
5. **Teen Female 3:** Mis profesores se pusieron muy emocionados cuando contesté la pregunta final. Mi equipo ganó las competencias académicas por tercera vez este año.
6. **Teen Female 2:** Di una presentación de guitarra en el auditorio durante la competencia de la Señorita Ciudad de México. Gané un millón de pesos para mis estudios universitarios.
7. **Teen Female 1:** Nos aburrimos mucho durante el partido. Los jugadores del otro equipo eran muy malos. Ganamos el campeonato fácilmente. El público gritaba de alegría.
8. **Teen Female 2:** El público comenzó a aplaudir y gritar cuando salí en mi vestido formal. Era un vestido rojo. Fue una competencia fenomenal. Era la más bella de las participantes.

Track 08: Audio Act. 6, Writing, Audio & Video Workbook, p. 109, (5:59)

In the past few years, there has been a growing interest in women's soccer. Listen as don Balón interviews Eva Barca, a rising women's soccer star. As you hear the different segments of the interview, read the following statements and tell whether each is *cierto* or *falso*. You will hear each segment twice.

1. **Adult Voice:** ¡Hola! Soy don Balón. Hoy voy a entrevistar a la jugadora fenomenal de La Liga Femenina del Fútbol, Eva Barca. Eva, gracias por estar aquí con nosotros.
   Teen Female: Gracias por invitarme. Gracias a usted y a su programa, hay más interés en las mujeres que juegan al fútbol. Ayer oí una entrevista de su programa con mi compañera de equipo, Susi Salsón. Usted entrevista tanto a mujeres como a hombres.
2. **Adult Voice:** Gracias. Trato de ser justo y, como dijiste, hay más interés en el fútbol femenino ahora.
   Teen Female: Sí, más interés… ¡pero menos dinero! Los hombres ganan miles de euros al mes. Las mujeres, no.
   Adult Voice: Poco a poco ustedes van a ganar más.
3. **Adult Voice:** ¿Viste los muñecos nuevos en las tiendas de juguetes esta semana? Hay un muñeco que tiene una pelota y una camiseta con el nombre *Eva*.
   Teen Female: Sí. Lo vi ayer cuando iba de compras con mi prima. ¡Es fantástico! Mi muñeco tiene muchos accesorios también. ¡No hay ningún muñeco de los jugadores masculinos!
4. **Adult Voice:** Dicen que los entrenadores de fútbol masculino gritan mucho y siempre están enojados. ¿Qué puedes decirme de los entrenadores de la Liga Femenina de Fútbol?
   Teen Female: Los entrenadores de la Liga Femenina no gritan todo el tiempo ni se enojan tanto. No se enojaron cuando el equipo perdió el primer partido. El entrenador nos pidió más prácticas en el estadio de fútbol. Hoy somos las campeonas de la Liga Femenina.
5. **Adult Voice:** La semana pasada leí que los aficionados del equipo Rayado se pusieron muy agitados cuando perdieron. ¿Cómo son los aficionados de la Liga Femenina?
   Teen Female: Todos los aficionados del fútbol son iguales, no importa si son aficionados del fútbol femenino o masculino. Los aficionados del fútbol femenino también se ponen muy agitados y se enojan cuando su equipo no gana.

Track 09: Audio Act. 7, Writing, Audio & Video Workbook, p. 110, (4:03)

How do contestants spend their free time during the *Señorita América del Sur* beauty pageant? Listen as some women talk about what their friend(s) in the pageant did last night, and as others talk about what they are doing today to calm themselves before the final competition begins. As you listen to each contestant, decide whether she is talking about last night or today. You will hear each set of statements twice.

1. **Adult Female 1:** A las nueve de la noche, Catrina y Ana se vistieron para salir con los amigos que vinieron anoche de Argentina. Fueron a un restaurante para cenar.
2. **Adult Female 2:** ¡Mira! Claudia duerme mientras espera la entrevista que tiene con el presentador.
3. **Adult Female 3:** Riqui durmió con su oso de peluche. Dice que le trae buena suerte.

4. **Adult Female 4:** Parece que Loli y Diana prefieren divertirse en el hotel. No están con el grupo esta mañana.
5. **Adult Female 5:** Carmen pidió una pizza grande del restaurante de la esquina para la cena de ayer. Ella come mucho cuando está nerviosa, y le encanta la pizza.
6. **Adult Female 6:** Todas las muchachas de la competencia de "Señorita América del Sur" fueron al centro a las siete de la noche, pero Lidia prefirió ir al gimnasio.
7. **Adult Female 7:** María está repitiendo sus líneas para dar una buena entrevista. Ella dice que la práctica hace la perfección. Ella sonríe todo el tiempo.
8. **Adult Female 8:** Luisa se divierte mucho mientras juega con los niños de la directora del concurso de belleza. A ella le gustan los niños.

Track 10: Audio Act. 8, Writing, Audio & Video Workbook, p. 110, (4:13)

Even though pets can not express their emotions through words, they can express themselves through their actions. As you hear each person describe his or her pet's behavior, match a picture to the pet. Write the number of each pet owner's description next to his or her dog. You will hear each description twice.

1. **Adult Female 1:** Mi perro Duncan no es muy paciente. Siempre quiere caminar conmigo y se aburre mucho cuando hablo con mis amigas. Al principio, él me espera pacientemente. Luego trata de forzarme a caminar.
2. **Adult Male 1:** Mi perra Sadie es muy deportista. Le gusta nadar conmigo en la piscina. Se divierte mucho cuando jugamos con la pelota en el agua. ¡Sadie siempre gana!
3. **Adult Female 2:** Mi perro se llama Arti. Él se vuelve loco cuando llego a la casa después de trabajar. Comienza a saltar por todas partes y corre por toda la casa como un loco. ¡Es muy gracioso!
4. **Adult Male 2:** Mi perro Rosty y mi gato no son amigos. A Rosty no le gusta cuando mi gato bebe agua de su plato. Él se enoja mucho cuando el gato lo hace.
5. **Adult Female 3:** Mi perro Chui no quiere a mi gato Calcetines. Chui se pone muy furioso cuando mis amigos abrazan a Calcetines. Chui muestra los dientes y mira a Calcetines muy feo.
6. **Adult Male 3:** Mi perro se llama Capitán. Es un perro muy bueno. Él busca el periódico cada mañana y luego se duerme a mis pies mientras lo leo. A mi perro le gusta jugar con los niños.

Track 11: Audio Act. 9, Writing, Audio & Video Workbook, p. 111, (4:51)

Yesterday in her popular talk show *Dime la verdad,* Lola Lozano had as her guests a group of famous soccer players. The question on the program was *¿Qué lo vuelve más loco?* In the table below, take notes about what each one said. Then use your notes to complete the sentences about each guest. You will hear each conversation twice.

1. **Lola:** Luis, como jugador de fúbol, ¿que cosa te vuelve más loco?
   Luis: Me vuelve loco cuando hay un empate en un partido importante. La competencia en nuestra liga siempre resulta muy intensa y nadie quiere terminar en un empate.
2. **Lola:** Y tú, Marisol, eres la Señorita Argentina y la jugadora más famosa de tu equipo. Muchas personas piensan que tienes una vida perfecta. ¿Qué te vuelve más loca?
   Marisol: Me encanta participar en los concursos de belleza, pero lo que más me vuleve loca es cuando el presentador me abraza cuando gano. Eso no me gusta tanto.
3. **Lola:** Enrique, eres el mejor entrenador de fútbol de la Liga Mexicana. ¿Qué te vuelve más loco?
   Enrique: El fútbol es mi vida. Me gusta mucho ese deporte, pero me vuelve loco cuando los aficionados se ponen muy agitados y se pelean en el estadio.
4. **Lola:** María está con nosotros para hablar sobre el fútbol femenino. María, ¿qué te vuelve más loca del fútbol?
   María: Me vuelve loca cuando los entrenadores de fútbol masculino dicen que las muchachas no deben jugar al fútbol. El fútbol es para toda la gente, no sólo para muchachos.
5. **Lola:** Aquí está Martín Gutiérrez, el goleador del equipo Rayados y el atleta del año. Martín, ¿qué te vuelve más loco?
   Martín: Me gusta cuando mi equipo gana todos los partidos de fútbol. Somos los campeones de la Liga Masculina de fútbol, pero me vuelve loco cuando el entrenador nos grita.

Track 12: *Pronunciación,* Regional variations of *ll* / *y* and *c* / *z*, Student Book, p. 308, (4:58)

The majority of Spanish speakers do not distinguish between *ll* and *y*, pronouncing both like *y* in the English word *yes*. Listen to and say these words and sentences as the majority of Spanish speakers would:

You will hear each word twice. After the word is pronounced the first time, there will be a pause so you can pronounce it. Then you will hear the word a second time.

rodilla	sellos
llamar	cepillo
joyas	rayas

Tiene que llevar un yeso.
La calle está cerca de la playa.

Note, however, that the pronunciation of *ll* and *y* varies around the Spanish-speaking world. In Argentina and Uruguay, *ll* and *y* are pronounced like the *s* in the English word *measure*. In other countries, the *ll* is pronounced with a hint of an *l*, much like the English *million*, but a bit softer.

Listen to and say the words and sentences above again, first as a speaker from Argentina or Uruguay would pronounce them, and then as many other Spanish speakers would.

Enjoy this chidren's riddle from Mexico:

A ver tú chiquillo,
cara de pillo,
si sabes contestar.
Es muy grande y muy feo
fuerte y fiero
y vive por el mar.

In Latin America and parts of Spain, *c* before *e* and *i* and *z* before a vowel are pronounced like the *s* in *sink*. In some parts of Spain, however, these letters are pronounced like the *th* in *think*.

Listen to and say the following words as most Spaniards would pronounce them:

cierto	azúcar
belleza	ciclismo
dice	buzón
abrazo	concierto
bronce	comenzar

¡Compruébalo! Try this tongue twister about an animal:

Gato cenizoso,
sal de ceniza
descenizósate, gato.

Track 13: *Repaso del capítulo*, Student Book, p. 316, (5:42)

Vocabulario y gramática

Escucha las palabras y expresiones que has aprendido en este capítulo.

See Student Book page 316 for vocabulary list.

Track 14: *Preparación para el examen*, Student Book, p. 317, (0:56)

Escuchar

Practice task

Listen as people talk about an awards show they saw on television. Try to identify their reactions to this type of show. Did they become angry? Emotional? Excited? Bored? Nervous?

ADULT FEMALE 1: Me puse loca anoche cuando vi el programa de Premios Velásquez. ¡Lupe Lazo ganó el premio para la actriz del año! Yo grité a la televisión.

ADULT FEMALE 2: Yo, no. Me aburrí y me dormí durante el programa. No puedo soportar esos programas ridículos.

Video Script

A primera vista: *El partido final*, (4:59)

Interviewer: …Y con este fenomenal gol, el equipo de los Lobos de Madero ganó a las Águilas del América y llegó al partido final del campeonato mexicano de fútbol. Hoy está con nosotros el jugador que metió el gol, Luis Campos, "la Pantera." Luis, gracias por estar aquí.

Luis Campos: Gracias por invitarme.

Interviewer: Este año tuvimos un campeonato muy interesante. Vimos muchos goles y todos los equipos estaban físicamente muy bien preparados.

Luis Campos: Así es. Competimos con equipos muy buenos y fue muy difícil llegar hasta el partido final. Tenemos jugadores muy buenos y nuestro entrenador conoce muy bien la liga…

Claudia: …Pues sí… Podemos ir al cine. O de compras… ¿Ahora? Estamos viendo la televisión… No sé, parece una entrevista. Manolo, ¿a quién están entrevistando?

Manolo: ¿A quién…? Es Luis Campos, "la Pantera." Hoy es el partido final del campeonato.

Claudia: Vaya… Entonces, como te decía…

Interviewer: …Y para recordarle a nuestro auditorio, durante este campeonato los Lobos ganaron 31 partidos, empataron seis y perdieron sólo tres.

Interviewer: Luis, ¿qué nos puedes decir del último partido que ganaron contra las Águilas?

Luis Campos: Bueno, fue un partido muy difícil. Ellos metieron el primer gol, pero cinco minutos después nosotros empatamos. Luego en el segundo tiempo metimos dos goles más y ganamos.

Interviewer: ¿Cómo te sentías tú al final del partido?

Luis Campos: Muy emocionado por el gol que metimos en el último minuto, y muy contento por el gran trabajo de todo el equipo durante el campeonato.

Interviewer: ¿Y ahora, qué piensas del partido final de hoy?

Luis Campos: Creo que va a ser un partido muy difícil para los dos equipos, pero pienso que vamos a ganar.

Claudia: …y entonces me puse furiosa. Pero es que ella me dijo que yo me podía llevar la falda…

Manolo: Oye, Claudia, esta entrevista nos interesa mucho. ¿Por qué no vas a hablar al cuarto?

Claudia: Uy… Espera, que aquí no se puede hablar… ¿Qué?… No sé. Voy a preguntarles. Oigan, Teresa dice que su tío trabaja en el estadio y que si queremos podemos ir a ver el partido allí.

Claudia: Creo que no quieren ir.

Ramón: ¿Ir adónde?

Claudia: Al estadio, a ver el partido allí.

Manolo and Ramón: ¡¿QUÉ?!

***GramActiva* Videos, (8:09)**

Preterite of *-ir* stem-changing verbs

Newspaper Host: Hello there. I have good news and bad news. Bad news: Some stem-changing verbs also have a stem-change in the preterite! Good news: Only two of their forms change in the preterite.

Typewriter Host: The two forms of the verb that change in the preterite are the *usted, él, ella* form and the *ustedes, ellos, ellas* form. These are the "bizarro" forms. With these two, the *e* changes to *i* and the *o* changes to *u-u-u-u-u-u-u-u*.

V.O.: In the mirror, *preferir* looks like this: *Preferir*. In the preterite, it looks like this:

preferí—Preferí la leche.
preferiste—Preferiste el agua.
prefirió—Prefirió la limonada.
preferimos—Preferimos el jugo de naranja.
preferisteis—Preferisteis té helado.
prefirieron—Prefirieron el café.

Host: In the oven, *pedir* looks like this: *Pedir*. In the preterite, it looks like this:

pedí—Pedí una hamburguesa.
pedíste—Pedíste un perrito caliente
pidió—Pidió un sándwich de jamón y queso.
pedimos—Pedimos sopa de verduras.
pedisteis—Pedisteis galletas.
pidieron—Pidieron ensalada.

Therapist: We are going deep, deep into your memories. You will remember more *-ir* verbs that change the *e* to *i* in the preterite tense.

Host V.O.: *Servir, repetir, repetir, repetir… Repetir, servir, sonreír, mentir, competir, reír, divertirse, vestirse,* and *sentirse*—whew—all change the *e* to an *i* in the preterite tense.

Typewriter Host: Let's say these verbs out loud. It'll be fun. After all, you haven't been embarrassed nearly enough today. We'll use the *usted* form. Like this: *repetir… repitió.* Ready?

servir
sonreír
mentir
competir

Host: Upside-down, *dormir* looks like this.

Host: In the preterite, *[gets out of handstand]* and right-side up, it looks like this:

Dormí.
Dormiste.
Durmió.
Dormimos.
Dormisteis.
Durmieron.

Ready for something else? How about a quiz?

Quiz

V.O.: Complete these sentences with the correct form of the preterite.
(dormir) Usted ______ bien.
Usted durmió bien.
(pedir) Ellos ______ el desayuno.
Ellos pidieron el desayuno.
(servir) La camarera nos ______ mucha comida.
La camarera nos sirvió mucha comida.
(divertir) Mis primos se ______ mucho en la fiesta.
Mis primos se divirtieron mucho en la fiesta.

Other reflexive verbs

Smiley Host: Hey everyone! Remember when we learned about reflexive verbs? Yes I know, it was four chapters ago, but it feels like yesterday.

Smiley Host V.O.: Remember when I combed the dog's hair, and then I combed my hair? I loved that part! And remember when I brushed the dog's teeth, and then I almost brushed my own teeth? Ha! What a scene! And who could forget my co-stars, the reflexive pronouns *me, te, se, nos, os,* and *se*? They're like family.

Smiley Host: But on my new show, *Other Reflexive Verbs*, I have a whole new family. I like to call my new family the "get verbs," because most of them show changes to a person, like "get angry," "get bored," or even "get married!" Here's a scene from our show. I hope you have as much fun watching it, as we did making it!

V.O.: *Aburrirse*—"to get bored."
Se aburre fácilmente.

V.O.: *Dormirse*—"to fall asleep."
Se duerme cuando tiene una cita aburrida.

V.O.: *Emocionarse*—"to be moved."
Se emociona por el anillo de bodas.

V.O.: *Casarse*—"to get married."
Se casan felizmente.

V.O.: *Volverse loco*—"to go crazy."
Se vuelve loca y sale rápidamente.

Smiley Host: Ha ha! Wasn't that a great scene? I can smell an Emmy. But we didn't talk about my favorite reflexive verb, *ponerse*, "to get"... well, to get all kinds of different emotions. Fire whoever is writing my dialogue.

V.O.: *Me pongo triste.*
Me pongo alegre.
Me pongo agitado.
Me pongo furioso.
Me pongo nervioso.

Smiley Host: My face is stuck! Let's try a quiz!

Quiz

V.O.: Complete these sentences with the correct reflexive verb.
(aburrirse) Yo ______ fácilmente.
Yo me aburro fácilmente.
(casarse) Nosotros ______ este fin de semana.
Nosotros nos casamos este fin de semana.
(ponerse) Ellos ______ nerviosos antes del examen.
Ellos se ponen nerviosos antes del examen.

Videomisterio: *En busca de la verdad,* **Episodio 7, (11:35)**

Julio: Bueno, ¿adónde vamos? Linda, ¿qué quieres ver?

Linda: No sé… ¡Hay tanto que ver en esta ciudad!… Jardines, museos, la Universidad, iglesias…

Julio: ¿Qué prefieres? Hoy decides tú.

Linda: El Museo del Quijote, claro, me interesa mucho.

Roberto: Y no olvides el de Diego Rivera. Fue su primera casa.

Julio: Sí, pero el del Quijote es más interesante… creo.

Roberto: ¿Desde cuándo te interesa tanto eso?

Julio: Todo el mundo conoce a… Cervante.

Roberto: Cervantes, si me permites, amigo.

Linda: Personalmente me gustaría ver los dos, el Museo del Quijote y la casa de Diego Rivera.

Roberto: Bueno, ¿adónde vamos primero?

Julio: Al de Diego Rivera, porque está más cerca.

Roberto: Tienes razón.

Linda: Bueno, vamos.

Roberto's V.O.: Primero fuimos al Museo de Diego Rivera. Diego Rivera fue un famoso muralista. Nació y vivió durante sus primeros años en esta casa. Su esposa, Frida Kahlo, también fue una artista muy importante. Luego Julio tuvo que irse y yo llevé a Linda al museo del Quijote.

Linda's V.O.: El Museo del Quijote es impresionante. Está dedicado a Miguel de Cervantes, el gran autor español que escribió *Don Quijote de la Mancha*. Este museo tiene una de las mejores colecciones de obras sobre Don Quijote en el mundo.

Roberto: Hay un grupo musical, una estudiantina, que viene aquí todas las noches, a eso de las nueve. ¿Quieres comer o tomar algo mientras esperamos?

Linda: Sí… Me encanta esta plaza.

Roberto: Aquí está el Café del Hotel Luna… siempre tienen buena comida.

Roberto: Papá, creo que tengo una pista para saber lo que pasó con el abuelo.

Tomás: ¿Una pista?

Roberto: Sí. Hablé con un viejo amigo de él, Chato Montesinos. El abuelo abrió una cuenta en un banco en los Estados Unidos, en San Antonio.

Tomás: Cuando tu abuelo se fue, le prometió a tu abuela que iba a volver, pero nunca lo hizo. Y ella nunca tuvo ninguna noticia de él, nada.

Daniela: ¿El abuelo… puede estar viviendo en algún lugar?

Tomás: Puede ser. ¿Y qué? Mi madre y yo nunca hablamos de él, ni siquiera mencionamos su nombre. Nuestro apellido es Toledo, el de tu abuela, no el de Federico.

Roberto: Sí, pero su nombre era Zúñiga. Federico Zúñiga.

Tomás: Así es, pero nunca lo hemos usado.

Daniela: Entonces Roberto y yo somos… Zúñiga…

Roberto: Tanto como Toledo. Zúñiga y Toledo. Por eso en el banco de San Antonio estaban confundidos.

Tomás: ¿Llamaste al banco?

Roberto: Sí, pero no van a decirnos nada hasta que un miembro de la familia vaya allí, con documentos y todo.

Berta: Vaya. ¿Y quién de nosotros puede ir? Para mí es imposible.

Tomás: Para mí también. Pero si Carmen y Linda están de acuerdo, Roberto, tú… puedes acompañarlas.

Roberto: Voy a verlas hoy. Puedo preguntarles.

Tomás: Bien. Y llama también a tu abuela. Dile lo que vas a hacer. Hijo, a veces es mejor no tocar el pasado.

Roberto: ¿No tocar el pasado? ¿Por qué nadie quería hablar sobre la verdad en nuestra familia?

Recepcionista: ¡Señorita Toledo! Un joven acaba de llamar y dejó un mensaje para Ud.

Linda: ¿Para mí?

Recepcionista: Sí. Aquí está su nombre. Roberto Toledo.

Linda: Ah, sí. Muchas gracias.

Turrón: El nombre que Ud. acaba de mencionar… Roberto Toledo… ¿Sabe Ud. su teléfono o su dirección?

Recepcionista: Señor, no podemos darle tal información. Si tiene algún motivo para saberla, debe hablar con el director…

Recepcionista: … como decía… ¡Señor…!

Roberto: Parece que hay un banco en San Antonio donde pueden saber algo sobre mi abuelo. Alguien de mi familia tiene que presentarse para obtener la información. Mis padres y yo pensamos si yo puedo…

Linda: ¡Tú vas con nosotras!

Carmen: Claro, no hay ningún problema. Oye, pero nosotras salimos en dos días. ¿Puedes viajar tan pronto? El boleto y todo…

Roberto: Creo que sí. Puedo arreglar todo muy rápido.

Linda: ¡Fabuloso!

Nombre

Fecha

Communicative Pair Activity **6A-1**

Estudiante **A**

Interview your partner about television, movies, sports, and current events. Record your partner's answers on the lines provided.

1. ¿En qué día de la semana vas al cine? ¿Cuánto tiempo dura una película?

2. ¿Qué película es la que más te gusta? ¿Por qué?

3. ¿Quién es tu actor favorito? ¿Y tu actriz favorita?

4. ¿Cuál es tu deporte favorito?

5. ¿Te gustan más los deportes de invierno o los deportes de verano?

6. ¿Cuál jugador(a) te gustaría conocer personalmente?

7. ¿Cuál es tu programa de televisión favorito?

8. ¿Cuál es tu película de ciencia ficción favorita?

9. ¿En tu casa les gusta ver las noticias en la televisión?

10. ¿Recuerdas alguna noticia importante que viste en un noticiero?

Realidades 2

Capítulo 6A

Nombre ______

Fecha ______

Communicative Pair Activity **6A-1**

Estudiante **B**

Interview your partner about television, movies, sports, and current events. Record your partner's answers on the lines provided.

1. ¿Te gusta ver los concursos de belleza en la televisión, o prefieres ver un partido de fútbol? ______
2. ¿Te gustan los programas deportivos? ______
3. ¿Qué evento importante recuerdas en la televisión? ¿Cuándo lo viste?
______
______
4. Cuando sales con tus amigos y amigas, ¿adónde prefieren ir a divertirse?
______
______
5. ¿Cuántas películas has visto este año? ¿Cuál te gustó más?
______
______
6. ¿Te gustan los programas de concursos en la televisión?
______
7. ¿Cuál es tu programa favorito de dibujos animados? ¿Qué personaje te gusta más?
______
______
8. ¿Practicas algún deporte? ¿Cuál? ¿Por qué?
______
______
9. ¿Recuerdas alguna película aburrida? ¿Te dormiste en el cine?
______
10. ¿Qué películas prefieres, las de horror o las cómicas?
______

Nombre ______________________________

Fecha ______________________________

Communicative Pair Activity 6A-2

Estudiante A

You and your partner are in charge of the sports equipment for a spring sports week for children at a nearby elementary school. You have taken inventory of the equipment available. Your partner has the list of the equipment needed. Ask your partner if the following items are needed and how many of each. Complete the table below to determine how many of each item you should buy. Follow the model.

—¿Necesitamos patines? *—¿Cuántos necesitamos?*

—Sí, los necesitamos. (No, no los necesitamos.) *—Necesitamos* ________ *.*

—¿Cuántos tenemos que comprar? *—Tenemos que comprar* ________ *.*

	Cuántos tenemos	Cuántos necesitamos	Cuántos tenemos que comprar
	15		
	26		
	17		

You have the list of the sports equipment needed for a fall sports week that you and your partner are organizing. Let your partner know how many of each item are needed.

	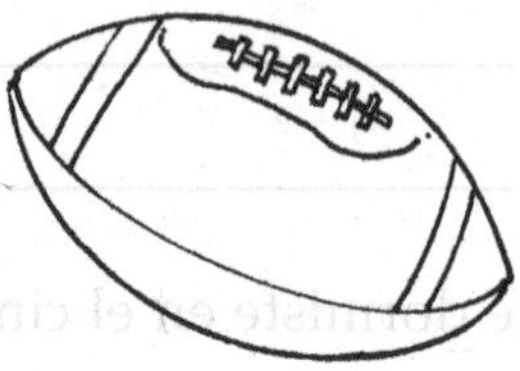	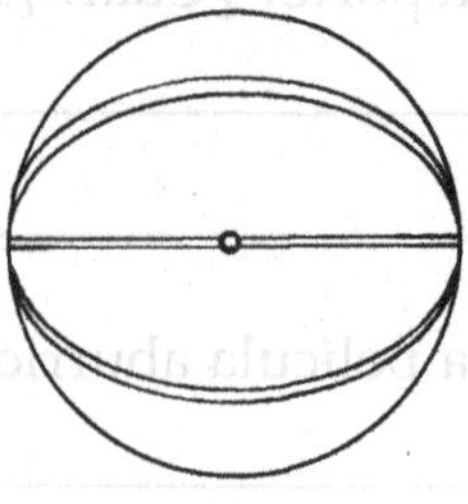	
35	**12**	**25**	**15**

Realidades 2

Capítulo 6A

Nombre ______________________________

Fecha ______________________________

Communicative Pair Activity **6A-2**

Estudiante **B**

You have the list of sports equipment needed for a spring sports week that you and your partner are organizing. Let your partner know how many of each item are needed.

30

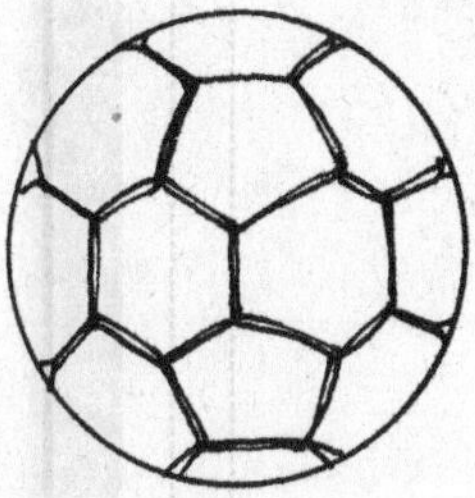

20

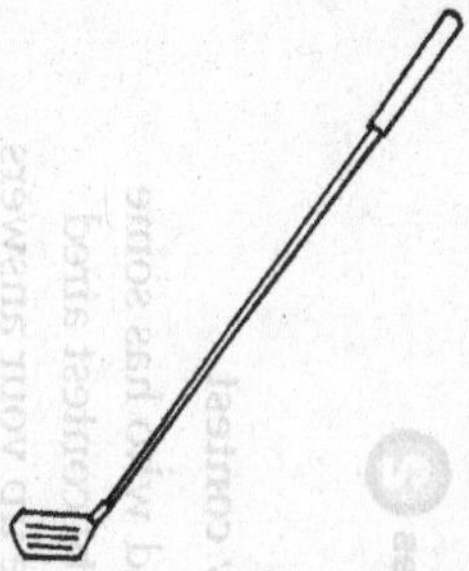

30

You and your partner are in charge of the sports equipment for a fall sports week at a nearby school. You have taken inventory of the equipment available. Your partner has the list of the equipment needed. Ask your partner if the following items are needed and how many of each. Complete the table below to determine how many of each item you should buy. Follow the model.

—¿Necesitamos patines?

—Sí, los necesitamos. (No, no los necesitamos.)

—¿Cuántos tenemos que comprar?

—¿Cuántos necesitamos?

—Necesitamos ________.

—Tenemos que comprar ________.

	Cuántos tenemos	Cuántos necesitamos	Cuántos tenemos que comprar
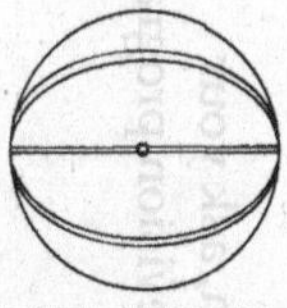	20		
	9		
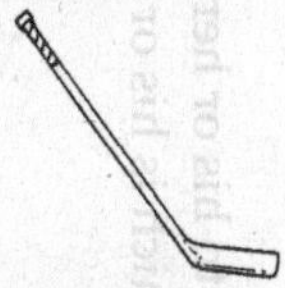	30		
	28		

Situation Cards

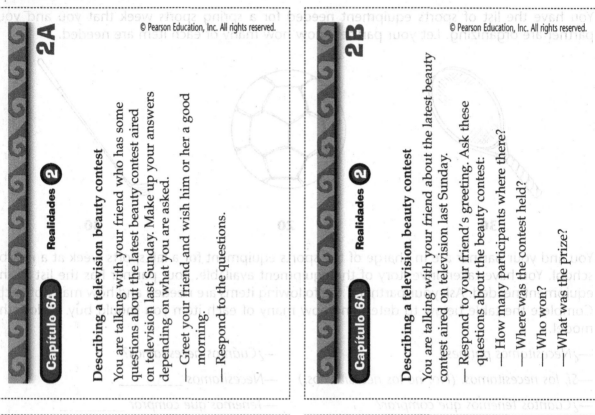

Capítulo 6A — Realidades 2 — **1A**

Naming and describing favorite television programs

You are a new student and are interested in finding out about the local television programs in your community.

— Introduce yourself.

— Respond to your new friend's question.

— Ask when he or she arrived in this community and if he or she has seen the local television programs.

— Answer your friend's question.

Capítulo 6A — Realidades 2 — **1B**

Naming and describing favorite television programs

You are talking to a new student about the local television programs in your community.

— Introduce yourself and ask where the new student is from.

— Respond to his or her questions. Then, ask your friend which is his or her favorite television program.

Capítulo 6A — Realidades 2 — **2A**

Describing a television beauty contest

You are talking with your friend who has some questions about the latest beauty contest aired on television last Sunday. Make up your answers depending on what you are asked.

— Greet your friend and wish him or her a good morning.

— Respond to the questions.

Capítulo 6A — Realidades 2 — **2B**

Describing a television beauty contest

You are talking with your friend about the latest beauty contest aired on television last Sunday.

— Respond to your friend's greeting. Ask these questions about the beauty contest:

— How many participants where there?

— Where was the contest held?

— Who won?

— What was the prize?

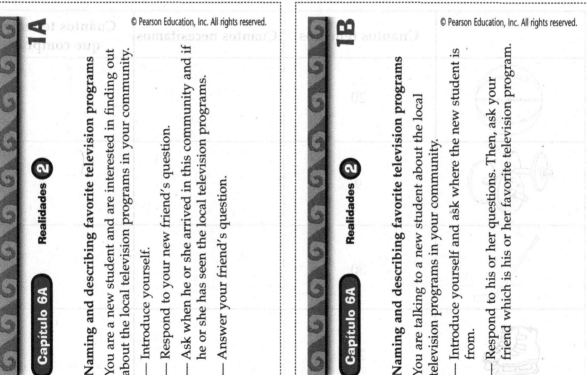

GramActiva

¿Viste el partido en la televisión?
Los programas que te gustan, p. 290

programa / película	descripción	canal / cine	actor / actriz

Vocabulary Clip Art

Vocabulary Clip Art

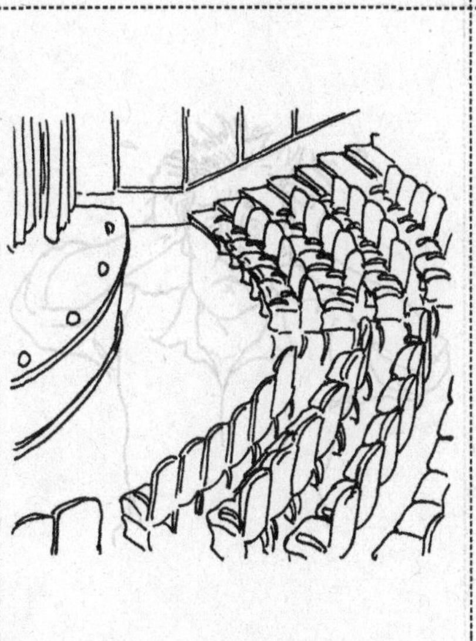

Capítulo 6A

Vocabulary Clip Art

Realidades 2

Capítulo 6A

Vocabulary Clip Art

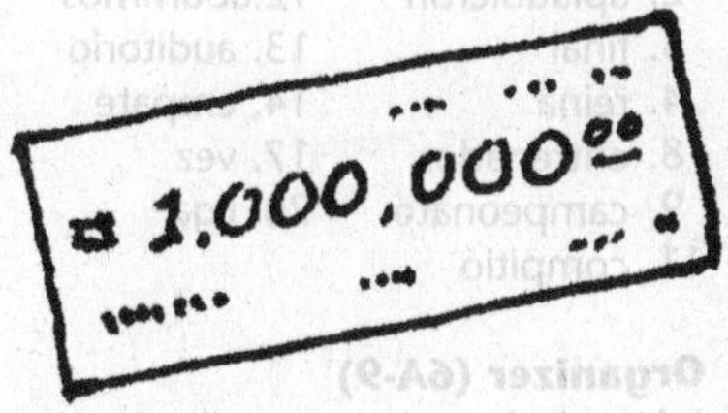

Capítulo 6A

Core Practice Answers

6A-A
1. Me interesan los programas de noticias.
2. Les encantan las telenovelas.
3. Nos gustan los programas deportivos.
4. Le interesan los dramas.
5. Te encantan los programas musicales.
6. Les gustan los programas de dibujos animados.
7. Nos interesan los programas educativos.
8. No me importa ver la tele.
9. Le gustan los programas de entrevistas.

6A-B
Wording of answers may vary.
1. Lee el periódico para saber qué programas hay en la televisión.
2. En el canal nueve dan un programa de concursos y en el doce dan un programa de la vida real.
3. Sara no quiere ver ninguno de los dos.
4. Sara no quiere verla porque no le gustan las películas violentas.
5. Sara quiere ir al cine.
6. Le interesa porque los actores son muy buenos.
7. Según José, las películas románticas son tontas.
8. Sara y José deciden ir a ver una película de ciencia ficción.

6A-1
1. El presentador
2. la reina
3. Los aficionados
4. el premio, millón
5. concurso, belleza
6. El entrenador
7. el auditorio

6A-2
1. emocionado
2. campeonato
3. por
4. liga
5. final
6. atletas
7. perdió
8. empate
9. compite
10. competencia
11. tanteo

B.
Panteras

6A-3
A.
Order of pictures should be (from left to right, top to bottom): 6, 5, 2, 8, 1, 7, 4, 3.

B.
1. falso
2. cierto
3. falso
4. falso
5. cierto
6. cierto
7. cierto

6A-4
Wording of answers may vary.
1. El equipo de San Fernando ganó el campeonato.
2. Ganaron en los últimos segundos del partido.
3. Metieron goles (en los primeros minutos del partido).
4. El tanteo fue de uno a uno.
5. Todos creían que el partido iba a terminar en un empate.
6. El público se volvió loco.
7. Se sintió alegre y emocionado.
8. Todo el mundo habla de su gol fenomenal.

6A-5
1. se rieron mucho
2. siguieron por la calle Miraflores
3. prefirió un restaurante italiano
4. pidieron espaguetis
5. sirvió la comida
6. se divirtieron mucho

6A-6
1. me aburrí
2. se enojó
3. se puso
4. se durmieron
5. se divirtió
6. me sentí
7. se volvieron
8. me lavé

6A-7
A.
1. Metió el gol final.
2. Los aficionados se pusieron locos, entonces no parece que se aburrieron.
3. El portero se puso furioso (se enojó).
4. El equipo del número once ganó el campeonato.
5. Sí, los jugadores compitieron con mucha emoción porque era un partido emocionante.

B.
6. Ganó el campeonato.
7. El tanteo final fue 3 a 2.
8. El número 11 hace una entrevista.
9. Sí, el público aplaude mucho.

Crucigrama (6A-8)
Horizontal:

1. emocionada	15. concurso
3. fenomenales	16. agitados
5. tanteo	18. premio
6. pusiste	19. enojó
7. gol	21. millones
10. volvieron	22. durmió
11. comentario	

Vertical:

2. aplaudieron	12. aburrimos
3. final	13. auditorio
4. reina	14. empate
8. entrenador	17. vez
9. campeonato	20. liga
11. compitió	

Organizer (6A-9)
I. Vocabulary Answers will vary.
II. Grammar
Wording of answers may vary.
1. The preterite of **-ir** stem changing verbs has a change in the vowel (*e* > *i*, *o* > *u*) in the third person singular and third person plural.
2. **divertirse:**

me divertí	nos divertimos
te divertiste	os divertisteis
se divirtió	se divirtieron

dormirse:

me dormí	nos dormimos
te dormiste	os dormisteis
se durmió	se durmieron

3. Spanish uses reflexive verbs express the idea of "to get" or "to become".

Nombre ______ Hora ______

Fecha ______ **AVSR 6A-1**

A ver si recuerdas: Verbs like *gustar* (p. 291)

- You are already familiar with the verb **gustar** and other verbs that function like it (**encantar, disgustar, importar, interesar**). Remember that the verb agrees in number with the item or action that follows it. The indirect object pronoun agrees with the person whose preferences are geing discussed.

A Juan → le encantan los deportes.
Juan loves sports.

A nosotros → nos importa el partido de tenis.
The tennis match is important to us.

A. Write the indirect object pronoun that corresponds to the person listed below. The indirect object pronouns are in the box below to help you.

me	*to me*	**nos**	*to us*
te	*to you (sing.)*	**os**	*to you (pl.)*
le	*to him/her* *to you (form.)*	**les**	*to them* *to you (pl.)*

Modelo Al profesor Rodríguez *le*

1. A Juliana ***le***
2. A nosotros ***nos***
3. A mí ***me***
4. A los doctores ***les***
5. A ti ***te***
6. A Juan y a Ramón ***les***
7. A ustedes ***les***
8. A mi hermano y a mí ***nos***
9. A la profesora ***le***
10. A usted ***le***

realidades.com • Web Code: jdd-0601

Realidades 2 — Nombre ______ Hora ______

Capítulo 6A — Fecha ______ **AVSR 6A-2**

Verbs like *gustar* (*continued*)

B. Look at the picture and corresponding noun for each number. Circle the correct form of the verb that could be used in a sentence about the noun.

Modelo  (encanta / (encantan)) las películas de horror

1.  (disgusta / (disgustan)) las telenovelas
2.  ((gusta) / gustan) el cine
3.  (interesa / (interesan)) los programas deportivos
4.  ((importa) / importan) la televisión
5.  (encanta / (encantan)) los programas musicales

C. Now complete these sentences, which are combined from exercises A and B. Write the appropriate indirect object pronoun in the first blank, and the correct form of the verb given in the second blank. Follow the model.

Modelo A mí ___*me*___ ___*encantan*___ (**encantar**) los programas musicales.

1. A Juan y a Ramón ___***les***___ ___***interesan***___ (**interesar**) los programas deportivos.
2. A mi hermano y a mí ___***nos***___ ___***importa***___ (**importar**) la televisión.
3. A Juliana ___***le***___ ___***gusta***___ (**gustar**) el cine.
4. A nosotros ___***nos***___ ___***encantan***___ (**encantar**) las películas de horror.
5. A ustedes ___***les***___ ___***disgustan***___ (**disgustar**) las telenovelas.
6. A ti ___***te***___ ___***encantan***___ (**encantar**) los programas musicales.

Realidades 2 — Nombre ______ Hora ______

Capítulo 6A — Fecha ______ **Vocabulary Flash Cards, Sheet 1**

Write the Spanish vocabulary word below each picture. Be sure to include the article for each noun.

 ***perder***	 ***el*** ***campeón***	 ***la*** ***campeona***
 ***el*** ***empate***	 ***el*** ***tanteo***	 ***el*** ***aficionado***
 ***la*** ***aficionada***	 ***el*** ***jugador***	 ***la*** ***jugadora***

Realidades 2 | Nombre ______ | Hora ______

Capítulo 6A | Fecha ______

Vocabulary Flash Cards, Sheet 2

Write the Spanish vocabulary word below each picture. Be sure to include the article for each noun.

 ***el entrenador***	 ***la entrenadora***	 ***el atleta***
 ***la atleta***	 ***aplaudir***	 ***meter un gol***
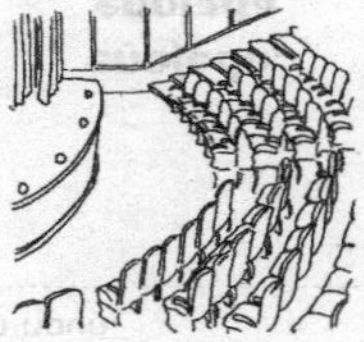 ***el auditorio***	 ***el premio***	 ***el presentador***

Realidades 2 | Nombre ______ | Hora ______

Capítulo 6A | Fecha ______

Vocabulary Flash Cards, Sheet 3

Write the Spanish vocabulary word or phrase below each picture. Be sure to include the article for each noun.

 ***la presentadora***	 ***el concurso de belleza***	 ***la reina***
 ***la entrevista***	 ***el comentario***	 ***alegre***
 ***el campeonato***	 ***un millón de / millones de***	 ***el público***

Nombre ______ Hora ______

Fecha ______ **Vocabulary Flash Cards, Sheet 4**

Copy the word or phrase in the space provided. Be sure to include the article for each noun.

enojado, enojada *enojado*, *enojada*	**furioso, furiosa** *furioso*, *furiosa*	**agitado, agitada** *agitado*, *agitada*
al final *al* *final*	**la competencia** *la* *competencia*	**fenomenal** *fenomenal*
la liga *la* *liga*	**por ... vez** *por* *...* *vez*	**resultar** *resultar*

Nombre ______ Hora ______

Fecha ______ **Vocabulary Flash Cards, Sheet 5**

Copy the word or phrase in the space provided. Be sure to include the article for each noun.

último, última *último*, *última*	**aburrirse** *aburrirse*	**enojarse** *enojarse*
volverse loco, loca *volverse* *loco*, *loca*	**dormirse** *dormirse*	**morirse** *morirse*
los campeones *los* *campeones*	**competir** *competir*	**entrevistar** *entrevistar*

Realidades 2 Nombre ______ Hora ______

Capítulo 6A Fecha ______ **Vocabulary Flash Cards, Sheet 6**

Copy the word or phrase in the space provided. These blank cards can be used to write and practice other Spanish vocabulary for the chapter.

ponerse + adjective *ponerse* + *adjective*		

Realidades 2 Nombre ______ Hora ______

Capítulo 6A Fecha ______ **Vocabulary Check, Sheet 1**

Tear out this page. Write the English words on the lines. Fold the paper along the dotted line to see the correct answers so you can check your work.

aplaudir	*to applaud*
competir	*to compete*
la competencia	*competition*
al final	*at the end*
fenomenal	*phenomenal*
resultar	*to result, to turn out*
último, última	*last, final*
el auditorio	*auditorium*
el comentario	*commentary*
entrevistar	*to interview*
el público	*audience*
aburrirse	*to get bored*
alegre	*happy*
emocionado, emocionada	*excited, emotional*
enojado, enojada	*angry*

Fold In ←

Realidades 2 | Nombre ____ Hora ____

Capítulo 6A | Fecha ____ **Vocabulary Check, Sheet 2**

Tear out this page. Write the Spanish words on the lines. Fold the paper along the dotted line to see the correct answers so you can check your work.

to applaud	***aplaudir***
to compete	***competir***
competition	***la competencia***
at the end	***al final***
phenomenal	***fenomenal***
to result, to turn out	***resultar***
last, final	***último, última***
auditorium	***el auditorio***
commentary	***el comentario***
to interview	***entrevistar***
audience	***el público***
to get bored	***aburrirse***
happy	***alegre***
excited, emotional	***emocionado, emocionada***
angry	***enojado, enojada***

Fold In ↓

Realidades 2 | Nombre ____ Hora ____

Capítulo 6A | Fecha ____ **Vocabulary Check, Sheet 3**

Tear out this page. Write the English words on the lines. Fold the paper along the dotted line to see the correct answers so you can check your work.

el aficionado, la aficionada	***fan***
el atleta, la atleta	***athlete***
el campeonato	***championship***
el empate	***tie***
el jugador, la jugadora	***player***
perder	***to lose***
el tanteo	***score***
el concurso de belleza	***beauty contest***
el premio	***prize***
la reina	***queen***
el presentador, la presentadora	***presenter***
agitado, agitada	***agitated***
furioso, furiosa	***furious***
dormirse	***to fall asleep***

Fold In ↓

Realidades 2 — Capítulo 6A

Nombre ______ Hora ______

Fecha ______

Vocabulary Check, Sheet 4

Tear out this page. Write the Spanish words on the lines. Fold the paper along the dotted line to see the correct answers so you can check your work.

fan	***el aficionado, la aficionada***
athlete	***el atleta, la atleta***
championship	***el campeonato***
tie	***el empate***
player	***el jugador, la jugadora***
to lose	***perder***
score	***el tanteo***
beauty contest	***el concurso de belleza***
prize	***el premio***
queen	***la reina***
presenter	***el presentador, la presentadora***
agitated	***agitado, agitada***
furious	***furioso, furiosa***
to fall asleep	***dormirse***

Fold In ↓

To hear a complete list of the vocabulary for this chapter, go to www.realidades.com and type in the Web Code jdd-0689. Then click on **Repaso del capítulo.**

Realidades 2 — Capítulo 6A

Nombre ______ Hora ______

Fecha ______

Guided Practice Activities 6A-1

Preterite of *-ir* stem-changing verbs (p. 302)

- In the preterite, verbs ending in **-ir**, like **preferir, pedir,** and **dormir,** have stem changes but only in the **usted/él/ella** and **ustedes/ellos/ellas** forms. The **e** changes to **i,** and the **o** to **u.**

  Mi mamá se d*u*rmió durante la película.
  Mis padres pref*i*rieron ver el concurso de belleza.
  En la liga comp*i*tieron los mejores equipos de México.

- Here are the preterite forms of **preferir, pedir,** and **dormir.**

preferir (e → i)		pedir (e → i)		dormir (o → u)	
preferí	preferimos	pedí	pedimos	dormí	dormimos
preferiste	preferisteis	pediste	pedisteis	dormiste	dormisteis
prefirió	**prefirieron**	**pidió**	**pidieron**	**durmió**	**durmieron**

A. Complete the following sentences by circling the correct form of the verb in parentheses. Then, draw a line beneath the vowel that represents the stem change. The first one is done for you.

1. Carlos (**prefirió** / **prefirieron**) asistir al partido el sábado.
2. Las niñas se (**durmió** / **durmieron**) en el auditorio.
3. Usted (**pidió** / **pedimos**) una entrevista al entrenador.
4. Ustedes (**preferiste** / **prefirieron**) ver este partido.
5. Las presentadoras (**pidió** / **pidieron**) a los voluntarios al final del programa.
6. Tomás se (**durmió** / **dormí**) antes de la competencia.
7. El campeón (**pidió** / **pedí**) un millón de dólares.
8. Lucía (**preferimos** / **prefirió**) entrevistar al público.
9. Mis hermanos (**dormiste** / **durmieron**) bien anoche.
10. Yo (**pidieron** / **pedí**) un café ayer en el café.

realidades.com • Web Code: jdd-0604

Realidades 2 | Nombre | Hora

Capítulo 6A | Fecha | Guided Practice Activities **6A-2**

Preterite of *-ir* stem-changing verbs (*continued*)

- Note the special spelling of the preterite forms of **reír**:
  reí, reíste, rió, reímos, reísteis, rieron
- Here are other **-ir** verbs with stem changes in the preterite tense:
  Verbs like **preferir: divertirse, mentir, sentirse**
  Verbs like **pedir: competir, despedirse, repetir, seguir, servir, vestirse**
  Verbs like **dormir: morir**
  Verbs like **reír: sonreír**

B. Sergio and Patricia went out on a Saturday night. Look at the pictures and fill in the blanks with the correct vowel that represents the stem change. Follow the model.

Modelo  Sergio y Patricia se div*i*rtieron mucho.

1.  Una tarde, Sergio y Patricia salieron a comer. Ellos s*i*guieron por la calle Miraflores.

2.  Sergio y Patricia p*i*dieron espaguetis.

3.  El camarero les s*i*rvió una comida muy buena.

4.  Después de la cena, Sergio y Patricia pref*i*rieron ir al cine.

5.  Sergio y Patricia se r*i*eron mucho.

© Pearson Education, Inc. All rights reserved.

Realidades 2 | Nombre | Hora

Capítulo 6A | Fecha | Guided Practice Activities **6A-3**

Preterite of *-ir* stem-changing verbs (*continued*)

C. Use the correct form of the verb in parentheses to complete each sentence. The first one is done for you.

1. Millones de aficionados ***siguieron*** al jugador. (**seguir**)
2. La reina ***sonrió*** mucho cuando ganó el concurso de belleza. (**sonreír**)
3. Pilar y yo nos ***reímos*** de los chistes que contó el presentador. (**reír**)
4. Al final, la reina de belleza se ***despidió*** del público. (**despedirse**)
5. El entrenador y su equipo se ***vistieron*** de rojo y blanco. (**vestirse**)
6. La presentadora ***repitió*** el tanteo para el público. (**repetir**)
7. Ustedes se ***sintieron*** alegres al final del partido. (**sentirse**)
8. Yo me ***divertí*** mucho en el campeonato. (**divertirse**)
9. La reportera dice que el jugador ***mintió***; él no rescató a la señora. (**mentir**)
10. Tú no ***competiste*** en el campeonato del año pasado. (**competir**)
11. Nosotros ***servimos*** una comida fantástica a los jugadores. (**servir**)
12. Ustedes ***prefirieron*** ver el partido en la tele. (**preferir**)
13. Eugenio y tú ***durmieron*** durante los comentarios. (**dormir**)
14. Yo ***pedí*** bebidas para los aficionados sentados cerca de mí. (**pedir**)
15. Resultó que nadie se ***murió*** en el accidente después del partido. (**morir**)

Other reflexive verbs (p. 305)

- Some reflexive verbs do not have the meaning of a person doing an action to or for himself or herself. These reflexive verbs describe a change. We say that someone "gets" or "becomes" something. Examples of these verbs are:

aburrirse	*to get bored*	**enojarse**	*to become angry*
casarse	*to get married*	**ponerse (furioso, -a; alegre;...)**	*to become (furious, happy, . . .)*
divertirse	*to have fun*	**volverse loco, -a**	*to go crazy*
dormirse	*to fall asleep*		

Ramiro se aburrió durante la película. *Ramiro got bored during the movie.*
Lalo se enojó al final del partido. *Lalo became angry at the end of the game.*

- Remember that reflexive verbs are used to say that people do something to or for themselves, and they use the reflexive pronouns **me, te, se, os,** and **nos**. Look at the conjugation of the verb **lavarse:**

yo	**me lavo**	nosotros/nosotras	**nos lavamos**
tú	**te lavas**	vosotros/vosotras	**os laváis**
usted/él/ella	**se lava**	ustedes/ellos/ellas	**se lavan**

A. Read the following sentences and write the correct reflexive pronoun in the blank. Then, match the meaning of the Spanish verb in the sentences with the English meanings on the right. Follow the model.

Modelo María ***se*** casó el domingo. ***c*** — a. went crazy
1. Yo ***me*** puse alegre con las noticias. ***f*** — b. had fun
2. Mis hermanos ***se*** enojaron cuando su equipo perdió. ***e*** — c. got married
3. Nosotros ***nos*** divertimos durante el campeonato. ***b*** — d. got bored
4. Juan ***se*** durmió durante el partido de ayer. ***g*** — e. got mad
5. Yo ***me*** aburrí mucho en el ballet. ***d*** — f. became happy
6. Tú ***te*** volviste loco cuando ganaste. ***a*** — g. fell asleep

Other reflexive verbs (*continued*)

B. Circle the verb in parentheses that completes the paragraph. Use the drawings to help you choose which verb to circle. The first one is done for you.

Ayer mi hermano y yo vimos un partido de fútbol en la televisión. Yo  (**me aburrí** / **me volví loco**) mucho porque no me gusta nada el fútbol y mi hermanito  (**se casó** / **se enojó**) conmigo. Entonces yo  (**me puse furioso** / **me divertí**) y mi hermanito pensó que era muy cómico y  (**se aburrió** / **se rió**). El partido de fútbol era muy aburrido y yo  (**me puse alegre** / **me dormí**). Cuando me desperté mi hermano no estaba en la sala y comencé a buscarlo.  (**Me volví loco** / **Me divertí**) porque estaba muy preocupado. Al fin encontré a mi hermanito ¡dormido debajo de su cama! No fue un día bueno para nosotros y no  (**nos divertimos** / **nos casamos**) mucho.

C. Complete the sentences telling the changes that took place in the different people. Write the preterite form of the reflexive verb in each sentence.

Modelo **(volverse loco)** Felipe ***se*** ***volvió*** ***loco*** cuando su equipo ganó el campeonato.

1. **(casarse)** Mis tíos ***se*** ***casaron*** al final de la estación.
2. **(ponerse furiosos)** Nosotros ***nos*** ***pusimos*** ***furiosos*** cuando el equipo perdió por tercera vez contra el mismo equipo.
3. **(divertirse)** Yo ***me*** ***divertí*** en el partido de ayer.
4. **(aburrirse)** Mis primos ***se*** ***aburrieron*** porque su equipo nunca ganaba.
5. **(ponerse agitada)** Marina ***se*** ***puso*** ***agitada*** con la reina del concurso.

Realidades 2 | Nombre ______ | Hora ______

Capítulo 6A | Fecha ______ | Guided Practice Activities 6A-5

Lectura: Los Juegos Panamericanos (pp. 310–311)

A. The reading in your textbook is about the **Juegos Panamericanos** or Pan-American Games, a sports event similar to the Summer Olympics. Using what you already know about the Summer Olympics can help you understand the reading. See if you can answer the questions below. ***Answers will vary.***

1. What are the Summer Olympics? ______
2. Who can participate in the Olympics? ______
3. What are five sports often featured in the Summer Olympics? ______, ______, ______, ______, ______

B. Read the following excerpts from your textbook reading. They contain many cognates (words that look and sound like English words) that will help you understand the excerpts. Write what you think some of these words mean in English in the spaces below.

> *Los Juegos Panamericanos se establecieron para promover la comprensión entre las naciones del continente americano. Los primeros Juegos se inauguraron el 25 de febrero en 1951 de Buenos Aires, con 2.513 atletas de 22 países.*
>
> *Todos los países de las Américas pueden mandar atletas a competir. Aproximadamente el 80 por ciento de los deportes de los Juegos Panamericanos se juegan en las Olimpíadas.*

1. Panamericanos ***Panamerican***
2. se establecieron ***established***
3. naciones ***nations***
4. febrero ***February***
5. atletas ***athletes***
6. Américas ***Americas***
7. competir ***compete***
8. Olimpíadas ***Olympics***

C. Now read the sentences below. Based on the excerpts in **part B,** write **Sí** if the sentence tells something that happens during the Pan-American Games. Write **No** if it doesn't happen during the Games.

1. Todos los países del mundo pueden participar en estos Juegos. ***No***
2. Las personas que participan en estos Juegos son atletas. ***Sí***
3. Todos los deportes de los Juegos Panamericanos también se juegan en las Olimpíadas. ***No***

realidades.com • Web Code: jdd-0606

Realidades 2 | Nombre ______ | Hora ______

Capítulo 6A | Fecha ______ | Guided Practice Activities 6A-6

Presentación oral (p. 313) *Answers will vary.*

Task: Prepare a review of your favorite television program and present it to your class.

A. Complete the following sentences about your favorite television program. Circle one option from the word lists for each sentence and write it in the blank.

una comedia	**la telenovela**
un programa deportivo	**una película de detectives**
un programa de concursos	**un programa de dibujos animados**

1. Mi programa favorito es ______

niños	**mayores**	**niños y mayores**

2. Este programa es para ______

me río mucho	**me enojo mucho**
me siento emocionado(a)	**me vuelvo loco(a)**

3. Cuando veo este programa ______

interesante	**divertido**	**fenomenal**	**alegre**

4. Este programa es ______

B. Now use the information from **part A** to complete the following sentences.

1. Mi programa favorito se llama ______ y es ______.
2. Este programa es para ______.
3. Cuando veo este programa ______.
4. Este programa es ______.

C. Use the sentences from **parts A** and **B** to practice your oral presentation. Go through the presentation several times. Try to:

- include all the information in the sentences
- use complete sentences and speak clearly

Antes de ver el video

Actividad 1

In this video you will hear an interview with a famous soccer player. Write six sentences the player might use to describe what happened in a recent game. Follow the model.

Modelo *El jugador metió un gol.*

1. **Answers will vary.**
2.
3.
4.
5.
6.

¿Comprendes?

Actividad 2

Read the following statements about the video and decide whether they are **cierto** or **falso.** If the statement is true, write ***cierto.*** If it is **falso,** rewrite the statement to make it true.

1. Manolo y Ramón están viendo una entrevista en la tele.
   Cierto.
2. Claudia tiene interés en la entrevista de Luis Campos.
   Falso, Claudia no tiene ningún interés en la entrevista.
3. Luis Campos es el mejor jugador de las Águilas del América.
   Falso, es el mejor jugador de los Lobos de Madero.
4. Manolo y Ramón tienen planes para ir al partido de hoy.
   Falso, Manolo y Ramón no piensan ir al partido.
5. Claudia sabe cómo pueden ver el partido en el estadio.
   Cierto.
6. Manolo y Ramón no quieren ir con Claudia al estadio para ver el partido.
   Falso, ellos tienen muchas ganas de ir al estadio para ver el partido.

Realidades 2 Nombre ____ Hora ____

Capítulo 6A Fecha ____ VIDEO

Actividad 3

Do you remember what happened in the video? Using the pictures to help you, summarize the video in your own words. Follow the model.

1 2 3 4

Modelo *Manolo y Ramón vieron una entrevista con "la Pantera", Luis Campos.*

1. Durante este campeonato, los Lobos ganaron 31 partidos, empataron seis y perdieron sólo tres.
2. Campos continúa la entrevista: "Ellos metieron el primer gol, pero cinco minutos después empatamos".
3. "Luego, en el segundo tiempo metimos dos goles más y ganamos", exclama "la Pantera".
4. Claudia les pregunta si quieren ir al partido, pero le parece a ella que no tienen interés.

Y, ¿qué más?

Actividad 4

If you were a reporter for the school newspaper, who would you interview? Why? Answer these questions. Then, write five questions you would ask during the interview. Follow the model.

Modelo *Voy a entrevistar a la presidenta del club de español. Quiero saber las actividades que planea para el semestre.*

Answers will vary.

Realidades 2 Nombre ____ Hora ____

Capítulo 6A Fecha ____ VIDEO

Actividad 5

The popular radio program **"Nuestra comunidad"** is highlighting three successful young women from the local Spanish-speaking community. As you listen to parts of their interviews, use the pictures below to decide whether the young woman speaking is Laura, Flor, or Isabel. Then, write the name of the young woman in the corresponding space. You will hear each set of statements twice.

Laura Flor Isabel

1. Laura	3. Isabel	5. Isabel	7. Laura
2. Flor	4. Laura	6. Flor	8. Flor

Actividad 6

In the past few years there has been a growing interest in women's soccer. Listen as Don Balón interviews Eva Barca, a rising women's soccer star. As you hear the different segments of the interview, read the following statements and tell whether each is **cierto** or **falso.** You will hear each segment twice.

1. Eva Barca escucha el programa de Don Balón. **(Cierto)** Falso
2. Don Balón sólo entrevista a las mujeres. Cierto **(Falso)**
3. Las mujeres ganan más dinero que los hombres. Cierto **(Falso)**
4. Hay un muñeco de Eva Barca. **(Cierto)** Falso
5. Según Eva, no hay muñecos de los hombres jugadores. **(Cierto)** Falso
6. Según Eva, su entrenador grita demasiado. Cierto **(Falso)**
7. Según Eva, los aficionados son iguales para las dos ligas. **(Cierto)** Falso

Realidades 2 Nombre Hora

Capítulo 6A Fecha **AUDIO**

Actividad 7

How do contestants spend their free time during the **"Señorita América del Sur"** beauty pageant? Listen as some women talk about what their friend(s) in the pageant did last night, and as others talk about what they are doing today to calm themselves before the final competition begins. As you listen to each contestant, decide whether she is talking about last night or today. You will hear each set of statements twice.

	1	2	3	4	5	6	7	8
Anoche	X		X		X	X		
Hoy		X		X			X	X

Actividad 8

Even though pets cannot express their emotions through words, they can express themselves through their actions. As you hear each person describe his or her pet's behavior, match a picture to the pet. Write the number of each pet owner's description underneath the picture of his or her dog. You will hear each description twice.

3

6

1

5

4

2

Realidades 2 Nombre Hora

Capítulo 6A Fecha **AUDIO**

Actividad 9

Yesterday in her popular talk show **"Dime la verdad,"** Lola Lozano had as her guests a group of famous soccer players. The question on the program was **"¿Qué lo vuelve más loco?"** In the table below, take notes about what each one said. Then, use your notes to complete the sentences about each guest. You will hear each conversation twice.

MIS NOTAS

1.

2.

3. Notes will vary.

4.

5.

1. Luis se vuelve loco cuando hay un empate.
2. Marisol se vuelve loca cuando el presentador la abraza.
3. Enrique se vuelve loco cuando los aficionados se pelean.
4. María se vuelve loca cuando los entrenadores masculinos dicen que las muchachas no deben jugar al fútbol.
5. Martín se vuelve loco cuando el entrenador grita.

Actividad 10

You and your friend are flipping through the channels, and you have each found one thing that you'd like to watch. Using the pictures below, describe each show in detail. The first description has been started for you.

1. 

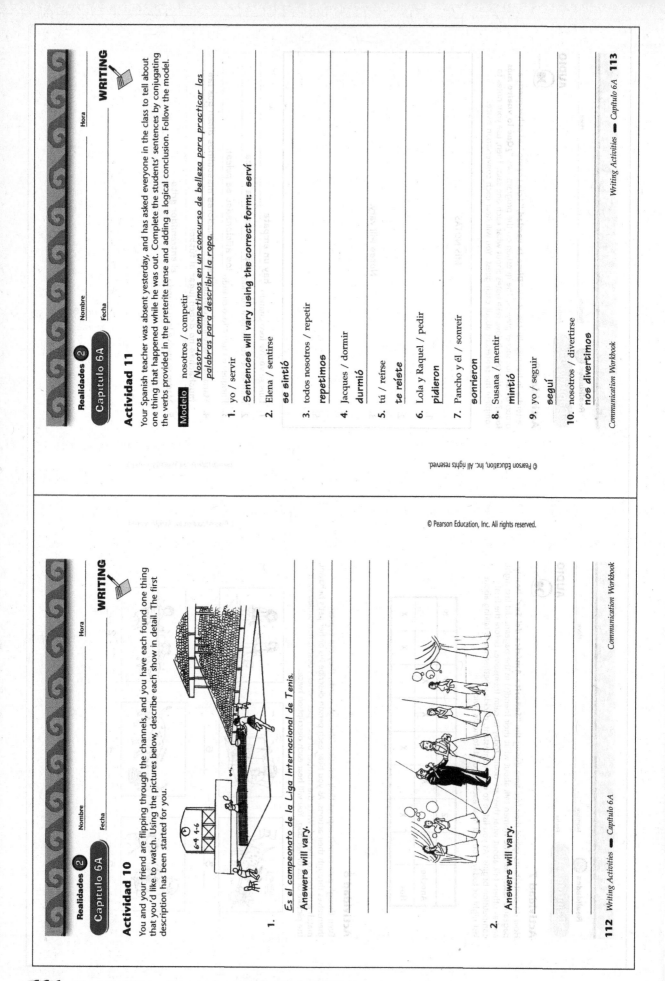

Es el campeonato de la Liga Internacional de Tenis.
Answers will vary.

2. 

Answers will vary.

Actividad 11

Your Spanish teacher was absent yesterday, and has asked everyone in the class to tell about one thing that happened while he was out. Complete the students' sentences by conjugating the verbs provided in the preterite tense and adding a logical conclusion. Follow the model.

Modelo nosotros / competir
Nosotros competimos en un concurso de belleza para practicar las palabras para describir la ropa.

1. yo / servir
Sentences will vary using the correct form: serví
2. Elena / sentirse
se sintió
3. todos nosotros / repetir
repetimos
4. Jacques / dormir
durmió
5. tú / reírse
te reíste
6. Lola y Raquel / pedir
pidieron
7. Pancho y él / sonreír
sonrieron
8. Susana / mentir
mintió
9. yo / seguir
seguí
10. nosotros / divertirse
nos divertimos

Actividad 12

Look at the scene below from Mariela and Pablo's wedding. Write at least six sentences to tell what is happening at the moment. You may want to use the verbs **casarse, enojarse, ponerse, aburrirse, dormirse,** and **divertirse.**

Answers will vary.

Actividad 13

Juanita just participated in a beauty pageant, and is writing a letter to her grandmother to tell her what it was like.

A. First, write sentences to help her describe where the event took place, who was there, and what everyone looked like. The first one is done for you.

Estuve en el Teatro Central. Answers will vary.

B. Next, list what Juanita and the other contestants probably did during the competition. The first one is done for you.

Yo me vestí en una hora. Answers will vary.

C. Finally, use your sentences from Part A and Part B to help Juanita write her letter to her grandmother. The letter has been started for you.

Querida abuela:
Hoy yo participé en un concurso de belleza. ¡Fue fantástico!
Answers will vary.

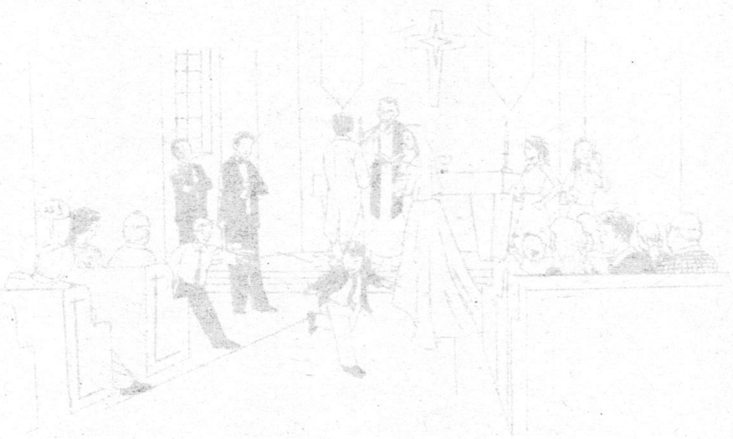

Test Preparation Answers

Reading Skills
p. 256 2. **C**
p. 257 2. **B**

Integrated Performance Assessment
p. 258
Answers will vary.

Capítulo 6B

School-to-Home Connection

Dear Parent or Guardian,

The theme of our current unit is *La televisión y el cine* (Television and movies). This chapter is called *¿Qué película has visto?* (What movie have you seen lately?).

Upon completion of this chapter students will be able to:

- discuss movie plots and characters
- talk about activities they have done
- understand cultural perspectives on movies

Students will also explore:

- the suffixes *–oso(a)* and *–dor(a)*

Our textbook, *Realidades,* helps with the development of reading, writing, and speaking skills through the use of strategies, process speaking, and process writing. In this chapter, students will:

- read movie reviews and compare movie ratings in different countries
- write a brief movie synopsis including their ideas for characters and a humorous plot

To reinforce and enhance learning, students can access a wide range of online resources on **realidades.com,** the personalized learning management system that accompanies the print and online Student Edition. Resources include the eText, textbook and workbook activities, audio files, videos, animations, songs, self-study tools, interactive maps, voice recording (RealTalk!), assessments, and other digital resources. Many learning tools can be accessed through the student Home Page on **realidades.com.** Other activities, specifically those that require grading, are assigned by the teacher and linked on the student Home Page within the calendar or the Assignments tab.

You will find specifications and guidelines for accessing **realidades.com** on home computers and mobile devices on MyPearsonTraining.com under the SuccessNet Plus tab.

realidades.com

For: Tips to Parents
Visit: www.realidades.com
Web Code: jce-0010

Check it out! At the end of the chapter, have your child tell you what his or her favorite movie is and its genre. Then have your child tell you what task he or she would enjoy most while making a movie.

Sincerely,

Capítulo 6B

Videocultura Script

Cine y televisión

Spanish version:

En la actualidad, la industria del cine y la televisión de América Latina y España goza de un gran éxito internacional.

Actores como Benicio del Toro, Javier Bardem y Penélope Cruz son ya estrellas reconocidas en el mundo entero.

Los directores de cine Alfonso Cuarón y Pedro Almodóvar han dirigido películas que cautivaron a una gran audiencia.

No importa de que país o lengua se trate, las películas son el resultado de un intenso proceso creativo y de una gran colaboración.

Además del cine, la televisión es una forma de entretenimiento muy popular en los países hispanos.

Uno de los tipos de programas de televisión más vistos en América Latina es la telenovela.

Estas series de telenovela entrelazan el romance, la aventura, el misterio y la historia en tramas que en algunos casos captan la atención de un país entero.

Las telenovelas se emiten diariamente, de cinco a seis veces por semana y duran varios meses.

Hoy en día, algunas de las telenovelas populares se emiten en los Estados Unidos a una creciente audiencia latina que sintoniza diferentes canales de televisión para hispanohablantes.

English version:

In Latin America and Spain, the television and movie industries are enjoying international success.

Movie actors such as Benicio del Toro, Javier Bardem, and Penélope Cruz are recognized around the world.

Talented film directors such as Alfonso Cuarón and Pedro Almodóvar create movies that appeal to a wide audience.

No matter the country or language, movies are the result of a collaborative, creative process.

In addition to going to the movies, watching television is a popular form of entertainment across the Spanish-speaking world.

One of the highest-rated television shows in Latin America is the *telenovela*.

These soap opera miniseries weave together romance, adventure, mystery, and history in storylines that often capture the attention of an entire country.

They generally appear five or six nights a week and end after a run of several months.

Today in the United States, popular *telenovelas* are broadcast to the growing Latino audience on the different Spanish television networks.

Input Script

Presentation

Input Vocabulary: Come to class wearing sunglasses and an ascot or other apparel to suggest that you are a movie star. Place the transparencies of the movies shown in the *A primera vista* on the screen. Tell students that when you are not teaching, you play small roles in movies. Point to the movies and describe the role you played in each one. Ask students if they saw each movie. Act disappointed when they respond no. Then distribute copies of the Vocabulary Clip Art showing different movie genres and have students cut them into individual images. Describe your upcoming roles in different kinds of movies and have students arrange the images on their desk in the order you mention them.

Input Dialogue 1: Tell students that they probably haven't seen *2050* because it just came out. Read the dialogue between the boys in *A primera vista*. Then ask students if they have seen different movies that have just come out in movie theaters by saying: *¿Has visto ____?* If they have seen the movie, ask them what it was like, using: *¿Qué tal fue?* Ask if the movie is out on video or DVD as well.

Input News Article: Read the behind-the-scenes article about the video *En busca de la verdad*. Then tell students: *¡No puedo creer que no mencionó el papel que yo hice: Hombre (Mujer) en la parada de autobús!* Ask for a volunteer to help you demonstrate your magnificent performance in the movie. Place two chairs at the front of the classroom and have the student sit next to you at the "bus stop." Have the student turn to you and ask: *¿Qué hora es?* With much drama, say: *Son… las diez*. Then distribute the following script to a group of five students (four actors and one director):

(Miguel y Cristina están hablando enfrente de la casa de Cristina.)

MIGUEL: Te amo, Cristina, y yo sé que tú me amas también. ¿Por qué no quieres casarte conmigo?

CRISTINA: ¡Porque, Miguel, como tú sabes, soy una extraterrestre! ¡Venimos de dos mundos diferentes!

SEÑOR BUSTAMENTE: *(Saliendo de la casa con la Señora Bustamente. Está furioso.)* ¡Cristina! ¡Vente por acá! ¡Te dije que no debes hablar con ese ser humano!

SEÑORA BUSTAMENTE: *(con emoción)* ¡Déjalos, Raúl! ¿No te recuerdas cómo fue para nosotros?

CRISTINA: ¿Qué? Mamá, ¿tú eres un ser humano?

SEÑORA BUSTAMENTE: Sí, mi hija.

(Cristina parece alegre, pero confudida.)

Have the group practice and present the script. Then ask the rest of the class about the performance: *¿Quién hizo el papel del papá? Quién fue el director (la directora)? ¿Qué tipo de película es?*

Comprehension Check

- Call out the names of different movies and have students tell you the genre of the movie in Spanish.
- Have students describe their favorite movies by telling the director, the actors, and the roles the actors played in the movie.

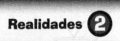

Audio Script

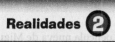

Audio DVD, Capítulo 6B

Track 01: *A primera vista, ¿Qué película has visto?*, Student Book, p. 320, (3:44)

Vocabulario y gramática en contexto

Vas a escuchar cada palabra o frase dos veces. Después de la primera vez hay una pausa para que puedas pronunciar la palabra o frase. Luego vas a escuchar de nuevo la palabra o frase.

violencia	los efectos especiales
el amor	el extraterrestre
alquila	la extraterrestre
robar	la detective
la ladrona	el detective
el ladrón	la película de acción
el crimen	una víctima

Lee en tu libro mientras escuchas el diálogo.

TEEN MALE 1: ¿Has visto la película *2050?* ¿Qué tal es?
TEEN MALE 2: Pues, me fascinan las películas de ciencia ficción, pero no he visto esa película todavía. Los críticos han escrito varios artículos sobre la película y todos la recomiendan. Creo que la película será muy popular con el público.
TEEN MALE 1: Bueno. ¿Se puede alquilar ya el video o DVD?
TEEN MALE 2: No. Todavía no.

Track 02: *A primera vista*, Student Book, p. 321, (4:08)

Vocabulario y gramática en contexto

Vas a escuchar cada palabra o frase dos veces. Después de la primera vez hay una pausa para que puedas pronunciar la palabra o frase. Luego vas a escuchar de nuevo la palabra o frase.

arrestar	hace el papel de
capturar	la actuación
la criminal	papeles
el criminal	el galán
está enamorado	la directora
se enamora de	la escena
un argumento	personajes principales
la dirección	

Más vocabulario
la estrella del cine
tratarse de

Lee en tu libro mientras escuchas la narración.

Detrás de *En busca de la verdad*

En busca de la verdad tiene un argumento muy básico. Se trata de tres generaciones de una familia mexicana. Roberto le pregunta a su abuela dónde está su abuelo, Federico, pero nadie sabe qué le pasó. Roberto decide buscar la verdad.

Dora Guzmán Trujillo, como directora, está en control de la dirección de la película. Roberto Castañeda hace el papel de Roberto. Vive en la ciudad de Querétaro y ha participado en muchas obras de teatro. Elia González hace el papel de Linda. Ella también vive en Querétaro y hace muchos años que es actriz. A los dos jóvenes les gusta la actuación y desean tener papeles cada vez más importantes en el cine, el teatro y la televisión.

Track 03: *A primera vista*, Act. 1, Student Book, p. 321, (2:51)

¿Qué película es?

Mira los carteles de las películas que hay en las páginas 320 y 321. Escucha las frases y señala el cartel de la película que corresponde a cada frase. Vas a escuchar las frases dos veces.

1. **MALE VOICE 1:** Carmen, mi amor. No puedo vivir sin ti. Te quiero.
2. **MALE VOICE 2:** ¡Vamos, rápido! Viene la policía. Toma las joyas ahora.
3. **MALE VOICE 3:** Mira, a la izquierda. ¡Hay tres extraterrestres con dos cabezas!
4. **FEMALE VOICE 1:** ¿Cómo murió la víctima?
5. **FEMALE VOICE 2:** Carlos. ¡Claro! Voy a casarme contigo. Eres el amor de mi vida.
6. **FEMALE VOICE 3:** Parece que es el crimen perfecto. No sabemos cómo ocurrió.
7. **MALE VOICE 4:** ¡Policía! Pongan las manos sobre la cabeza. ¡Rápido!

Track 04: *A primera vista*, Act. 2, Student Book, p. 321, (2:48)

¿Cuánto sabes de las películas?

Escucha las frases y contesta las preguntas. Vas a escuchar las frases dos veces.

1.	a. el personaje principal	b. el director
2.	a. la directora	b. el actor
3.	a. los extraterrestres	b. los efectos especiales
4.	a. se enamoran de ellos	b. los capturan

1. En la película *Violencia en la ciudad*, Manuel Farol hace el papel del detective. ¿Es Manuel el personaje principal o el director?
2. En una película, ¿la persona que está en control de todos los aspectos de la actuación es la directora o el actor?
3. En la película *2050*, ¿los personajes que vienen de otro planeta son los extraterrestres o los efectos especiales?
4. Cuando los detectives llegan a la escena de un crimen, ¿que hacen con los criminales? ¿Se enamoran de ellos o los capturan?

Track 05: *A primera vista, Videohistoria*, Student Book, pp. 322–323, (2:04)

El mosquito

Lee en tu libro mientras escuchas la *Videohistoria*.

See Student Book pages 322–323 for script.

Track 06: ***Manos a la obra*****, Act. 6, Student Book, p. 325, (2:04)**

Escucha y escribe

Escucha las siguientes descripciones y escríbelas en una hoja de papel. Luego decide quién del recuadro hace cada acción y escribe su nombre al lado de la frase. Vas a escuchar las descripciones dos veces.

1. Se enamora de la mujer bonita.
2. Viene de otro planeta.
3. Captura y arresta a los criminales.
4. Habla con los actores sobre sus papeles.
5. Dice que la película es un fracaso o un éxito.
6. Roba el banco o la joyería.
7. Mata a alguien o hace otro crimen.

Track 07: Audio Act. 5, Writing, Audio & Video Workbook, p. 119, (4:33)

The drama class is trying to decide on the cast of their upcoming spring production *Aquella noche*. Match the name of the person with his or her suggested role by marking an *X* in the corresponding square in the grid. You will hear each set of statements twice.

ADULT FEMALE TEACHER: Esta obra de teatro se trata de un muchacho rico y su novia, quien es víctima de un ladrón de joyas. El detective encuentra al ladrón de joyas con la ayuda de un extraterrestre. La obra tiene un argumento muy interesante y divertido.

1. **TEEN MALE 1:** Bueno, tenemos que decidir quién va a hacer el papel del galán de la obra. Tiene que ser muy guapo… ¡Ya sé!, Fernando es ideal. Es el muchacho más popular de la escuela y es muy buen actor.
2. **TEEN FEMALE 1:** La novia de Fernando, María, puede ser la víctima. Son una pareja ideal y a él le encantaría salvar la vida de su novia. Están enamorados ya.
3. **TEEN MALE 2:** A ver… ¡Ah!, Matilde puede ser la extraterrestre porque a ella le gustan las películas de ciencia ficción. Ella habla de extraterrestres todo el tiempo en la clase de ciencias. Es perfecta para el papel. Me vuelve loco algunas veces.
4. **TEEN FEMALE 2:** Antonio es perfecto para el papel del ladrón que roba las joyas de la muchacha rica. Él tiene cara de muchacho malo, pero es muy guapo.
5. **TEEN MALE 3:** ¿Quién va a a hacer el papel de detective?

ADULT FEMALE TEACHER: Déjame pensar un momento… Sí, Alberto es muy bueno en el papel de policía. Él puede ser el detective que investiga el crimen contra la novia del galán.

6. **TEEN MALE 4:** Y recomiendo a Carmen para dirigir la obra de teatro. Ella trabaja muy bien.

ADULT FEMALE TEACHER: Perfecto, todos de acuerdo.

Track 08: Audio Act. 6, Writing, Audio & Video Workbook, p. 119, (6:57)

Listen as people talk about movies they have seen. As you hear each opinion, fill in the grid below by writing or circling the correct answer. You do not need to write complete sentences. You will hear each set of statements twice.

1. **ADULT FEMALE 1:** ¿Has visto la película nueva de Miguel León? Hay que verla. Hace el papel de ladrón. El argumento es bastante complicado. Al principio, todos piensan que su personaje es un detective que trata de salvar a la heroína, María. Me gusta más la escena cuando Miguel la besó a ella. El beso fue tan romántico. Pero, poco a poco, aprendemos que es un criminal que quiere el dinero de ella. Es muy buena película.
2. **ADULT MALE 1:** Anoche alquilé una película de ciencia ficción. Se trata de un niño que ve un extraterrestre en su dormitorio cada noche. Tiene un argumento bastante básico. La primera noche que lo visitó, el niño se asustó mucho. Pero más tarde, el niño y el extraterrestre se hacen buenos amigos. Me gustaron los efectos especiales, pero en realidad, la película fue un fracaso. Debes alquilar otra película.
3. **ADULT FEMALE 2:** La última película de Juan Antonio Mendoza fue un tremendo éxito. El argumento es complicado. La película trata de un detective que busca a un ladrón de obras de arte. Cuando el detective está cerca de encontrar al ladrón, éste se escapa rápidamente. Me gustó la escena en que se cayó cuando robaba una obra de arte del Museo del Prado en España. ¡Qué gracioso! Te va a encantar la película. Es fantástica.
4. **ADULT MALE 2:** Anoche fui a ver la película *Los monstruos hambrientos*. No gastaron más de quinientos dólares en la producción de la película. Los personajes principales eran muy aburridos. Me gustan las películas de horror, pero esta fue un fracaso completo. El argumento es muy básico y te hacía dormir. Lo único que me gustó fue la escena con las pizzas y los monstruos. No debes verla porque es una pérdida de dinero.
5. **ADULT FEMALE 3:** Ayer fui al cine con mi novio para ver una película de Javier Miranda. ¡Qué muchacho tan guapo! Es mi galán favorito. Su actuación fue fantástica. Fue una película muy romántica. El galán se enamoró de una muchacha muy pobre, pero a su familia no le gustaba la idea de que ellos se casaran. Me gustó cuando se casaron al final de la película. Los críticos la recomiendan como una de las mejores películas del año, pero tiene un argumento básico. Debes ir al cine para ver esta película.

Track 09: Audio Act. 7, Writing, Audio & Video Workbook, p. 120, (4:44)

In today's episode of *Dime la verdad*, Lola Lana interviews actors and actresses on the set of a popular *telenovela*. She quickly learns that they all have very different movie preferences. As you listen, write the number of the interview underneath the corresponding poster. You will hear each set of statements twice.

1. **ADULT FEMALE 1:** Me fascinan las películas de los años cuarenta porque los personajes principales siempre se enamoran. Me encantan los musicales de aquellos años. Yo soy una persona muy romántica. No me gustan las películas de hoy: son tan violentas.

2. **Adult Male 1:** Las películas de los años cincuenta me encantan, especialmente las de detectives. La ropa de los detectives de esos años era tan elegante y los sombreros me gustan mucho porque son muy bonitos. Me aburren las películas románticas. Los actores se besan todo el tiempo.
3. **Adult Male 2:** Me parece que las películas de los años noventa son las mejores. Me interesan especialmente las películas de acción y aventuras. A mi novia le molesta ver películas de acción, pero a mí no me importa. Me molesta tener que ver una película romántica porque me aburren completamente y me dan dolor de cabeza.
4. **Adult Male 3:** Me encanta ir al cine a ver películas de ciencia ficción. Creo que hay extraterrestres que nos visitan. Me fascinan los efectos especiales en las películas de extraterrestres. Yo tengo un vestido de extraterrestre que me queda muy bien. Mi mamá dice que estoy loco.
5. **Adult Female 2:** Las películas clásicas de los años veinte son las mejores. El héroe de la película rescata a la estrella y se besan al final. Esas películas son muy románticas. A veces lloro tanto que los ojos me duelen toda la noche.

Track 10: *Manos a la obra,* Act. 18, Student Book, p. 332, (1:45)

Escucha y escribe

Tus amigos están viendo una película, pero tú llegaste tarde. Ahora te están diciendo lo que ha pasado. Escribe lo que te dijeron. Después pon las frases en orden según los dibujos. Vas a escuchar las frases dos veces.

1. Los médicos le han puesto una venda a la víctima en el hospital.
2. Nadie ha muerto, pero los paramédicos han tenido que ayudar a una víctima.
3. Los detectives han capturado y arrestado a los criminales.
4. Los ladrones han hecho una explosión y han robado el banco.

Track 11: Audio Act. 8, Writing, Audio & Video Workbook, p. 120, (4:13)

Even though Julia's grandmother only missed one episode of her favorite *telenovela*, she is eager to hear about what she missed. As Julia tells her about the last episode, answer the questions below about what has happened with each character. You will hear each conversation twice.

1. **Grandmother:** Dime, Julia. ¿Qué ha pasado en mi telenovela? ¿Todo está bien con Javier? Algunas veces se porta mal.
   Julia: Javier es el galán, ¿no?
   Grandmother: Sí. Hace el papel del médico.
   Julia: Creo que él ha muerto en un accidente.
   Grandmother: ¡Ay! ¡No me digas!
2. **Grandmother:** ¿Y Marlena? La pobrecita. Ella es la novia de Javier. ¿Qué ha pasado con ella?
   Julia: Después de oír las noticias de Javier, ella se ha vuelto loca. Creo que está en el hospital.
   Grandmother: ¡Ay! ¡No me digas!
3. **Grandmother:** ¿Qué ha pasado con Marco? Tenía planes de casarse con Victoria. No me gusta Victoria. Es una mujer tan mala.
   Julia: Marco no se ha casado todavía.
4. **Grandmother:** ¿Y qué le ha pasado a Victoria?
   Julia: Victoria se ha caído de la escalera de su casa y ha estado en el hospital casi muerta por varios días. Marco la ha visitado varias veces.
5. **Grandmother:** Y a mi ángel, Marisol, ¿qué le ha pasado?
   Julia: Marisol le ha escrito una carta de amor a Marco. Ella ha llorado tanto por el amor de Marco…
   Grandmother: ¡Qué horror! Pobrecita Marisol.

Track 12: Audio Act. 9, Writing, Audio & Video Workbook, p. 121, (4:09)

You and your classmates are creating storyboards to outline the plots of your upcoming class movies. Listen as one student describes the plot line for his project. Take notes on each part of the plot in the top half of each of the storyboard boxes below. Then draw a quick sketch in the bottom half of each box. You will hear the story twice.

1. Es un argumento básico, pero muy cómico también. Trata de Enrique, un muchacho que va de cámping con algunos amigos.
2. Enrique ha aprendido a cocinar recientemente. A Enrique no le molesta cocinar para todos. Él pone la carne en la sartén que ha traído de su casa.
3. Pero un momento…, ¿dónde está la carne? Estaba en la sartén hace un minuto. Enrique está enojado. Un ladrón le robó la carne.
4. Él busca la carne como un detective por todos lados. Enrique busca al ladrón detrás de un árbol.
5. ¿Quién se está comiendo la carne? ¡Oh, no! ¡Es un oso muy grande!
6. El oso corre hacia Enrique.
7. De repente, Enrique se cae. Le pierna le duele mucho. El oso está muy cerca. ¡Qué horror morirse en los dientes de un oso!
8. En el último momento, sus amigos llegan con una cámara y todos se ríen. El oso no es un oso. Es su mejor amigo, vestido de oso.

Track 13: *Repaso del capítulo,* Student Book, p. 342, (5:54)

Vocabulario y gramática

Escucha las palabras y expresiones que has aprendido en este capítulo.

See Student Book page 342 for vocabulary list.

Track 14: *Preparación para el examen,* Student Book, p. 343, (1:20)

Escuchar

Practice task

Listen as you hear a film critic interview people as they leave the movie *Mil secretos*. What did they think of: a) the actors; b) the director; c) the special effects; d) the theme; and e) future award possibilities.

EL CRÍTICO: Buenas tardes, señorita. ¿Qué piensa de *Mil secretos?*

ADULT FEMALE 1: Me fascina el argumento de la película—una chica que se enamora de un criminal. Marco Antonio hace el papel del galán. La escena con ella y Marco en el restaurante fue fantástica.

EL CRÍTICO: Gracias. ¿Y Ud., señor? ¿Qué piensa?

MALE ADULT 2: Fue un fracaso. No va a tener mucho éxito. El director fue horrible. ¡Nunca he visto efectos especiales tan malos! ¡Yo busqué la salida a los diez minutos!

Video Script

A primera vista: *El mosquito*, (7:12)

PROFESOR: …Y ahora, antes de terminar, la tarea es hacer una película de dos o tres minutos. El argumento puede estar basado en algún cuento o un libro.
MANOLO: ¿Podemos tener efectos especiales?
PROFESOR: Por supuesto. Puede tratarse de monstruos y extraterrestres.
MANOLO: Muy bien. Pues yo ya tengo una idea.
PROFESOR: Entonces tú puedes ser el director. Ahora tienes que escoger a los actores.
MANOLO: Bien. A ver… Necesito tres actores. El personaje principal tiene que ser alguien…
CLAUDIA: ¡Yo! Yo quiero ser el personaje principal.
MANOLO: Bueno, Claudia, es que vas a tener que hacer el papel de…
CLAUDIA: No importa. Yo quiero hacerlo.
MANOLO: Está bien. Ahora necesito a dos actores más. ¿Teresa? Ahora, a alguien más.

MANOLO: ¿Listos?
PROFESOR: Buenos días. ¿Cómo están? ¿Están todos listos? Y bien, ¿qué película vamos a ver primero?
PROFESOR: A ver… ¿Manolo?

El mosquito
RAMÓN: Mañana tengo el examen y no sé nada.
CLAUDIA: ¡No, no me mates, por favor!
RAMÓN: ¿Qué has dicho? ¿Tú hablas?
CLAUDIA: Sí. Yo puedo hablar en inglés y en español.
RAMÓN: No lo puedo creer… Pues tengo que matarte. Tengo que estudiar y tú me molestas.
CLAUDIA: ¡Espera, espera! Puedo ayudarte.
RAMÓN: ¿Cómo puedes ayudarme tú?
CLAUDIA: Yo sé leer. Puedo ayudarte a estudiar.
RAMÓN: ¡Caramba! Vamos a ver si eso es verdad.
RAMÓN: A ver. Lee lo que dice aquí.
CLAUDIA: Espera… Aquí dice que el primer Presidente de los Estados Unidos fue George Washington.
RAMÓN: ¡Increíble!
CLAUDIA: No me vas a matar, ¿verdad?
RAMÓN: No sé… ¿Y cómo puedes ayudarme en el examen?
CLAUDIA: Muy fácil. Tu puedes descansar y dormir ahora y yo voy a estudiar. Mañana puedo esconderme aquí. Desde allí te puedo explicar todo.
RAMÓN: ¡Buena idea! Puedes empezar ahora.Tienes que estudiar desde esta página hasta ésta. Yo me voy a dormir. Hasta mañana.

TERESA: ¡Ramón, despiértate ya! Es muy tarde y hoy tenemos el examen. ¿Estudiaste?
RAMÓN: ¿Cómo? Sí, sí estudié.
TERESA: Parece que estudiaste mucho. Este libro…
CLAUDIA: ¡¡¡NOOOOOO!!!
RAMÓN: ¡Teresa! ¡¿Qué has hecho?!

***GramActiva* Videos, (6:41)**
Verbs that use the indirect object

REAR-VIEW MIRROR GUY: Let's take a look back at indirect objects.
The dog brought me the coffee. *Me* is the indirect object. Or as we say in *español, El perro me trajo el café.*
CHEERLEADER: Give me a *me!*
EXTRAS: *¡Me!*
CHEERLEADER: Give me a *te!*
EXTRAS: *¡Te!*
CHEERLEADER: Give me a *le!*
EXTRAS: *¡Le!*
CHEERLEADER: Give me a *nos!*
EXTRAS: *¡Nos!*
CHEERLEADER: Give me an *os!*
EXTRAS: *¡Os!*
CHEERLEADER: Give me a *les!*
EXTRAS: *¡Les!*
CHEERLEADER: What's that spell?
EXTRAS: *METELENOSOSLES…*
HOST: There are a lot of verbs in Spanish that use indirect object pronouns. Look at these sentences.
Me gustan las comedias.
Nos interesa la actuación.
Can you see the indirect objects?
There they are! *Me* and *nos* are indirect objects.
V.O.: *¿Te gusta este coche?*
Me encanta este coche.
¡Nos encanta la vaca!
HOST: Remember that sometimes we add *a* plus a pronoun to emphasize or make clear if you're talking about a he, a she, a you formal or monsters from outer space.
V.O.: *A él le fascina la gente.*
A ella le interesan los coches.
¿A Uds. les interesa la prueba?

Quiz
V.O.: Complete the sentences with the correct indirect object pronoun.
A Juan ______ gustan los dramas.
A Juan le gustan los dramas.
A ellas ______ encantan las comedias.
A ellas les encantan las comedias.
A mí ______ fascina la fotografia.
A mí me fascina la fotografía.
A nosotros ______ gustan los efectos especiales.
A nosotros nos gustan los efectos especiales.

The present perfect

DETECTIVE: A mystery. I have seen this sort of thing before. I should know. I have worked on many cases and I have done a good job on every one of them. How do I do it, you ask? It takes a keen eye, and a good grasp of the present perfect.

DETECTIVE: I have seen. *He visto.*
I have worked. *He trabajado.*
I have done. *He hecho.*
The present perfect is simple. It's used to say what you have done. Now if only I could figure out what happened to that chicken.

HANDYMAN: Hold it right there. The present perfect is a bit more complicated than that. Here are two things you want to watch out for. First, in English, you use the helping verb "to have." In Spanish, you also use the helping verb "to have"—*haber*. This isn't the same "have" as *tener*. *Haber* is a special word that you use with the present perfect.

V.O.: *He, has, ha, hemos, habéis, han.*

HANDYMAN: Two. Your main verb has to be in the form of a past participle. Take the stem of the verb and add *-ado* for *-ar* verbs or add *-ido* for *-er* and *-ir* verbs.
hablar becomes *hablado*
comer becomes *comido*
vivir becomes *vivido*
The present perfect is a very handy thing to know. Watch.

V.O.: Hmm… *la pista.*
He encontrado muchas pistas como esa pista.
Siempre me he preguntado, ¿es importante?
Siempre he seguido la dirección correcta.

HANDYMAN: Watch for verbs with irregular participles. Like these: *hecho, dicho, escrito,* and *visto*.

V.O.: *He visto muchos crímenes.*
He hecho el análisis.
Algunas personas han dicho, "Eso puede ser peligroso."
Pero sólo es peligroso para el pollo.
¿Quién ha matado al pollo?
¡Ah ha!

HANDYMAN: One more thing to keep in mind. When you use object and reflexive pronouns with the present perfect, you put the pronoun before the form of *haber*.
"We have written it." *Lo hemos escrito.*
"I have brushed my teeth." *Me he cepillado los dientes.*

DETECTIVE V.O.: *¡Es mi mamá! ¡Lo has matado!*
Mmm… tú has preparado muy bien el pollo.
Nunca he comido un pollo tan sabroso.

Quiz

V.O.: Make a sentence using the present perfect.
(trabajar) Yo ______ en casa.
Yo he trabajado en casa.
(hacer) Ellos ______ los efectos especiales.
Ellos han hecho los efectos especiales.
(escribir) Usted ______ el guión.
Usted ha escrito el guión.
(ver) Nosotros ______ el monstruo.
Nosotros hemos visto el monstruo.

Videomisterio: *En busca de la verdad*, Episodio 8, (6:41)

ROBERTO'S V.O.: Mientras yo me preparaba para viajar a San Antonio, el misterioso hombre seguía haciendo preguntas sobre mi familia por toda la ciudad. Nadie sabía quién era o de dónde venía.

TURRÓN: ¿Conoce usted al doctor Toledo?
PEDRO: Claro, Tomás Toledo.
TURRÓN: ¿Se llama también doctor Zúñiga?
PEDRO: ¿Zúñiga? No, para nada. Se llama Toledo. Doctor Tomás Toledo.

TURRÓN: Busco información sobre un posible cliente de Uds.
CLERK: ¿Tomás Toledo? Tendrá que hablar con la directora. No podemos dar información sobre nuestros clientes.
TURRÓN: ¿Es Tomás Toledo o Tomás Zúñiga?
CLERK: Señor, ya le dije que no puedo…
TURRÓN: Sí, sí, está bien…

TURRÓN: …¿Y qué más me puede decir sobre la familia Toledo? ¿Tienen problemas de dinero? ¿Usan el nombre de Zúñiga?

TOMÁS: No veo nada, ¿tose mucho?
SR. TOS: Sí, mucho.
TOMÁS: Pues yo no encuentro nada.
SR. TOS: Pues yo le digo que tengo algo.
TOMÁS: Mire, tome esta medicina y si sigue tosiendo, regrese para hacerle más pruebas, un examen completo.
SR. TOS: Bueno… Por cierto, ¿sabe que por ahí anda un hombre haciendo preguntas sobre Ud.?
TOMÁS: ¿Qué?
SR. TOS: Sí, ayer habló conmigo y me preguntó varias cosas.
TOMÁS: ¿Qué cosas?
SR. TOS: Cosas… Como por ejemplo, si Ud. tiene problemas económicos, si usa el nombre de Tomás Zúñiga…
BERTA: Parece que hay un hombre por allí que está haciendo preguntas sobre nuestra familia.
TOMÁS: Sí, ya lo oí de otra gente.
BERTA: ¿Y sabes qué cosas preguntaba?
TOMÁS: Dónde vivimos, si tenemos problemas económicos, qué se yo.
BERTA: Tomás, ¿qué crees que quiera esta persona? No me gusta nada.
TOMÁS: No te preocupes. A mí tampoco me gusta pero por ahora no podemos hacer nada.

ROBERTO'S V.O.: Desafortunadamente Carmen y Linda tenían que regresar a San Antonio. Mi familia les ofreció una cena de despedida. Y también invitamos a Julio.
LINDA: ¡Cómo he disfrutado este viaje!
CARMEN: Así es. Linda y yo les agradecemos su gran hospitalidad. Pasamos una semana estupenda.
LINDA: Y yo quiero agradecer a Julio, a Dani y a Roberto por enseñarme esta magnífica ciudad.

Roberto: Pues entonces yo tengo que agradecerles a Carmen y a Linda, porque me voy a quedar en su casa en San Antonio.

Berta: Ay, hijo. Yo todavía no estoy muy segura si tu viaje a los Estados Unidos es una buena idea.

Roberto: Mamá, es la única forma de saber qué es lo que le pasó al abuelo.

Tomás: Cierto. Te deseo mucha suerte, hijo. Espero que puedas encontrar la respuesta a este misterio de tantos años.

Linda: ¡Me encanta esta ciudad! Gracias por todo.

Julio: Creo que todos nos divertimos mucho.

Roberto: Cierto. ¿Oye y cuándo vas a regresar a Guanajuato?

Linda: Probablemente en la primavera, con el intercambio entre nuestras escuelas.

Roberto: Y vas a quedarte más tiempo la próxima vez, ¿verdad?

Linda: Seguro.

Julio: Bueno, pues yo los dejo aquí. Tengo que ir a ver… a Josefina.

Roberto: ¿Josefina?

Julio: Sí, es una chica de la escuela, la del restaurante del otro día. Bueno… voy a ir a verla. Fue un placer conocerte, Linda. Eres una chica muy simpática.

Linda: Gracias por todo, Julio. Buena suerte.

Realidades 2

Capítulo 6B

Nombre ______

Fecha ______

Communicative Pair Activity **6B-1**

Estudiante **A**

Last weekend your classmates decided to go to the movies, but they could not agree which one to watch. There were too many types of movies playing! They finally decided that each person would go to a different type of movie and you want to know which type of movie each person saw. Use the following questions to ask your partner who saw what.

1. ¿Qué tipo de película vieron Pedro y María?
2. ¿Qué tipo de película vieron Luisa y Valentina?
3. ¿Qué tipo de película vio José?
4. ¿Qué tipo de película vieron Eduardo y Gabriela?
5. ¿Qué tipo de película vieron Marcela y Ana?
6. ¿Qué tipo de película vio Andrés?

Your partner was very kind in giving you all the previous information. In exchange, he or she wants to ask you if you know the names given to different types of movies. Answer his or her questions and write your answers in the spaces provided.

1. ______
2. ______
3. ______
4. ______
5. ______
6. ______

Last weekend you and your classmates decided to go to the movies, but you could not agree on which one to watch. There were too many types of movies playing! You finally decided that each person would go to a different type of movie. Your partner, however, could not go and he or she wants to know which type of movie each one of you saw. Use the following cues to answer his or her questions.

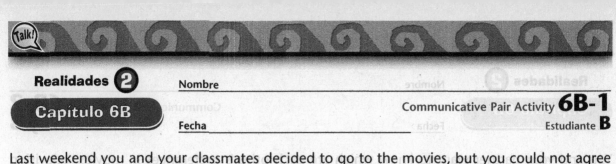

Pedro y María

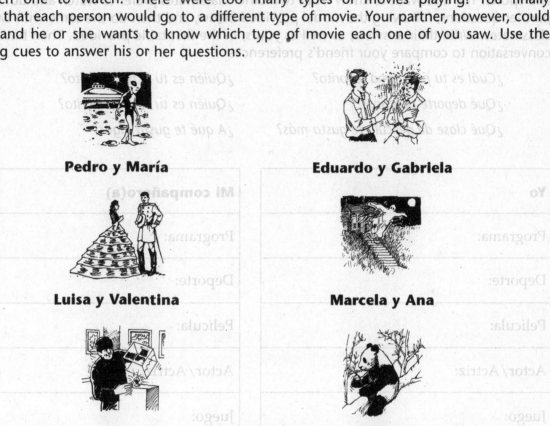

Eduardo y Gabriela

Luisa y Valentina

Marcela y Ana

José

Andrés

Now you want to find out if your partner knows the names given to different types of movies. Ask him or her the following questions and write his or her answers in the spaces provided.

1. Cómo se llaman las películas con astronautas y extraterrestres?
____
2. ¿Cómo se llaman las películas donde el galán se enamora con una mujer bonita?
____
3. ¿Cómo se llaman las películas con agentes secretos? ______________________
4. ¿Cómo se llaman las películas donde la gente se ríe mucho? ______________________
5. ¿Cómo se llaman las películas donde la gente siempre está asustada?
____
6. ¿Cómo se llaman las películas? ______________________

Realidades 2

Capítulo 6B

Nombre

Fecha

Communicative Pair Activity **6B-2**

Estudiantes **A y B**

You and your partner want to know which are each other's preferences in movies, television and sports. You also want to know what two other classmates prefer to watch and do. Ask your partner questions, following the model provided below, and then do the same with two other classmates. Write their answers, as well as yours, in the first table provided. Then have a short conversation to compare your friend's preferences.

¿Cuál es tu programa favorito?
¿Qué deporte practicas?
¿Qué clase de película te gusta más?
¿Quién es tu actor favorito?
¿Quién es tu actriz favorita?
¿A qué te gusta jugar?

Yo
Programa:
Deporte:
Película:
Actor/Actriz:
Juego:

Mi compañero(a)
Programa:
Deporte:
Película:
Actor/Actriz:
Juego:

Mi amigo(a)
Programa:
Deporte:
Película:
Actor/Actriz:
Juego:

Mi amigo(a)
Programa:
Deporte:
Película:
Actor/Actriz:
Juego:

Situation Cards

1A

Capítulo 6B Realidades 2

Talking about a movie or a television show

You are talking with a friend about the movies or TV shows you like.

— Ask your friend which TV show or movie he or she likes most.

— Ask which TV show or movie he or she dislikes most.

1B

Capítulo 6B Realidades 2

Talking about a movie or a television show

You are talking with a friend about the movies or TV shows you like.

— Respond to your friend's questions. Be sure to give a reason.

— Then, ask your partner the same questions.

2A

Capítulo 6B Realidades 2

Summarizing the plot and describing the characters of a movie or television show

You and a friend are asked to create the plot of a soap opera.

— Begin by suggesting the opening.

— Continue developing the plot by adding another detail.

— Continue until you finalize your plot.

— Then, discuss with your friend who you want to star in your soap opera.

2B

Capítulo 6B Realidades 2

Summarizing the plot and describing the characters of a movie or television show

You and a friend are asked to create the plot of a soap opera.

— Add details to the plot your friend has started.

— Continue until you are satisfied with the plot.

— Discuss with your partner who you want as the actor and actress in your soap opera.

GramActiva

¿Qué película has visto?
Las películas que hemos visto, p. 334

	Total para el grupo	Total para la clase
¿Cuántas películas han visto?		
¿Qué clase de películas?		
¿Dónde las han visto?		

Vocabulary Clip Art

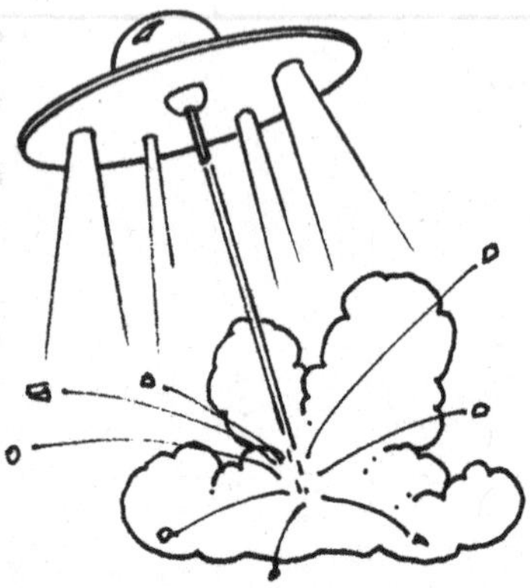

Vocabulary Clip Art

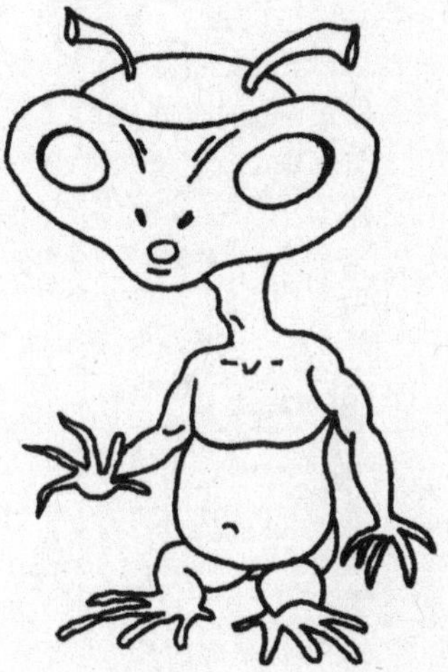

Vocabulary Clip Art

Core Practice Answers

6B-1
1. extraterrestres
2. galán
3. personajes
4. amor
5. película de acción
6. ladrones
7. estrella (del cine)
8. detectives, criminal
9. la víctima

6B-2
1. críticos
2. recomiendan
3. fascinó
4. he visto
5. director
6. argumentos
7. efectos
8. hace el papel
9. actuación
10. arresta
11. robó
12. trata de
13. se enamora de

6B-3
1. basado
2. violencia
3. un fracaso
4. el papel
5. éxito
6. un argumento
7. roba, mata
8. captura

6B-4
1. Se trata de un crimen.
2. Los personajes principales son los ladrones y las víctimas.
3. Unos ladrones roban el banco.
4. Sí, un ladrón mata a un policía y los otros ladrones usan violencia para poder robar el dinero.
5. Sí, los empleados del banco son víctimas del robo y el policía es víctima de la pistola del ladrón.
6. Answers will vary.

6B-5
1. Les encantan los postres.
2. Me duele un diente.
3. Nos interesa la historia.
4. Le queda mal la falda que tiene.
5. Les parece triste el argumento.
6. No le gusta la violencia.
7. Le fascinan las películas.
8. Te molestan mucho los mosquitos.

6B-6
1. Margarita y yo ya la hemos pedido.
2. Isabel ya las ha hecho.
3. Luis y Paco ya los han traído.
4. yo ya la he puesto.
5. Francisco ya la ha llamado.
6. Nosotros ya la hemos escogido.
7. Carlos ya la ha roto.
8. Marta ya la ha arreglado.

6B-7
1. Jesús ha tenido que estudiar para el examen.
2. Yo he visto una película policíaca.
3. Javier le ha escrito a Sarita esta semana.
4. Los ladrones han robado el dinero de la casa.
5. Nosotros hemos alquilado un video de la tienda.
6. La crítica ha hecho comentarios sobre la película.
7. La policía les ha capturado a los criminales.
8. Pilar me ha recomendado una película romántica.
9. Linda ha tratado de matar el mosquito.
10. el mosquito ha bajado en el libro de Juan.

Crucigrama (6B-8)
Horizontal:
1. recomendó
3. extraterrestre
6. visto
10. arrestado
13. mató
16. argumento
17. basado
19. fascinó
21. fracaso
24. enamorados

Vertical:
2. crítico
4. violencia
5. éxito
7. ladrones
8. director
9. efectos
11. alquilado
12. personaje
14. trata
15. galán
18. escena
20. capturó
22. actuación
23. papel

Organizer (6B-9)
I. Vocabulary Answers will vary.
II. Grammar
Wording of answers may vary.
1. Answers will vary, but must include eight of the following verbs: aburrir, doler, encantar, fascinar, gustar, importar, interesar, molestar, parecer, quedar.
2. The present perfect tense is formed with the auxiliary verb **haber** and the past participle.
3. Object pronouns in the present perfect are placed immediately before the form of **haber**.
4.
   Row 1: dicho, hecho, roto
   Row 2: devuelto, muerto, visto
   Row 3: escrito, puesto, vuelto

Realidades 2 | Nombre | Hora

Capítulo 6B | Fecha | **Vocabulary Flash Cards, Sheet 1**

Write the Spanish vocabulary word or phrase below each picture. Be sure to include the article for each noun.

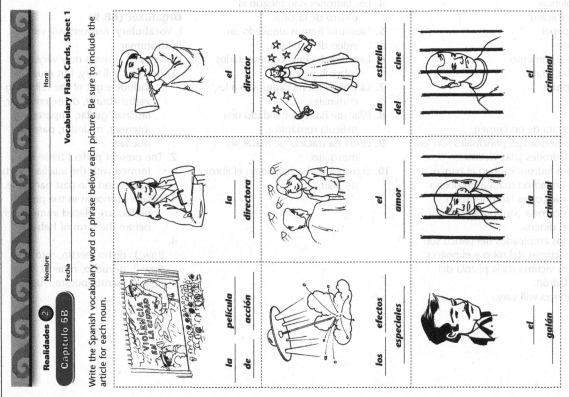

 ***la película de acción***	 ***la directora***	 ***el director***
 ***los efectos especiales***	 ***el amor***	 ***la estrella del cine***
 ***el galán***	 ***la criminal***	 ***el criminal***

Realidades 2 | Nombre | Hora

Capítulo 6B | Fecha | **Vocabulary Flash Cards, Sheet 2**

Write the Spanish vocabulary word below each picture. If there is a word or phrase, copy it in the space provided. Be sure to include the article for each noun.

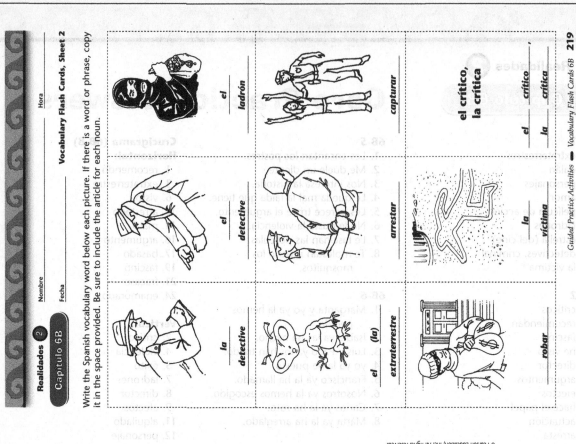

 ***la detective***	 ***el detective***	 ***el ladrón***
 ***el (la) extraterrestre***	 ***arrestar***	 ***capturar***
 ***robar***	 ***la víctima***	**el crítico, la crítica** ***el crítico, la crítica***

Realidades 2 — Capítulo 6B

Nombre ____ Hora ____

Fecha ____ **Vocabulary Flash Cards, Sheet 3**

Copy the word or phrase in the space provided. Be sure to include the article for each noun.

fascinar *fascinar*	**el fracaso** *el* *fracaso*	**he visto** *he* *visto*
has visto *has* *visto*	**matar** *matar*	**¿Qué tal es...?** *¿Qué* *tal es ...?*
recomendar *recomendar*	**será** *será*	**tener éxito** *tener* *éxito*

Realidades 2 — Capítulo 6B

Nombre ____ Hora ____

Fecha ____ **Vocabulary Flash Cards, Sheet 4**

Copy the word or phrase in the space provided. Be sure to include the article for each noun.

tratarse de *tratarse* *de*	**la violencia** *la* *violencia*	**la actuación** *la* *actuación*
el argumento *el* *argumento*	**la dirección** *la* *dirección*	**alquilar** *alquilar*
hacer el papel de *hacer el* *papel de*	**el personaje principal** *el personaje* *principal*	**no... todavía** *no ... todavía*

Realidades 2 Nombre ______ Hora ______

Capítulo 6B Fecha ______ **Vocabulary Flash Cards, Sheet 5**

Copy the word or phrase in the space provided. Be sure to include the article for each noun. These blank cards can be used to write and practice other Spanish vocabulary for the chapter.

enamorarse (de) *enamorarse* *(de)*	**(estar) enamorado, enamorada de** *(estar)* *enamorado*, *enamorada de*	**el crimen** *el* *crimen*
la ladrona *la* *ladrona*	**la escena** *la* *escena*	**estar basado, basada en** *estar basado*, *basada en*
el papel *el* *papel*		

Realidades 2 Nombre ______ Hora ______

Capítulo 6B Fecha ______ **Vocabulary Check, Sheet 1**

Tear out this page. Write the English words on the lines. Fold the paper along the dotted line to see the correct answers so you can check your work.

alquilar	*to rent*
el amor	*love*
arrestar	*to arrest*
capturar	*to capture*
el (la) criminal	*criminal*
enamorarse (de)	*to fall in love (with)*
robar	*to rob, to steal*
tener éxito	*to succeed, to be successful*
el fracaso	*failure*
tratarse de	*to be about*
he visto	*I have seen*
el director, la directora	*director*
la escena	*scene*
el papel	*role*
la víctima	*victim*

Fold In ←

Vocabulary Check, Sheet 2

Tear out this page. Write the Spanish words on the lines. Fold the paper along the dotted line to see the correct answers so you can check your work.

to rent	***alquilar***
love	***el amor***
to arrest	***arrestar***
to capture	***capturar***
the criminal	***el (la) criminal***
to fall in love (with)	***enamorarse (de)***
to rob, to steal	***robar***
to succeed, to be successful	***tener éxito***
failure	***el fracaso***
to be about	***tratarse de***
I have seen	***he visto***
director	***el director, la directora***
scene	***la escena***
role	***el papel***
victim	***la víctima***

Fold In

Vocabulary Check, Sheet 3

Tear out this page. Write the English words on the lines. Fold the paper along the dotted line to see the correct answers so you can check your work.

la estrella (del cine)	***(movie) star***
el (la) detective	***detective***
el galán	***leading man***
el ladrón, la ladrona	***thief***
la película de acción	***action film***
los efectos especiales	***special effects***
el (la) extraterrestre	***alien***
la actuación	***acting***
el argumento	***plot***
el crimen	***crime***
matar	***to kill***
el crítico, la crítica	***critic***
fascinar	***to fascinate***
¿Qué tal es...?	***How is (it)...?***

Fold In

Tear out this page. Write the Spanish words on the lines. Fold the paper along the dotted line to see the correct answers so you can check your work.

(movie) star	*la estrella (del cine)*
detective	*el (la) detective*
leading man	*el galán*
thief	*el ladrón, la ladrona*
action film	*la película de acción*
special effects	*los efectos especiales*
alien	*el (la) extraterrestre*
acting	*la actuación*
plot	*el argumento*
crime	*el crimen*
to kill	*matar*
critic	*el crítico, la crítica*
to fascinate	*fascinar*
How is (it)...?	*¿Qué tal es...?*

Fold In

To hear a complete list of the vocabulary for this chapter, go to www.realidades.com and type in the Web Code jdd-0699. Then click on **Repaso del capítulo.**

Verbs that use indirect object pronouns (p. 328)

- Many verbs that use indirect object pronouns, such as **aburrir, doler, encantar, fascinar, gustar,** and **importar,** use a similar construction:

  indirect object pronoun + verb + subject

  Le + encantan + las películas de acción.
  He likes action movies.

- You can use **a** + a noun or a pronoun with these verbs for emphasis or to make something clear:

  A Rodrigo le gustan las flores.
  Rodrigo likes flowers.

  or:

  A él le gustan las flores.
  He likes flowers.

- Here are the indirect object pronouns:

(A mí)	me	(A nosotros/a nosotras)	nos
(A ti)	te	(A vosotros/a vosotras)	os
(A usted/A él/A ella)	le	(A ustedes/A ellos/A ellas)	les

A. Circle the correct indirect object pronoun to complete each sentence. Follow the model.

Modelo A María (**le** / les) encantan las películas románticas.

1. A mí (te / **me**) aburre este programa.
2. A nosotros (**nos** / les) molestan los videojuegos.
3. A mi padre y a mí (**nos** / te) importan los actores de Hollywood.
4. A Pablo y a Ramón (le / **les**) fascina el cine.
5. A los directores (**les** / le) encanta trabajar con actores famosos.
6. ¡A ti (me / **te**) duele la cabeza después de ver tantas películas!

realidades.com
• Web Code: jdd-0613

Verbs that use indirect object pronouns (*continued*)

B. In the sentences below, fill in the first blank with the correct indirect object pronoun. Then, write the correct ending for each verb using the words that come after it as clues. Use the pictures to help you guess the correct indirect object pronouns. The first one is done for you.

1. A Maricarmen ***le*** interes***an*** las comedias.

2. A ellos ***les*** molest***a*** esperar mucho tiempo.

3. ¿A Ud. ***le*** parec***en*** interesantes los efectos especiales?

4. A mí ***me*** import***a*** el campeón de la liga.

5. A Sara y a Pilar ***les*** qued***an*** bien las camisas.

C. Write questions using the elements given and indirect object pronouns to ask the various people about their entertainment preferences. Follow the model.

Modelo A ti / gustar / ir al cine
¿*A ti te gusta ir al cine*?

1. A Juan / molestar / las películas de horror
   ¿***A Juan le molestan las películas de horror***?
2. A Uds. / interesar / los actores
   ¿***A Uds. les interesan los actores***?
3. A Steven Spielberg / importar / la ciencia ficción
   ¿***A Steven Spielberg le importa la ciencia ficción***?
4. A los criminales / fascinar / las películas de acción
   ¿***A los criminales les fascinan las películas de acción***?
5. A mí / parecer / tristes / los dramas
   ¿***A mí me parecen tristes los dramas***?

The present perfect (p. 331)

- Use the present perfect tense to tell what a person has done.
- To form this tense, use present-tense forms of **haber** + the past participle:
  Hemos alquilado dos películas.
  We have rented two movies.
- To form the past participle of a verb, drop the ending of the infinitive and add **-ado** for **-ar** verbs and **-ido** for **-er** and **-ir** verbs.

	alquilar	vivir		alquilar	vivir
he	alquilado	vivido	**hemos**	alquilado	vivido
has	alquilado	vivido	**habéis**	alquilado	vivido
ha	alquilado	vivido	**han**	alquilado	vivido

A. Complete the sentences below with the correct form of the verb **haber**.

Modelo Tú *has* vivido en Atlanta, ¿verdad?

1. Mis amigos ***han*** ido al cine todos los viernes por dos años.
2. Yo nunca ***he*** alquilado una película de horror.
3. Los directores ***han*** trabajado mucho en esta película.
4. El actor ***ha*** practicado mucho para este papel.
5. Nosotros ***hemos*** oído que es una película muy buena.

- Most verbs that have two vowels together in the infinitive have a written accent on the í of the past participle:
  caer → caído oír → oído leer → leído

B. Write the past participle form of the following verbs. Follow the model.

Modelo robar *robado*

1. matar ***matado***
2. hablar ***hablado***
3. perder ***perdido***
4. traer ***traído***
5. leer ***leído***
6. aprender ***aprendido***
7. caer ***caído***
8. oír ***oído***

Realidades 2 Nombre ______ Hora ______

Capítulo 6B Fecha ______ **Guided Practice Activities 6B-3**

The present perfect (*continued*)

C. Write the present perfect form of the verb in parentheses in each sentence to tell what things have happened in a recent action movie. Note that in the forms of the present perfect, the past participle does not change; the ending will always be *-o*. Follow the model.

Modelo (**filmar**) El director Mario Fernández *ha* *filmado* una nueva película.

1. (**matar**) En la película, unos criminales ***han*** ***matado*** a algunas personas.
2. (**robar**) Ellos ***han*** ***robado*** su dinero también.
3. (**esconder**) Un criminal ***ha*** ***escondido*** el dinero en el campo.
4. (**capturar**) Los detectives ***han*** ***capturado*** a todos los criminales.
5. (**ir**) Mis amigos y yo ***hemos*** ***ido*** al cine a ver la película tres veces.
6. (**leer**) Yo ***he*** ***leído*** los artículos de los críticos en el periódico.
7. (**crear**) Según los críticos, Fernández ***ha*** ***creado*** efectos especiales fantásticos.
8. (**tener**) Las películas del director Fernández siempre ***han*** ***tenido*** éxito.
9. (**oír**) Y tú, ¿ ***has*** ***oído*** decir algo bueno sobre esta película?

- These verbs have irregular past participles:

decir → ***dicho***	**poner →** ***puesto***
escribir → ***escrito***	**romper →** ***roto***
hacer → ***hecho***	**ver →** ***visto***
morir → ***muerto***	**volver →** ***vuelto***

D. Look at the following verbs. Write **I** (for Irregular) if the verb has an irregular past participle form. If not, write **R** (for Regular). Then, in the second blank, write in the past participle form for each verb, paying close attention to spelling. Follow the model.

Modelo alquilar *R* *alquilado*

1. volver ***I*** ***vuelto***
2. hacer ***I*** ***hecho***
3. escribir ***I*** ***escrito***
4. comer ***R*** ***comido***
5. decir ***I*** ***dicho***
6. vivir ***R*** ***vivido***
7. ver ***I*** ***visto***
8. morir ***I*** ***muerto***

© Pearson Education, Inc. All rights reserved.

Realidades 2 Nombre ______ Hora ______

Capítulo 6B Fecha ______ **Guided Practice Activities 6B-4**

The present perfect (*continued*)

E. The following sentences describe a movie. Use the correct form of **haber** plus the past participle of the verb in parentheses to complete the sentences. Follow the model.

Modelo Yo *he* *visto* (**ver**) una película policíaca.

1. El director ***ha*** ***dicho*** (**decir**) que el argumento es malo.
2. Nadie ***ha*** ***muerto*** (**morir**) en esta escena.
3. Luis y Damián ***han*** ***hecho*** (**hacer**) los papeles de las víctimas.
4. Nosotras ***hemos*** ***escrito*** (**escribir**) el argumento para la película.
5. ¿Tú ***has*** ***puesto*** (**poner**) el coche en la última escena?
6. La estrella ***ha*** ***roto*** (**romper**) el vaso otra vez.

F. Marta is talking about movies. Rewrite her statements by replacing the underlined words with the pronoun in parentheses and placing it before the form of **haber** for each sentence. Follow the model.

Modelo Yo he alquilado <u>la película</u>. (la)
Yo *la he alquilado*.

1. Los detectives han arrestado <u>a las ladronas</u>. (las)
   Los detectives ***las han arrestado***.
2. Los actores han leído la escena <u>al director</u>. (le)
   Los actores ***le han leído*** la escena.
3. El galán ha capturado <u>a los extraterrestres</u>. (los)
   El galán ***los ha capturado***.
4. El director ha pedido ayuda <u>a nosotros</u>. (nos)
   El director ***nos ha pedido*** ayuda.
5. La directora ha escrito <u>el argumento</u>. (lo)
   La directora ***lo ha escrito***.
6. El crítico ha dicho su opinión <u>a mí</u>. (me)
   El crítico ***me ha dicho*** su opinión.

Realidades 2 Nombre ______ Hora ______

Capítulo 6B Fecha ______ **Guided Practice Activities 6B-4a**

The present perfect (*continued*)

- When you use object or reflexive pronouns with the present perfect, the pronoun goes right before the form of **haber**:

  ¿Has visto la película? Sí, la he visto. *Have you seen the movie? Yes, I have seen it.*

G. Complete the following sentences by writing the correct reflexive pronoun and the present perfect form of the verbs in parentheses. Use the pictures to help you with meaning. Follow the model. *Note: Some verbs have regular past participles, some require accent marks, and some have irregular past participles.*

Modelo (caerse) La actriz __*se*__ __*ha*__ __*caído*__.

1. (volverse) ¡El director __*se*__ __*ha*__ __*vuelto*__ loco!

2. (enojarse) Yo __*me*__ __*he*__ __*enojado*__ muchas veces cuando veo películas de horror.

3. (casarse) ¡Qué romántico! Los dos actores famosos __*se*__ __*han*__ __*casado*__.

4. (dormirse) ¿Tú __*te*__ __*has*__ __*dormido*__ viendo una película de acción?

5. (divertirse) Nosotros __*nos*__ __*hemos*__ __*divertido*__ viendo las comedias mexicanas.

6. (vestirse) Los críticos __*se*__ __*han*__ __*vestido*__ con elegancia para estos premios.

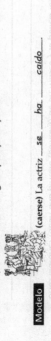

realidades.com • Web Code: jdd-0614

Realidades 2 Nombre ______ Hora ______

Capítulo 6B Fecha ______ **Guided Practice Activities 6B-5**

Lectura: La cartelera del cine (pp. 336–337)

A. First, read the title and subtitles and look at the pictures in the textbook reading. These can give you an idea of what the reading is about or what is the "big picture." *Then, circle the best option for the choices below.*

1. This reading is about
   (a.) movies. **b.** sports. **c.** politics.
2. Each section has a summary and a
   a. comedy. **(b.)** review. **c.** drama.

B. You will notice that each movie review begins with some basic facts. Read the following fact excerpt from your textbook reading. Then answer the questions below.

> *X-Men: Primera generación*
> *EE.UU., 2011 / Clasificación: PG-13 / Director: Matthew Vaughn / Actores: James McAvoy, Michael Fassbender, Jennifer Lawrence, Kevin Bacon*

1. What is the second part of the movie called? __***Primera generación***__
2. Who is the director __***Matthew Vaughn***__
3. In what year was the movie made? __***2011***__
4. What is the classification of the movie? __***PG-13***__

C. Read the following ***Crítica*** or review section for ***El caballero oscuro.*** Circle the answer that best completes each of the statements below.

> ***El caballero oscuro*** *es genial, con diálogos divertidos y acción sin límites. Hay que mencionar la actuación de Heath Ledger, quien es, sin duda, el protagonista estrella de esta película. De la saga Batman, éste es el mejor trabajo hasta el momento.*

1. El crítico de *El caballero oscuro* piensa que la película es
   a. incoherente. **(b.)** genial.
2. Al crítico le gusta
   (a.) la actuación de Heath Ledger. **b.** la música.
3. El crítico dice que la película es
   (a.) la mejor de la saga Batman. **b.** muy larga.

realidades.com • Web Code: jdd-0615

Realidades 2 | Nombre ______ | Hora ______

Capítulo 6B | Fecha ______ | **Guided Practice Activities 6B-6**

Presentación escrita (p. 339) *Answers will vary.*

Task: Think about and write a good movie idea for a class contest. Describe the main characters, the plot, and the scenes. Then draw a few scenes from the movie.

A. Fill in the blanks with information about the kind of movie you would like to write. You can choose an option from the list, or make up your own.

1. Me gustaría escribir ______

una película de acción	una película romántica	un drama
una película de ciencia ficción	una película policíaca	una comedia
una película de horror		

2. Los personajes principales de mi película pueden ser ______

ladrones y policías	una familia y sus amigos
extraterrestres	criminales

B. Read the following plot descriptions to get ideas for your movie. You can use these descriptions or make up your own. Then write a brief outline of your plot below.

- Los personajes desean encontrar algo que alguien escondió hace muchos años.
- Los extraterrestres vienen a visitarnos.
- Unos ladrones roban una pintura *(painting)* de un museo y la policía los busca.

______

______

______

______

C. In the following boxes, sketch four scenes from the movie plot you described in **part B**.

Antes de ver el video

Actividad 1

The next video is about a short movie that Manolo directs. Think about movies you have seen recently and answer the following questions using words from your vocabulary.

1. ¿Qué clase de película fue? **Answers will vary.**
2. ¿Quiénes eran los actores principales?
3. ¿Quién era el (la) director(a)?
4. ¿De qué trataba?
5. ¿Había mucha violencia o era más un cuento de enamorados?

¿Comprendes?

Actividad 2

Answer the following questions in complete sentences in order to better understand the video.

1. ¿Qué está haciendo Ramón en su habitación?
   Ramón *está estudiando* para su examen de mañana.

2. ¿Quién entra a la habitación cuando Ramón está estudiando?
   Un mosquito (Claudia) *entra* en la habitación.

3. ¿Qué quiere hacer Ramón con el periódico?
   Ramón *quiere matar* el mosquito con el periódico.
4. ¿En qué idiomas puede hablar el mosquito?
   El mosquito *puede hablar* en inglés y en español.
5. ¿Por qué Ramón no mata el mosquito?
   Ramón no lo mata porque el mosquito puede ayudarlo en el examen.

6. ¿Dónde se va a esconder el mosquito el día del examen para explicarle todo a Ramón?
   El mosquito *se va a esconder* en la oreja de Ramón.

7. ¿Quién mata el mosquito y cómo lo hace?
   Teresa mata el mosquito cuando cierra el libro.

Actividad 3

In the chart below are quotes from the video. Next to each quote, write the name of the character who said it and the role he or she played in the movie. Follow the model.

	Frase u oración	Personaje	Papel
Modelo	"¡¡¡NOOOOOOOO!!!"	*Claudia*	*mosquito*
1.	"Tengo que estudiar y tú me molestas."	Ramón	estudiante
2.	"¡Yo quiero hacer el personaje principal!"	Claudia	mosquito
3.	"¡Ramón, despiértate ya!"	Teresa	amiga de Ramón/ estudiante
4.	"A ver... necesito tres actores."	Manolo	director
5.	"¡No, no me mates, por favor!"	Claudia	mosquito
6.	"¿Podemos tener efectos especiales?"	Manolo	director
7.	"Parece que estudiaste mucho."	Teresa	amiga de Ramón/ estudiante
8.	"Pero, Teresa, ¿qué has hecho?"	Ramón	estudiante

Y, ¿qué más?

Actividad 4

Now that you have seen the movie made by the characters from the video, think about a film that you might like to create. In the spaces below, list the characters and describe the plot and the scene to get you started.

Los personajes: Answers will vary.

El argumento: ____

La escena: ____

Actividad 5

The drama class is trying to decide on the cast of their upcoming spring production **"Aquella noche."** Match the name of the person with his or her suggested role by marking an X in the corresponding square in the grid. You will hear each set of statements twice.

	El (la) ladrón (ladrona)	El galán	El (la) extra-terrestre	El (la) detective	El (la) director(a)	La víctima
Fernando		X				
María						X
Matilde			X			
Antonio	X					
Alberto				X		
Carmen					X	

Actividad 6

Listen as people talk about movies they have seen. As you hear each opinion, fill in the grid below by writing or circling the correct answer. You do not need to write complete sentences. You will hear each set of statements twice.

	¿La recomienda?	¿El argumento?	¿Qué cosa(s) le gustó/gustaron más?
1.	**Sí** / No	Básico / **Complicado**	(Possible answers listed. Wording may vary.) El beso
2.	Sí / **No**	**Básico** / Complicado	Los efectos especiales
3.	**Sí** / No	Básico / **Complicado**	Cuando el detective se cayó
4.	Sí / **No**	**Básico** / Complicado	La escena con las pizzas
5.	**Sí** / No	**Básico** / Complicado	Cuando se casaron

Realidades 2 Nombre ____ Hora ____

Capítulo 6B Fecha ____ AUDIO

Actividad 7

In today's episode of **"Dime la verdad,"** Lola Lana interviews actors and actresses on the set of a popular **telenovela.** She quickly learns that they all have very different movie preferences. As you listen, write the number of the interview underneath the corresponding poster. You will hear each set of statements twice.

2

4

1

3

5

Actividad 8

Even though Julia's grandmother only missed one episode of her favorite **telenovela,** she is eager to hear about what she missed. As Julia tells her about the last episode, answer the questions below about what has happened with each character. You will hear each conversation twice.

¿Qué ha pasado?

1. Javier **ha muerto.**
2. Marlena **se ha vuelto loca.**
3. Marco **no se ha casado.**
4. Victoria **se ha caído de una escalera / ha estado en un hospital.**
5. Marisol **ha escrito una carta de amor / ha llorado.**

Realidades 2 Nombre ____ Hora ____

Capítulo 6B Fecha ____ AUDIO

Actividad 9

You and your classmates are creating storyboards to outline the plots of your upcoming class movies. Listen as one student describes the plot line for his project. Take notes on each part of the plot in the top half of each of the storyboard boxes below. Then, draw a quick sketch in the bottom half of each box. You will hear the story twice.

Notes will vary.

NOTES and SKETCHES			
#1	#2	#3	#4
drawing of a camping scene	**drawing of a male teen cooking meat in a frying pan**	**drawing of same teen looking angrily at frying pan without meat**	**drawing of same teen looking behind a tree (for the meat)**
#5	#6	#7	#8
drawing of a bear eating meat	**drawing of bear running after same teen**	**drawing of same teen fallen on ground; bear coming closer**	**drawing of bear shown as a human in costume**

Actividad 10

Look at the movie theater marquee below. For each movie, write at least three sentences to tell what you think it might be about. The first one has been started for you.

1. *"Un verano que recordar" es una película romántica.*
   Answers will vary.
2. Answers will vary.
3. Answers will vary.

Actividad 11

A. You are interested in hosting an exchange student from Spain. Fill out the form below so that your school can find you a compatible student.

Nombre Answers will vary.
Edad *(age)*
Actividad(es) que te gusta(n)
Comida(s) que te encanta(n)
Clase(s) que te interesa(n)
Tipo(s) de película(s) que te fascina(n)
Cosa(s) que te disgusta(n)

B. Now, read Ramiro's form below and write complete sentences to compare your interests with his. Follow the model.

Nombre *Ramiro Fuentes*
Edad *16*
Actividad(es) que te gusta(n) *esquiar, leer, ir al cine*
Comida(s) que te encanta(n) *la carne, la pasta, los pasteles*
Clase(s) que te interesa(n) *ciencias naturales, inglés*
Tipo(s) de película(s) que te fascina(n) *románticas, de horror*
Cosa(s) que te disgusta(n) *la televisión, los gatos*

Modelo *A Ramiro le gusta leer pero a mí me disgusta. Prefiero más escribir.*

1.
2.
3.
4.
5.

C. Based on your interests, do you think you and Ramiro are compatible? Why or why not? Write your answer in Spanish in one or two complete sentences.

Realidades 2 Nombre ________ Hora ________

Capítulo 6B Fecha ________ WRITING

Actividad 12

Before becoming a host family to a Mexican exchange student, your family is asked to provide a list of things you have done to become familiar with Mexican culture. Under each category below, write three sentences about your real or imaginary experiences. The first one has been done for you.

Answers will vary; use correct forms of present perfect.

Los viajes

Nosotros *hemos viajado a Cancún y hemos visitado las ruinas mayas.*

Yo ________

Mi hermano ________

Los deportes

Mi familia y yo ________

Mi clase de español ________

Mis padres ________

Las clases

Yo ________

Mi hermano(a) ________

Mis hermanos(as) ________

Las comidas

Mi madre ________

Yo ________

Toda la familia ________

Realidades 2 Nombre ________ Hora ________

Capítulo 6B Fecha ________ WRITING

Actividad 13

You are writing a review for the school newspaper of a movie that you saw recently.

A. First, write down the information requested below to give some background information about the movie. You may use your imagination.

1. Nombre del actor principal **Answers will vary.**

   Otras películas de él ________

2. Nombre de la actriz principal ________

   Otras películas de ella ________

3. Nombre del director (de la directora) ________

   Otras películas de él (ella) ________

B. Now, write five sentences about your opinion of the movie. Tell what you liked, what you disliked, what interested you, etc. about the plot, acting, and directing of the movie.

Answers will vary.

C. Now, write your review for the paper, using the information from Part A and Part B to help you.

Answers will vary.

Test Preparation Answers

Reading Skills
p. 259 2. **C**
p. 260 2. **A**

Integrated Performance Assessment
p. 261
Answers will vary.

Practice Test: Ray Suarez
p. 263

1. B
2. J
3. A
4. H
5. Las respuestas variarán pero pueden incluir: ¿A quién le gustaría entrevistar que nunca ha entrevistado? ¿Qué evento fue el más interesante (triste, feliz, emocionante, peligroso) para Ud. como reportero? ¿Qué le gusta más (o menos) de su trabajo?
6. Las respuestas y las razones variarán.

Table of Contents

Tema 7: Buen provecho

Capítulo 7A: ¿Cómo se hace paella?

Capítulo 7B: ¿Te gusta comer al aire libre?

Theme Project

¡Buen provecho!
Una comida especial

Overview:

You will plan a menu for a special meal. Include ingredients for an appetizer, a salad, a main dish, and a dessert, at least one of which needs to be from a Spanish-speaking country. Then you will present your menu to the class.

Resources:

Internet search access, digital or print photos, page layout/word processing software and/or poster board, markers, photos, glue or tape, scissors

Sequence:

STEP 1. Review instructions with your teacher.

STEP 2. Submit a rough draft of the proposed menu. Work with a partner and present your drafts to each other.

STEP 3. Create layouts of the menus, leaving room for photos or drawings.

STEP 4. Submit a draft of the menu.

STEP 5. Present your special meal menu to the class.

Assessment:

Your teacher will provide you with a rubric to assess this project.

Theme 7 Project: Una comida especial

Project Assessment Rubric

RUBRIC	Score 1	Score 3	Score 5
Evidence of Planning	No written draft or sketch provided.	Draft was written and layout created, but not corrected.	Evidence of corrected draft and layout.
Use of Illustrations	No photos/ visuals included.	Very few photos/visuals included.	Several photos/ visuals included.
Presentation	Contains details that develop ideas about meals.	Includes a partial list of meals and their ingredients.	Includes a complete list of meals and their ingredients.

21st Century Skills Rubric: Promote Communication

RUBRIC	Score 1	Score 3	Score 5
Subject knowledge	Demonstrates little knowledge of the topic	Demonstrates some knowledge of the topic	Demonstrates accurate knowledge of the topic
Organization and coherence	Poorly organized information; audience does not understand presentation	Generally organizes information; audience understands some of the presentation	Organizes information coherently; audience understands presentation
Decision-making based on feedback	Does not listen to or accept group feedback; does not take notes	Listens to some feedback and takes notes	Listens to feedback, takes notes, and asks follow-up questions

School-to-Home Connection

Dear Parent or Guardian,

The theme of our current unit is *Buen provecho* (Enjoy your meal!). This chapter is called *¿Cómo se hace la paella?* (How do you prepare paella?).

Upon completion of this chapter students will be able to:

- talk about food and cooking
- tell others what not to do
- describe what people generally do
- understand cultural perspectives on recipes and food preparation

Students will also explore:

- dividing words into syllables in Spanish

Our textbook, *Realidades,* helps with the development of reading, writing, and speaking skills through the use of strategies, process speaking, and process writing. In this chapter, students will:

- read poems about two common foods
- speak about how to prepare their favorite dish

To reinforce and enhance learning, students can access a wide range of online resources on **realidades.com,** the personalized learning management system that accompanies the print and online Student Edition. Resources include the eText, textbook and workbook activities, audio files, videos, animations, songs, self-study tools, interactive maps, voice recording (RealTalk!), assessments, and other digital resources. Many learning tools can be accessed through the student Home Page on **realidades.com.** Other activities, specifically those that require grading, are assigned by the teacher and linked on the student Home Page within the calendar or the Assignments tab.

You will find specifications and guidelines for accessing **realidades.com** on home computers and mobile devices on MyPearsonTraining.com under the SuccessNet Plus tab.

realidades.com

For: Tips to Parents
Visit: www.realidades.com
Web Code: jce-0010

Check it out! At the end of the chapter, have your child name six items in the kitchen. Then have him or her tell what they are used for.

Sincerely,

Capítulo 7A

Videocultura Script

La cocina mexicana

Spanish version:

La gastronomía mexicana es famosa en todo el mundo por sus muchos sabores, olores y colores.

Estos sabores vienen de la variedad de especias y vegetales frescos que se venden en los mercados en México.

Las civilizaciones antiguas azteca y maya comían el maíz, los frijoles, los chiles, los tomates, las calabazas, las papas y el chocolate.

Estas comidas son todavía muy importantes para la cocina mexicana.

La comida mexicana es diferente en cada región. Por ejemplo, en el norte de México, cocinan mucho con carne. En el sureste, cocinan mucho con vegetales y pollo.

La cocina mexicana es peculiar y creativa. Por eso, a mucha gente alrededor del mundo le encanta.

English version:

Mexican cooking is known for its variety of flavors, colorful presentation, and spicy taste.

Its strong flavors and delicious aromas come from a variety of fresh spices such as chili peppers and local ingredients found in the many markets all over the country.

Mexican cuisine is based on the foods of the ancient Aztecs and Mayan Indians.

They ate foods such as corn, beans, chili peppers, tomatoes, squash, potatoes, sweet potatoes, and chocolate.

These foods are still very important in Mexico and their influence has spread to cuisines found around the world.

Mexican food varies in taste and style from region to region in the country.

For instance, in northern Mexico, you will find more beef and meat dishes with wheat tortillas being common.

In central and southern Mexico, dishes include vegetables such as avocado and tomatoes, meats such as pork and chicken.

Mexican food has an identity of its own. Its wide range of flavors and unique combinations are what make it one the most creative and delicious cuisines of the world.

Input Script

Presentation

Input Vocabulary and Dialogue: Present the vocabulary by playing the role of a new TV cooking show chef: *El (La) Matador(a)* who will prepare the recipe on p. 349. Come to class wearing an apron, a chef's hat, and, if possible, a matador's cape. You might do the presentation in the Home Economics kitchen at your school. Or, draw the kitchen shown on p. 348 on the chalkboard. Introduce yourself as *Jefe (Jefa) El (La) Matador(a).* Give your chef character a very colorful personality and use a fun catchphrase such as *¡Olé!* to encourage audience participation (shout *¡Olé!* after each step and have students shout it after you).

Choose a volunteer to be your cooking assistant. Place the transparency of the kitchen on the screen. Distribute Vocabulary Clip Art images to students and have them cut them into individual images. Then lead your assistant on a tour of the kitchen by pointing to the items on the transparency or by pointing out the chalkboard drawings or the real kitchen items. Then quiz your volunteer and the rest of the class by calling out the names of the items and having them hold up the correct Clip Art images. Quiz them on the cooking actions by calling out the verbs and having them act out the motions.

Next, have your assistant read the first line of the dialogue on p. 349: *¿Qué vamos a preparar?* Read the boy's response. Then review the recipe. If you like, change recipes by reading each ingredient in the recipe and stating: *¿Cien gramos de camarones? ¡Uy! ¡No tenemos 100 gramos de camarones!, ¿Azafrán? ¡No tenemos azafrán!,* and so forth. Then proceed to make another recipe. First review all the ingredients. Call on students to give the names of food items they have already learned. Then prepare the recipe (if you like, pantomime the actual mixing of ingredients). Describe your actions as you perform them and have students hold up the appropriate Clip Art images.

You might prepare the finished dish ahead of time. Pull it from the oven at the end of the show and give samples to students.

Comprehension Check

- Give commands to students for them to put certain items in the refrigerator, oven, sink, or microwave and have them carry out or pantomime the actions.
- Say that you are going to do appropriate actions *(Voy a añadir una cucharada de sal al caldo.),* and illogical actions *(Voy a hervir los camarones por tres horas.),* and have students tell you: *¡Buena idea!* or *¡No es una buena idea!*
- Describe the steps to creating different recipes and have students hold up the Clip Art images of the actions you mention. Then have students guess the dish you described.

Audio Script

Audio DVD, Capítulo 7A

Track 01: *A primera vista, ¿Cómo se hace la paella?*, Student Book, p. 348, (4:33)

Vocabulario y gramática en contexto

Vas a escuchar cada palabra o frase dos veces. Después de la primera vez hay una pausa para que puedas pronunciar la palabra o frase. Luego vas a escuchar de nuevo la palabra o frase.

enlatado	calentar
enlatada	la sartén
congelado	frito
congelada	frita
el refrigerador	el fuego
el microondas	batir
fresco	mezclar
fresca	pelar
el horno	picar
probar	el pedazo
el fregadero	añadir
al horno	freír
la estufa	hervir
la olla	

Track 02: *A primera vista,* Student Book, p. 349, (2:06)

Vocabulario y gramática en contexto

Lee en tu libro mientras escuchas la narración.

TEEN FEMALE: ¿Qué vamos a preparar?

TEEN MALE: Una receta que aprendí de mi abuela que vivía en Valencia. Se llama arroz a banda. Es un arroz típico de la provincia de Alicante y ha sido el favorito de mi familia. Aquí está la lista de los ingredientes que necesitamos.

Vas a escuchar cada palabra o frase dos veces. Después de la primera vez hay una pausa para que puedas pronunciar la palabra o frase. Luego vas a escuchar de nuevo la palabra o frase.

el caldo	la salsa
el vinagre	la cucharada
el ajo	los camarones
el aceite	los mariscos

Track 03: *A primera vista,* Act. 1, Student Book, p. 349, (2:13)

La cocina típica

¿Qué hay en tu cocina? Escucha mientras Ignacio describe una cocina típica. Mira los dibujos y las fotos, y señala el objeto o los objetos que menciona. Vas a escuchar las frases dos veces.

1. En la cocina hay comida enlatada.
2. Siempre hay aceite y vinagre.
3. Debes lavar las verduras en el fregadero antes de cocinarlas.
4. Todas las cocinas tienen una sartén y una olla.
5. Mucha gente no tiene un microondas.
6. Muchas personas prefieren comer la comida fresca.
7. Necesito una cucharada de sal.

Track 04: *A primera vista,* Act. 2, Student Book, p. 349, (2:38)

¿Lógico o no?

¿Sabes cocinar? Levanta una mano si lo que oyes es lógico y levanta las dos manos si no es lógico. Vas a escuchar las frases dos veces.

1. A veces hay que cortar el pollo en pedazos pequeños.
2. Es importante picar el caldo.
3. Vamos a beber el aceite.
4. A muchas personas les gusta freír el pollo.
5. Es importante abrir la lata antes de usar las zanahorias enlatadas.
6. Normalmente se usa leche congelada para cocinar.
7. Las verduras frescas son mejores para la salud que las verduras enlatadas.
8. Normalmente se mezclan con las manos los ingredientes de una receta.

Track 05: *A primera vista, Videohistoria,* Student Book, pp. 350–351, (2:10)

¿Cómo se hace la paella?

Lee en tu libro mientras escuchas la *Videohistoria.*

See Student Book pages 350–351 for script.

Track 06: *Manos a la obra,* Act. 5, Student Book, p. 353, (2:02)

La cocina de mi tía

Escucha mientras la tía Juanita describe su cocina. Dibuja y escribe los nombres de las cosas que menciona. Luego compara tu dibujo con el de otro estudiante. Vas a escuchar las descripciones dos veces.

1. En mi cocina hay un refrigerador nuevo.
2. Al lado del refrigerador hay un fregadero.
3. Al otro lado del refrigerador están la estufa y el horno.
4. Encima de la estufa hay una sartén y una olla.
5. Delante del fregadero hay una mesa con un microondas.
6. Al lado del microondas hay un libro de recetas.

Track 07: Audio Act. 5, Writing, Audio & Video Workbook, p. 129, (3:18)

Alejandro's older sister has been trying to teach him the basics of cooking. Listen to the questions he asks her during one of their phone conversations. If the question seems logical, circle the word *lógico* and if the question seems illogical, circle the word *ilógico.* You will hear each question twice.

1. Necesito probar el vinagre antes de usarlo, porque tiene que ser fresco. Tengo que beber mucho, ¿no?
2. Debo picar el ajo y luego calentarlo en el aceite. Es mejor usar la sartén, ¿no?

3. Tengo que cocinar la comida congelada por cinco minutos en el fregadero, ¿no?
4. Necesito pelar las cebollas antes de mezclarlas en la ensalada, ¿no?
5. Puedo servir un caldo de vinagre bien calentado para el almuerzo, ¿no?
6. Es una buena idea probar un pedazo del bistec antes de servirlo, ¿no?
7. Debo poner los camarones en el refrigerador antes de usarlos en mi receta, ¿no?
8. Necesito comprar todos los ingredientes antes de preparar la receta, ¿no?

Track 08: Audio Act. 6, Writing, Audio & Video Workbook, p. 129, (2:56)

Both Ignacio and Javier think they are expert cooks. As they are preparing *paella*, each wants to make sure the other is doing it right. Listen to their conversations, and match each one to one of the pictures below. Write the number of the conversation in the blank underneath the corresponding picture. You will hear each conversation twice.

1. **Teen Male 1:** ¡Ay! No te olvides del aceite. ¡Está hirviendo ya! Debes tener cuidado. Vas a incendiar la cocina.
2. **Teen Male 2:** ¿Camarones congelados? ¡Qué asco! Los congelados no son tan sabrosos como los frescos.
3. **Teen Male 1:** No se puede servir paella con espaguetis. Las verduras frescas son más saludables. Hay muchas en el refrigerador.
4. **Teen Male 2:** No vamos a usar tanto ajo. Nuestras novias no van a besarnos si hay demasiado ajo.
5. **Teen Male 1:** ¡No! ¡No usamos el horno! La paella se prepara en una sartén. Necesitas apagar el fuego del horno.
6. **Teen Male 2:** ¡Ay de mí! ¿Por qué tiras los mariscos? Vamos a picar los demás para una ensalada.

Track 09: Audio Act. 7, Writing, Audio & Video Workbook, p. 130, (3:04)

Listen as different people give Roberto advice about cooking. As you listen to each piece of advice, decide whether the person is advising him on: a) getting ready to cook; b) things to do while he's cooking; or c) things to do after he's finished cooking. Place an X in the appropriate box in the grid below. You will hear each piece of advice twice.

1. No piques el ajo antes de pelarlo.
2. No dejes las ollas sucias en el fregadero.
3. Mientras calientas el aceite, no lo dejes encima de la estufa.
4. Compra todos los ingredientes frescos por la mañana.
5. No frías los camarones en un aceite barato.
6. No pagues demasiado por los mariscos.
7. No olvides apagar el horno.
8. No añadas la sal y pimienta hasta el fin, cuando lo comes.
9. No uses el microondas para cocinar la carne.
10. No vayas al supermercado sin una lista de ingredientes.

Track 10: *Pronunciación*, Dividing words into syllables, Student Book, p. 359, (4:37)

In Spanish, you divide words into syllables after a vowel sound or between most double consonants. Listen to and say these words.

You will hear each word twice. After the word is pronounced the first time, there will be a pause so you can pronounce it. Then you will hear the word a second time.

ca-ma-ro-nes	en-cien-do
ma-ris-cos	her-vir
fres-co	con-ge-la-do

However, you do not separate most combinations of a consonant followed by *l* or *r*. Listen to and say these words:

You will hear each word twice. After the word is pronounced the first time, there will be a pause so you can pronounce it. Then you will hear the word a second time.

do-ble	vi-na-gre
re-fres-cos	fre-ga-de-ro
in-gre-dien-tes	re-fri-ge-ra-dor

When two strong vowels *(a, e, o)* appear together, each is pronounced individually, forming two syllables. Listen to and say these words:

You will hear each word twice. After the word is pronounced the first time, there will be a pause so you can pronounce it. Then you will hear the word a second time.

pa-e-lla	fe-o
mi-cro-on-das	to-a-lla
tra-e-mos	hé-ro-e

Track 11: Audio Act. 8, Writing, Audio & Video Workbook, p. 130, (2:34)

Listen as a counselor at a Spanish Immersion Camp tells the campers what things are going to be like at the camp for the summer. Draw a circle around the things that do happen, and an X over the pictures of the things that don't happen. You will hear each statement twice.

1. Se habla español todo el día.
2. Se come en el comedor.
3. Se prohíbe escuchar música después de apagar las luces.
4. Se debe llegar a tiempo a las clases de conversación.
5. Se usa el gimnasio para levantar pesas y hacer ejercicios.
6. No se sirve comida en las cabinas.
7. Se cierra la piscina a las diez de la noche.
8. Se permite ir de compras cada sábado en la ciudad.

Track 12: Audio Act. 9, Writing, Audio & Video Workbook, p. 131, (4:35)

Ryan's friend, Carmen, asks him to come to dinner at her home. Some of the things he eats are very familiar, but others are not. Listen as they talk about what is on the dinner table. Write the number of each conversation under the corresponding item on the dinner table. You will hear each conversation twice.

1. **Teen Male:** ¿Qué es esto?
   Teen Female: Tienes que probarlo. Es muy popular en España. Es un caldo de ajo.
   Teen Male: ¿Cómo se hace?
   Teen Female: Es muy fácil. Tienes que pelar y picar el ajo. Luego lo pones en el caldo para hervir por cinco minutos. Es muy sabroso, ¿no?
2. **Teen Male:** Ésta la reconozco. Pero has añadido algunas frutas que no conozco. ¿Qué son?
   Teen Female: Es una ensalada de frutas con uvas, plátanos y manzanas. A mi madre le gusta añadir papaya y mangos.
3. **Teen Male:** Normalmente no me gustan las verduras, pero éstas son diferentes.
   Teen Female: ¡No me gustan las verduras tampoco, pero mi madre añade algunos ingredientes secretos! En las judías verdes ella mezcla un poco de jamón y queso.
   Teen Male: Son deliciosas.
4. **Teen Male:** Ese plato es como la foto de nuestro libro de español. Me gustan todos los ingredientes: los mariscos, los guisantes, el arroz y el pollo.
   Teen Female: Mi madre es de la ciudad de Valencia, en España. Ella tiene la receta especial para la paella de mi abuela.
5. **Teen Male:** Ah… el olor de estos camarones es irresistible. Es el olor de ajo, ¿no?
   Teen Female: Sí. Se sirve muy caliente con pan. Es importante hervir los camarones en el aceite con el ajo. Es la comida favorita de nuestra profesora de español.

Track 13: *Repaso del capítulo,* Student Book, p. 370, (5:04)

Vocabulario y gramática

Escucha las palabras y expresiones que has aprendido en este capítulo.

See Student Book page 370 for vocabulary list.

Track 14: *Preparación para el examen,* Student Book, p. 371, (1:07)

Escuchar

Practice task

Listen as Gabriel's sister Valeria gives him cooking instructions over the phone. See if you can identify: a) what he wants to cook; b) what ingredients he still needs to buy; and c) the first few steps in the recipe.

Valeria: Diga.

Gabriel: Valeria, soy yo, Gabriel. Tengo una cebolla, un ajo, unos tomates y unos mariscos. ¿Es bastante para hacer una paella? ¿Cómo se hace?

Valeria: Necesitas comprar un pollo y unas verduras, como guisantes.

Gabriel: ¿Qué hago primero?

Valeria: Primero, pica la cebolla y el ajo. Luego corta los tomates en pedazos.

Gabriel: Un momento. Necesito un lápiz para escribir.

Video Script

A primera vista: *¿Cómo se hace la paella?*, (7:14)

Ignacio: Hola, Javier, ¿cómo estás?

Javier: Bien… ¿Qué haces por aquí?

Ignacio: Es que… tú sabes cocinar muy bien, ¿verdad?

Javier: Más o menos… ¿por qué?

Ignacio: Javier… ¿cómo se hace la paella?

Javier: ¿La paella? ¿Por qué quieres saberlo?

Ignacio: Porque… quiero preparar una comida especial para Ana, para su cumpleaños. Pero sólo sé sacar productos congelados del refrigerador, y calentarlos en el microondas.

Javier: Ahh…

Ignacio: He probado la paella que tú preparas, y es deliciosa… ¿Me enseñas la receta?

Javier: Bueno, está bien. Pero primero vamos al supermercado a comprar los ingredientes.

Javier: Vamos a necesitar camarones, y otros mariscos…

Ignacio: ¿Camarones?

Javier: ¡Ay, gambas! No, no uso ingredientes congelados. Sólo uso ingredientes frescos… por eso mi paella es tan rica. No uso ingredientes enlatados tampoco. Todo tiene que ser fresco. Ah, ajos frescos. Le dan un sabor delicioso…

Ignacio: A mí me gustan las patatas fritas. ¿Se puede servir la paella con patatas fritas?

Javier: No, no, no, no… Se sirve con una ensalada.

Ignacio: Bueno, ¿enciendo el horno?

Javier: ¡No! No se puede usar el horno para hacer la paella. Se prepara encima de la cocina.

Ignacio: ¡Ah!…

Ignacio: ¿Pongo el aceite en la olla?

Javier: Deja esa olla, y escucha bien. Primero tienes que calentar el aceite, en una sartén grande; como ésta.

Ignacio: Bien.

Javier: ¡No tires el aceite!… Y no añadas más. Tienes más que suficiente.

Javier: Primero vamos a freír los ajos…

Ignacio: ¿Así?

Javier: ¡No Ignacio! Tienes que picar los ajos primero.

Ignacio: ¿Picar?

Javier: Sí, picar… cortar los ajos en pedazos muy pequeños.

Ignacio: Voy a encender la cocina…

Javier: Vale.

Javier: A ver… el aceite tiene que estar bien caliente. No, todavía no está… Yo preparo los mariscos. Tú, no te olvides del aceite… No dejes que se caliente demasiado.

Javier: ¡Ignacio! ¡Apaga la cocina! ¡Hombre! ¿En qué estabas pensando?

Ignacio: En nada… Bueno, en la sorpresa de Ana cuando…

Javier: Pues, así, creo que va a recibir una gran sorpresa, pero no va a ser buena…

Ignacio: No sé, Javier. Me gusta más cocinar en el microondas. Los ingredientes no se queman… ¿Se puede hacer la paella en el microondas?

Javier: No, Ignacio, no se puede…

Ignacio: Bueno, vale. Vamos a seguir.

Javier: Quieres decir, vamos a empezar otra vez…

Ignacio: Pues, sí, venga… ¿Uso ésta?

***GramActiva* Videos, (6:28)**
Negative *tú* commands

Football Coach: Bernard! Don't block with your face! Fernando! Don't hold the ball in the air. Chris… Chris don't do that! Yelling at your players means *nada* if you don't know negative *tú* commands. Fortunately, I do.

Coach: Don't run! *¡No corras!*

Coach: Don't jump! *¡No saltes!*

Coach: Don't do… uh… that. *No hagas… uh… eso.*

Coach/Madden V.O.: Let's take a look at that play again. Don't run. You take your verb, *correr*, and make it into the *yo* form, *corro*. Then you drop the *o* and add *-as*, because it's an *-er* verb. *-ir* verbs work the same way. *No corras.*

Coach/Madden V.O.: How about an *-ar* verb? Here, the command is "don't jump."
Saltar is the verb. The *yo* form is *salto*. Drop the *o* and add *-es* because it's an *-ar* verb. *No saltes*. It's simple. So don't forget it!

Football Coach: Listen up! Verbs that end in *-car*, *-gar*, and *-zar* have a spelling change! *C* changes to *qu*. *G* changes to *gu*. And *z* changes to *c*. Now drop and gimme three verbs!

Football Player 1: *¡Tocar! ¡No toques!*

Football Player2: *¡Jugar! ¡No juegues!*

Football Player 3: *¡Abrazar! ¡No abraces!*

Guitar Guy: *Amor… amor…*

Gal: *No. No toques la guitarra.*
No. No juegues con eso.
No. No me abraces.

Guy: *Qué lástima.*

Coach: All right, rookies! Let me hear your irregular negative *tú* commands! And make them snappy!

Football Players: *Dar, no des.*
Estar, no estés.
Ir, no vayas.
Ser, no seas.

Coach: Again!

Football Players: *Dar, no des.*
Estar, no estés.
Ir, no vayas.
Ser, no seas…

Coach: Oh, one more thing. Remember, you attach pronouns to the end of the affirmative command
¿Hago ejercicio?
Sí, hazlo.

But, with negative commands, pronouns always go right before the verb
¿Hago ejercicio?
No, no lo hagas.

V.O.: *¡No mires el libro!* [Don't look at it!] *¡No lo mires!* *No salgas. Tenemos la prueba.* [Don't leave! We have a quiz!]

Quiz

V.O.: Complete the sentences with the correct affirmative command.
(usar) No ______ a estufa.
No uses la estufa.
(tocar) No ______ la guitarra en la clase.
No toques la guitarra en la clase.
(ir) No te ______ tan pronto.
No te vayas tan pronto.

The impersonal *se*

COOK SHOW HOST: *Se prohíbe correr en la cocina.* Running is prohibited in the kitchen. Remember that when you're cooking, and remember that when you're using the impersonal *se.*

HOST: We use the impersonal se when something is DONE to the subject.
The door is closed.
The book is opened.
To get this idea across in Spanish, we use the word *se* plus the *usted* or the *ustedes* form of the verb, depending on whether the subject is singular or plural.
Let's look at an example.
Se abre la puerta.
How about a less creepy example:
Se habla español. [Spanish is spoken here.]
Se vende pan. [Bread is sold here.]
Se venden libros. [Books are sold here.]
But not that one.

COOK SHOW HOST V.O.: *Calentar. Se calienta el aceite en la sartén.*
Cortar. Se corta el ajo.
Poner. Se pone el ajo en la sartén.
Freír. Se fríen los camarones con el ajo en el aceite.
Al final, un galón de helado.
Mmm… tengo hambre.

LUISA: *¡Hola! Me llamo Luisa, y soy locutora de radio.*
En España, tenemos muchos letreros con "se."
Se habla español.
Se alquila apartamento.
Se vende casa.
Y otra vez.
Se presenta la prueba.

Quiz

V.O.: Complete the sentences using the correct impersonal form.
(vender) ______ aceite.
Se vende aceite.
(comprar) ______ libros y revistas.
Se compran libros y revistas.
(necesitar) ______ secretaria bilingüe.
Se necesita secretaria bilingüe.

Videomisterio: *En busca de la verdad,* Episodio 9, (8:23)

ROBERTO'S V.O.: Al día siguiente Linda, su mamá y yo salimos para San Antonio. Ellas, para regresar a casa y yo, para buscar la verdad sobre mi abuelo.

TOMÁS: Roberto, llévate estos documentos. Puedes necesitarlos en San Antonio.

ROBERTO: ¿Qué son?

TOMÁS: Tres certificados de nacimiento, el de mi padre, el mío y el tuyo. ¿Tienes tu pasaporte?

ROBERTO: Sí, y también mi credencial de estudiante.

BERTA: Bueno, váyanse ya. El vuelo sale en tres horas.

CARMEN: Enrique, Paco: Roberto Toledo. Roberto, él es mi esposo Enrique y mi hijo Paco.

ENRIQUE: Bienvenido, Roberto.

ROBERTO: Muchas gracias, Señor.

PACO: ¿Oye, juegas al fútbol?

LINDA: A Paco le encanta el fútbol.

ROBERTO: Sí, juego un poco.

ENRIQUE: Pueden hablar de fútbol más tarde. Vamos adentro.

CARMEN: Nuestra casa es tu casa.

ROBERTO: Gracias, señora.

LINDA'S V.O.: Al día siguiente teníamos mucho que hacer.

ENRIQUE: Y bien, ¿qué van a hacer hoy?

LINDA: Primero vamos a mi escuela. Ya he perdido cuatro días de clases. Roberto puede dar una vuelta por ahí.

CARMEN: Buena idea. Así podrás conocer la escuela de Linda.

ROBERTO: Así es. Y luego, en la tarde, vamos al Banco de la Frontera.

ENRIQUE: Carmen me contó lo de tu abuelo. ¿Nunca han oído nada de él?

ROBERTO: No. No sabemos nada.

PACO: Buenos días a todos… y adiós.

ENRIQUE: Pues te deseo suerte. Llámenme si me necesitan. Linda tiene mi número.

ROBERTO: Muchas gracias.

ROBERTO: Mira, es esta oficina.

ROBERTO: Buenas tardes, Señor. Me llamo Roberto Toledo. Yo hablé con Ud. por teléfono hace una semana, desde Guanajuato.

De León: Ah, sí, lo recuerdo perfectamente. Por lo de Federico Zúñiga. Pero siéntense. ¿Me trajo los documentos que le pedí?

De León: Vamos a ver… La cuenta de su abuelo es muy antigua. Por cierto, ¿cuál es su dirección aquí, en San Antonio?

Linda: Se está quedando con nosotros. Calle Abemar, 200.

De León: ¿El teléfono, por favor?

Linda: 210-555-0011.

De León: Federico Zúñiga… Pero su apellido es Toledo. ¿Me lo puede explicar?

Roberto: Como le dije por teléfono, Toledo es el apellido de nuestra abuela y de nuestra familia. Mi padre nunca conoció a su padre y por eso no usamos el Zúñiga.

De León: Vaya… Pues no sé si pueda decirles mucho.

Roberto: Pero mire, si yo he venido aquí por eso, para ver que pasó con mi abuelo.

De León: Pero es que es una cuenta muy antigua. De más de cincuenta años.

Roberto: ¿Pero no tienen por lo menos la dirección de mi abuelo? Puede que tenga una cuenta en otro banco.

De León: Lo siento, pero aquí no podemos darle más información. Las cuentas tan antiguas como ésta son transferidas automáticamente a un centro en Austin. Creo que van a tener que ir allí.

Roberto: Pero, ¿por qué tanto misterio?

De León: Porque hay consideraciones legales. En un caso como éste… cuando se trata de la cuenta de un soldado…

Linda: Bueno, entonces… ¿qué hacemos?

De León: Ésta es la dirección en Austin donde tienen que ir. Todavía tienen tiempo para ir hoy. Aquí está el número de cuenta de Federico.

De León: Sin la presencia del Sr. Toledo, digo Zúñiga, su padre, no sé si les puedan ayudar.

Linda: Creo que las respuestas a todas nuestras preguntas están en Austin.

Linda: Creo que es aquí.

Roberto: Buenas tardes. Venimos de parte del Señor De León, de San Antonio. Él nos dijo que aquí podrían ayudarnos. Estamos buscando a mi abuelo, Federico Zúñiga. Ésta es su cuenta.

Secretaria: Generalmente damos información sólo al heredero más cercano. El señor Zúñiga, ¿tiene esposa o hijos?

Roberto: Sí, mi abuela y mi padre, pero ellos no pudieron venir. Yo estoy aquí en su lugar.

Secretaria: ¿Cuántos años tiene Ud.?

Roberto: Diecinueve, señorita.

Secretaria: Esperen aquí. Voy a hablar con el señor Turrón.

Secretaria: Pasen, por favor. El señor Turrón los quiere ver.

Turrón: Bienvenidos. Mi nombre es Alfredo Turrón y yo estoy a cargo del caso de Federico Zúñiga. Siéntense, por favor. Sr. Toledo, este es un caso muy especial y antes de darle toda la información, teníamos que estar seguros de su identidad.

Roberto: ¿Un caso especial?

Turrón: Así es. La semana pasada yo mismo viajé a Guanajuato, para hacer una pequeña investigación sobre su familia.

Roberto: Entonces… ¿Ud. es el hombre que estaba haciendo preguntas sobre nosotros por toda la ciudad?

Turrón: Sí. Le voy a explicar todo… Este archivo contiene las respuestas a todas sus preguntas…

Your partner has asked you to help make *guacamole* for a party in Spanish class. Ana, Rita, and José are also going to help. Do you have everything that the recipe calls for? Tell your partner what ingredients are needed and how much of each one. Ask your partner if he or she has the ingredients in the proper amounts. Then make a list of the items that must be purchased. Finally, ask your partner who should do each task involved in making the *guacamole*. Record the answers on the lines provided. Follow the model.

Necesitamos ocho aguacates. ¿Los tenemos?

Guacamole	**Tenemos que comprar:**
8 aguacates	______________
4 tomates	______________
2 cebollas	______________
jugo de 2 limones	______________
salsa picante al gusto	______________
sal, pimienta y chiles al gusto	______________

1. ¿Quién debe comprar los ingredientes? ______________
2. ¿Quién debe picar los tomates? ______________
3. ¿Quién debe picar las cebollas? ______________
4. ¿Quién debe mezclar el guacamole? ______________

Your partner will tell you what ingredients are needed to make *gazpacho*. Then you will tell him or her which ingredients are on hand and how much there is of each. If the item is not on your list, someone will have to buy it. Finally, tell your partner who should do the tasks he or she asks about. Follow the model.

—¿Quién debe comprar los ingredientes?

—Felipe debe comprarlos.

Los ingredientes que tenemos:

2 tomates
ajo
16 onzas de jugo de tomate
1 cebolla
vinagre
otras verduras al gusto

comprar los ingredientes: Felipe y yo
picar los tomates y las cebollas: Andrés
picar los pimientos y el ajo: Celia
cortar los pepinos: tu compañero(a)

Nombre ______________________

Fecha ______________________

Communicative Pair Activity **7A-1**

Estudiante **B**

Your partner will tell you what ingredients are needed to make *guacamole.* Then you will tell him or her which ingredients are on hand and how much there is of each. If the item is not on your list, someone will have to buy it. Finally, tell your partner who should do the tasks he or she asks about. Follow the model.

—¿Quién debe comprar los ingredientes?

—Tú debes comprarlos.

Los ingredientes que tenemos:			
pimienta, sal	salsa picante	**picar los tomates:**	José
3 cebollas	chiles	**picar las cebollas:**	tu compañero(a)
6 aguacates	1 tomate	**mezclar el guacamole:**	Ana y yo

comprar los ingredientes: Rita

Your partner has asked you to help make *gazpacho* for a party in Spanish class. Felipe, Andrés, and Celia are also going to help. Do you have everything that the recipe calls for? Tell your partner what ingredients are needed and how much of each one. Ask your partner if she or he has the ingredients in the proper amounts. Then make a list of the items that must be purchased. Finally, ask your partner who should do each task involved in making the *gazpacho.* Record the answers on the lines provided. Follow the model.

Necesitamos seis tomates. ¿Los tenemos?

Gazpacho	**Tenemos que comprar:**
6 tomates	______________________
32 onzas de jugo de tomate	______________________
2 cebollas	______________________
vinagre	______________________
2 pimientos verdes	______________________
aceite	______________________
ajo	
2 pepinos	

1. ¿Quién debe comprar los ingredientes? ______________________
2. ¿Quién debe picar los tomates y las cebollas? ______________________
3. ¿Quién debe picar los pimientos y el ajo? ______________________
4. ¿Quién debe cortar los pepinos? ______________________

Realidades 2

Capítulo 7A

Nombre ____________________

Fecha ____________________

Communicative Pair Activity **7A-2**

Estudiante **A**

You are attending school in Mexico and living with the Fernández family. La señora Fernández asks you to go to the market to buy fruit to make a fruit salad for dinner. First, ask your partner if the following fruits are available in the fruit stand at the market. Then ask how much they will cost. Record the information on the lines provided. Follow the model.

¿Venden piñas en el mercado? ¿Cuánto cuestan las piñas?

Sí/No _____ **pesos/kg**

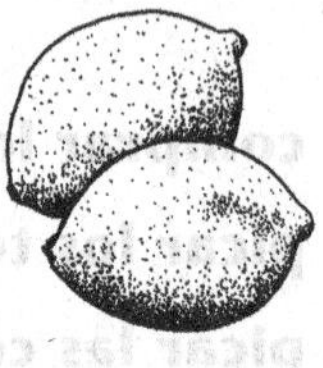

Sí/No _____ **pesos/kg**

Sí/No _____ **pesos/kg**

Sí/No _____ **pesos/kg**

Sí/No _____ **pesos/kg**

Sí/No _____ **pesos/kg**

Sí/No _____ **pesos/kg**

Sí/No _____ **pesos/kg**

Sí/No _____ **pesos/kg**

You have just returned from the supermarket. Tell your partner whether the items that he or she wants to buy are currently available, based on the pictures below. Then answer his or her questions about the prices in *pesos.* Follow the model.

—¿Venden papas en el supermercado?

—Sí, venden papas. (No, no venden papas.)

—¿Cuánto cuestan las papas?

—Cuestan ____ *pesos el kilo.*

VERDURAS

$10/kg

$18/kg

$9/kg

$8/kg

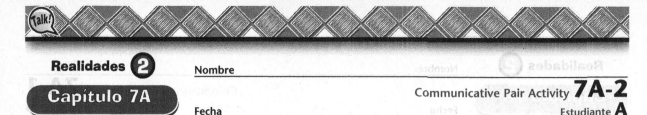

$12/kg

Realidades 2

Capítulo 7A

Nombre ____________________

Fecha ____________________

Communicative Pair Activity **7A-2**

Estudiante **B**

You have just returned from the fruit stand at the market. Tell your partner whether the items that he or she wants to buy are currently available, based on these pictures. Then answer his or her questions about the prices in *pesos*. Follow the model.

—*¿Venden piñas en el mercado?*

—*Sí, venden piñas. (No, no venden piñas.)*

—*¿Cuánto cuestan las piñas?*

—*Cuestan ____ pesos el kilo.*

$14/kg

$20/kg

$18/kg

$25/kg

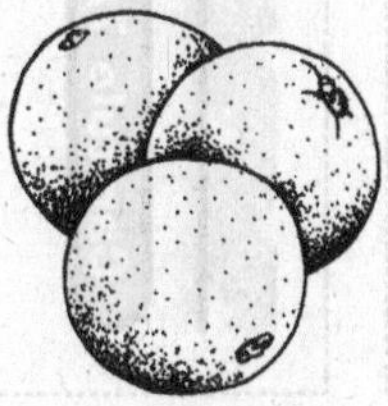

$10/kg

$12/kg

You are attending school in Mexico and living with the Ramírez family. La señora Ramírez asks you to go to the supermarket to buy various items to make a casserole for dinner. First, ask your partner if the following items are available in the supermarket. Then ask how much they cost. Record the information on the lines provided. Follow the model.

¿Venden papas en el supermercado? ¿Cuánto cuestan las papas?

Sí/No _____ **pesos/kg**

Sí/No _____ **pesos/kg**

Sí/No _____ **pesos/kg**

Sí/No _____ **pesos/kg**

Sí/No _____ **pesos/kg**

Situation Cards

1A

Capítulo 7A — Realidades 2

Describing and recommending different types of food

Together with a friend, you are planning a Spanish Club dinner. Think of three dishes you would like to prepare.

— Suggest the first dish. Then, ask your friend what you will need to prepare it.

— Suggest the second dish and ask about the ingredients.

— Suggest the third dish and ask about what you will need to prepare it.

1B

Capítulo 7A — Realidades 2

Describing and recommending different types of food

Together with a friend, you are planning a Spanish Club dinner.

— Respond to your friend's questions.

— Then, suggest beverages to accompany the meal.

— Respond to your friend's questions.

2A

Capítulo 7A — Realidades 2

Recommending and suggesting various foods and dishes

You invite your friend to your favorite restaurant. Think about which restaurant is your favorite.

— Greet your friend and invite him or her to eat with you.

— Suggest a restaurant (your favorite).

— Respond to your friend's questions.

2B

Capítulo 7A — Realidades 2

Recommending and suggesting various foods and dishes

A friend approaches you in the mall and invites you to eat at his or her favorite restaurant.

— Accept and ask where he or she is going to eat.

— Ask why he or she wants to go there.

— Ask what he or she suggests you order.

— Ask when you are going and how you'll get there.

GramActiva

¿Cómo se hace la paella?
¿Cómo comes?, p. 344

la cena	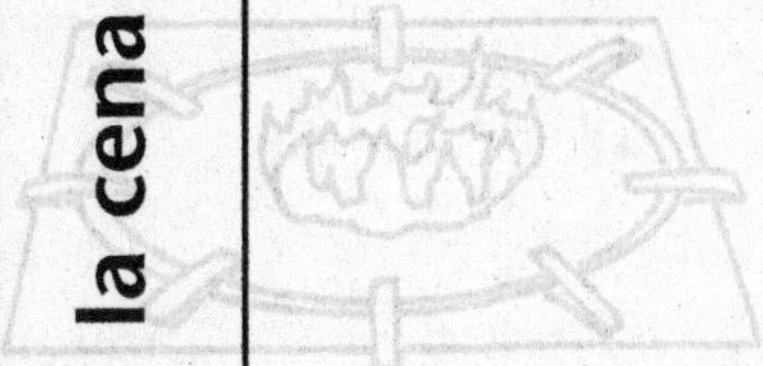		
el almuerzo			
el desayuno			

Vocabulary Clip Art

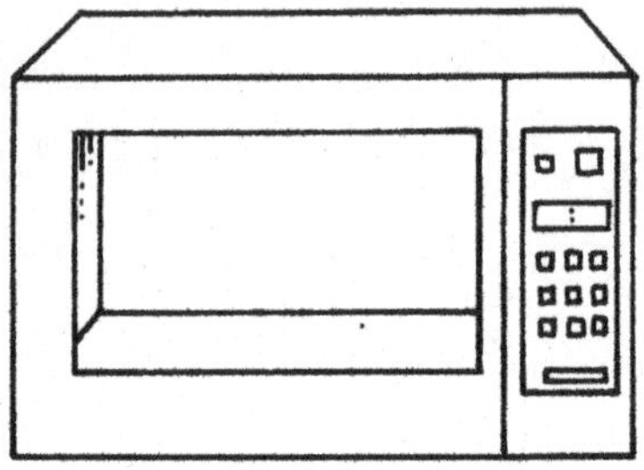

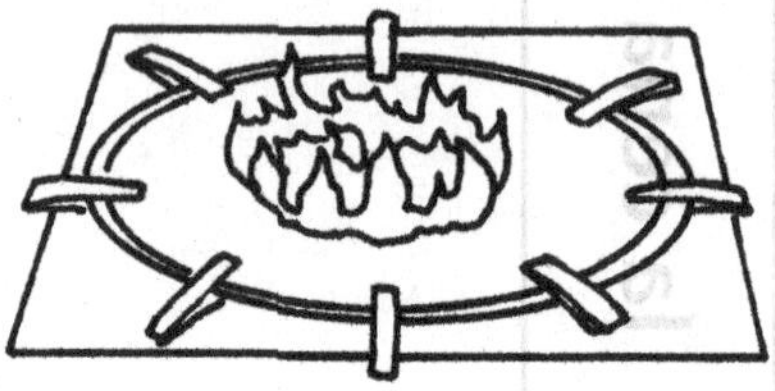

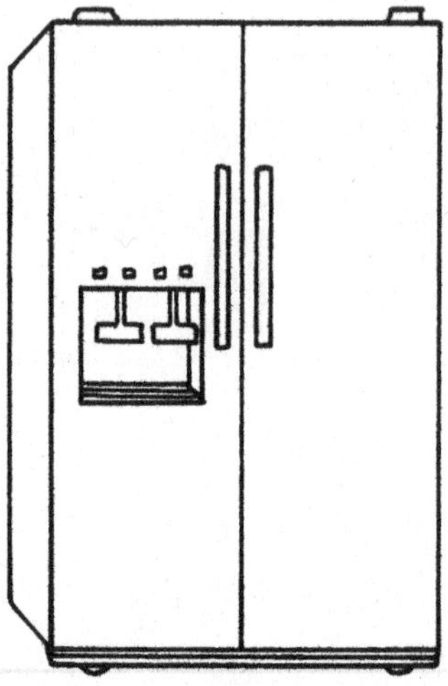

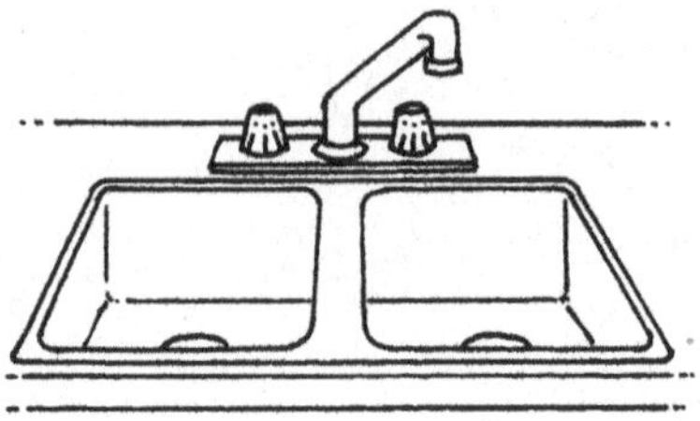

Vocabulary Clip Art

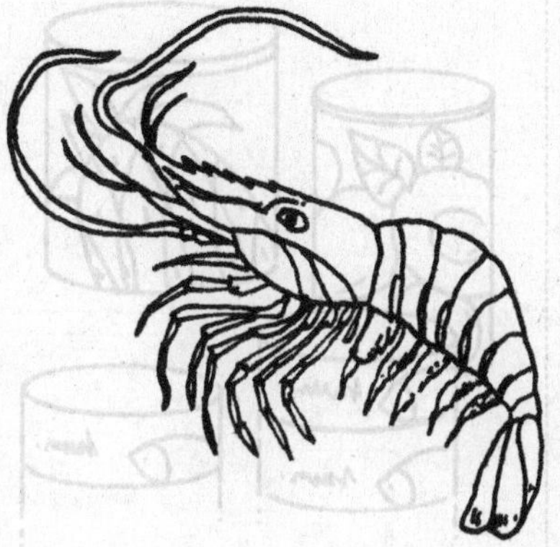
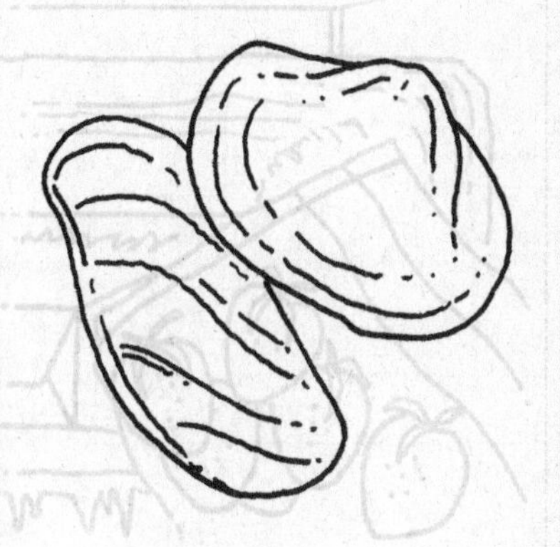

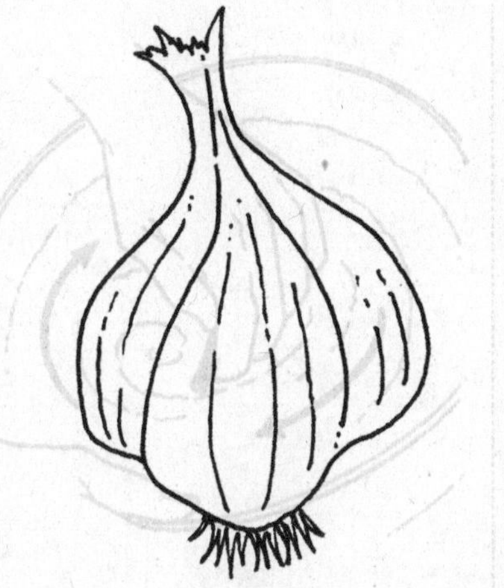
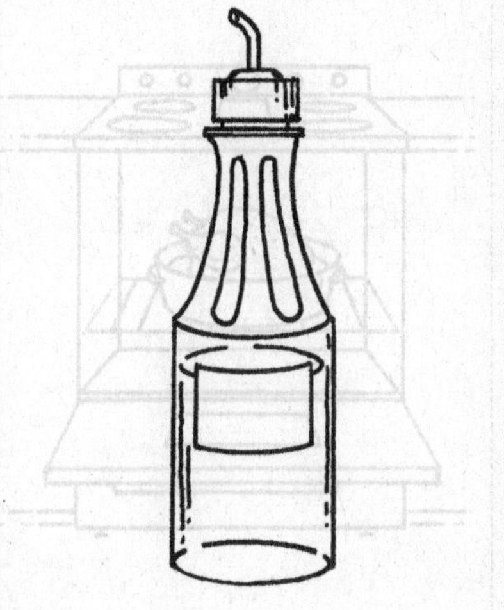

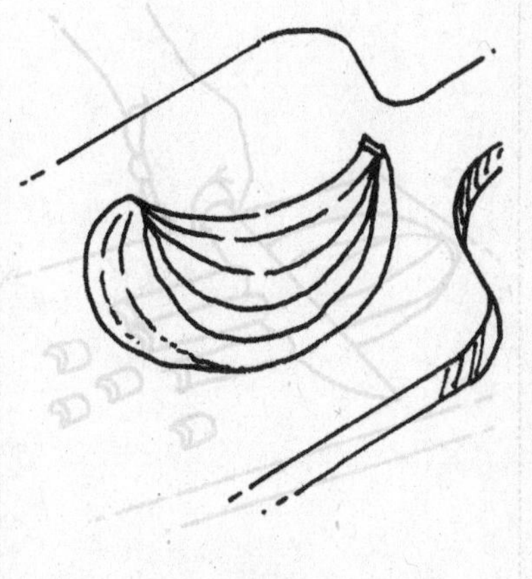

Vocabulary Clip Art

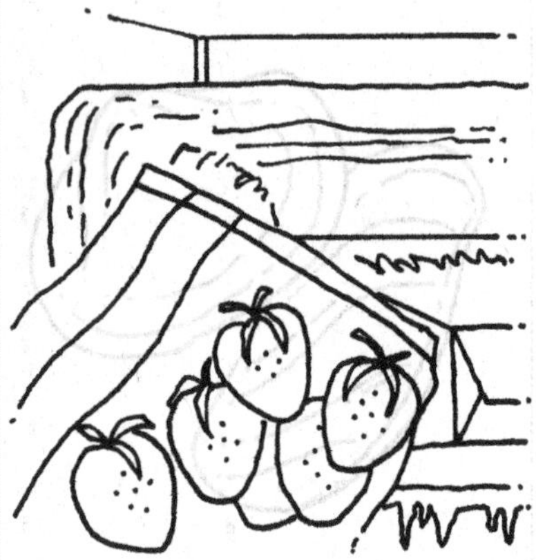

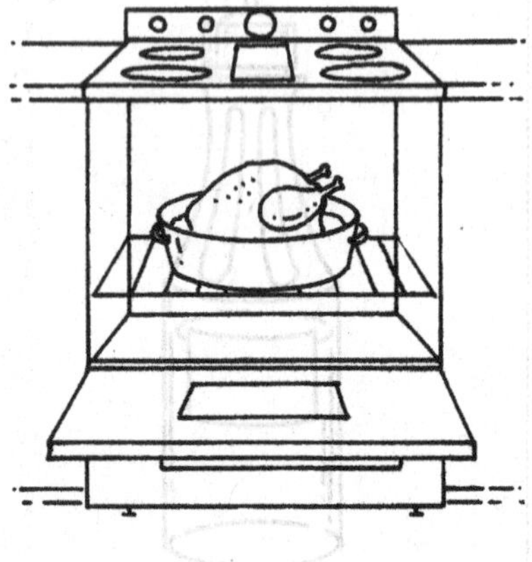

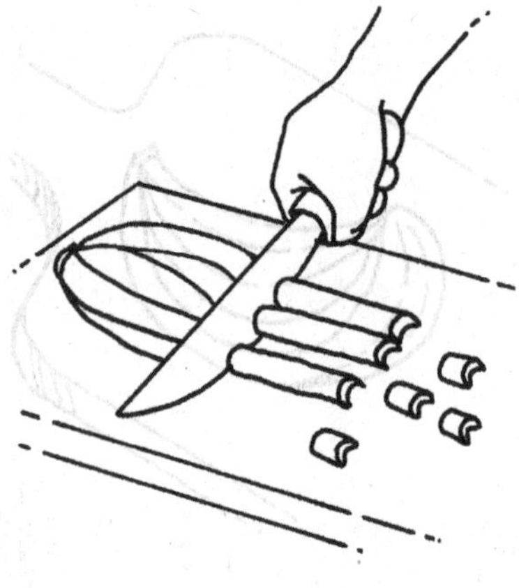

Realidades 2

Capítulo 7A — Vocabulary Clip Art

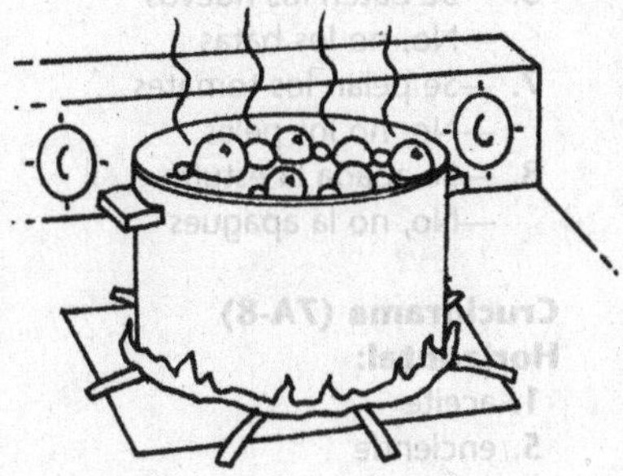
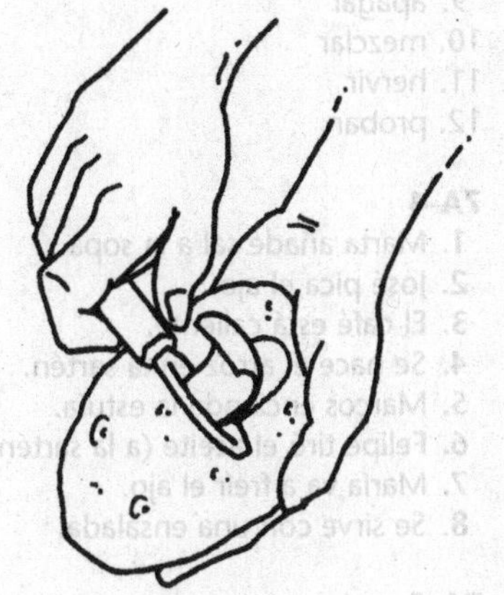

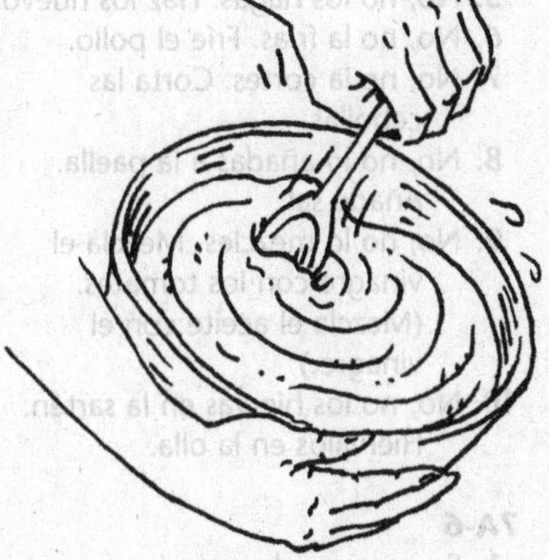

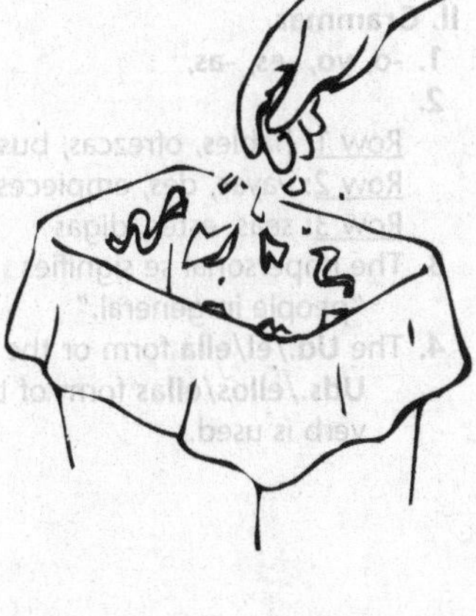

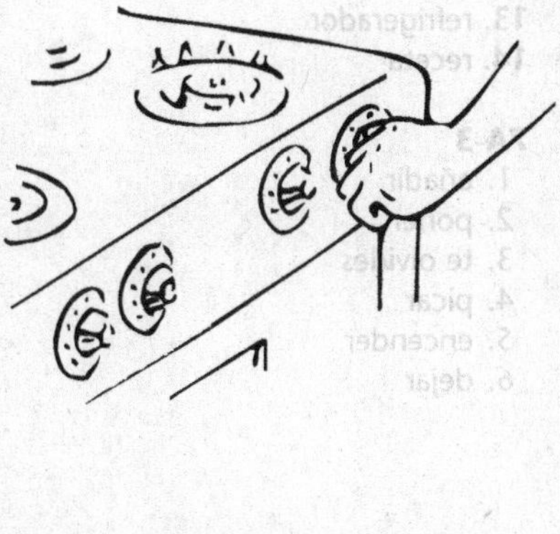

Core Practice Answers

7A-A
1. Conozco
2. Hago
3. Mantengo
4. Digo
5. Pongo
6. Salgo
7. Le ofrezco
8. Tengo
9. Oigo
10. Les obedezco

7A-B
1. comen cereal
2. mantiene la salud
3. hago ejercicios
4. beben, agua
5. come unas frutas
6. come bistec
7. come pescado

7A-1
1. la sartén
2. la estufa
3. el microondas
4. el horno
5. el refrigerador
6. el fregadero
7. olla
8. el fuego

7A-2
1. añadir
2. camarones
3. salsa
4. enlatadas
5. fresca
6. ingredientes
7. horno
8. calentar
9. mezclo
10. aceite
11. cucharada
12. ajo
13. refrigerador
14. receta

7A-3
1. añadir
2. poner
3. te olvides
4. picar
5. encender
6. dejar
7. Se sirve
8. pelar, freír
9. apagar
10. mezclar
11. hervir
12. probar

7A-4
1. Marta añade sal a la sopa.
2. José pica el ajo.
3. El café está caliente.
4. Se hace el arroz en la sartén.
5. Marcos enciende la estufa.
6. Felipe tiró el aceite (a la sartén).
7. María va a freír el ajo.
8. Se sirve con una ensalada.

7A-5
1. No, no lo piques. Pica los ajos.
2. No, no la tires. Tira el agua.
3. No, no lo pongas en el microondas. Ponlo en la olla.
4. No, no los peles. Pela las papas.
5. No, no los hagas. Haz los huevos.
6. No, no la frías. Fríe el pollo.
7. No, no la cortes. Corta las cebollas.
8. No, no lo añadas a la paella. Añade sal.
9. No, no lo mezcles. Mezcla el vinagre con los tomates. (Mezcla el aceite con el vinagre.)
10. No, no los hiervas en la sartén. Hiérvalos en la olla.

7A-6
1. Se usan muchos mariscos
2. Se sirve una ensalada.
3. Se pone, en el horno
4. Se añade sal
5. se usa comida enlatada
6. Se prepara, en la sartén
7. Se calientan, en el microondas
8. Se baten los huevos

7A-7
1. —Se calienta la salsa
—No, no la calientes
2. —Se fríen los ajos
—No, no los frías
3. —Se enciende la estufa
—No, no la enciendas
4. —Se deja la olla en la estufa
—No, no la dejes en la estufa
5. —Se mezclan los ingredientes
—No, no los mezcles
6. —Se baten los huevos
—No, no los batas
7. —Se pelan los tomates
—No, no los peles
8. —Se apaga la estufa
—No, no la apagues

Crucigrama (7A-8)
Horizontal:
1. aceite
5. enciende
7. frescas
8. hierve
10. cucharada
12. mariscos
16. olvides
17. bate
18. olla
19. fregadero
20. sartén
21. ingredientes

Vertical:
2. tires
3. piques
4. peles
5. enlatada
6. prueba
9. fritas
10. congelada
11. refrigerador
12. microondas
13. calienta
14. horno
15. pedazos

Organizer (7A-9)
I. Vocabulary Answers will vary.
II. Grammar
1. **-o, yo, -es, -as,**
2. <u>Row 1</u>: hables, ofrezcas, busques
<u>Row 2</u>: vayas, dés, empieces
<u>Row 3</u>: seas, estés, digas
3. The impersonal se signifies "people in general."
4. The **Ud./él/ella** form or the **Uds./ellos/ellas** form of the verb is used.

Realidades 2 — Capítulo 7A

Nombre ____ Hora ____

Fecha ____ **AVSR 7A-1**

A ver si recuerdas: Verbs with irregular *yo* forms (p. 345)

- As you know, some verbs have irregular **yo** forms in the present tense. These fall into two categories:

  Verbs with irregular **-go** forms:

salir → yo salgo	**poner → yo pongo**	**hacer → yo hago**
caer → yo caigo	**decir → yo digo**	**venir → yo vengo**

  Verbs with irregular **-zco** forms:

conocer → yo conozco	**parecer → yo parezco**
obedecer → yo obedezco	**ofrecer → yo ofrezco**

A. Change the following verbs from the **tú** form to the **yo** form. Follow the model.

Modelo pones *pongo*

1. sales	***salgo***	**5.** obedeces	***obedezco***
2. conoces	***conozco***	**6.** caes	***caigo***
3. dices	***digo***	**7.** haces	***hago***
4. ofreces	***ofrezco***	**8.** vienes	***vengo***

B. Elena is living with her aunt and uncle for the summer. Complete her e-mail by writing the **yo** form of the verbs given. The first one is done for you.

Estimada Mónica:

¿Cómo estás? Yo estoy muy bien aquí con mis tíos, pero yo *tengo* (**tener**) mucho trabajo. Yo me levanto y ***me*** ***pongo*** (**ponerse**) la ropa muy temprano. Después, yo ***salgo*** (**salir**) de la casa para trabajar con mi tío. Yo siempre ***hago*** (**hacer**) lo que él necesita y yo nunca le ***digo*** (**decir**) que estoy cansada. ¡Es trabajo divertido!

A ver si recuerdas: Verbs with irregular *yo* forms (*continued*)

Bueno, yo ya ***conozco*** (**conocer**) a muchas personas del pueblo. ¡Todos dicen que yo ***me*** ***parezco*** (**parecerse**) mucho a mi tío! Al final del día, cuando ***vengo*** (**venir**) a la casa, siempre le ***ofrezco*** (**ofrecer**) un poco de ayuda a mi tía, que está preparando la cena. En total, yo ***tengo*** (**tener**) una vida muy interesante aquí.

Un abrazo,

Elena

C. Answer the following questions in complete sentences, paying special attention to the verbs with irregular **yo** forms.

Modelo ¿Siempre dices la verdad?
Sí, yo siempre ***digo la verdad***.

1. ¿Te pareces a alguien de tu familia?
   Sí, yo ***me parezco*** a mi ***familia***.
2. ¿Siempre obedeces a tus padres?
   No, yo no ***obedezco a mis padres*** siempre.
3. ¿A veces sales por la noche con tus amigos?
   Sí, yo ***salgo por la noche*** a veces ***con mis amigos***.
4. ¿Conoces a alguna persona famosa?
   No, no ***conozco a ninguna persona famosa***.
5. ¿Tienes mucha tarea esta noche?
   Sí, yo ***tengo mucha tarea esta noche***.
6. ¿Haces la tarea por la tarde o por la noche?
   Yo ***hago la tarea por la tarde***.

Write the Spanish vocabulary word below each picture. Be sure to include the article for each noun.

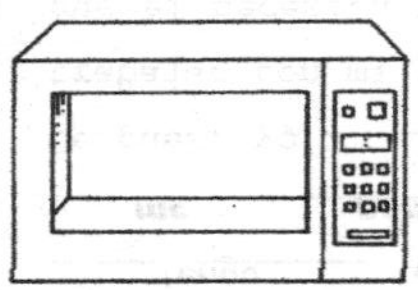

el
microondas

la
estufa

el
fuego

la
sartén

la
olla

el
horno

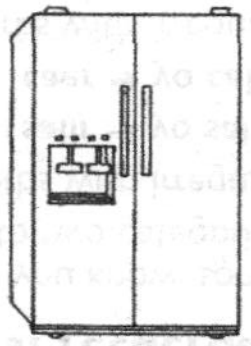

el
refrigerador

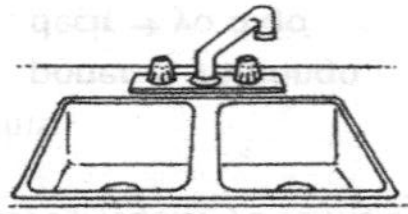

el
fregadero

el
ingrediente

Realidades 2 Nombre Hora

Capítulo 7A Fecha **Vocabulary Flash Cards, Sheet 2**

Write the Spanish vocabulary word below each picture. Be sure to include the article for each noun.

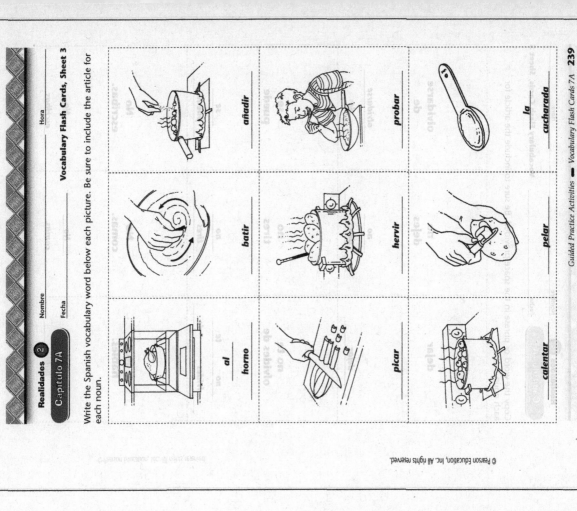

	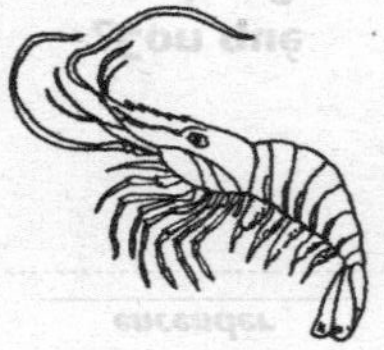	
la	***el***	***los***
receta	***camarón***	***mariscos***

el	***el***	***el***
caldo	***ajo***	***aceite***
		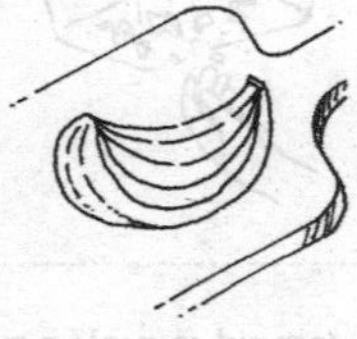
el	***la***	***el***
vinagre	***salsa***	***pedazo***

Realidades 2 Nombre Hora

Capítulo 7A Fecha **Vocabulary Flash Cards, Sheet 3**

Write the Spanish vocabulary word below each picture. Be sure to include the article for each noun.

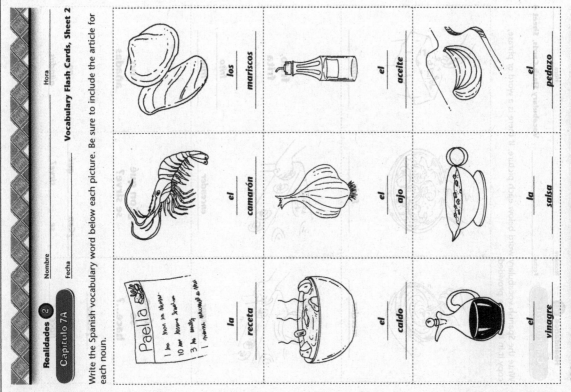

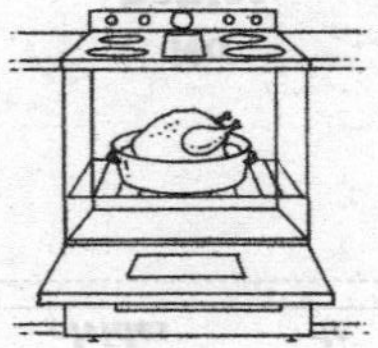	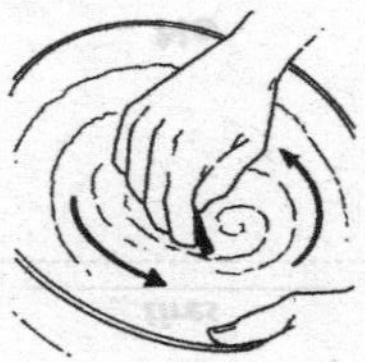	
al		
horno	***batir***	***añadir***
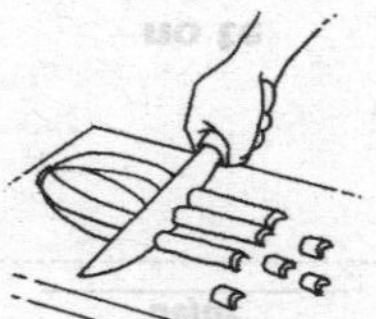		
picar	***hervir***	***probar***
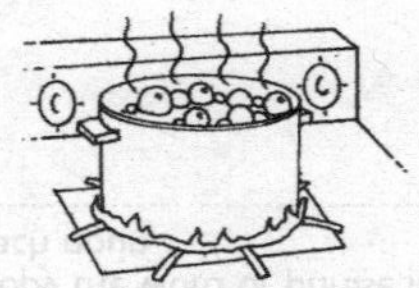	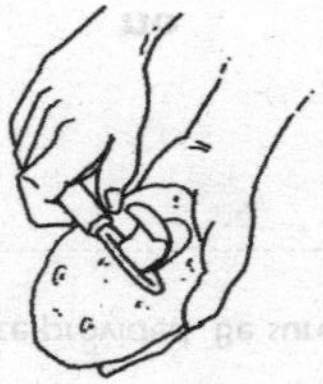	
		la
calentar	***pelar***	***cucharada***

Realidades 2 | Nombre ______ | Hora ______

Capítulo 7A | Fecha ______ | **Vocabulary Flash Cards, Sheet 4**

Write the Spanish vocabulary word below each picture. If there is a word or phrase, copy it in the space provided.

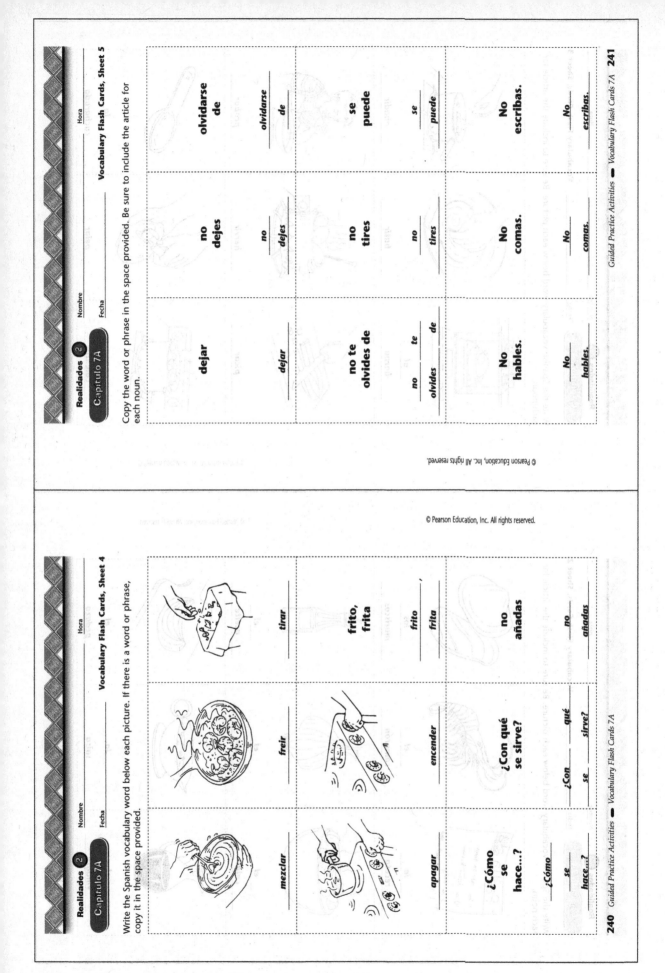

 *mezclar*	 *freir*	 *tirar*
 *apagar*	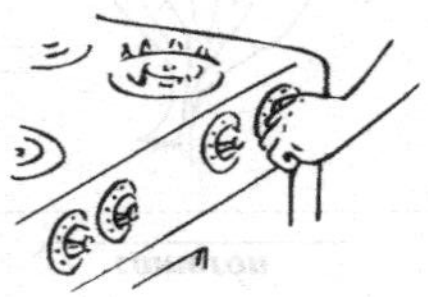 *encender*	**frito, frita** *frito*, *frita*
¿Cómo se hace...? *¿Cómo* *se* *hace...?*	**¿Con qué se sirve?** *¿Con* *qué* *se* *sirve?*	**no añadas** *no* *añadas*

Realidades 2 | Nombre ______ | Hora ______

Capítulo 7A | Fecha ______ | **Vocabulary Flash Cards, Sheet 5**

Copy the word or phrase in the space provided. Be sure to include the article for each noun.

dejar *dejar*	**no dejes** *no* *dejes*	**olvidarse de** *olvidarse* *de*
no te olvides de *no* *te* *olvides* *de*	**no tires** *no* *tires*	**se puede** *se* *puede*
No hables. *No* *hables.*	**No comas.** *No* *comas.*	**No escribas.** *No* *escribas.*

Copy the word or phrase in the space provided. These blank cards can be used to write and practice other Spanish vocabulary for the chapter.

congelado, congelada *congelado*, *congelada*	**enlatado, enlatada** *enlatado*, *enlatada*	**fresco, fresca** *fresco*, *fresca*

Tear out this page. Write the English words on the lines. Fold the paper along the dotted line to see the correct answers so you can check your work.

la salsa	*salsa, sauce*
el aceite	*cooking oil*
el ajo	*garlic*
la olla	*pot*
el refrigerador	*refrigerator*
el fuego	*fire, heat*
caliente	*hot*
el horno	*oven*
añadir	*to add*
tirar	*to spill, to throw away*
freír	*to fry*
mezclar	*to mix*
probar	*to taste, to try*
la receta	*recipe*
olvidarse de	*to forget about/to*

Fold In

Realidades 2 Nombre ____ Hora ____

Capítulo 7A Fecha ____ **Vocabulary Check, Sheet 2**

Tear out this page. Write the Spanish words on the lines. Fold the paper along the dotted line to see the correct answers so you can check your work.

salsa, sauce	***la salsa***
cooking oil	***el aceite***
garlic	***el ajo***
pot	***la olla***
refrigerator	***el refrigerador***
fire, heat	***el fuego***
hot	***caliente***
oven	***el horno***
to add	***añadir***
to spill, to throw away	***tirar***
to fry	***freír***
to mix	***mezclar***
to taste, to try	***probar***
recipe	***la receta***
to forget about/to	***olvidarse de***

Fold In ←

Realidades 2 Nombre ____ Hora ____

Capítulo 7A Fecha ____ **Vocabulary Check, Sheet 3**

Tear out this page. Write the English words on the lines. Fold the paper along the dotted line to see the correct answers so you can check your work.

el caldo	***broth***
la estufa	***stove***
el fregadero	***sink***
el pedazo	***piece, slice***
la sartén	***frying pan***
calentar	***to heat***
hervir	***to boil***
el ingrediente	***ingredient***
picar	***to chop***
apagar	***to turn off***
dejar	***to leave, to let***
encender	***to turn on, to light***
fresco, fresca	***fresh***

Fold In ←

Tear out this page. Write the Spanish words on the lines. Fold the paper along the dotted line to see the correct answers so you can check your work.

broth	***el caldo***
stove	***la estufa***
sink	***el fregadero***
piece, slice	***el pedazo***
frying pan	***la sartén***
to heat	***calentar***
to boil	***hervir***
ingredient	***el ingrediente***
to chop	***picar***
to turn off	***apagar***
to leave, to let	***dejar***
to turn on, to light	***encender***
fresh	***fresco, fresca***

Fold In

To hear a complete list of the vocabulary for this chapter, go to www.realidades.com and type in the Web Code jdd-0789. Then click on **Repaso del capítulo.**

Negative *tú* commands (p. 356)

- Negative commands are used to tell someone what *not* to do.
- To form negative **tú** commands, drop the **-o** of the present-tense **yo** form and add:
  -es for **-ar** verbs
  usar → uso: No uses el microondas. *Don't use the microwave.*
  -as for **-er** and **-ir** verbs
  encender → enciendo: No enciendas el horno. *Don't turn on the oven.*

A. Look at the following sentences and add the correct endings to the verbs to make negative **tú** commands. Use the verbs in parentheses for reference. Follow the model.

Modelo Jaime, no com*as* todas las frutas. **(comer)**

1. Raquel, no tir***es*** el pollo en el aceite caliente. **(tirar)**
2. Tadeo, no cort***es*** el ajo en pedazos tan pequeños. **(cortar)**
3. Susana, no beb***as*** el café si está muy caliente. **(beber)**
4. Mario, no us***es*** tanto aceite en el sartén. **(usar)**
5. Julia, no añad***as*** el ajo ahora. **(añadir)**

- Remember that some verbs have irregular **yo** forms, which are used to form the negative commands.
  salir → salgo No salga de la casa. *Don't leave the house.*

B. Complete the statements below by writing the correct negative **tú** commands of the verbs given. Follow the model.

Modelo (poner) *No pongas* las manos en la masa.

1. (salir) ***No salgas*** sin comer algo.
2. (decir) ***No digas*** mentiras (*lies*).
3. (hacer) ***No hagas*** eso, por favor.
4. (obedecer) ***No obedezcas*** a tus amigos malos.

realidades.com
• Web Code: jdd-0704

Negative *tú* commands (*continued*)

- Remember that stem-changing verbs will still have the same stem changes to form the negative commands. Also, if the verb is reflexive, the reflexive pronoun will be placed the same way.

  dormirse → te duermas

  ¡No te duermas en la clase! *Don't fall asleep in class!*

C. Look at the following verbs in the infinitive. Write the negative command form for each. Follow the model.

Modelo divertirse *No te diviertas.*

1. encender ***No enciendas.***
2. calentar ***No calientes.***
3. probar ***No pruebes.***
4. hervir ***No hiervas.***
5. caerse ***No te caigas.***
6. parecerse ***No te parezcas.***
7. olvidarse ***No te olvides.***
8. dormirse ***No te duermas.***

- With negative **tú** commands, some verbs such as **picar** (*to chop*), **pagar** (*to pay*), and **empezar** (*to start*) have spelling changes: **c** changes to **qu**, **g** changes to **gu**, and **z** changes to **c**.

  picar → no piques **pagar → no pagues** **empezar → no empieces**

D. Your parents have given you a list of things not to do on the weekend. Complete their list by writing the correct negative **tú** commands of the verbs given. Follow the model.

Modelo *No* *empieces* la tarea a las nueve de la noche los domingos. (empezar)

1. ***No*** ***almuerces*** en restaurantes caros. (**almorzar**)
2. ***No*** ***busques*** problemas en la calle. (**buscar**)
3. ***No*** ***juegues*** con las personas malas. (**jugar**)
4. ***No*** ***llegues*** a casa después de las diez de la noche. (**llegar**)
5. ***No*** ***saques*** cosas de la casa de otra persona sin pedirlas. (**sacar**)

realidades.com
• Web Code: jdd-0704

Negative *tú* commands (*continued*)

- Some verbs have irregular negative **tú** commands:

  dar → no des **estar → no estés**
  ir → no vayas **ser → no seas**

E. For each of the following sentences, write the appropriate negative **tú** command of the verb in parentheses.

1. No ***des*** (**dar**) dulces a tu hermano antes del almuerzo.
2. No ***estés*** (**estar**) en la cocina antes de la cena.
3. No ***vayas*** (**ir**) al mercado hoy.
4. No ***seas*** (**ser**) tan desordenada.

- Remember that pronouns are attached to the verb when they are added to the affirmative command form. Note: An accent mark is written on the verb when the added pronoun makes three or more syllables.

  —¿Añado la sal? *Do I add the salt?*
  —Sí, añádela. *Yes, add it.*

F. Read the following questions and unfinished answers. Place the correct pronoun in the spaces provided to finish the answers. Remember to add an accent, if necessary, to the affirmative command in each answer. Follow the model.

Modelo —¿Mezclo los ingredientes en la taza?
—Sí, mézcla*los* en la taza.

1. —¿Añado el aceite a la sartén?
   —Sí, añáde***lo*** a la sartén.
2. —¿Tiro los huesos del pollo?
   —Sí, tíra***los***.
3. —¿Apago el fuego de la estufa?
   —Sí, apága***lo***.
4. —¿Pongo la mesa antes de la cena?
   —Sí, pon***la*** antes de la cena.
5. —¿Saco los platos después de la comida?
   —Sí, sáca***los*** después de la comida.

realidades.com
• Web Code: jdd-0704

Negative *tú* commands (*continued*)

- Pronouns always go right before the verb when writing negative commands.
  —¿Pongo los platos en la mesa?
  Should I put the plates on the table?
  —No, no *los pongas* en la mesa en este momento.
  No, don't put them on the table right now.

G. Señor Báez is giving a class on cooking. Nacho is having trouble with many of the tasks. Follow the conversation below by writing in señor Báez' responses using negative **tú** commands. Remember to correctly place the pronouns in each. The first one is done for you.

1. NACHO: ¿Debo apagar el horno?
   SEÑOR BÁEZ: No, *no lo apagues*
2. NACHO: ¿Debo hacer el arroz?
   SEÑOR BÁEZ: No, ***no lo hagas***
3. NACHO: ¿Debo pelar los tomates?
   SEÑOR BÁEZ: No, ***no los peles***
4. NACHO: ¿Debo picar los huevos?
   SEÑOR BÁEZ: No, ***no los piques***
5. NACHO: ¿Debo freír la ensalada?
   SEÑOR BÁEZ: No, ***no la frías***
6. NACHO: ¿Debo poner el pan en el microondas?
   SEÑOR BÁEZ: No, ***no lo pongas*** allí.
7. NACHO: ¿Debo mezclar la leche con los tomates?
   SEÑOR BÁEZ: No, ***no la mezcles*** con los tomates.
8. NACHO: ¿Debo hervir los huevos en la sartén?
   SEÑOR BÁEZ: No, ***no los hiervas*** en la sartén.

The impersonal *se* (p. 360)

- In Spanish, to say that people in general do a certain thing, you use **se** + the **usted/él/ella** or **ustedes/ellos/ellas** form of the verb. This is called the impersonal **se**.
  Aquí se sirve el pan tostado con mantequilla. *Here they serve the toast with butter.*
  Se comen tortillas frecuentemente. *Tortillas are eaten frequently.*

A. Look at the pictures and read the sentences that describe what people do in general when they prepare food. Circle the appropriate impersonal **se** expression in parentheses to complete each sentence.

1. En mi casa el pollo (**se hace** / **se tira**) con sal y ajo.

2. Para preparar la salsa (**se calienta** / **se pica**) el ajo.

3. El plato principal (**se sirve** / **se hierve**) con ensalada.

4. En mi casa (**se come** / **se bebe**) mucha fruta.

5. La comida (**se pica** / **se calienta**) en el microondas.

The impersonal *se* (*continued*)

- Note: The **usted/él/ella form** of the verb is used when the thing following it is singular and the **ustedes/ellos/ellas** form is used when the thing following it is plural.

Se pela la papa.	*The potato is pealed.*
Se pelan las papas.	*The potatoes are pealed.*

B. Complete the following rules by circling the appropriate impersonal **se** expression to tell what is done or not done. Follow the model.

Modelo No (**se fríen** / **se fríe**) los camarones. [circled: se fríen]

1. (**Se sirven** / **Se sirve**) pan con mariscos. [circled: Se sirve]
2. (**Se calienta** / **Se calientan**) el pan en el horno. [circled: Se calienta]
3. No (**se añade** / **se añaden**) sal a la sopa. [circled: se añade]
4. (**Se dejan** / **Se deja**) el ajo en la cocina. [circled: Se deja]
5. No (**se hierve** / **se hierven**) los mariscos. [circled: se hierven]

C. Complete the following recipe to prepare **arroz con mariscos**. Use the impersonal **se** form of the verb in parentheses to complete each instruction. The first one is done for you. Be careful to choose between the singular and plural verb forms.

Arroz con mariscos

1. *Se calienta* (**calentar**) el aceite en la sartén.
2. ***Se preparan*** (**preparar**) los mariscos con sal.
3. ***Se pela*** (**pelar**) el ajo y
4. ***se corta*** (**cortar**) en pedazos.
5. ***Se mezclan*** (**mezclar**) los mariscos y el ajo.
6. ***Se hierve*** (**hervir**) agua en una olla.
7. ***Se añade*** (**añadir**) arroz y sal al caldo.
8. ***Se mezclan*** (**mezclar**) los mariscos con el arroz.

Lectura: "Oda al tomate" y "Oda a la cebolla" (pp. 364–365)

A. The two poems in your textbook reading are about tomatoes and onions. What words would you use to describe a tomato or an onion? Write them below.

tomato: ______, ______, ______, ______

onion: ______, ______, ______, ______

B. These poems use many descriptive words to tell us about tomatoes and onions. Some of these words are listed below. Circle the letter of the English meaning of each word.

1. **redonda** — a. small — (b.) round
2. **clara** — (a.) clear — b. dark
3. **pobres** — a. rich — (b.) poor
4. **constelación** — a. condition — (b.) constellation
5. **planeta** — (a.) planet — b. plantation

C. Look at the excerpt of **"Oda a la cebolla"** below. Read it aloud and look back at your answers from **part B** if you need help with the meaning of certain words. Then, write **C (cierto)** or **F (falso)** for each sentence below.

(...) cebolla,
clara como un planeta,
y destinada
a relucir (*shine*),
constelación constante,
redonda (*round*) *rosa*
de agua sobre la mesa
de las pobres gentes.

1. According to the poet, the onion is like a planet. ***C***
2. An onion is also like a tomato. ***F***
3. *Redonda rosa de agua* means that it is like a white flower. ***C***
4. The poet says that everyone has an onion on their table. ***F***

Realidades 2 Nombre ____________ Hora ______

Capítulo 7A Fecha ____________ **Guided Practice Activities 7A-6**

Presentación oral (p. 367)

Task: Imagine you are a guest on a television cooking show. You will be telling the audience how to prepare your favorite main dish.

A. Write the name of your favorite dish below. Then place an *X* next to the ingredients in the chart that you need to prepare that dish. ***Answers will vary.***

Mi plato favorito es ______________________.

Ingredientes			
____ huevos	____ caldo	____ carne	____ tomate
____ agua	____ pollo	____ lechuga	____ ajo
____ leche	____ sal	____ cebolla	____ pimienta
____ camarones	____ queso	____ aceite	____ mariscos

B. Use the ingredients you chose in **part A.** Think about the steps you would follow to prepare your dish. You can use the verbs for food preparation from the list or others you have learned in this chapter. ***Answers will vary.***

se mezcla	se corta	se sirve	se pone	se añade

Now, complete the recipe card below. Include the name of the dish, the ingredients you need, and the steps to prepare this dish.

Nombre del plato: ____________

Ingredientes: ____________

Preparación:

1. Primero, ____________
2. Luego, ____________
3. Después, ____________
4. Al final, ____________

C. Use your recipe card to practice your presentation. Remember to include the ingredients, describe the steps to prepare the dish, and to speak clearly.

Antes de ver el video

Actividad 1

List eight ingredients that you would need to prepare your favorite dish.

Answers will vary.

¿Comprendes?

Actividad 2

Javier is teaching Ignacio how to make paella. The steps he takes and the things he tells Ignacio are listed below, but they are in the wrong order. Order them correctly by writing a **1** to indicate the first thing Javier said and a **7** to indicate the last thing he said.

a. __6__ ¡No tires el aceite! Y no añadas más. Ya tienes más que suficiente.

b. __3__ No uso ingredientes congelados. Sólo uso ingredientes frescos... por eso mi paella es tan rica.

c. __2__ Bueno, está bien. Pero primero vamos al supermercado..., a comprar los ingredientes.

d. __5__ *Primero tienes que calentar el aceite, en una sartén grande; como ésta.*

e. __4__ No te olvides del aceite, y no dejes que se caliente demasiado.

f. __7__ Quieres decir, vamos a volver a empezar otra vez...

g. __1__ Quiero preparar una comida especial para Ana, para su cumpleaños.

Actividad 3

You have just finished watching Javier and Ignacio have a cooking adventure. Answer the questions below in complete sentences. Follow the model.

Modelo ¿Adónde van Javier e Ignacio?
Ignacio y Javier van al supermercado a comprar los ingredientes para hacer una paella.

1. ¿Qué sabe cocinar Ignacio?
Ignacio no sabe cocinar; sólo sabe sacar productos congelados del refrigerador y calentarlos en el microondas.

2. ¿Cómo es la paella de Javier? ¿Por qué?
La paella que prepara Javier es deliciosa. Es tan deliciosa porque no usa ingredientes congelados ni enlatados, sólo ingredientes frescos.

3. ¿Qué van a necesitar los jóvenes para hacer la paella?
Ellos van a necesitar camarones y otros mariscos.

4. ¿Dónde se prepara la paella?
La paella se prepara encima de la cocina.

5. ¿Qué tiene que hacer Ignacio con los ajos antes de cocinarlos?
Ignacio tiene que picar los ajos primero o cortarlos en pedazos muy pequeños.

6. ¿Por qué piensa Javier que Ana va a recibir una gran sorpresa, que no va a ser buena?

Javier piensa que Ana va a recibir una gran sorpresa, pero no va a ser buena, porque la paella se va a quemar.

Y, ¿qué más?

Actividad 4

Do you like to have big dinner parties or intimate dinners for two? What would you prepare for such a dinner? Write a short paragraph to tell about your ideal gathering and its menu. Follow the model.

Modelo *A mí me gusta reunirme con mis mejores amigos.*

En estas reuniones, me gusta cocinar algo como un pescado en salsa de queso. Invito a varios amigos, y ellos traen los otros platos: la ensalada, la bebida y el postre.

Nos ponemos a cocinar todos, y escuchamos música mientras preparamos la cena. Al terminar, todos comemos una comida muy rica, y todos quedamos contentos de compartir una noche tan agradable.

Answers will vary.

Actividad 5

Alejandro's older sister has been trying to teach him the basics of cooking. Listen to the questions he asks her during one of their phone conversations. If the question seems logical, circle the word **lógico** and if the question seems illogical, circle the word **ilógico.** You will hear each question twice.

1. lógico (ilógico)
2. (lógico) ilógico
3. lógico (ilógico)
4. (lógico) ilógico
5. lógico (ilógico)
6. (lógico) ilógico
7. (lógico) ilógico
8. (lógico) ilógico

Actividad 6

Both Ignacio and Javier think they are expert cooks. As they are preparing paella, each wants to make sure the other is doing it right. Listen to their conversations, and match each one to one of the pictures below. Write the number of the conversation in the blank underneath the corresponding picture. You will hear each conversation twice.

5

3

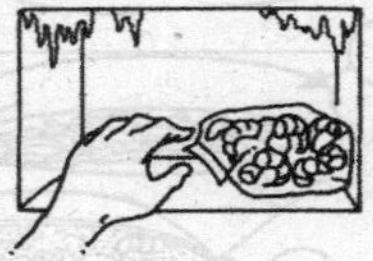
2

1

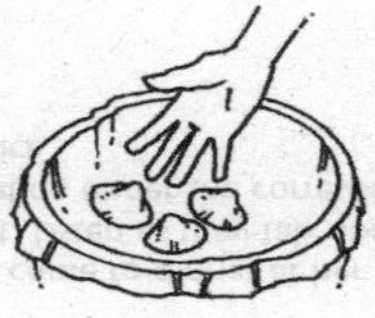
6

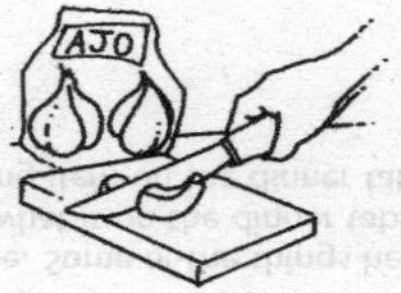

4

Actividad 7

Listen as different people give Roberto advice about cooking. As you listen to each piece of advice, decide whether the person is advising him on: a) getting ready to cook; b) things to do while he's cooking; or c) things to do after he's finished cooking. Place an **X** in the appropriate box in the grid below. You will hear each piece of advice twice.

	1	2	3	4	5	6	7	8	9	10
Antes de cocinar...	X			X		X				X
Cuando cocinas...			X		X				X	
Después de cocinar...		X					X	X		

Actividad 8

Listen as a counselor at a Spanish Immersion Camp tells the campers what things are going to be like at the camp for the summer. Draw a circle around the things that do happen, and an **X** over the pictures of the things that don't happen. You will hear each statement twice.

Actividad 9

Ryan's friend, Carmen, asks him to come to dinner at her home. Some of the things he eats are very familiar, but others are not. Listen as they talk about what is on the dinner table. Write the number of each conversation under the corresponding item on the dinner table. You will hear each conversation twice.

Actividad 10

Your mother is running late and calls you from the store to tell you to get dinner started. Use the pictures below to write what she tells you to do. Follow the model.

Modelo *Fríe el pollo en una sartén*.

Answers will vary. Possible answers:

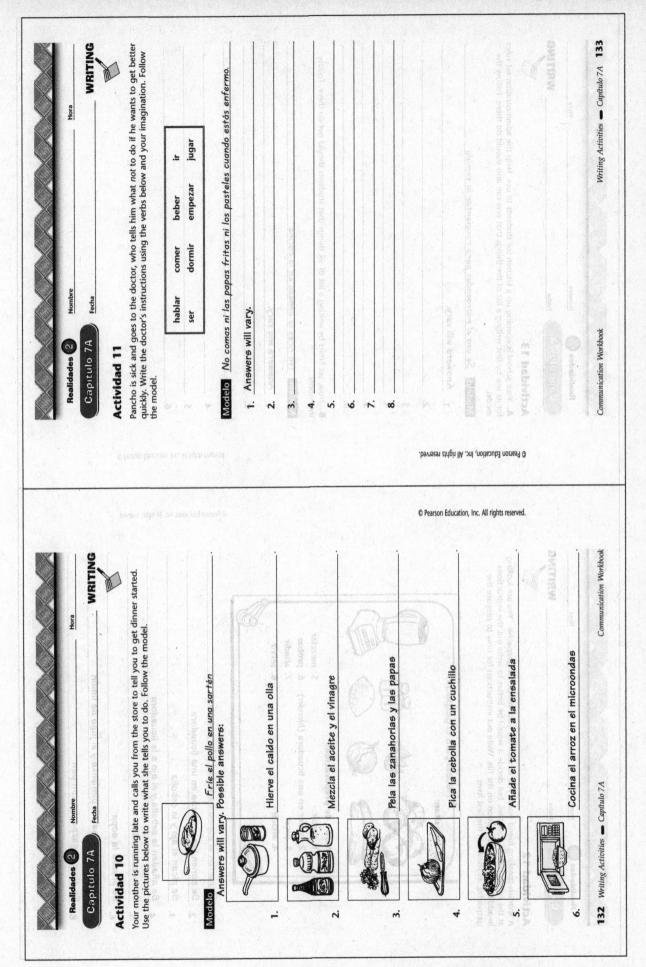

1. Hierve el caldo en una olla.

2. Mezcla el aceite y el vinagre.

3. Pela las zanahorias y las papas.

4. Pica la cebolla con un cuchillo.

5. Añade el tomate a la ensalada.

6. Cocina el arroz en el microondas.

Actividad 11

Pancho is sick and goes to the doctor, who tells him what *not* to do if he wants to get better quickly. Write the doctor's instructions using the verbs below and your imagination. Follow the model.

hablar	comer	beber	ir
ser	dormir	empezar	jugar

Modelo *No comas ni las papas fritas ni los pasteles cuando estás enfermo.*

1. Answers will vary.
2. ______
3. ______
4. ______
5. ______
6. ______
7. ______
8. ______

Actividad 12

A Spanish-speaking friend wants you to mail her your recipe for gazpacho. You are looking at the recipe card in your files, but decide it would be better to write out the instructions in addition to the information on the file. Write out instructions for how to prepare the gazpacho, as shown in the first item.

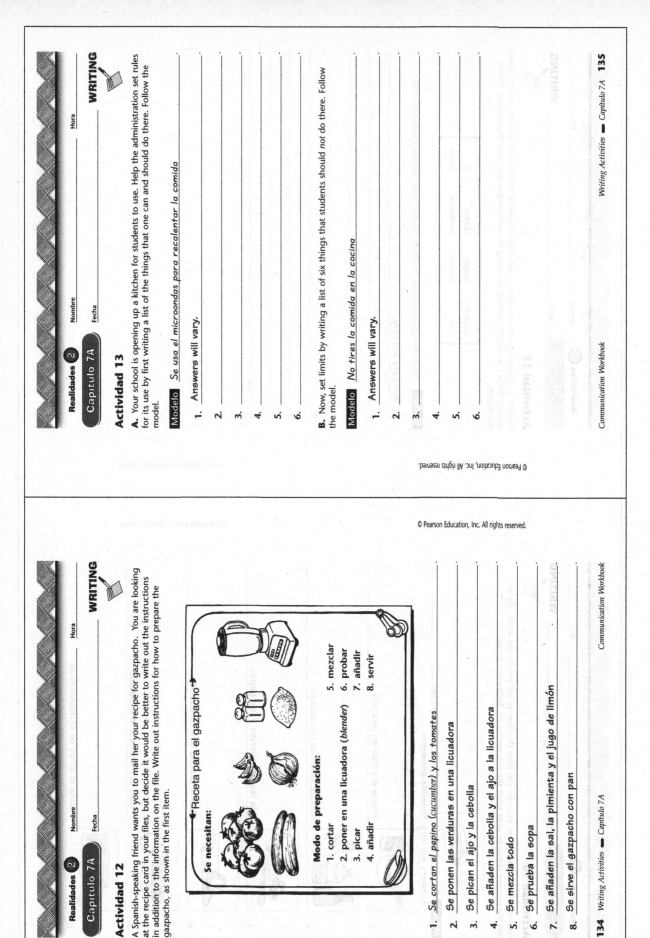

Receta para el gazpacho

Se necesitan:

Modo de preparación:

1. cortar
2. poner en una licuadora (*blender*)
3. picar
4. añadir
5. mezclar
6. probar
7. añadir
8. servir

1. *Se cortan el pepino (cucumber) y los tomates*.
2. Se ponen las verduras en una licuadora.
3. Se pican el ajo y la cebolla.
4. Se añaden la cebolla y el ajo a la licuadora.
5. Se mezcla todo.
6. Se prueba la sopa.
7. Se añaden la sal, la pimienta y el jugo de limón.
8. Se sirve el gazpacho con pan.

Actividad 13

A. Your school is opening up a kitchen for students to use. Help the administration set rules for its use by first writing a list of the things that one can and should do there. Follow the model.

Modelo *Se usa el microondas para recalentar la comida*.

1. Answers will vary.
2. ______
3. ______
4. ______
5. ______
6. ______

B. Now, set limits by writing a list of six things that students should *not* do there. Follow the model.

Modelo *No tires la comida en la cocina*.

1. Answers will vary.
2. ______
3. ______
4. ______
5. ______
6. ______

Realidades 2

Capítulo 7A

Test Preparation Answers

Reading Skills
p. 265 2. **D**
p. 266 2. **C**

Integrated Performance Assessment
p. 267
Answers will vary.

Realidades 2

Capítulo 7B

School-to-Home Connection

Dear Parent or Guardian,

The theme of our current unit is *Buen provecho* (Enjoy your meal!). This chapter is called *¿Te gusta comer al aire libre?* (Do you enjoy eating outside?).

Upon completion of this chapter students will be able to:

- discuss food and outdoor cooking
- give instructions about what to do or not to do
- indicate duration, exchange, reason, and other expressions
- understand cultural perspectives on special foods and outdoor food vendors

Students will also explore:

- compound words

Our textbook, *Realidades,* helps with the development of reading, writing, and speaking skills through the use of strategies, process speaking, and process writing. In this chapter, students will:

- read about a forest in Puerto Rico
- prepare a barbecue cookbook with emphasis on flavors drawn from the cuisines of the Spanish-speaking world

To reinforce and enhance learning, students can access a wide range of online resources on **realidades.com,** the personalized learning management system that accompanies the print and online Student Edition. Resources include the eText, textbook and workbook activities, audio files, videos, animations, songs, self-study tools, interactive maps, voice recording (RealTalk!), assessments, and other digital resources. Many learning tools can be accessed through the student Home Page on **realidades.com.** Other activities, specifically those that require grading, are assigned by the teacher and linked on the student Home Page within the calendar or the Assignments tab.

You will find specifications and guidelines for accessing **realidades.com** on home computers and mobile devices on MyPearsonTraining.com under the SuccessNet Plus tab.

realidades.com

For: Tips to Parents
Visit: www.realidades.com
Web Code: jce-0010

Check it out! At the end of the chapter, have your child name three things used to prepare food outdoors. Then have your child name his or her favorite food to eat outdoors.

Sincerely,

Capítulo 7B

Videocultura Script

La cocina mexicana

Spanish version:

La gastronomía mexicana es famosa en todo el mundo por sus muchos sabores, olores y colores.

Estos sabores vienen de la variedad de especias y vegetales frescos que se venden en los mercados en México.

Las civilizaciones antiguas azteca y maya comían el maíz, los frijoles, los chiles, los tomates, las calabazas, las papas y el chocolate.

Estas comidas son todavía muy importantes para la cocina mexicana.

La comida mexicana es diferente en cada región. Por ejemplo, en el norte de México, cocinan mucho con carne. En el sureste, cocinan mucho con vegetales y pollo.

La cocina mexicana es peculiar y creativa. Por eso, a mucha gente alrededor del mundo le encanta.

English version:

Mexican cooking is known for its variety of flavors, colorful presentation, and spicy taste.

Its strong flavors and delicious aromas come from a variety of fresh spices such as chili peppers and local ingredients found in the many markets all over the country.

Mexican cuisine is based on the foods of the ancient Aztecs and Mayan Indians.

They ate foods such as corn, beans, chili peppers, tomatoes, squash, potatoes, sweet potatoes, and chocolate.

These foods are still very important in Mexico and their influence has spread to cuisines found around the world.

Mexican food varies in taste and style from region to region in the country.

For instance, in northern Mexico, you will find more beef and meat dishes with wheat tortillas being common.

In central and southern Mexico, dishes include vegetables such as avocado and tomatoes, meats such as pork and chicken.

Mexican food has an identity of its own. Its wide range of flavors and unique combinations are what make it one the most creative and delicious cuisines of the world.

Input Script

Presentation

Input Vocabulary: Come to class wearing a flannel shirt and jeans with dots of calamine lotion on your face to show that you've been camping in a mosquito-infested area. Bring a picnic basket filled with the fruit pictured on p. 374 of *A primera vista.* Place the transparency showing picnic foods on the screen. Distribute copies of the Vocabulary Clip Art and have students cut them into individual pieces. Describe the camping trip you went on last weekend in which you ran into a few problems. Say: *El fin de semana pasado, fui de cámping con mi amigo(a). Nos gusta mucho comer al aire libre. Y a mí me gustan mucho las frutas. Entonces, llevé en esta cesta…*. Pull each type of fruit out of the basket as you name it in Spanish. Then say: *Pero a mi amigo(a) no le gustan las frutas. Me dijo—¿Por qué llevas tantas frutas? No necesitamos…* Name the fruits again and have students hold up the Clip Art images of the fruit this time.

Next say: *Mi amigo(a) llevó la mostaza, la salsa de tomate, la mayonesa y…* Name the kinds of meat your friend brought, using the transparency, gestures, and pantomime to convey meaning. Say: *Le dije—¿Por qué llevas tanta carne? Mi amigo(a) dijo—Llevé tanta carne porque me gusta…* Name the meats again and have students hold up the Clip Art image.

Continue the story, using the transparency, gestures, and pantomime to convey meaning. Have students hold up the Clip Art of the items you mention. Say: *Cuando llegamos, teníamos mucha hambre. Dije—Voy a encender el fuego ahora. ¿Me puedes dar los fósforos? Mi amigo(a) dijo—¡Lo siento! ¡Se me olvidaron los fósforos! Vamos a dar una caminata. Quizás hay otras personas que van de cámping y podemos pedir prestado algunos fósforos. Yo le dije—No estoy seguro(a). Mira las nubes en el cielo. Va a llover. Y me dijo—No va a llover. Aquí está un sendero. ¡Vamos! Le dije—Bueno, pero llevo mi cesta de fruta. Tengo hambre.*

¡Bueno, no encontramos a ninguna persona! Pero, encontramos a muchos mosquitos y moscas. ¡Fue horrible! ¡Afortunadamente, los insectos se fueron… cuando comenzó a llover! Estábamos completamente mojados. Y no teníamos ropa seca con nosotros. Entonces, regresamos. ¡Cuando llegamos, vimos un oso comiendo toda la carne que mi amigo(a) había llevado! Después que el oso se fue, comimos la fruta que yo había llevado. Mi amigo(a) me dijo—¡Buena idea que nosotros llevamos toda esta fruta! ¡¿Nosotros?!

Then have pairs of students read the dialogues on pp. 374–375. After each section, discuss the similarities and differences between your camping experience and the ones portrayed in the dialogues.

Comprehension Check

- Act indecisive about which foods to pack for a camping trip. Quickly place Clip Art images of food in the picnic basket, pull some out, put others in, take more out. Have students tell you which fruits you ended up with.
- Make logical and illogical remarks about camping. Have students give a "thumbs-up" for logical remarks and a "thumbs-down" for illogical remarks.

Audio Script

Audio DVD, Capítulo 7B

Track 01: *A primera vista, ¿Te gusta comer al aire libre?*, Student Book, p. 374, (4:24)

Vocabulario y gramática en contexto

Lee en tu libro mientras escuchas el diálogo.

TEEN FEMALE: Voy a encender el fuego ahora. ¿Me puedes dar los fósforos?

TEEN MALE: Claro. ¿Qué vamos a comer?

TEEN FEMALE: Carne de res a la parrilla, tortillas de maíz y guacamole. También tengo una salsa que está hecha con chiles verdes y es bien picante. Y de postre, piña y sandía. Las dos son muy dulces.

TEEN MALE: ¡Fabuloso! Gracias por hacer todas las preparaciones.

TEEN FEMALE: De nada. Me encanta comer al aire libre.

Vas a escuchar cada palabra o frase dos veces. Después de la primera vez hay una pausa para que puedas pronunciar la palabra o frase. Luego vas a escuchar de nuevo la palabra o frase.

hacer una parrillada	la carne de res
el fósforo	el pavo
la piedra	a la parrilla
el durazno	la chuleta de cerdo
el melón	el pollo asado
el aguacate	asar
las cerezas	la salsa de tomate
la sandía	la mostaza
la piña	la mayonesa
la cesta	

Track 02: *A primera vista,* Student Book, p. 375, (2:57)

Vocabulario y gramática en contexto

Lee en tu libro mientras escuchas el diálogo.

TEEN MALE 1: ¡Ay! No me gustan nada los mosquitos. Hay muchos por aquí.

TEEN MALE 2: Sí, y hay moscas y hormigas también. ¡Qué problema!

TEEN FEMALE 1: Pedro y Roberto, traigan más leña para la fogata. Si no, la fogata se va a apagar. Pónganla aquí muy cerca.

TEEN MALE 2: Ahora, no. Vamos a dar una caminata por una hora.

TEEN FEMALE 1: Tengan cuidado. Dicen que va a llover.

TEEN MALE 2: Gracias. ¡Hasta pronto!

ADULT MALE: Una hora después…

TEEN MALE 1: No entren en la cabaña. Están mojados. Aquí, dentro de la cabaña, todo está seco. ¡Y dejen las botas sucias fuera!

TEEN MALE 2: ¿Qué dicen? ¡Abran la puerta ahora!

Vas a escuchar cada palabra o frase dos veces. Después de la primera vez hay una pausa para que puedas pronunciar la palabra o frase. Luego vas a escuchar de nuevo la palabra o frase.

las nubes	la leña
el cielo	la hormiga
dar una caminata	la mosca
el sendero	secos
la fogata	mojados

Track 03: *A primera vista,* Act. 1, Student Book, p. 375, (2:07)

¿Cierta o falsa?

Escucha las siguientes frases. Según la información de la escena de la página anterior indica si son ciertas o falsas. Señala con el pulgar hacia arriba si la frase es cierta y con el pulgar hacia abajo si es falsa. Vas a escuchar las frases dos veces.

1. Los dos van a comer al aire libre.
2. Van a apagar la fogata con los fósforos.
3. Los dos van a comer pollo asado.
4. De postre, van a comer fruta.
5. El pavo es un pollo grande.
6. El aguacate es carne.
7. El chico preparó toda la comida.

Track 04: *A primera vista,* Act. 2, Student Book, p. 375, (2:55)

Al aire libre

Escucha las frases y preguntas sobre un día al aire libre. Escoge la respuesta correcta para cada pregunta. Vas a escuchar las frases dos veces.

1. **TEEN FEMALE 1:** Ramón, ¿puedes encender el fuego?
   NARRATOR: ¿Qué necesita Ramón, la piedra o el fósforo?
2. **TEEN MALE 1:** Creo que va a llover. Mira el cielo.
   NARRATOR: ¿Qué se ve en el cielo, unas nubes o un pavo?
3. **TEEN FEMALE 1:** Mira. Está lloviendo y la leña está fuera.
   TEEN MALE 1: ¡Ay! ¿Cómo vamos a encender la fogata?
   NARRATOR: ¿Cómo está la leña, mojada o seca?
4. **TEEN FEMALE 1:** Voy a preparar una ensalada de frutas.
   NARRATOR: ¿Qué necesita, la piña o la chuleta de cerdo?
5. **TEEN MALE 1:** Vamos a cocinar a la parrilla esta noche.
   NARRATOR: ¿Qué van a comer, el durazno o la carne de res?
6. **TEEN FEMALE 1:** Las hamburguesas están listas para comer.
   NARRATOR: ¿Qué necesitamos para ellas, la mostaza o la sandía?

Track 05: *A primera vista, Videohistoria,* Student Book, pp. 370–371, (2:37)

Un día al aire libre

Lee en tu libro mientras escuchas la *Videohistoria.*

See Student Book pages 370–371 for script.

Track 06: *Manos a la obra,* Act. 5, Student Book, p. 378, (2:13)

Escucha y escribe

Seis personas van a hablar de comer al aire libre. Escribe lo que dicen. Después indica si a la persona le gusta o no le gusta comer al aire libre. Vas a escuchar las frases dos veces.

1. Me encanta el olor de la carne asada a la parrilla.
2. Me molestan mucho las hormigas y las moscas.
3. El sabor de la comida siempre es mejor al aire libre.
4. Los domingos hay puestos en el parque con comida muy sabrosa.
5. Encender una fogata con leña y fósforos es demasiado trabajo.
6. Muchas veces el suelo está mojado y no es cómodo comer allí.

Track 07: Audio Act. 5, Writing, Audio & Video Workbook, p. 139, (4:06)

The Cruz and Ramos families are getting together for their annual barbecue. Listen as they talk about what they brought in their picnic baskets. As you listen to each family member talk about a particular food item, look at the pictures below of the picnic baskets. Then, write C in the blank if you think a member of the Cruz family is speaking, and write *R* in the blank if you think a member of the Ramos family is speaking. You will hear each set of statements twice.

1. **Adult Female 1:** ¿Tienes hambre, mi amor? Mientras preparas la parrilla, puedes comer un durazno. Aquí lo tienes.
2. **Adult Male 1:** ¿Dónde están los fósforos? ¿Quién los tiene? Ah, aquí están, en la cesta.
3. **Adult Female 2:** Parece que a las moscas les gusta la piña de nuestra cesta. Necesito matarlas. ¿Dónde está el matamoscas?
4. **Teen Male 1:** Papi, ¿tienes la carne de res? En la otra cesta hay un pavo, pero no quiero pavo. Prefiero la carne de res. ¿Dónde está? Ah, sí. La veo en nuestra cesta.
5. **Adult Female 1:** Mi amor, ¿dónde está la sandía? No la encuentro en la cesta. Sabes que a los niños les gusta la sandía bien fría.
6. **Teen Female 1:** Mami, quiero la salsa de tomate, pero no la encuentro. El sabor de la carne de res es mejor con salsa de tomate.
7. **Adult Male 2:** ¡Ah!, aquí está el aguacate. Quiero hacer un sándwich de pavo, queso y mucho aguacate. ¡Son deliciosos!
8. **Teen Male 2:** Quiero algo dulce para el postre. ¡Ya sé! Hay un melón muy delicioso en la cesta.

Track 08: Audio Act. 6, Writing, Audio & Video Workbook, p. 140, (3:03)

Some people prefer the great outdoors and others prefer the comforts of being indoors. As you listen to each conversation, determine whether the person is talking about eating outdoors or inside at a restaurant. Fill in the grid below as you listen. You will hear each set of statements twice.

1. No quiero comer aquí. El suelo aquí está mojado. Vamos a buscar un lugar seco.
2. La carne asada es la especialidad aquí. El camarero me dijo que toda su carne viene de la Argentina.
3. Me gusta cocinar así. El pollo asado a la parrilla es muy delicioso.
4. No me gusta comer aquí. Las moscas quieren mi comida y los mosquitos me molestan todo el tiempo.
5. ¡Esta carne de res está muy grasosa! El menú la describe como una comida saludable. ¡Qué horrible! El chef no sabe cocinar muy bien.
6. La chuleta de cerdo es muy deliciosa, pero no puedo comerla porque no tengo ni cuchillo ni tenedor. Camarero, un cuchillo y un tenedor, por favor.

Track 09: Audio Act. 7, Writing, Audio & Video Workbook, p. 140, (3:14)

You are helping the Scoutmaster, Señor Naranjo, assign tasks for the boys in his troop to do at summer camp. Your job is to write each task in the chart below so that each pair of boys knows what to do. You will hear each task twice.

1. Dani y Benito. Cuando lleguemos, queremos hacer la fogata. Uds. dos recogan leña. Y no traigan leña mojada. Tiene que estar muy seca.
2. Adán y Miguel, a Uds. dos les gusta dar caminatas. Busquen piedras para la fogata. Tengan cuidado y quédense en el sendero.
3. David y Enrique, Uds. dos saben cocinar a la parrilla, ¿no? Por favor, preparen la carne de res para asar.
4. Jaime y Pepe, no hablen tanto y hagan la ensalada de frutas para el postre de los muchachos.
5. Arturo y Benito, vayan a comer al comedor. ¿Dónde estaban Uds. dos? Llegan muy tarde para comer.
6. Raúl y Tomas, no pierdan el tiempo jugando y hagan la fogata para cocinar la comida.

Track 10: *Manos a la obra,* Act. 24, Student Book, p. 389, (3:11)

Supermercado El Ranchero

Lee las preguntas sobre un anuncio. Luego escucha el anuncio para el supermercado El Ranchero. Escribe la letra correcta para cada pregunta. Vas a escuchar el anuncio dos veces.

¿Tiene planes para hacer una parrillada este fin de semana? ¡Pues, venga al supermercado El Ranchero! Empezando mañana por la mañana, Ud. puede encontrar los precios más bajos para todo lo que Ud. necesita para hacer la parrillada perfecta. Por ejemplo, en la carnicería tenemos carne de res para asar o fajitas de pollo por sólo dos dólares y cuarenta y nueve centavos por libra. Chuletas de cerdo por sólo dos dólares y noventa y nueve centavos por libra. Y por supuesto, también tenemos frutas y verduras frescas a los mejores precios. Y no se olvide de pasar por nuestra taquería. Allí tenemos pollos enteros asados, con arroz, frijoles, salsa y tortillas de maíz o de harina, todo por sólo doce dólares y noventa y nueve centavos. ¡Y por un tiempo limitado, le damos dos pollos enteros por el precio de uno! Por favor, no pierda esta gran oportunidad para comprar con los mejores precios la comida más fresca en el supermercado El Ranchero.

Track 11: Audio Act. 8, Writing, Audio & Video Workbook, p. 141, (3:59)

Listen as people talk about what they did on behalf of their friends or relatives last week. As you listen to each conversation, fill in the grid below with the following information: 1) what he or she did; 2) on whose behalf he or she did it; and 3) the amount of time it took. For the first column, choose from the following statements:
a) *Preparó una cena.*; b) *Trabajó en una computadora.*;
c) *Estudió matemáticas.*; d) *Limpió el apartamento.* You will hear each set of statements twice.

1. **Teen Female 1:** El sábado pasado yo fui a la casa de mi hermana mayor. Trabajé por dos horas con su computadora. Sin su computadora, ella no podía comunicarse con la familia por correo electrónico. Lo hice por ella porque la quiero mucho. ¡Ella me pagó con una cena a la parrilla!
2. **Adult Male 1:** Cuando entré por la puerta del apartamento de mi hijo, todo estaba en mucho desorden. Yo limpié la cocina y el baño por tres horas. Lo hice por él porque estudia mucho y no tiene tiempo para limpiar.
3. **Teen Male 1:** La semana pasada fui a la casa de mi abuela. Quería darle una sorpresa inolvidable. Cociné por cinco horas en su apartamento. Preparé una cena muy sabrosa con pavo asado en salsa de mostaza, ensalada de papas y muchas frutas para el postre. Me gustó verla muy feliz cuando entró por la puerta.
4. **Teen Male 1:** A mi amigo Juan no le gustan las matemáticas. Él necesitaba ayuda para el examen general de matemáticas. Yo le ayudé por ser mi mejor amigo. Estudié matemáticas con él por ocho horas en la biblioteca.

Track 12: Audio Act. 9, Writing, Audio & Video Workbook, p. 141, (3:50)

Listen as guests on a cruise ship listen to instructions from the Activity Director about the upcoming "ship-to-shore" camping trip. She gives lots of advice on what to do on their expedition. As you listen to each piece of advice, decide whether she is talking about trekking in the woods or getting ready for the evening barbecue and bonfire. Put an *X* in the correct box below. You will hear each piece of advice twice.

1. Nunca caminen solos en los senderos. Vayan acompañados con uno de sus compañeros.
2. Recogan la leña seca y las piedras para la fogata.
3. Saquen las cerezas y los duraznos de la cesta. A todos les gusta algo dulce después de comer la carne asada.
4. Recuerden Uds.... No toquen las plantas ni coman nada en el bosque.
5. Pongan en la cesta mostaza, mayonesa y salsa de tomate.
6. No lleven los zapatos que llevan al trabajo para caminar por los senderos. Si los usan les van a doler los pies mucho.
7. Tomen agua mientras caminan por los senderos.
8. Lleven fósforos en la cesta. Es muy difícil hacer una fogata sin ellos.
9. Pongan la carne de res en jugo de piña antes de cocinarla. ¡Es muy deliciosa!
10. Hablen con la gente si se pierden. Las personas que viven aquí son muy buenas y pueden mostrarles el camino.

Track 13: *Repaso del capítulo*, Student Book, p. 396, (5:01)

Vocabulario y gramática
Escucha las palabras y expresiones que has aprendido en este capítulo.

See Student Book page 396 for vocabulary list.

Track 14: *Preparación para el examen*, Student Book, p. 397, (1:02)

Escuchar
Practice task
A group of teenagers is discussing whether to have a picnic or a dinner at someone's home next Saturday to welcome a group of new students. As you listen to their opinions, decide whether the person is in favor or not in favor of an outdoor picnic.

Beto: Es más difícil preparar la comida con leña y fósforos. Si llueve el sábado, es imposible.
Héctor: Estoy de acuerdo. Queremos hablar con los estudiantes que nos visitan. No queremos pasar el tiempo buscando las piedras y leña.
Ana: Es más informal y divertido comer al aire libre. Recojan Uds. las piedras y leña el viernes.

Video Script

A primera vista: *Un día al aire libre*, (8:16)

CLAUDIA: ¡Qué idea tan buena! ¡Me encanta ir al parque y comer al aire libre!

TERESA: Ay sí, a mí también. ¡Y el Desierto de los leones es el sitio perfecto!

MANOLO: Pues, yo soy de la ciudad y comer en el campo no me gusta.

RAMÓN: ¿Por qué no te gusta?

MANOLO: No me gustan ni las moscas ni los mosquitos.

CLAUDIA: Ay, Manolo, por favor. Vivimos en la ciudad, mejor, un parque.

TERESA: Oye, ¿qué traes en la cesta?

CLAUDIA: Carne de res, tortillas de harina, frijoles. Ah, y también guacamole.

TERESA: ¡Qué rico! Ya tengo mucha hambre. Mira, ya llegamos. Allí está el parque.

CLAUDIA: Miren, vamos a ver lo que hay allí.

MANOLO: Vámonos. Vámonos.

RAMÓN: ¡Ya!

MANOLO: ¡Ya vámonos!

TERESA: Mira, aquí lo podemos poner.

CLAUDIA: Pero está mojado. Mejor buscamos un sitio que esté seco.

MANOLO: Hace frío. ¿Qué hay de beber?

RAMÓN: Sí. Yo también tengo sed.

CLAUDIA: Pues, no traje bebidas. Mejor las compramos aquí, en un puesto.

MANOLO: ¿No trajiste bebidas?

RAMÓN: ¿Qué tal allí? Está seco.

CLAUDIA: Perfecto. Vamos.

RAMÓN: Pongan la comida aquí. ¿Me ayudas?

MANOLO: Tengo sed. ¿Venden bebidas por aquí?

RAMÓN: Manolo, ¿quieres dar una caminata?

MANOLO: ¿Dar una caminata? Quiero un refresco.

RAMÓN: Sí, podemos comprar un refresco también. ¿Quieren acompañarnos?

CLAUDIA: Gracias, pero vamos a quedarnos aquí, a charlar.

MANOLO: Está bien. Vamos.

RAMÓN: ¡Uumm, chuletas de cerdo! ¡Qué olor tan bueno!

MANOLO: Sí. Un poco grasosas, pero muy ricas. ¡Ahora tengo sed y hambre!

RAMÓN: ¿Permiten hacer fogatas aquí?

MANOLO: Pues, parece que sí.

RAMÓN: Vamos por este sendero.

MANOLO: Vamos.

MANOLO: Otro mosquito. Y ahora, una mosca. ¡Uf! No me gustan las moscas ni en el campo ni en el parque.

TERESA: ¿Me pasas las tortillas?

CLAUDIA: Pues, no están aquí.

TERESA: ¿Estás segura?

CLAUDIA: Y tampoco está la carne de res.

TERESA: ¿Y los frijoles?

CLAUDIA: Pues, esta mañana tenía tanta prisa que… olvidé la comida en la mesa.

TERESA: Pues, ¿qué vamos a comer?

MANOLO: Tenemos hambre. ¡Vamos a comer! ¿Podemos ayudar en algo?

TERESA: Tenemos un problema…

RAMÓN: ¿Qué tipo de problema?

CLAUDIA: Toda la comida que preparé…

MANOLO: Sí…

RAMÓN: Por favor…

MANOLO: Bien. Estamos en un parque donde hay muchos puestos y podemos comprar de todo, ¿no? Vamos a comer allí. ¿Qué queremos? Chuletas de cerdo, carne de res, arroz… ¡Que bien! Claudia no puede cocinar muy bien. La comida de aquí, del parque, será mucho mejor…

CLAUDIA: ¿Qué dicen?

MANOLO: Nada…

***GramActiva* Videos, (7:33)**
***Usted* and *ustedes* commands**

FOOTBAL COACH: Mr. Simpson! Photocopy those documents! Mrs. Watermeier, send out that report! Ms. Smith… Ms. Smith… you uh, you… Formal commands aren't as fun as ordering around your football team, but hey, a job's a job.

REAR-VIEW MIRROR GUY: Formal commands are similar to informal commands. Remember them? Let's take a look back and reVIEW them. Get it? ReVIEW? Ha! Rack up another one for the funny machine.

REAR-VIEW MIRROR GUY: To make an informal command, you use the *usted* form of a verb and let *-er* rip.
¡Trae las llaves!
Llena el tanque.
Lava la coche.
All right. But for formal commands, say, to this gas station attendant, it's a little bit different.
¡Traiga las llaves!
Llene el tanque.
Lave el coche.

COACH: To give a command using *usted*, take the present-tense *yo* form of the verb and replace the *-o* at the end with *-e* when it's an *-ar*, like this.

V.O.: *Lavar. Lavo. Lave.*

COACH: If it's an *-er* or *-ir* verb, replace the *yo* form *-o* with an *-a*, like this.

V.O.: *Traer. Traigo. Traiga.*

REAR-VIEW MIRROR GUY: If you want to give a formal command to more than one person, just add an *n*.
Laven el coche.
No tiren las cosas.

Coach: Verbs ending in *-car, -gar,* and *-zar* have spelling changes with the negative *tú* commands. Those same changes also occur with the *usted* and *ustedes* commands. So keep practicing!

V.O.: *Sacar. Saque. Saquen.*

V.O.: *Pagar. Pague. Paguen.*

V.O.: *Cruzar. Cruce. Crucen.*

Coach: All right! Great practicing! Now, one more thing. When you use a pronoun with an affirmative command, the pronoun attaches to the end of the verb. But with negative commands, the pronoun comes right before the verb.

Extras: *Lavamos el coche?*

Coach: *Si, lávenlo.*

¡No! No lo laven.

¡Lávenlo!

¡No! ¡No lo laven!

Quiz

V.O.: Make a command with the following words.

(Ud.) <u>preparar</u> una ensalada.

Prepare una ensalada.

(Uds.) <u>traer</u> la leña.

Traigan la leña.

(Ud.) <u>comprar</u> la harina.

Compre la harina.

Uses of *por*

Therapist: Deep, deep in your subconscious, lie hidden memories of the word *por*. It has many, many uses. When I count to three, you will remember all the different uses of *por*. One. Two. Three.

Host V.O.: Length of distance. Length of time.

Therapist: Good job. Here's a biscuit.

V.O.: *Cocina el pavo por diez minutos.* [Cook the turkey for ten minutes.]

Nosotros manejamos por cien millas. [We drove for a hundred miles.]

Host: You can use *por* to talk about movement through something.

Singer's V.O.: *Paso por el parque, paso por la parque.*

Paso por la letra O, paso por la letra O.

Rear-view mirror guy: You can use *por* to talk about exchanging stuff.

Friend: *¿Cuánto por los peces?*

Rear-view mirror guy: *Diez dólares.*

Guitar Guy: *Por* can be used to show a motive or reason, kind of like the phrase "for the sake of" in English.

Te canto por amor.

La cucaracha, la cucaracha…

Sick Host: *Por* can also be used to show an action done for someone in their place.

¡Estoy enfermo!

Aaron, lava los platos por mí.

Johnnie, arregla el cuarto por tu hermano. Ouch.

Old Man: And finally, another use of por is like the phrase "by means of." *We talked by means of the phone yesterday.* Okay, no one says it that way. We'd say, "We talked on the phone yesterday," but in Spanish it's "We talked by means of the phone."

Nos hablamos por teléfono.

Not now, sonny, I'm explaining grammar.

Here's another example.

Nos escribimos por correo electrónico.

Scarecrow: *¿Hola?*

Host: I sent that letter by plane. *Mandé esa carta por avión.*

Typewriter Host: Fact is, you can find the word *por* just about anywhere: *por ejemplo, por favor, por lo general, por supuesto, por todas partes, por eso, por la mañana, por la tarde, por la noche, por primera vez.* Ah! One more place where you can find the word *por*. On the quiz.

Quiz

V.O.: Match the reasons and the sentences to explain the use of *por*:

Pagué poco por el coche.

On behalf… In exchange for.

In exchange for.

Viajé por avión.

By means of… through.

By means of.

Trabajé por tres horas.

On behalf of… Length of time.

Length of time.

Videomisterio: *En busca de la verdad,* Episodio 10, (8:23)

Turrón: …Este archivo contiene las respuestas a todas sus preguntas. Su abuelo, Federico Zúñiga, fue un gran hombre…

Roberto: ¿Fue?

Turrón: Su abuelo murió hace muchos años, en la Segunda Guerra Mundial. Murió como soldado en el ejército de los Estados Unidos.

Roberto: Yo sabía que él entró al ejército, pero esto…

Turrón: Lo que usted no sabe es que su abuelo murió como un héroe.

Roberto: ¿Qué dice Ud.?

Turrón: Mire… Este archivo contiene todo lo que su abuelo dejó.

Linda: ¿Quién es esta mujer?

Roberto: Creo que es… Sí, es mi abuela Nela.

Turrón: Ésta es la cuenta de ahorro de su abuelo. Está cerrada, pero el dinero todavía está allí. Una póliza de seguro, nombrando como beneficiaria a su esposa, Nela, o en su ausencia, a cualquier miembro sobreviviente de su familia. Y esto es quizás lo más importante, que nadie se presentó a recibir durante tantos años: una Medalla de honor de los EE UU. Jóvenes, gracias a Uds., ya podemos cerrar este caso.

Roberto: Señor, ¿podemos llevarnos todo esto?

Turrón: Por supuesto. Esto le pertenece a su familia. Sólo necesitamos hacer copias de los documentos.

Roberto: Tengo que regresar a Guanajuato, con mi familia.

Roberto's V.O.: Al fin iba a volver a México con la verdad sobre mi abuelo.

Linda: Qué bien que por fin se resolvió este misterio.

Carmen: Roberto, cuando llegues a Guanajuato, no olvides de saludar a tu mamá y a toda la familia de nuestra parte.

Roberto: Es increíble, todo lo que ha pasado. Y, Linda, todo comenzó con tu viaje a México. Sin ti, no sé…

Linda: Ha sido una gran aventura.

Roberto: Pero no va a ser la última.

Linda: Claro que no. Nos volveremos a ver en la primavera, con el intercambio y todo. Aquí y en Guanajuato.

Roberto: Sí. Son sólo unos meses. Estaremos en contacto. Señora, muchas gracias por todo. Paco…

Paco: La próxima vez vamos a jugar al fútbol, eh…

Roberto: Claro. Linda, gracias por todo. Cuídate mucho.

Linda: Tu también.

Tomás: Bienvenido, hijo.

Roberto: Hola, papá. Aquí traigo las respuestas a todas nuestras preguntas sobre el abuelo.

Tomás: Todos estos años sin saber nada… Nunca me ha gustado tocar el pasado, pero esta vez tú has tenido la razón. Gracias, hijo.

Roberto: ¿Ya hablaron con la abuela?

Berta: Por supuesto. Nos está esperando. Vamos a ir a visitarla esta noche.

Nela: Nunca me imaginé todo esto. Tanto tiempo… tanto tiempo. Pero como dicen, mejor tarde que nunca.

Roberto: Así es. Ahora ya sabemos que Federico murió como un héroe.

Tomás: Y que sentía un profundo amor por México y por su familia mexicana.

Nela: Muchas gracias, Roberto y gracias a todos por estar aquí en un momento tan importante para mí. Ahora ya sabemos que Federico fue un hombre muy bueno. Por fin se ha resuelto el misterio de mi vida. Esta medalla… Ahora regreso.

Nela: Federico…

Federico: Ahora ya sabes la verdad, Nela. Por qué no regresé y por qué nunca te llamé. No me olvides…

Tomás: Mamá, ¿estás bien?

Nela: Sí, sí, hijo. Ahora voy.

Nela: ¡Y ahora hay que celebrar, por la memoria de Federico! A ver, Dani, pon algo de música. Berta, en la cocina hay un pastel; tráelo. Y tú, Tomás, ayúdale. ¿Y Roberto? ¿Dónde está Roberto?

Sofía: Mire, le traje estos dulces, Señora Toledo.

Nela: Puedes llamarme Señora Zúñiga.

Roberto's V.O.: Y así es como termina esta historia. Gracias a la ayuda de Linda, yo fui en busca de la verdad sobre mi abuelo Federico y la encontré. En cuanto a Linda y yo… bueno, ésa es otra historia.

Roberto: ¿Linda? Hola, ¿como estás…?

Nombre ____________________

Fecha ____________________

Communicative Pair Activity **7B-1**

Estudiante **A**

Each of us has his or her own eating preferences. Write your answers to the following questions on line A. Then ask your partner the same questions and record his or her answers on line B.

1. ¿Qué clase de comidas prefieres, las picantes o las no picantes?
   A. ____________________
   B. ____________________
2. Cuando sales a cenar con tu familia, ¿qué tipo de restaurante prefieres?
   A. ____________________
   B. ____________________
3. ¿Te gustan las verduras frescas o enlatadas?
   A. ____________________
   B. ____________________
4. ¿Dónde hacen las compras de comida en tu casa?
   A. ____________________
   B. ____________________
5. ¿Cuando vas de cámping con tus amigos(as), te gusta cocinar o llevar sándwiches?
   A. ____________________
   B. ____________________
6. ¿Cuál es tu comida favorita?
   A. ____________________
   B. ____________________
7. ¿Qué te gusta más, las verduras, la carne o los postres?
   A. ____________________
   B. ____________________
8. ¿Cuál es tu fruta favorita? ¿Puedes hacer jugo de ella?
   A. ____________________
   B. ____________________

Nombre ______________________

Communicative Pair Activity **7B-1**

Fecha ______________________ Estudiante **B**

Each of us has his or her own eating preferences. Write your answers to the following questions on line A. Then ask your partner the same questions and record his or her answers on line B.

1. ¿Qué comida del día es tu favorita, el desayuno, el almuerzo o la cena?
   A. ______________________
   B. ______________________
2. ¿Sabes preparar algún plato? ¿Cuál es el ingrediente principal?
   A. ______________________
   B. ______________________
3. ¿Te gusta comer al aire libre, en un picnic? ¿Por qué?
   A. ______________________
   B. ______________________
4. ¿Qué es lo que más te gusta de comer en un restaurante?
   A. ______________________
   B. ______________________
5. ¿Prefieres los jugos de frutas naturales o los refrescos?
   A. ______________________
   B. ______________________
6. ¿Qué te gusta comer en el desayuno?
   A. ______________________
   B. ______________________
7. Escribe algunas de las comidas que comiste esta semana en la escuela.
   A. ______________________
   B. ______________________
8. ¿Cómo prefieres tus sándwiches? ¿Te gustan con tomate, lechuga y queso?
   A. ______________________
   B. ______________________

Nombre ______________________

Fecha ______________________

Communicative Pair Activity **7B-2**
Estudiante **A**

You are going to spend the weekend camping with a group from your school at a remote lake. Although there are separate cabins for the boys and the girls, there is only one bathroom, one mirror, and a very small eating area. You and your partner decide it is necessary to make a schedule. When you check, you discover that your notes are incomplete. Ask your partner questions based on your notes. Follow the model.

¿A qué hora se despierta Valeria?

¿A qué hora se desayuna Valeria?

¿Cuándo se peina Valeria?

¿Cuándo se baña Valeria?

¿A qué hora se acuesta Valeria?

Yo
Despertarse: 6:15 A.M.
Desayunar:
Peinarse:
Bañarse: por la mañana
Acostarse:

Mi compañero(a)
Despertarse:
Desayunar: 7:00 A.M.
Peinarse: después de despertarse
Bañarse:
Acostarse: 10:45 P.M.

Valeria
Despertarse: 6:00 A.M.
Desayunar: 6:30 A.M.
Peinarse: antes de desayunar
Bañarse:
Acostarse:

Camilo
Despertarse: 7:15 A.M.
Desayunar:
Peinarse:
Bañarse:
Acostarse: 10:00 P.M.

Realidades 2

Capítulo 7B

Nombre ____________________

Fecha ____________________

Communicative Pair Activity **7B-2**

Estudiante **B**

You are going to spend the weekend camping with a group from your school at a remote lake. Although there are separate cabins for the boys and the girls, there is only one bathroom, one mirror, and a very small eating area. You and your partner decide it is necessary to make a schedule. When you check, you discover that your notes are incomplete. Ask your partner questions based on your notes. Follow the model.

¿A qué hora se despierta Valeria?

¿A qué hora se desayuna Valeria?

¿Cuándo se peina Valeria?

¿Cuándo se baña Valeria?

¿A qué hora se acuesta Valeria?

Yo
Despertarse: 6:30 A.M.
Desayunar:
Peinarse:
Bañarse: por la noche
Acostarse:

Mi compañero(a)
Despertarse:
Desayunar: 6:45 A.M.
Peinarse: después de desayunar
Bañarse:
Acostarse: 10:15 P.M.

Valeria
Despertarse:
Desayunar:
Peinarse:
Bañarse: por la noche
Acostarse: 10:30 P.M.

Camilo
Despertarse:
Desayunar: 7:45 A.M.
Peinarse: antes de desayunar
Bañarse: por la mañana
Acostarse:

Situation Cards

Capítulo 7B **Realidades 2** **1A**

Talking about food preferences

You are talking to a friend from Mexico and you want to know what they traditionally eat there.

— Ask your friend what is a typical Mexican meal.

— Ask him or her if Mexican food is always very spicy.

— Ask him or her if he or she knows food from the United States.

Capítulo 7B **Realidades 2** **1B**

Talking about food preferences

Pretend you are from Mexico and you are talking to a friend about Mexican food.

— Respond to your friend's questions.

— Then, ask him or her to tell you two typical dishes of the United States.

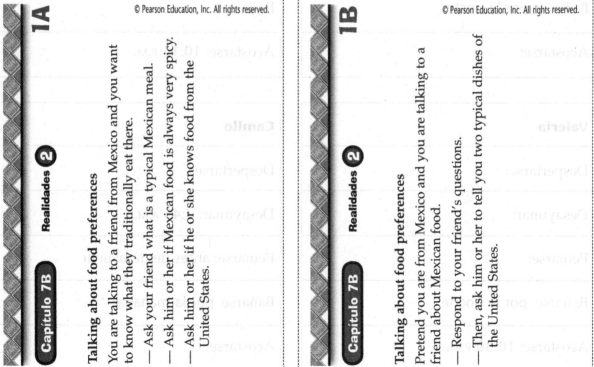

Capítulo 7B **Realidades 2** **2A**

Talking about food preferences

You are talking with a friend about the best hot dog. Ask him or her questions to find out how he or she prefers to eat them.

— Ask your friend if he or she likes hot dogs with onions.

— Respond to your friend's question. Then ask him or her if he or she likes them with mustard and ketchup.

— Respond to your friend's question. Ask him or her if he or she prefers hot dogs or hamburgers.

Capítulo 7B **Realidades 2** **2B**

Talking about food preferences

You are talking with a friend about the best hot dog. Ask him or her questions to find out how he or she prefers to eat them.

— Respond to your friend's question. Then ask him or her if he or she likes hot dogs boiled or baked.

— Respond to your friend's question. Ask him or her if he or she likes hot dogs with cheese.

— Respond to your friend's question.

GramActiva

¿Te gusta comer al aire libre?

¿Adentro o al aire libre?, p. 381

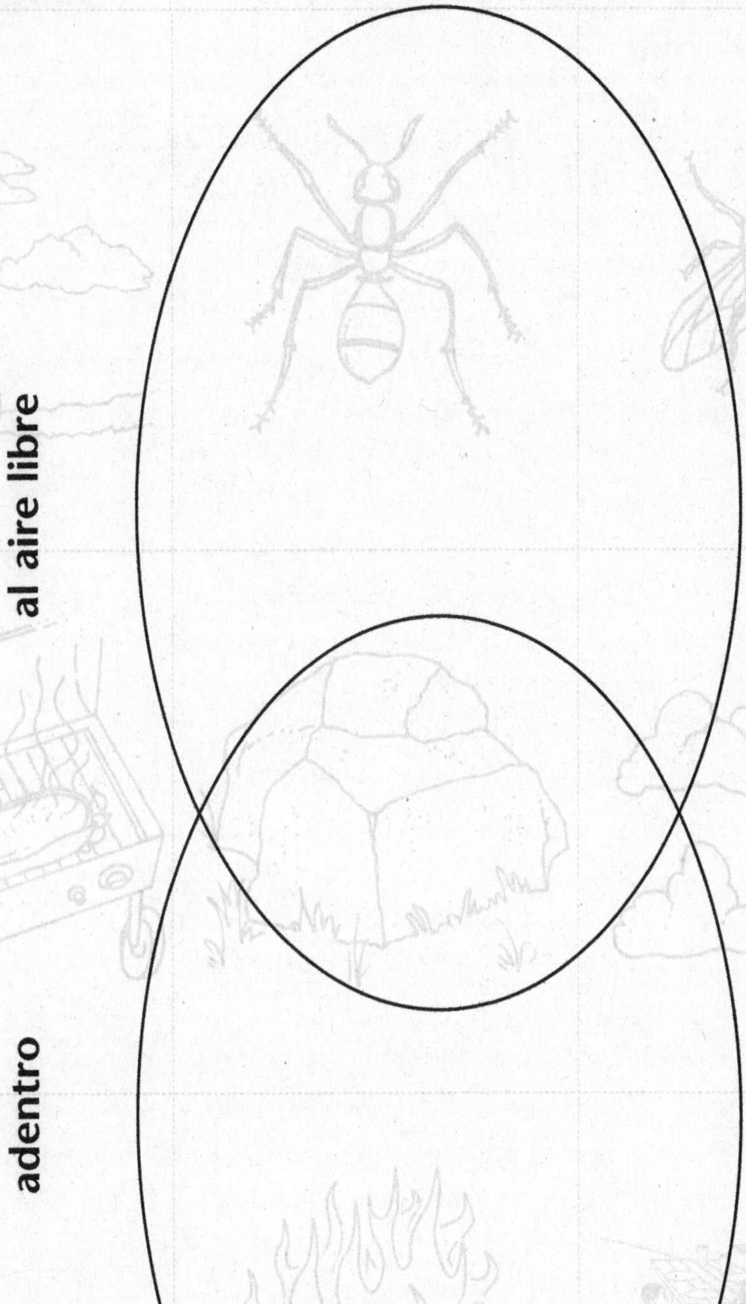

Vocabulary Clip Art

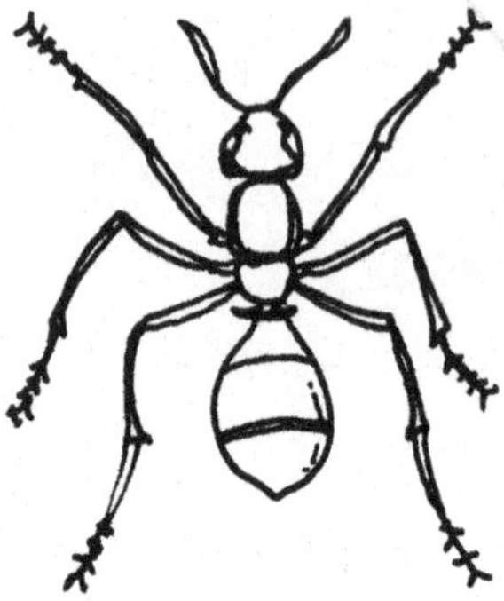

Vocabulary Clip Art

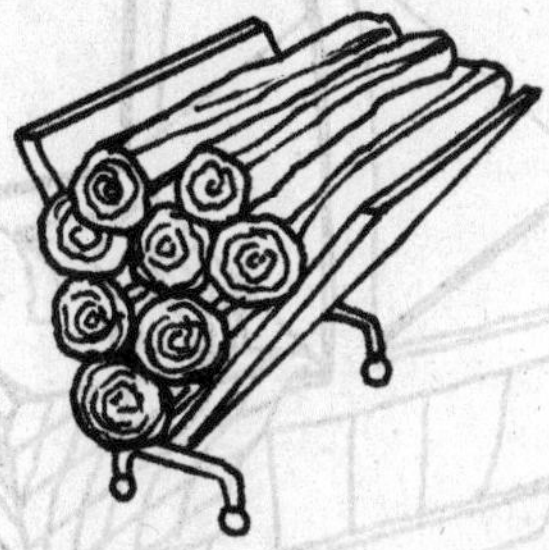

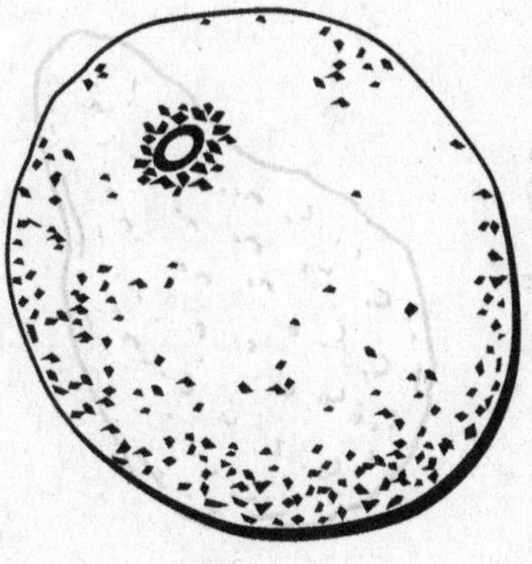

Vocabulary Clip Art

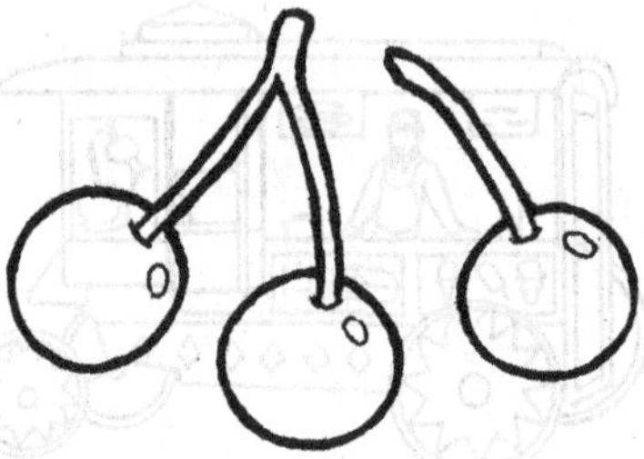

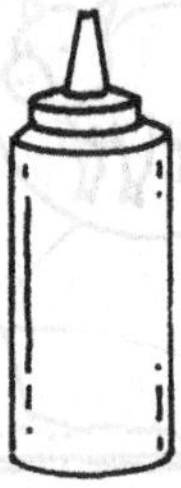

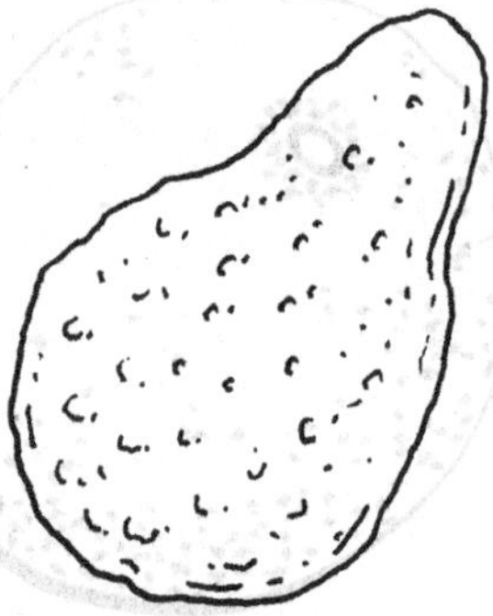

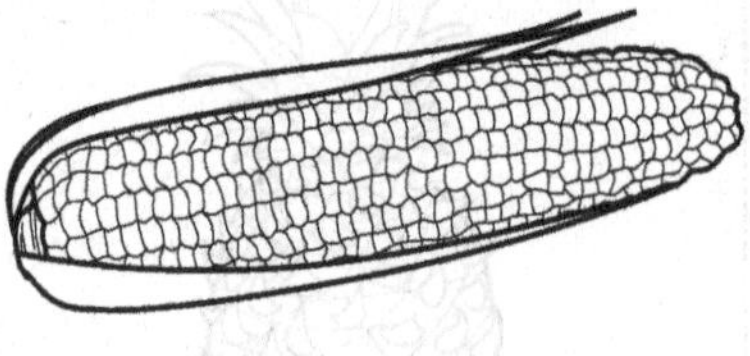

Vocabulary Clip Art

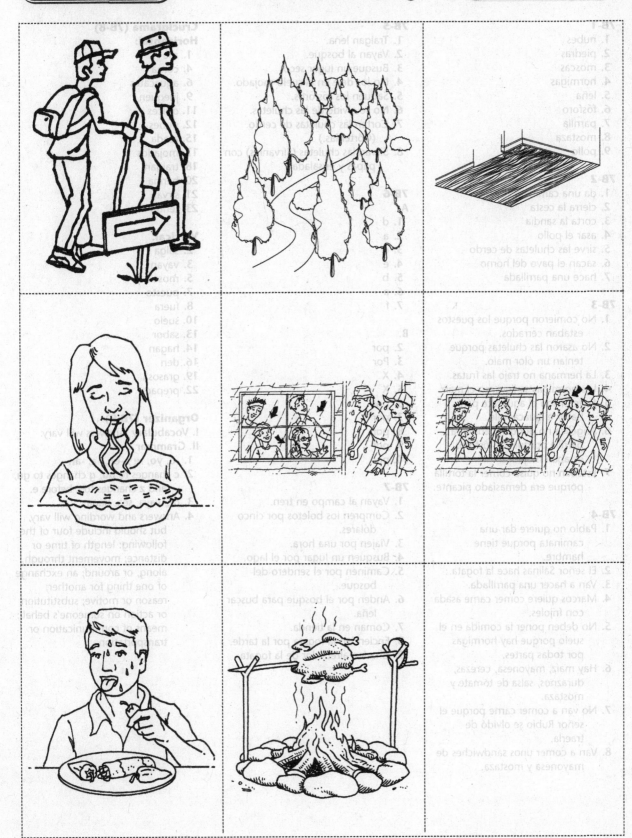

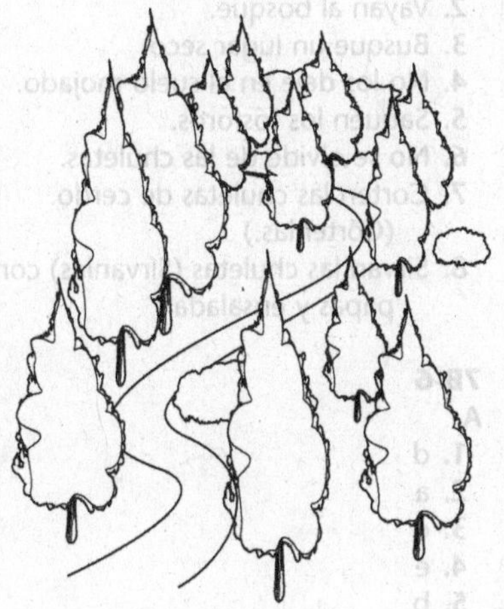

Capítulo 7B

Core Practice Answers

7B-1
1. nubes
2. piedras
3. moscas
4. hormigas
5. leña
6. fósforo
7. parrilla
8. mostaza
9. pollo

7B-2
1. da una caminata
2. cierra la cesta
3. corta la sandía
4. asar el pollo
5. sirve las chuletas de cerdo
6. sacan el pavo del horno
7. hace una parrillada

7B-3
1. No comieron porque los puestos estaban cerrados.
2. No asaron las chuletas porque tenían un olor malo.
3. La hermana no trajo las frutas.
4. Las hormigas se llevaron el maíz.
5. Se le olvidó el aguacate para hacer el guacamole.
6. Angélica no pudo encender la parrilla porque los fósforos estaban mojados.
7. Esteban no quiso comer la tortilla porque era demasiado picante.

7B-4
1. Pablo no quiere dar una caminata porque tiene hambre.
2. El señor Salinas hace la fogata.
3. Van a hacer una parrillada.
4. Marcos quiere comer carne asada con frijoles.
5. No deben poner la comida en el suelo porque hay hormigas por todas partes.
6. Hay maíz, mayonesa, cerezas, duraznos, salsa de tomate y mostaza.
7. No van a comer carne porque el señor Rubio se olvidó de traerla.
8. Van a comer unos sándwiches de mayonesa y mostaza.

7B-5
1. Traigan leña.
2. Vayan al bosque.
3. Busque un lugar seco.
4. No los deje en el suelo mojado.
5. Saquen los fósforos.
6. No se olvide de las chuletas.
7. Corten las chuletas de cerdo. (Córtenlas.)
8. Sirvan las chuletas (Sírvanlas) con papas y ensalada.

7B-6

A.
1. d
2. a
3. c
4. e
5. b
6. a
7. f

B.
2. por
3. Por
4. X
5. X
6. por
7. por
8. por
9. por
10. por

7B-7
1. Vayan al campo en tren.
2. Compren los boletos por cinco dólares.
3. Viajen por una hora.
4. Busquen un lugar por el lago.
5. Caminen por el sendero del bosque.
6. Anden por el bosque para buscar leña.
7. Coman en la tienda.
8. Enciendan la fogata por la tarde.
9. Charlen alrededor de la fogata.

Crucigrama (7B-8)

Horizontal:
1. ase
4. coma
6. aguacates
9. jueguen
11. dulces
12. nubes
15. asada
17. mojados
18. traigan
20. harina
21. sirvan
23. tenga

Vertical:
2. salga
3. vayan
5. moscas
7. puesto
8. fuera
10. suelo
13. sabor
14. hagan
16. den
19. grasosa
22. prepare

Organizer (7B-9)

I. Vocabulary Answers will vary.

II. Grammar
1. **-o, yo, -e , -en, -a, -an**
2. **c** changes to **qu**, **g** changes to **gu**, and **z** changes to **c** before **e**.
3. dé, vaya, sea, haga
4. Answers and wording will vary, but should include four of the following: length of time or distance; movement through, along, or around; an exchange of one thing for another; reason or motive; substitution or action on someone's behalf; means of communication or transportation

Realidades 2 | Nombre ____________ | Hora ______

Capítulo 7B | Fecha ____________ | **Vocabulary Flash Cards, Sheet 1**

Write the Spanish vocabulary word or phrase below each picture. Be sure to include the article for each noun.

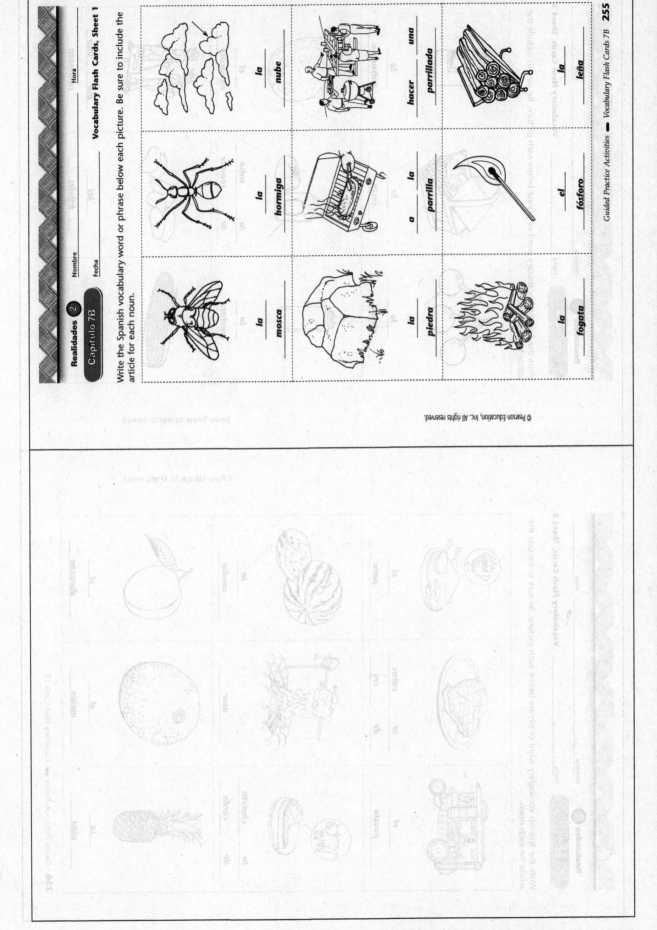

 ***la mosca***	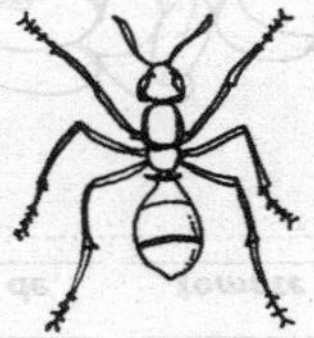 ***la hormiga***	 ***la nube***
 ***la piedra***	 ***a la parrilla***	 ***hacer una parrillada***
 ***la fogata***	 ***el fósforo***	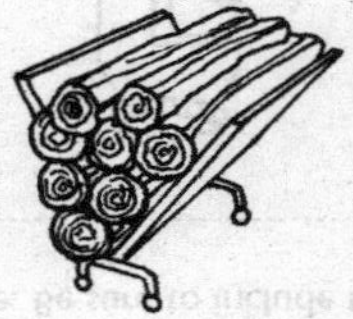 ***la leña***

Realidades 2 | Capítulo 7B

Nombre ____________ Hora ______

Fecha ____________

Vocabulary Flash Cards, Sheet 2

Write the Spanish vocabulary word or phrase below each picture. Be sure to include the article for each noun.

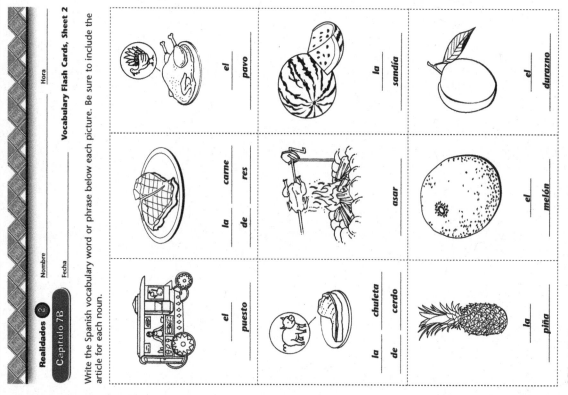

 *el puesto*	 *la carne de res*	 *el pavo*
 *la chuleta de cerdo*	 *asar*	 *la sandía*
 *la piña*	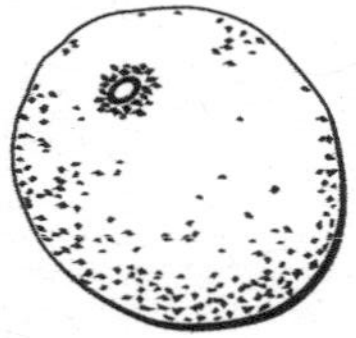 *el melón*	 *el durazno*

Realidades 2 | Capítulo 7B

Nombre ____________ Hora ______

Fecha ____________

Vocabulary Flash Cards, Sheet 3

Write the Spanish vocabulary word or phrase below each picture. Be sure to include the article for each noun.

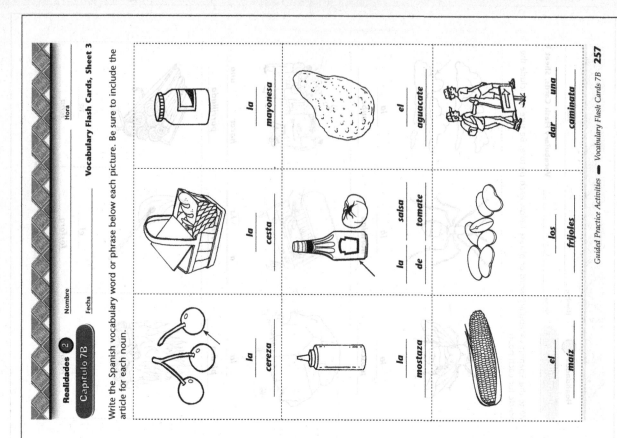

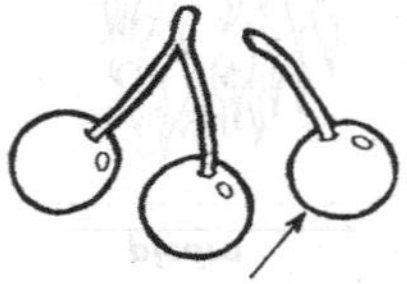 *la cereza*	 *la cesta*	 *la mayonesa*
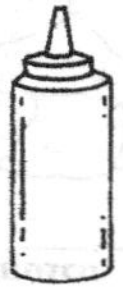 *la mostaza*	 *la salsa de tomate*	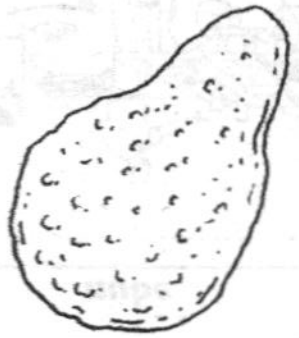 *el aguacate*
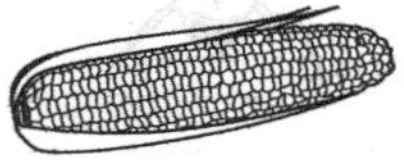 *el maíz*	 *los frijoles*	 *dar una caminata*

Realidades 2 | Nombre ______ | Hora ______

Capítulo 7B | Fecha ______

Vocabulary Flash Cards, Sheet 4

Write the Spanish vocabulary word below each picture. If there is a word or phrase, copy it in the space provided. Be sure to include the article for each noun.

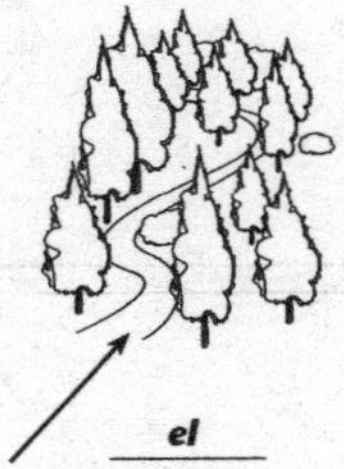 *el* *sendero*	 *el* *olor*	 *secos*, *secas*
 *picante*	 *mojados*, *mojadas*	**asado, asada** *asado*, *asada*
fuera (de) *fuera* *(de)*	**dentro de** *dentro* *de*	**el cielo** *el* *cielo*

Realidades 2 | Nombre ______ | Hora ______

Capítulo 7B | Fecha ______

Vocabulary Flash Cards, Sheet 5

Copy the word or phrase in the space provided. Be sure to include the article for each noun. These blank cards can be used to write and practice other Spanish vocabulary for the chapter.

la harina *la* *harina*	**dulce** *dulce*	**grasoso, grasosa** *grasoso*, *grasosa*
acompañar *acompañar*	**al aire libre** *al* *aire* *libre*	**el suelo** *el* *suelo*
el sabor *el* *sabor*		

Vocabulary Flash Cards, Sheet 6

These blank cards can be used to write and practice other Spanish vocabulary for the chapter.

______	______	______
______	______	______
______	______	______

Vocabulary Check, Sheet 1

Tear out this page. Write the English words on the lines. Fold the paper along the dotted line to see the correct answers so you can check your work.

al aire libre	***outdoors***
el cielo	***sky***
dentro de	***inside***
fuera (de)	***outside***
la nube	***cloud***
la piedra	***rock***
el aguacate	***avocado***
la chuleta de cerdo	***pork chop***
los frijoles	***beans***
la harina	***flour***
el maíz	***corn***
el sabor	***taste***
dulce	***sweet***
picante	***spicy***
acompañar	***to accompany***

Fold In ↓

Realidades 2 | Nombre | Hora

Capítulo 7B | Fecha

Vocabulary Check, Sheet 2

Tear out this page. Write the Spanish words on the lines. Fold the paper along the dotted line to see the correct answers so you can check your work.

outdoors	***al aire libre***
sky	***el cielo***
inside	***dentro de***
outside	***fuera (de)***
cloud	***la nube***
rock	***la piedra***
avocado	***el aguacate***
pork chop	***la chuleta de cerdo***
beans	***los frijoles***
flour	***la harina***
corn	***el maíz***
taste	***el sabor***
sweet	***dulce***
spicy	***picante***
to accompany	***acompañar***

Fold In

Realidades 2 | Nombre | Hora

Capítulo 7B | Fecha

Vocabulary Check, Sheet 3

Tear out this page. Write the English words on the lines. Fold the paper along the dotted line to see the correct answers so you can check your work.

el sendero	***trail***
el suelo	***ground, floor***
la fogata	***bonfire***
el fósforo	***match***
la leña	***firewood***
a la parrilla	***on the grill***
el puesto	***(food) stand***
asado, asada	***grilled***
asar	***to grill, to roast***
la carne de res	***steak***
la cereza	***cherry***
la cesta	***basket***
la mayonesa	***mayonnaise***
la mostaza	***mustard***

Fold In

Tear out this page. Write the Spanish words on the lines. Fold the paper along the dotted line to see the correct answers so you can check your work.

trail	*el sendero*
ground, floor	*el suelo*
bonfire	*la fogata*
match	*el fósforo*
firewood	*la leña*
on the grill	*a la parrilla*
(food) stand	*el puesto*
grilled	*asado, asada*
to grill, to roast	*asar*
steak	*la carne de res*
cherry	*la cereza*
basket	*la cesta*
mayonnaise	*la mayonesa*
mustard	*la mostaza*

Fold In ←

To hear a complete list of the vocabulary for this chapter, go to www.realidades.com and type in the Web Code jdd-0799. Then click on **Repaso del capítulo.**

Usted and *ustedes* commands (p. 382)

- Use the **usted** command form to tell someone older than you what to do or what *not* to do. Use the **ustedes** form to tell a group of people what to do or what *not* to do.
  Coma Ud. el arroz. **Beban Uds. la leche.**
- **-ar** verbs use **-e** for **Ud.** commands, and **-en** for **Uds.** commands; **-er** and **-ir** verbs use **-a** for **Ud.** commands, and **-an** for **Uds.** commands.
- The commands for **viajar, comer,** and **servir** are shown below.

verbs ending in *-ar*			verbs ending in *-er*			verbs ending in *-ir*		
viajar	usted	ustedes	comer	usted	ustedes	servir	usted	ustedes
yo viajo	viaje	viajen	yo como	coma	coman	yo sirvo	sirva	sirvan

A. Write the correct ending for the **usted** or **ustedes** command form for each of the infinitives below. The first one is done for you.

1. abrir — abr *an* Uds.
2. batir — bat *a* Ud.
3. calentar — calient *e* Ud.
4. entrar — entr *en* Uds.
5. añadir — añad *an* Uds.
6. tirar — tir *e* Ud.
7. hervir — hierv *an* Uds.
8. pelar — pel *e* Ud.

B. Write the correct **usted** or **ustedes** command form for each sentence using the verbs in parentheses. Follow the model.

Modelo (hervir) No *hierva* Ud. el agua.

1. (cortar) No *corte* Ud. los huevos.
2. (preparar) No *preparen* Uds. el desayuno.
3. (freír) No *fríen* Uds. el pescado.
4. (probar) No *pruebe* Ud. el tocino.
5. (encender) No *encienda* Ud. el horno.

realidades.com
• Web Code: jdd-0713

Usted and *ustedes* commands (*continued*)

- Affirmative and negative **usted** and **ustedes** commands have the same spelling changes and irregular forms as the negative **tú** commands:

(hacer)	**Haga Ud.**	**Hagan Uds.**
(buscar)	**Busque Ud.**	**Busquen Uds.**
(almorzar)	**Almuerce Ud.**	**Almuercen Uds.**

C. Write the correct **usted/ustedes** command for each verb in parentheses. Follow the model.

Modelo (poner) *Pongan* Uds. los platos en el fregadero.

1. (hacer) ***Hagan*** Uds. un picnic para sus amigos.
2. (picar) No ***pique*** Ud. el durazno.
3. (buscar) No ***busque*** Ud. la fogata sin leña.
4. (tener) ***Tenga*** Ud. cuidado con las hormigas.
5. (almorzar) No ***almuercen*** Uds. sin vasos.

- If you want to use a pronoun such as **lo, la, los,** or **las** with an affirmative command, attach it to the end of the command. You will need to add a written accent mark in the commands.

—**¿Dónde ponemos la leña?** *Where do we put the firewood?*

—**Pónganla en un lugar seco.** *Put it in a dry place.*

D. Rewrite the following commands, replacing the underlined words with pronouns (**lo, la, los,** or **las**). Remember to add written accents where necessary. Follow the model.

Modelo Preparen la comida. *Prepárenla*

1. Compre las hamburguesas. ***Cómprelas***
2. Traigan los frijoles. ***Tráiganlos***
3. Busque la leña. ***Búsquela***
4. Asen el pollo. ***Ásenlo***
5. Piquen los tomates. ***Píquenlos***
6. Coma las galletas. ***Cómalas***

Usted and *ustedes* commands (*continued*)

- If you want to use a pronoun with a negative command, put it right before the command.

—**¿Encendemos la fogata?** *Should we light the fire?*

—**No, no la enciendan.** *No, don't light it.*

E. Eugenia and señora López are discussing some things students shouldn't do when camping. Fill in señora López's responses with the correct **usted/ustedes** command forms of the verbs in parentheses. The first one is done for you.

1. EUGENIA: ¿Lavamos las ollas aquí? (lavar)
   SEÑORA LÓPEZ: No, *no los laven* allí.
2. EUGENIA: ¿Traemos la mostaza para encender el fuego? (traer)
   SEÑORA LÓPEZ: No, ***no la traigan*** para encender el fuego.
3. EUGENIA: ¿Sacamos los fósforos ahora? (sacar)
   SEÑORA LÓPEZ: No, ***no los saquen*** ahora.
4. EUGENIA: ¿Buscamos un parque en la ciudad para la fogata? (buscar)
   SEÑORA LÓPEZ: No, ***no lo busquen*** en la ciudad.
5. EUGENIA: ¿Servimos las chuletas luego? (servir)
   SEÑORA LÓPEZ: No, ***no las sirven*** luego.
6. EUGENIA: ¿Dejamos los fósforos en el bosque? (dejar)
   SEÑORA LÓPEZ: No, ***no los dejen*** en el bosque.

Uses of *por* (p. 386)

The preposition **por** is used in many ways.

- To tell about time or distance: **Yo dormí por ocho horas.** *I slept for eight hours.*
- To tell about movement: **Vamos a caminar por el sendero.** *Let's walk along the path.*
- To tell about exchanging one thing for another: **No pagué mucho por la piña.** *I didn't pay much for the pineapple.*
- To tell about a reason: **Yo fui al mercado por unas cerezas.** *I went to the market for some cherries.*
- To tell about an action on someone's behalf: **Encendí la parrilla por Luisa.** *I lit the grill for Luisa.*
- To tell about a way of communication or transportation: **¿Vas a viajar por avión?** *Are you going to travel by plane?*

A. Choose the best ending from the word bank to complete each sentence below. Use the context clues given to help you decide. Follow the model.

por avión	~~por tres horas~~	por la leche	por el sendero	por mis padres

Modelo Nosotros preparamos la cena *por tres horas*. (*how much time?*)

1. Vamos a viajar ***por avión***. (*what form of transportation?*)
2. Voy a cocinar ***por mis padres***. (*on whose behalf?*)
3. Tú vas a caminar ***por el sendero***. (*how did you move?*)
4. Voy a la tienda ***por la leche***. (*for what?*)

B. Each of these sentences below ends with an expression that uses **por.** Write the letter of the best ending for each sentence.

1. Yo dormí ***b***.
   a. por la camisa **b.** por dos horas
2. Lupe va a la tienda ***b***.
   a. por avión **b.** por el periódico
3. Me gusta viajar ***b***.
   a. por dos tomates **b.** por avión
4. ¿Cuánto dinero pagaste ***b***?
   a. por el sendero **b.** por esa piña
5. Voy a preparar la carne ***a***.
   a. por mi hermano **b.** por teléfono

Lectura: El Yunque (pp. 390–391)

A. Your textbook reading is about a national park called **El Yunque.** What kind of things do you think you'll read about in the reading? Add two more questions to the list about things you think the reading may describe.

¿Dónde está el parque? ¿Qué hay en el parque? ¿Qué tipos de plantas hay?

Answers will vary. , ______

B. Read the following selections from the reading about **El Yunque.** As you read, find answers to some of the questions in **part A** and write them below.

> *El Yunque es una de las atracciones más visitadas de Puerto Rico. . . . Más de 240 especies de árboles coexisten con animales exóticos, como el coquí y la boa de Puerto Rico.*

> *La mejor forma de explorar este parque es caminando por las varias veredas (paths) que pasan por el bosque.*

1. ¿Dónde está el parque? El parque ésta en ***Puerto Rico***.
2. ¿Qué hay en el parque? Hay ***muchos árboles y animales exóticos (como el coquí y la boa) de Puerto Rico***
3. ¿Qué tipos de plantas hay? Hay ***más de 240 especies de árboles***

C. Look at the following advice from the reading about walking in **El Yunque.** After you read the selection, place a ✓ next to those sentences that are true.

> *Consejos para el caminante*
> *1 Nunca camine solo. Siempre vaya acompañado.*
> *2 Traiga agua y algo para comer.*
> *3 Use repelente para insectos.*
> *4 No abandone las veredas para no perderse (to get lost).*
> *5 No toque (touch) las plantas del bosque.*

1. Never walk alone in the park. ✓
2. Don't take food or water with you. ______
3. Use insect repellent. ✓
4. Don't walk along the paths. ______
5. Touch the plants in the forest. ______

Presentación escrita (p. 393)

Task: You will write and illustrate a poster on safety and fun at an outdoor cookout.

A. Read and circle the sentences below that tell about something you need for an outdoor cookout. ***Answers may vary but students should underline nos. 1, 2, 4, and 6.***

1. Se necesitan fósforos.
2. Se debe comprar carne.
3. Se debe buscar un lugar mojado.
4. Se necesita leña.
5. Se debe llevar regla y lápiz.
6. Se debe comprar agua o refrescos.
7. Se debe mirar una película.

B. Now, read and circle the commands below that provide good advice before, during, and after a cookout.

1. Tengan cuidado con la parrilla caliente.
2. Lleven sus videojuegos.
3. Compren carne para asar.
4. Busquen un lugar seco para hacer la fogata.
5. Lleven repelente para mosquitos.
6. No jueguen cerca de un lago.
7. No tiren nada en el parque.
8. No apaguen la fogata antes de salir.

C. Using your answers from **parts A** and **B**, write a short paragraph. Mention how to stay safe and have fun before, during, and after the cookout. You may use the sentence starters below.

Antes de hacer una parrillada, ustedes necesitan ____

El lugar debe ____

Para hacer la fogata deben ____

No jueguen ustedes con ____

Antes de salir, ____

D. Review the spelling and vocabulary on your poster. Check that your paragraph includes the appropriate commands and is easy to understand.

E. Use artwork to illustrate your sentences on the poster.

Realidades 2 Nombre ______ Hora ______

Capítulo 7B Fecha ______ **VIDEO**

Antes de ver el video

Actividad 1

Make a list of six things you would bring to a picnic.

1. Answers will vary.
2.
3.
4.
5.
6.

Now, name three activities you might do on a picnic.

1. Answers will vary.
2.
3.

Finally, name two things that could happen to spoil your picnic.

1. Answers will vary.
2.

¿Comprendes?

Actividad 2

All of the following sentences are incorrect. Rewrite them to make them correct.

1. Manolo es del campo y no le gusta comer en la ciudad.
   Manolo es de la ciudad y no le gusta comer en el campo.

2. Claudia trae en la canasta toda la comida que preparó.
   Claudia no trae nada en la canasta.

Realidades 2 Nombre ______ Hora ______

Capítulo 7B Fecha ______ **VIDEO**

3. Los muchachos van al parque en el coche de Claudia.
   Los muchachos van al parque en autobús.

4. En el parque nadie hace fogatas.
   En el parque, muchos hacen fogatas or En el parque, no está prohibido hacer fogatas.

5. En el parque no hay puestos de comida; no pueden comprar nada.
   En el parque hay muchos puestos y pueden comprar de todo.

6. A Manolo le encanta la comida que hace Claudia.
   Manolo piensa que Claudia no cocina muy bien.

Actividad 3

Answer the following questions in complete sentences based on the video.

1. ¿Por qué a Manolo no le gusta comer en el campo?
   A Manolo no le gusta comer en el campo porque no le gustan ni las moscas ni los mosquitos.
2. ¿Por qué Claudia no puede darles bebidas a los amigos?
   Claudia no puede darles bebidas porque no las trajo.
3. ¿Por qué escogen un sitio para sentarse por fin?
   Escogen un sitio porque está seco y no quieren un sitio mojado.
4. ¿Quiénes dan una caminata por el parque?
   Manolo y Ramón dan la caminata por el parque.
5. ¿Qué comida trajo Claudia? ¿Por qué?
   Claudia no trajo ninguna comida porque se le olvidó.

Y, ¿qué más?

Actividad 4

Picnics are a fun summer activity. Make a list telling what kind of food and beverage you like to bring to a picnic, who you like to invite, and where you like to have it. Use complete sentences. The first one has been done for you.

1. *Me gusta traer una canasta con mucha comida cuando quiero hacer un picnic.*
2. Answers will vary.
3. ______
4. ______
5. ______
6. ______
7. ______

Actividad 5

The Cruz and Ramos families are getting together for their annual barbecue. Listen as they talk about what they brought in their picnic baskets. As you listen to each family member talk about a particular food item, look at the pictures below of the picnic baskets. Then, write **C** in the blank if you think a member of the Cruz family is speaking, and write **R** in the blank if you think a member of the Ramos family is speaking. You will hear each set of statements twice.

1. C
2. C
3. R
4. R
5. C
6. R
7. C
8. R

Realidades 2 | Nombre | Hora

Capítulo 7B | Fecha | AUDIO

Actividad 6

Some people prefer the great outdoors and others prefer the comforts of being indoors. As you listen to each conversation, determine whether the person is talking about eating outdoors or inside at a restaurant. Fill in the grid below as you listen. You will hear each set of statements twice.

	1	2	3	4	5	6
	X		X	X		
		X			X	X

Actividad 7

You are helping the Scoutmaster, Sr. Naranjo, assign tasks for the boys in his troop to do at summer camp. Your job is to write each task in the chart below so that each pair of boys knows what to do. You will hear each task twice.

Carlos y Ramón	*Lleven los sacos de dormir.*
1. Dani y Benito	Recojan leña.
2. Adán y Miguel	Busquen piedras.
3. David y Enrique	Preparen la carne de res.
4. Jaime y Pepe	Hagan la ensalada de frutas.
5. Arturo y Benito	Vayan al comedor.
6. Raúl y Tomás	Hagan la fogata.

Realidades 2 | Nombre | Hora

Capítulo 7B | Fecha | AUDIO

Actividad 8

Listen as people talk about what they did on behalf of their friends or relatives last week. As you listen to each conversation, fill in the grid below with the following information: 1) what he or she did; 2) on whose behalf he or she did it; and 3) the amount of time it took. For the first column, choose from the following statements: **a) Preparó una cena; b) Trabajó en una computadora; c) Estudió matemáticas; d) Limpió el apartamento.** You will hear each set of statements twice.

	¿Qué hizo?	¿Por quién lo hizo?	¿Por cuánto tiempo lo hizo?
1.	b	Su hermana mayor	dos horas
2.	d	Su hijo	tres horas
3.	a	Su abuela	cinco horas
4.	c	Su amigo Juan	ocho horas

Actividad 9

Listen as guests on a cruise ship listen to instructions from the Activity Director about the upcoming "ship-to-shore" camping trip. She gives lots of advice on what to do on their expedition. As you listen to each piece of advice, decide whether she is talking about trekking in the woods or getting ready for the evening barbecue and bonfire. Put an X in the correct box below. You will hear each piece of advice twice.

	1	2	3	4	5	6	7	8	9	10
Consejos para el caminante	X			X		X	X			X
Consejos para hacer una barbacoa y fogata		X	X		X			X	X	

Actividad 10

Look at the picture below of the picnic Adriana recently had with her family. Help her write a letter to her pen pal describing the picnic. The letter has been started for you.

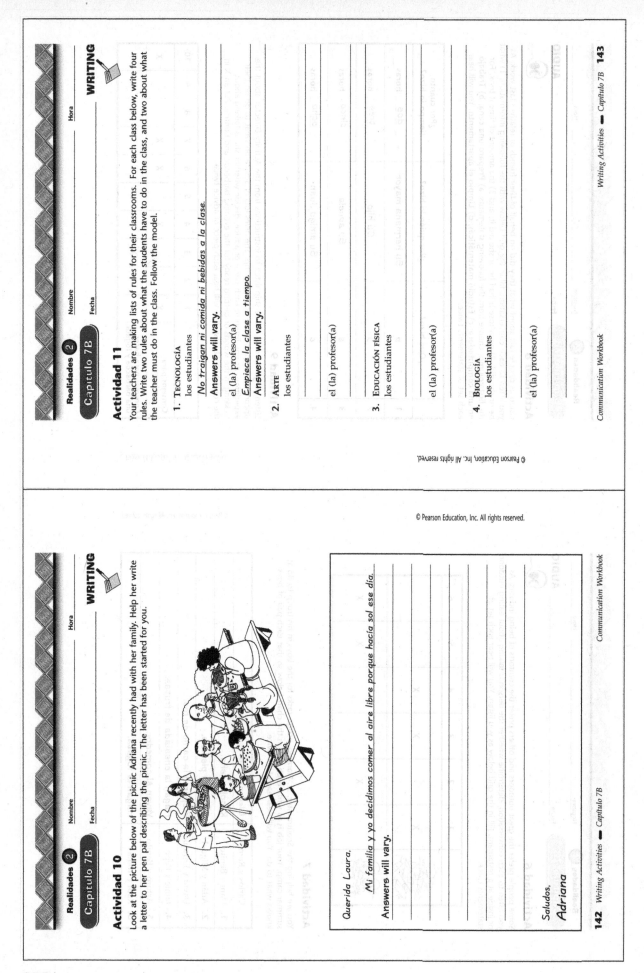

Querida Laura,

Mi familia y yo decidimos comer al aire libre porque hacía sol ese día.

Answers will vary.

Saludos,
Adriana

Actividad 11

Your teachers are making lists of rules for their classrooms. For each class below, write four rules. Write two rules about what the students have to do in the class, and two about what the teacher must do in the class. Follow the model.

1. TECNOLOGÍA
   los estudiantes
   No traigan ni comida ni bebidas a la clase.
   Answers will vary.
   el (la) profesor(a)
   Empiece la clase a tiempo.
   Answers will vary.
2. ARTE
   los estudiantes
   el (la) profesor(a)
3. EDUCACIÓN FÍSICA
   los estudiantes
   el (la) profesor(a)
4. BIOLOGÍA
   los estudiantes
   el (la) profesor(a)

Realidades 2 Nombre Hora

Capítulo 7B Fecha **WRITING**

Actividad 12

Answer the following questions in complete sentences that include the word **por**, where applicable.

Possible answers below.

1. ¿Qué fue la última cosa que compraste? ¿Cuánto pagaste?
   Compré unos pantalones cortos. Pagué veinte dólares por ellos.
2. Por lo general, ¿gastas mucho cuando vas de compras? ¿Por qué?
   Me gusta más andar por la calle porque no me gusta gastar mucho dinero.
3. Cuando quieres mandar una tarjeta a un amigo, ¿cómo la mandas?
   La mando por correo electrónico.
4. ¿Cómo te comunicas con tus amigos durante un viaje?
   Les hablo por teléfono.
5. ¿Cómo viaja tu familia si quiere ir de vacaciones?
   Mi familia viaja en coche.
6. ¿Cuándo fue la última vez que viajaste con tu familia? ¿Por cuánto tiempo estuvieron de vacaciones?
   Mi famila y yo hicimos un viaje el año pasado. Estuvimos allí por una semana.
7. ¿Uds. caminaron mucho allí? Si no, ¿cómo pasaron de un lugar a otro?
   Sí, caminamos por todas partes.
8. ¿Cómo es un día normal para ti? ¿En qué es diferente un día de vacaciones?
   Por la mañana voy a la escuela, por la tarde juego deportes y por la noche ceno con mi familia y hago la tarea.
   Durante las vacaciones no tengo que ir a la escuela. Me divierto por la mañana, por la tarde y por la noche.

Realidades 2 Nombre Hora

Capítulo 7B Fecha **WRITING**

Actividad 13

Your entire Spanish class is coming to your house for a barbecue next weekend. They have asked you to e-mail them and let them know what to bring. Write three complete sentences for each group. Follow the model.

Modelo Celia y Ramón: *Vengan a mi casa a las once. Traigan la mayonesa, la mostaza y la salsa de tomate. No se olviden del cuchillo para servirlos.*

1. La Srta. Arrojo: **Answers will vary.**
2. Catrina, Ramona y Carlos:
3. Luisa y David:

B. Luisa and David would also like to bring a fruit salad, and have asked you to send them the directions from a cookbook for making one. Write at least six instructions you would find in the recipe for making a fruit salad. The first one has been done for you.

Compren las uvas, las manzanas, los plátanos y la piña en el supermercado.

Answers will vary.

Realidades 2

Capítulo 7B

Test Preparation Answers

Reading Skills
p. 268 2. **C**
p. 269 2. **A**

Integrated Performance Assessment
p. 270
Answers will vary.

Practice Test: Flan de piña
p. 272

1. D
2. F
3. B
4. J
5. Las respuestas variarán sobre los ingredientes y si se usan en postres típicos de los Estados Unidos o de otros países. Compruebe que los estudiantes nombren ingredientes que indican que entienden la consistencia y el sabor de las natillas y los ingredientes que saben bien en ellas.
6. Answers will vary but may include: The best advice to give someone writing a recipe is to break it down into lists of supplies and ingredients needed, to write clear and complete steps, and to try it out themselves. The best advice for someone following a recipe is to read it carefully all the way through, to make sure that he or she has all the items needed, and to watch the time and temperatures given.

Table of Contents

Tema 8: Cómo ser un buen turista

Capítulo 8A: Un viaje en avión

Capítulo 8B: Quiero que disfrutes de tu viaje

Theme Project

Cómo ser un buen turista

Cómo ser un buen turista

Overview:

You will create a poster that displays good travel habits. You will write the letters in the words *"Cómo ser un buen turista"* in bold, block letters down the center of the poster. Each piece of advice that you give must be written in smaller writing and must incorporate one of the letters of the phrase *"Cómo ser un buen turista."* For example:

Es importante que **C**ambies el dinero a la casa de cambio.
Es necesario que no **O**lvides tu pasaporte.
Es importante que **M**andes tarjetas postales a tu familia.
Es necesario que no **O**fendas a la gente.

After writing your list of travel habits, you will decorate your poster with photos or drawings.

Resources:

Page layout/word processing software and digital photos and/or poster board, markers

Sequence:

STEP 1. Review instructions with your teacher.

STEP 2. Submit a rough draft of your acrostic list of rules. Work with a partner and present your drafts to each other.

STEP 3. Create layouts, leaving room for photos and descriptions.

STEP 4. Submit a draft of your poster.

STEP 5. Present your poster to the class, explaining each rule and describing selected pictures.

Assessment:

Your teacher will provide you with a rubric to assess this project.

Theme 8 Project: Cómo ser un buen turista

Project Assessment Rubric

RUBRIC	Score 1	Score 3	Score 5
Evidence of Planning	No written draft or poster layout provided.	Draft was written and layout created, but not corrected.	Evidence of corrected draft and layout.
Use of Illustrations	No photos/ visuals included.	Very few photos/visuals included.	Several photos/ visuals included.
Presentation	Contains details that develop ideas about appropriate travel behavior.	Gives a partially complete list of advice (some letters used).	Gives a complete list of advice (all letters used).

21st Century Skills Rubric: Encourage Critical Thinking and Problem Solving

RUBRIC	Score 1	Score 3	Score 5
Identify source	Does not identify author of source	Identifies author of source	Identifies identify of source and states purpose
Evaluate information for fact or opinion	Does not evaluate information	Creates list of up to six facts and options from source	Creates a list of more than seven facts or opinions from source
Draw conclusions	Does not draw conclusions	Draws conclusions but does not explain reasons why	Draws conclusions and explains reasons why

Realidades 2

Capítulo 8A

School-to-Home Connection

Dear Parent or Guardian,

The theme of our current unit is *Cómo ser un buen turista* (How to be a good tourist). This chapter is called *Un viaje en avión* (An airplane trip).

Upon completion of this chapter students will be able to:

- talk about visiting an airport
- plan for a trip to a foreign country
- make suggestions about safe travel
- read about and recommend travel destinations in Hispanic countries
- understand cultural perspectives in traveling

Students will also explore:

- the correct pronunciation of linking sounds

Our textbook, *Realidades,* helps with the development of reading, writing, and speaking skills through the use of strategies, process speaking, and process writing. In this chapter, students will:

- read a travel article about Ecuador
- speak about a country they would like to travel to

To reinforce and enhance learning, students can access a wide range of online resources on **realidades.com,** the personalized learning management system that accompanies the print and online Student Edition. Resources include the eText, textbook and workbook activities, audio files, videos, animations, songs, self-study tools, interactive maps, voice recording (RealTalk!), assessments, and other digital resources. Many learning tools can be accessed through the student Home Page on **realidades.com.** Other activities, specifically those that require grading, are assigned by the teacher and linked on the student Home Page within the calendar or the Assignments tab.

You will find specifications and guidelines for accessing **realidades.com** on home computers and mobile devices on MyPearsonTraining.com under the SuccessNet Plus tab.

realidades.com

For: Tips to Parents
Visit: www.realidades.com
Web Code: jce-0010

Check it out! At the end of the chapter, have your child name three items he or she would need to take on a trip. Then ask for two suggestions for planning a trip.

Sincerely,

Videocultura Script

Viajar en Centroamérica

Spanish version:

América Central se sitúa justo al sur de México. En este istmo estrecho, se encuentran siete países de abundante belleza natural, historia, cultura y gente acogedora.

Un buen plan de viaje debe incluir una visita a la ciudad capital de uno de estos países, para conocer personas y lugares interesantes.

La influencia indígena se ve en la vida cotidiana. En Guatemala, el 40 por ciento de la población es de ascendencia maya.

Aparte de la gente y los sitios turísticos, puedes probar comida deliciosa. *Casamiento*, una combinación de arroz y frijoles, *plátanos* o *pupusas*, es la versión salvadoreña de la tortilla.

La verdadera belleza de estos países está en su naturaleza, lejos de las ciudades grandes.

Las islas de Roatán en Honduras reciben visitantes de todo el mundo que llegan para ver la impresionante vida marina.

En Nicaragua, hay muchísimos volcanes, como Concepción y Maderas.

Costa Rica es uno de los países con mayor biodiversidad del mundo. Hay selvas tropicales en las que puedes observar muchísimos animales y plantas.

América Central es sin duda una región perfecta para explorar e ir de vacaciones.

English version:

Central America is located just south of Mexico. The narrow isthmus contains seven countries that are known for their history, culture, natural beauty, and welcoming people.

A trip to any country in Central America offers an amazing opportunity. You can start in the capital city of one of these countries.

You can also see the history of the region in its people. In Guatemala, 40% of the population are of Mayan descent, and you may encounter the indigenous influence in everyday life.

In addition to the people and places, you can try authentic dishes such as *casamiento*, the combination of black beans and rice popular in El Salvador, fried bananas called *plátanos*, or *pupusas*, a version of the tortilla.

In any of the countries in Central America, you'll want to leave the big city to discover its diverse natural beauty.

In the Roatán islands in Honduras, visitors come from around the world for snorkeling and diving. The blue waters are teeming with marine life and stunning coral reefs.

In Nicaragua you can climb the impressive volcanoes such as Concepción and Maderas.

Costa Rica offers some of the greatest biodiversity in the world. You can visit dense tropical rain forests and misty cloud forests, observing the many plants and animals.

If you are looking for a vacation that combines history, culture, great food, and a variety of activities, add Central America as a future destination!

Input Script

Presentation

Input Vocabulary: Come to class dressed up as the Tin Man *(Hombre de Hojalata)* from *The Wizard of Oz*. Place the transparency showing the travel agency on the screen. Distribute copies of the Vocabulary Clip Art and have students cut them into individual images. Then describe how you went to a travel agency in Oz to buy a plane ticket to visit Dorothy in Kansas. Point to the images in the transparency as you talk about your conversation with the travel agent, how you bought electronic tickets, how you needed to stop over in Emerald City, and how you needed to arrive early to pass through security. Describe how you packed your suitcases, being very careful not to pack anything not allowed on airplanes. Then pull out a checklist and name the preparations again as you pretend to check them off. Have students raise the Clip Art images of the words you mention.

Then tell of the terrible problem you had at the airport trying to go through security because you kept setting off the the metal detector. The airport employees "wanded" you, made you take off your shoes, and so forth, until you finally got it through to them that you were the Tin Man from *The Wizard of Oz*.

Place the transparency of the airport and interior of an airplane on the screen. Describe how you boarded the plane, found your seat by the window, chatted with the other passengers and the flight attendants and said hello to the pilots. Say that you wanted to remember everything, so you took pictures of the passengers, the flight attendants, the pilot, and even the aisle and window. Have students hold up the Clip Art images of the people and things you took pictures of.

Describe your arrival. Tell how angry you got when you passed through customs and the customs agent made a joke by asking you if you were bringing any flying monkeys into the country!

Input Dialogues: Revert back to your true identity and have a volunteer role-play the first and last dialogues with you. Present the flight announcements and then have volunteers practice saying the announcements aloud in their most official-sounding voice.

Comprehension Check

- Tell students short anecdotes, real or imaginary, of things that have happened to you while traveling by air. Have them hold up the Clip Art images of the words you mention.
- Play the role of a security agent and have students pass through security. Ask to see their ticket, boarding pass, and passport, and to give you their luggage. Students will give you their Clip Art images of these items.
- Have students perform a skit in which two passengers argue over who gets the window seat. You will play the role of flight attendant. Help them with any vocabulary words they need to present their skit.

Capítulo 8A Audio Script

Audio DVD, Capítulo 8A

Track 01: *A primera vista, Un viaje en avión,* Student Book, p. 402, (3:45)

Vocabulario y gramática en contexto

Lee en tu libro mientras escuchas el diálogo.

TEEN FEMALE: Mi hermano Antonio y yo vamos a hacer un viaje a Nicaragua para visitar a nuestros abuelos. Para planear el viaje, fuimos con nuestros padres a una agencia de viajes.

ADULT MALE: Les he hecho las reservaciones. Tienen dos boletos de ida y vuelta entre Miami y Managua. Aquí están sus boletos electrónicos. Van a recibir sus tarjetas de embarque en el aeropuerto. Ya tienen los asientos 8D y 8F. Antes de llegar a Managua van a hacer escala en Tegucigalpa, Honduras, porque no hay vuelo directo a Managua.

TEEN FEMALE: Muchas gracias, Señor Salazar. ¿Y que más necesitamos?

ADULT MALE: Necesitan sus pasaportes. Las líneas aéreas sugieren que lleguen al aeropuerto dos horas antes de la salida del vuelo para facturar el equipaje. También insisten en que pasen por la inspección de seguridad.

Vas a escuchar cada palabra o frase dos veces. Después de la primera vez hay una pausa para que puedas pronunciar la palabra o frase. Luego vas a escuchar de nuevo la palabra o frase.

la tarjeta de embarque	la agencia de viajes
hacer la maleta	los turistas
la maleta	el agente de viajes
el equipaje	el pasaporte

Más vocabulario

sugerir

Track 02: *A primera vista,* Student Book, p. 403, (3:35)

Vocabulario y gramática en contexto

Vas a escuchar cada palabra o frase dos veces. Después de la primera vez hay una pausa para que puedas pronunciar la palabra o frase. Luego vas a escuchar de nuevo la palabra o frase.

la piloto	la puerta de embarque
el piloto	la empleada
la ventanilla	el anuncio
el pasajero	registrar
la pasajera	la aduanera
el pasillo	el aduanero
el auxiliar de vuelo	la aduana
la auxiliar de vuelo	

Lee en tu libro mientras escuchas el diálogo.

ADULT FEMALE: Lo sentimos mucho. Hay un pequeño retraso en la salida del vuelo 342 con destino a Tegucigalpa, Honduras. Dentro de veinte minutos tendremos más información sobre la salida del vuelo 342.

ADULT FEMALE: El vuelo 342 con destino a Tegucigalpa está listo. En unos minutos vamos a abordar. Favor de pasar a la puerta número 17 de la Terminal A.

ADULT MALE: Bienvenido a Managua. ¿Qué tiene?

TEEN MALE: Una maleta y una mochila.

ADULT MALE: Pase a la izquierda. Tendremos que ver qué cosas tiene dentro de su equipaje. Ese señor va a registrar el equipaje. Aquí está su pasaporte.

Track 03: *A primera vista,* Act. 1, Student Book, p. 403, (3:23)

En el aeropuerto

Estás en un aeropuerto esperando tu vuelo. Oyes muchas conversaciones entre los pasajeros y muchos anuncios. Si escuchas buenas noticias, señala con el pulgar hacia arriba. Si escuchas malas noticias, señala con el pulgar hacia abajo. Vas a escuchar las frases dos veces.

1. ¡Ay! No tengo mi pasaporte. ¿Dónde está?
2. El vuelo número 17 con destino a Caracas, Venezuela, está listo. Pronto vamos a abordar.
3. —Señorita, no tengo un asiento.
   —Tiene que esperar el próximo vuelo.
4. Puedo hacer sus reservaciones a un precio muy barato.
5. El avión todavía no ha llegado. Hay un retraso de media hora. Lo siento.
6. Señor, Ud. no puede abordar el avión con esta maleta. Es demasiado grande.
7. La inspección de seguridad sólo tomó cinco minutos. ¡Fue muy rápido!
8. Muy buenas tardes. Soy el Capitán Gallego. Tengo treinta y dos años de experiencia como piloto. Bienvenidos al vuelo número 22 con destino a Lima, Perú.

Track 04: *A primera vista,* Act. 2, Student Book, p. 403, (2:45)

¿Quién lo dice?

Escucha cada frase y en una hoja de papel escribe quién lo dijo: una pasajera, una agente de viajes, una auxiliar de vuelo o una aduanera. Vas a escuchar las frases dos veces.

1. **ADULT FEMALE 1:** Bienvenidos abordo. ¿Sabe Ud. dónde está su asiento?
2. **ADULT FEMALE 2:** Muy bien. Aquí en la computadora dice que hay un vuelo directo entre Chicago y la Ciudad de México.
3. **ADULT FEMALE 3:** Señor, ¿puede Ud. abrir la mochila? Tengo que registrarla a mano.

4. **Adult Female 4:** Señorita, ¿a qué hora va a salir el avión?
5. **Adult Female 1:** ¿Quisiera Ud. un refresco, café o jugo?
6. **Adult Female 3:** ¿Por cuánto tiempo quiere Ud. quedarse en Guatemala?
7. **Adult Female 2:** Es importante llegar al aeropuerto dos horas antes de la salida de un vuelo internacional.
8. **Adult Female 3:** Bienvenidos a Montevideo. Necesito ver su pasaporte.

Track 05: *A primera vista, Videohistoria,* Student Book, pp. 404–405, (2:10)

¡Buen viaje!

Ana y Elena van a Londres para estudiar inglés. Compran los boletos para el viaje en una agencia de viajes, pero hay un problema. Lee para saber qué pasa.

Lee en tu libro mientras escuchas la *Videohistoria.*

See Student Book pages 404–405 for script.

Track 06: *Manos a la obra,* Act. 5, Student Book, p. 406, (2:18)

Escucha y escribe

Hay cosas que vas a necesitar para tu viaje. Escucha estos consejos y escribe la cosa que necesitas. Vas a escuchar las frases dos veces.

1. Cuando viajas a un país extranjero, lo necesitas como identificación.
2. La haces antes de salir de casa. Pones tu ropa y otras cosas dentro de ella.
3. La recibes en el aeropuerto y la necesitas para abordar el avión.
4. Es el boleto que necesitas para ir a un lugar y volver al aeropuerto de donde sales.
5. Es el vuelo que prefieres si no quieres hacer escala durante el viaje.
6. Lo facturas cuando llegas al aeropuerto.

Track 07: Audio Act. 5, Writing, Audio & Video Workbook, p. 149, (5:50)

Listen to the messages recorded by different airlines for customers to listen to as they wait for the next available agent to take their phone call. As you listen to each announcement, identify which picture best matches each taped message. Write the number of the conversation in the blank under the corresponding picture. You will hear each message twice.

1. Es importante tener muchas actividades planeadas para los niños que viajan con Ud. Si quieren los sentamos cerca de la ventanilla para ver mejor las montañas durante el día y las luces de las ciudades por la noche. Si les gusta dibujar, pueden imaginar que las nubes que ven por la ventanilla son animales.
2. Prepárense para conocer una nueva forma de viajar. Con nosotros no tienen que hacer una escala en diez ciudades diferentes. Tenemos más vuelos directos que todas las líneas aéreas. Hay tres vuelos directos de Dallas a Madrid y dos vuelos directos de Miami a San Juan al día.
3. Los pasajeros con destino a ciudades de Europa deben inscribirse en el Departamento de Estado dos meses antes de la fecha del viaje para recibir su pasaporte a tiempo. Recuerden que la aduana del país que visitan necesita ver su pasaporte. Por favor, tengan el pasaporte en la mano para que la espera sea más corta.
4. Es necesario presentarse en el aeropuerto tres horas antes de los vuelos internacionales. Las inspecciones de seguridad toman mucho tiempo. Tengan la tarjeta de embarque en la mano para que pasen las inspecciones más rápidamente. Por favor, tengan paciencia. Gracias por su atención.
5. Es muy importante facturar el equipaje antes de abordar el avión. Solo permitimos maletas pequeñas en el avión. Las maletas grandes no se pueden poner debajo del asiento ni en el compartimiento superior. Traigan al avión una o dos maletas pequeñas porque no tenemos suficiente espacio para poner muchas maletas.

Track 08: Audio Act. 6, Writing, Audio & Video Workbook, p. 149, (7:11)

Several Spanish club members just got back from a summer trip to Europe with their teacher. On the way home from the airport, two girls talk about what happened on the trip and how their classmates acted. As you listen, decide whether the student they are talking about was a *buen turista* or *mal turista* and mark the grid below with your answer. You will hear each conversation twice.

1. **Teen Female 1:** Me encantó el viaje. ¡Estoy lista para regresar a Madrid ahora mismo!
   Teen Female 2: De acuerdo. ¡Pero SIN Susana! ¿La viste en el avión? Insistió en tener un asiento de ventanilla. Finalmente, Chris le dio el suyo.
   Teen Female 1: Y todos los españoles que iban en el avión lo miraron.
2. **Teen Female 2:** Me gustó mucho nuestro viaje en tren de Madrid a Barcelona. Me encantó dormir en el tren.
   Teen Female 1: ¿Pudiste dormir? Yo, no, porque Daniel tocó guitarra desde la salida de Madrid hasta llegar a Barcelona.
   Teen Female 2: Sí. Aún les molestó a los empleados del tren.
3. **Teen Female 2:** A mí me gustó el viaje en avión que hicimos de Barcelona a París porque conocimos a muchos estudiantes extranjeros en el vuelo.
   Teen Female 1: ¿Recuerdas al niño que lloraba durante el retraso? Jason le dio la galleta que recibió en el almuerzo y el niño dejó de llorar. Y cuando la madre supo que Jason hablaba español, nos dijo que los jóvenes estadounidenses son fabulosos.
4. **Teen Female 2:** Me encantó el viaje en avión de Madrid a Sevilla. ¡Sevilla es una ciudad muy hermosa! ¡La agente de viajes tenía razón!
   Teen Female 1: A mí me gustó también, pero no creo que a los españoles les guste que John insiste en llevar maletas grandes a todas partes, especialmente a los restaurantes. Él se portó tan mal con los camareros.

5. **Teen Female 1:** Insisto en que Granada es la ciudad más hermosa de España. Los edificios son muy grandes. Y la gente es tan buena… No hay ciudad igual en ningún otro lado.
Teen Female 2: Sí, es verdad. Granada es muy bonita. Parece que Ian regresa a Granada el verano próximo. Los españoles lo quieren mucho porque es muy amable con todo el mundo. Él siempre espera con mucha paciencia su turno en la línea para pasar las inspecciones de seguridad.
6. **Teen Female 2:** Me gusta más viajar en tren que en avión. Me encanta mirar por la ventanilla del tren. El avión va muy rápido y no veo nada.
Teen Female 1: Prefiero el avión porque es más rápido. Así no tengo que viajar por mucho tiempo con Daniel. Él es tan impaciente… Le pregunta cada cinco minutos al auxiliar si ya llegamos o si no hemos llegado. Me vuelve loca.

Track 09: *Manos a la obra,* Act. 11, Student Book, p. 410, (2:29)

Escucha y escribe

Escucha a una persona que viaja mucho dar recomendaciones sobre su viaje. Escribe sus seis recomendaciones. Después subraya el verbo en la expresión de recomendación y traza un círculo alrededor del verbo que indica lo que debes hacer. Vas a escuchar las frases dos veces.

1. Les sugiero que compren un boleto de ida y vuelta.
2. Insisten en que pasen por la inspección de seguridad.
3. Les prohíben que lleven tijeras o cuchillos en el avión.
4. Les recomiendo que no facturen la maleta que tiene sus medicinas.
5. Prefieren que lleguen al aeropuerto dos horas antes de la salida del vuelo.
6. Quieren que tengan su pasaporte siempre durante el viaje.

Track 10: Audio Act. 7, Writing, Audio & Video Workbook, p. 150, (3:56)

When her friends and family find out that Elisa is going on a school trip to Europe, they all have advice for her about her initial plane trip to Madrid. As you listen to each person's advice, match his or her suggestion to the corresponding picture below. Write the number of the conversation underneath the correct drawing. You will hear each suggestion twice.

1. **Adult Female 1:** Hija mía, quiero que tengas un viaje fantástico. ¡Va a ser muy difícil despedirme en el aeropuerto! Quiero que me envíes una tarjeta postal cuando llegues a Madrid. Puedes escribirla durante el vuelo.
2. **Adult Male:** Elisa, no olvides que las inspecciones de seguridad toman mucho tiempo. Te recomiendo que llegues tres horas antes de la salida de tu vuelo. Prefiero que comas tu desayuno temprano para llevarte al aeropuerto a tiempo.
3. **Teen Male:** Yo fui a España el año pasado. Los españoles hablan muy rápido. No entendía nada de lo que decían. Te recomiendo que practiques español antes de ir a Europa. Debes leer revistas y periódicos españoles.
4. **Teen Female:** El viaje a Madrid es muy largo y son seis horas más tarde allá. Te sugiero que duermas en el avión. Así en Madrid te sientes muy bien y no estás tan cansada como la gente que no duerme en el avión.
5. **Adult Female 2:** Quiero que hagas sólo una maleta. Es preferible que lleves poco equipaje. Si llevas mucho equipaje, gastas más tiempo en las inspecciones de seguridad y tienes que llevarlas de un sitio a otro. Es un problema.

Track 11: Audio Act. 8, Writing, Audio & Video Workbook, p. 150, (7:23)

Listen to a panel of seasoned travelers and school officials as they give suggestions to students who are taking a trip next month. As you listen to each suggestion, decide whether it is a: a) *Sugerencia para planear el viaje;* b) *Sugerencias para el aeropuerto y durante el vuelo;* c) *Sugerencias para cuando viajan por las ciudades que visitan;* or d) *Sugerencias sobre qué comprar como recuerdo del viaje.* Write the correct letter in each space below. You will hear each suggestion twice.

1. Recomiendo que sean bien educados en el aeropuerto. Como jóvenes de nuestra escuela, deben portarse bien. Uds. representan a los otros estudiantes y a sus familias.
2. Insisto en que todas las jóvenes vayan a una tienda para comprarse un bolso de cuero como recuerdo de su viaje a España. Son muy bonitos y cuestan menos dinero que en los Estados Unidos.
3. Sugiero que Uds. sean pacientes cuando pasen por la inspección de seguridad antes de llegar a la puerta de embarque. Algunas veces los empleados insisten en que les den sus llaves, sus zapatos y su abrigo para registrarlos.
4. Recomiendo que Uds. vayan a una agencia de viajes. Muchas veces se pueden comprar cheques de viajero allí. Pienso que los cheques de viajero son mejores que el dinero en efectivo para el viaje. Todos los hoteles, los restaurantes y las tiendas los aceptan.
5. Yo sé que sus padres prefieren que siempre estén con el grupo y con su profesora cuando visiten las ciudades. Su profesora necesita saber que Uds. están listos cuando el autobús turístico tiene que salir.
6. Es importante que sepan que los ladrones buscan a los turistas para quitarles el dinero. Les sugiero que estén alertas a las personas que estén cerca de Uds. Quiero que lleven el dinero dentro de los zapatos.
7. En Europa hay muchas tiendas que venden pequeños recuerdos de las ciudades que visitamos. Les sugiero que vayan a esas tiendas porque todo es muy barato y muy bonito. A veces tienen precios especiales muy buenos. Así pueden traerles un recuerdo a todos sus amigos.

8. Les recomiendo que vayan a la biblioteca de la escuela y que busquen información de los países que van a visitar. Quiero que sepan cuáles ciudades van a visitar durante el viaje a Europa. Si sabemos las que queremos visitar, no perderemos tiempo.
9. Insisto en que todos los estudiantes de mi grupo estén preparados para las inspecciones de seguridad. Quiero que tengan su tarjeta de embarque y una tarjeta de identidad en la mano siempre, porque piden estos documentos en varios lugares del aeropuerto.
10. Quiero que sean muy amables con la gente que ven en la calle. No quiero que nadie piense que somos malos turistas. Les prohíbo que den su número de teléfono o dirección a cualquier persona.

Track 12: Audio Act. 9, Writing, Audio & Video Workbook, p. 151, (4:22)

People sometimes encounter difficulties while traveling. As you listen to each of these three people discuss his or her problem, determine what the problem is and circle the appropriate answer. You will hear each discussion twice.

1. **ADULT MALE:** Soy el señor Machado. Compré este boleto para un vuelo directo a Buenos Aires hace dos meses. Y le dije al agente de viajes que necesitaba llegar antes de las ocho de la mañana. Me parece que este vuelo no llega hasta las once. Es imposible. Tengo una reunión muy importante a las diez. Tengo que llegar a tiempo.
   ADULT FEMALE 1: Lo siento, Señor Machado. Vamos a ver… recomiendo que cambie al vuelo que hace escala en Santiago, Chile. Este vuelo va a llegar a Buenos Aires a las nueve y media.
2. **ADULT FEMALE 2:** ¡Buenas tardes! Soy la señora Manizales. Llegamos en el vuelo de San Juan, Puerto Rico. Mi hija llevó su oso de peluche al avión. El oso es su mejor amigo. Pero el problema es que se me olvidó el oso de peluche en el avión porque estaba muy emocionada. Quiero que lo busque, si es posible.
   ADULT FEMALE 1: ¡Qué pena! Necesito que tenga paciencia y espere en la terminal del aeropuerto mientras llamo al avión para que busquen el oso de peluche. Un momento, por favor.
3. **ADULT MALE:** ¡María, este aeropuerto es horrible! Mira toda la gente que espera las inspecciones de seguridad. No puedo creer lo que veo. Hacen todo tan lentamente. No vamos a llegar nunca al avión. ¡Qué horrible!
   ADULT FEMALE 3: Luis, quiero que sepas que las inspecciones de seguridad son necesarias. Te sugiero que tengas paciencia. No quiero tener que llamar a un médico porque eres tan impaciente. Tenemos tiempo; no hay que ser impaciente.

Track 13: *Repaso del capítulo*, Student Book, p. 422, (7:23)

Vocabulario y gramática

Escucha las palabras y expresiones que has aprendido en este capítulo.

See Student Book page 422 for vocabulary list.

Track 14: *Preparación para el examen*, Student Book, p. 423, (0:57)

Escuchar

Practice task

A student from Spain gives travel tips to students who are thinking of traveling there this summer. Decide if the suggestion includes: a) planning tips; b) packing tips; c) airport arrival tips; or d) in-flight tips.

TEEN FEMALE: Hola. Soy Marisol, de Barcelona. Sugiero que llames a tu agente de viajes muy pronto. En el verano muchos turistas quieren viajar a España. ¡Es muy popular! Recomiendo que viajes en el mes de junio. Hace mucho calor en julio y agosto.

Video Script

A primera vista: *¡Buen viaje!*, (6:06)

Ana: Señorita, ¿a qué hora cierra la agencia de viajes?

Agente: A la una y media.

Ana: ¡Ay! Elena llega tarde para todo. Siempre le sugiero, vamos a planear todo con tiempo suficiente, pero ella no me escucha…

Agente: Ten paciencia, seguramente llega pronto.

Ana: Perdón.

Ana: ¡Elena! Ven, rápido. Es muy tarde.

Elena: Tranquila, ya voy. Ya voy.

Ana: Vamos. La agente de viajes nos está esperando.

Elena: Hola, ¿qué tal?

Agente: A ver. ¿En qué os puedo ayudar?

Ana: Queremos un billete para Londres.

Agente: ¿A Londres?

Elena: Sí. Vamos a estar allí dos semanas, para estudiar inglés.

Agente: Muy bien. ¿Y cómo queréis ir? ¿En avión?

Ana: Pues sí, ¿no?

Agente: Aquí hay un vuelo directo. En clase turista.

Elena: ¿En clase turista? ¿Y cuánto cuesta?

Agente: El billete de ida y vuelta cuesta doscientos dos con ochenta y seis euros. Es un buen precio.

Ana: No sé. ¿Tienes algo más?

Agente: Bueno, ¿os gustaría ir en tren?

Elena: ¿En tren? ¿Desde Madrid a Londres?

Ana: ¡Claro! ¡Qué buena idea! Podemos ir en tren a Francia, y después cruzar el canal.

Agente: Podéis comprar un billete de tren, el "Europass," desde Madrid a París. Desde París, podéis ir a Londres en el "Eurostar."

Elena: ¿El Eurostar?

Agente: Sí, es un tren que va desde París a Londres, por un túnel, debajo del agua.

Elena: Pero, ¿no es muy caro?

Agente: No. Os sugiero que compréis un billete para estudiantes. Es más barato. Muchos estudiantes extranjeros viajan así. Es muy divertido.

Elena: ¿Y cuánto dura el viaje?

Agente: Bueno, de Madrid a París son doce horas. De París a Londres, aproximadamente dos horas y quince minutos.

Elena: Es un viaje muy largo, ¿no?

Ana: Ay, Elena. Puedes dormir durante el viaje.

Elena: No sé. Un tren, en un túnel, en el agua…

Agente: No te preocupes. Te va a gustar. Tienes que pasar por el control de pasaporte, pero no tienes que hacer escala. Aquí hay uno para el 26 de junio. La salida de París es a las 8:07 de la mañana. La llegada a Londres es a las 10:18. ¿Qué os parece?

Ana: ¿Lleva retraso?

Agente: No. Generalmente no lleva retraso.

Ana: ¿Hacemos la reserva?

Elena: ¡Vale!

Agente: Aquí los tenéis. ¡Buen viaje!

Ana: Muchas gracias. Vamos a celebrarlo.

Elena: Vale.

Ana: ¿Por qué no tomamos un refresco?

Elena: Ana, estoy tan emocionada. ¿Puedo ver los billetes?

Ana: Sí, claro.

Ana: ¿Dónde están? ¿Los tienes tú?

Elena: No, no los tengo. ¿No te los dio a ti?

Ana: Está cerrado. ¿Qué hacemos?

Elena: Mira, allí están, encima de la mesa.

Ana: Abren esta tarde, ¿no? ¿A qué hora?

Elena: Ana, por favor. A las cuatro y media. ¡Ten paciencia!

***GramActiva* Videos, (7:26)**
The present subjunctive

Scarecrow: Introducing, the subjunctive! Hey, I suggest you relax. The subjunctive is easy. All you need are your *usted* command forms.

Foreman: I want you to pay attention. *Quiero que preste atención.* If you just want to say "Pay attention!" then you'd say *Preste atención.* But Spanish is a subtle language. We like to make commands sound pleasant, so we add *quiero que* and then we have the subjunctive. *Quiero que preste atención.*

Coach: *¡Laven el coche!* Oh, all right, I'll be nice. I'll add on "I need." *Necesito que laven el coche.* And make it snappy!

Rear-view mirror guy: *Llene el tanque.* Uh, I mean, *Recomiendo que llene el tanque.*

V.O.: To make the present subjunctive, take the *yo* form of the verb, drop the *-o* and add the subjunctive ending. The endings for *-ar* verbs and *-er* or *-ir* verbs flipflop.

V.O.: The endings for *-ar* verbs in the subjunctive are: *-e, -es, -e, -emos, -éis,* and *-en.*
Using the verb *usar* we get:
Use, uses, use, usemos, uséis, usen.

V.O.: The endings for *-er* and *-ir* verbs in the subjunctive are: *-a, -as, -a, -amos, -áis,* and *-an.*
Using the verb *comer* we get: *coma, comas, coma, comamos, comáis, coman.*

Coach: If you spot verbs like *recomendar, querer, sugerir, preferir, decir,* or *necesitar* followed by a *que,* you'll need the subjunctive tense in the next part of the sentence. But be careful. Remember, you only use subjunctive if one person wants someone else to do something, or wants something to happen.

Coach V.O.: For example,
I need to wash the car.
Necesito lavar el coche. That's not subjunctive.
I need YOU to wash the car.
Necesito que TÚ laves el coche. Now that's subjunctive.
Let's try that again.
Necesito llenar el tanque.
Necesito que tú llenes el tanque.

Scarecrow: One more thing. The subjunctive uses the same spelling changes and irregular *yo* forms that are found in negative commands.

No quiero que vengas tarde.

Quiero que hagas la tarea ahora mismo.

V.O.1: Let's watch as renowned travel expert and radio show host Luisa uses the subjunctive tense.

Luisa: *Aquí Luisa. ¿Cuál es su pregunta?*

V.O.2: *Quiero viajar a España.*

Luisa: *Yo recomiendo que hable con un agente de viajes.*

Aquí Luisa. ¿Cuál es su pregunta?

V.O.3: *Necesito un boleto más barato.*

Luisa: *Sugiero que compre un boleto de ida y vuelta.*

Aquí Luisa. ¿Cuál es su pregunta?

V.O.4: *Ud. es fantástica. Quiero una cita con Ud.*

Luisa: *Prefiero que no llame más.*

That's all the time we have for Travel Radio, folks.

It's time for a quiz.

Quiz

V.O.: Form the subjunctive using the verb in parenthesis.

(viajar) Quiero que tú ______ a España.

Quiero que tú viajes a España.

(estudiar) Sugerimos que ellos ______.

Sugerimos que ellos estudien.

(llegar) Recomienda que nosotros ______ temprano al aeropuerto.

Recomienda que lleguemos temprano al aeropuerto.

(leer) Prefiero que él ______ los letreros.

Prefiero que él lea los letreros.

Irregular subjunctive verbs

Coach: Heads up people! We have lots of irregular subjunctive verbs to put in our playbook!

I want to see *dar, estar, ir, saber,* and *ser*—Let's get moving!

Cheerleaders: *Dar.*

Dé, des, dé, demos, deis, den.

Quiero que me dé la letra "A."

Bees V.O.: *Estar.*

Esté, estés, esté, estemos, estéis, estén.

No quiero que esté aquí.

Roadworkers: *Ir.*

Vaya, vayas, vaya, vayamos, vayáis, vayan.

Necesitamos que vayas a New Jersey.

Driver: But that's the road for Cleveland!

Graduates: *Saber.*

Sepa, sepas, sepa, sepamos, sepáis, sepan.

Queremos que sepan las reglas.

Hamlet: *Ser.*

Sea, seas, sea, seamos, seáis, sean.

Quiero que seas famoso como yo.

Coach: That was a lot of verbs. So what are you waiting for? Get practicing! Bring me the quiz!

Quiz

V.O.: Form the subjunctive using the verb in parenthesis.

(estar) Quiero que tú ______ contento.

Quiero que tú estés contento.

(ir) Recomendamos que ustedes ______ de vacaciones.

Recomendamos que ustedes vayan de vacaciones.

(ser) Tus padres prefieren que tú ______ ordenada.

Tus padres prefieren que tú seas ordenada.

(dar) Sugiero que me ______ el boleto.

Sugiero que me des el boleto.

Nombre ______________________________

Fecha ______________________________

Communicative Pair Activity **8A-1**

Estudiante **A**

This summer, some of your classmates traveled to South America for vacation with their families. Ask your partner to which country your friends went. Record his or her answers on the lines provided.

1. ¿Dónde pasaron Yadira y Pepe sus vacaciones? ______________________________
2. ¿Dónde pasaron Lina y Jaime sus vacaciones? ______________________________
3. ¿Dónde pasó Santiago sus vacaciones? ______________________________
4. ¿Dónde pasó Paco sus vacaciones? ______________________________
5. ¿Dónde pasaron Luis y Lupita sus vacaciones? ______________________________
6. ¿Dónde pasó Enrique sus vacaciones? ______________________________
7. ¿Dónde pasaron Marcela y Giovanna sus vacaciones? ______________________________
8. ¿Dónde pasó Lucas sus vacaciones? ______________________________

Use the map below to answer your partner's questions. Also be prepared to answer a question about yourself.

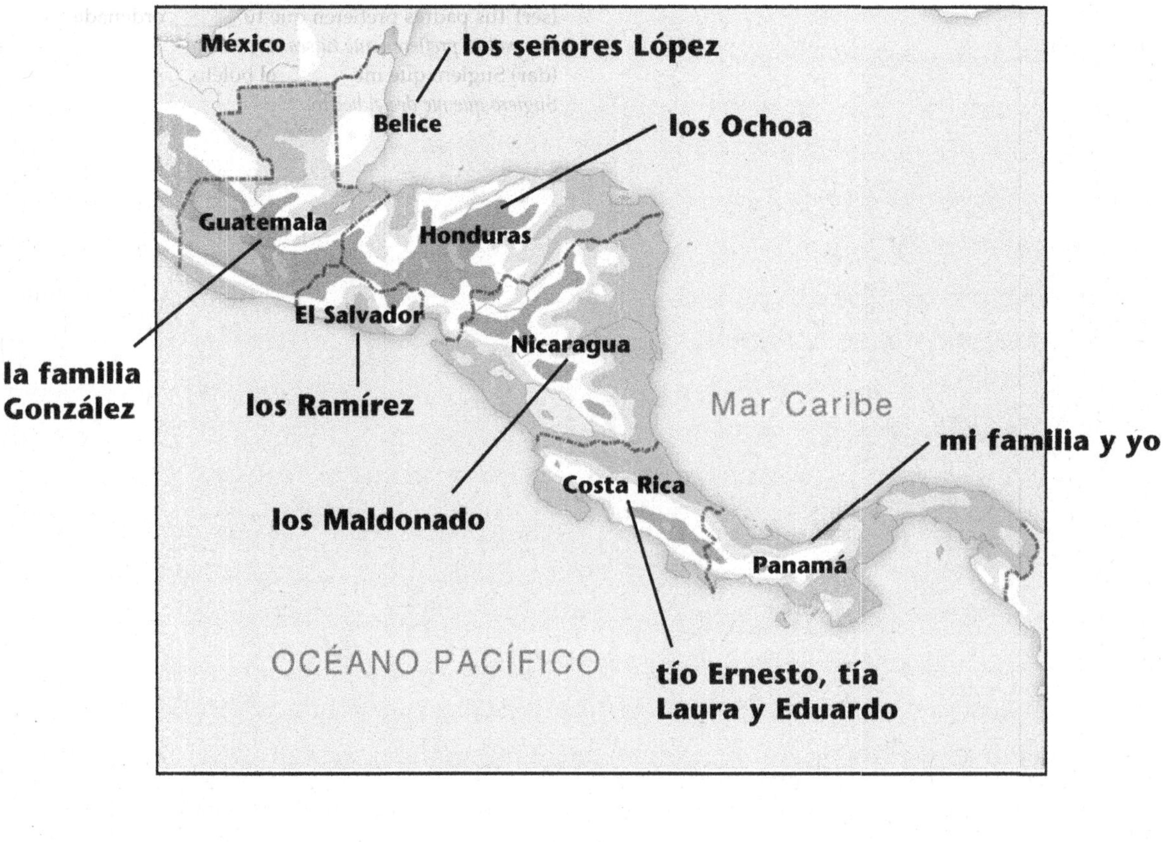

Nombre ______________________

Communicative Pair Activity **8A-1**

Fecha ______________________ Estudiante **B**

Use the map below to answer your partner's questions. Also be prepared to answer a question about yourself.

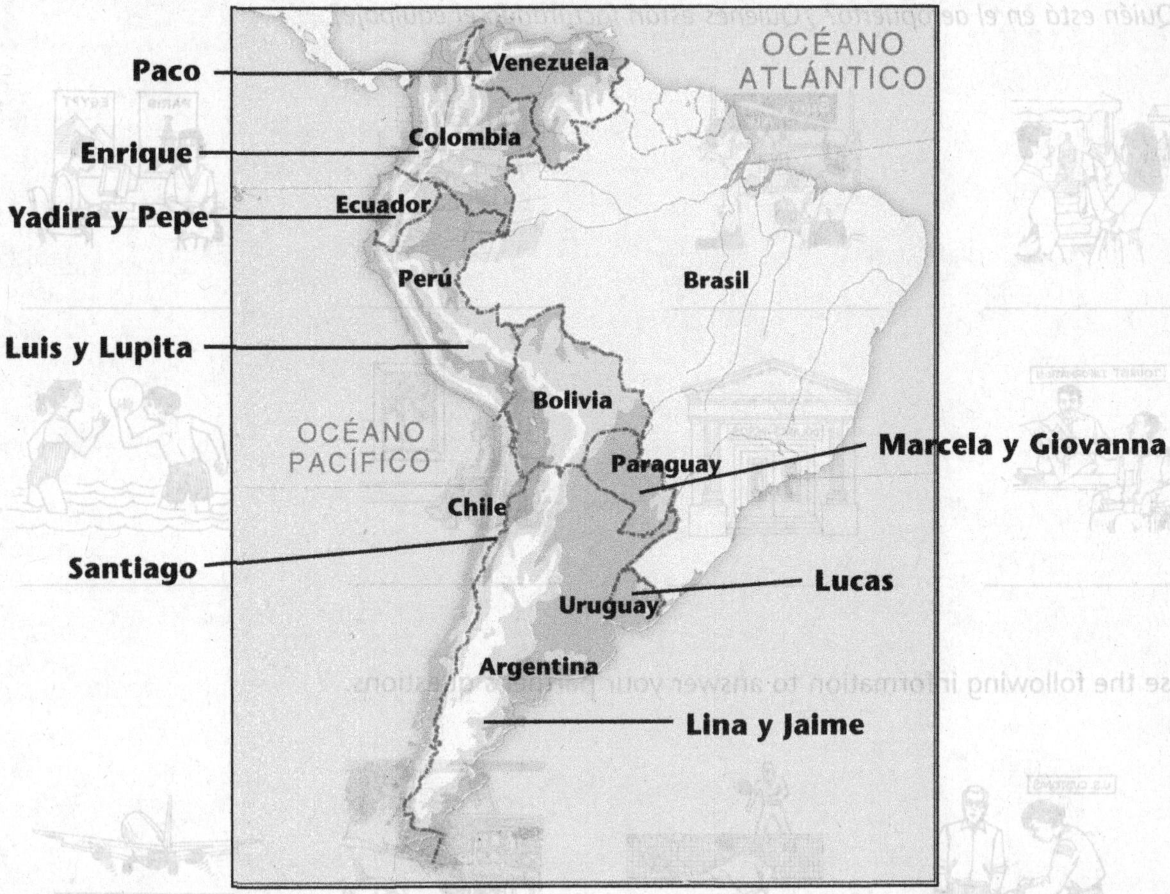

Last year your family and your family's friends went on vacation to different countries in Central America and the Caribbean. Ask your partner to play the role of your cousin and ask him or her where all these people enjoyed their vacations. Record your partner's answers on the lines provided.

1. ¿Dónde pasaron los Maldonado sus vacaciones? ______________________
2. ¿Dónde pasaron los Ochoa sus vacaciones? ______________________
3. ¿Dónde pasaron los señores López sus vacaciones? ______________________
4. ¿Dónde pasó la familia González sus vacaciones? ______________________
5. ¿Dónde pasaron los Ramírez sus vacaciones? ______________________
6. ¿Dónde pasaron tío Ernesto, tía Laura y Eduardo sus vacaciones? ______________________
7. ¿Dónde pasaste tú tus vacaciones con tu familia? ______________________

Nombre ______________________________

Fecha ______________________________

Communicative Pair Activity **8A-2**
Estudiante **A**

Many of your friends are taking trips for vacation. Ask your partner who is in each of the following places. Record the answers on the lines provided. Follow the model.

¿Quién está en el aeropuerto? ¿Quiénes están facturando el equipaje?

____

____

____

____

____

____

____

____

Use the following information to answer your partner's questions.

Amanda

Ramiro y Miguel

Arturo

los Gutiérrez

Carolina

Juanita y Cristina

Augusto

Pepe

Realidades 2

Capítulo 8A

Nombre ______________________________

Fecha ______________________________

Communicative Pair Activity **8A-2**

Estudiante **B**

Use the following information to answer your partner's questions.

Adriana

Jorge y Marta

Roberto y el empleado

los Pérez

Marcela y el agente de viaje

Luis

Gonzalo y Elena

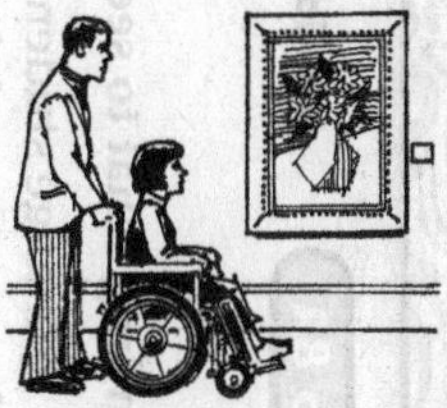

Mario y Carmen

Many of your friends work at the airport or are in the travel industry. Others are taking trips for vacation. Ask your partner who works at the following jobs or who is currently on vacation. Record the answers on the lines provided. Follow the model.

¿Quiénes están haciendo un viaje en avión?

____

____

____

____

____

____

____

____

Situation Cards

Capítulo 8A **Realidades 2** **1A**

Discussing travel destinations

You are talking with a friend about places to visit outside the United States. Think of a country you'd like to visit.

— Ask your friend where he or she would like to go on a trip outside the United States.
— Respond to your friend's choice by asking why and what he or she would like to do there.
— Respond to your friend's answers with your own opinion.
— Ask how he or she will travel there.

Capítulo 8A **Realidades 2** **2A**

Recommending what to see in your community

You are an exchange student from Spain and you want to know what to see and do in your new community.

— Ask your friend which places he or she recommends that you visit.
— Ask why you should visit each location.
— Then, mention that your parents are coming to see you and ask what hotel he or she suggests they stay in.

Capítulo 8A **Realidades 2** **1B**

Discussing travel destinations

You are talking with a friend about places to visit outside the United States. Think of a country you'd like to visit.

— Answer your friend's questions.
— Express your opinion about his or her choice of destinations.
— Answer your friend's question.

Capítulo 8A **Realidades 2** **2B**

Recommending what to see in your community

The Spanish exchange student in your school is asking you what to see and do in your community.

— Think of three places he or she should visit.
— Respond to your friend's questions.

GramActiva

Un viaje en avión

Dos medios de transporte, p. 409

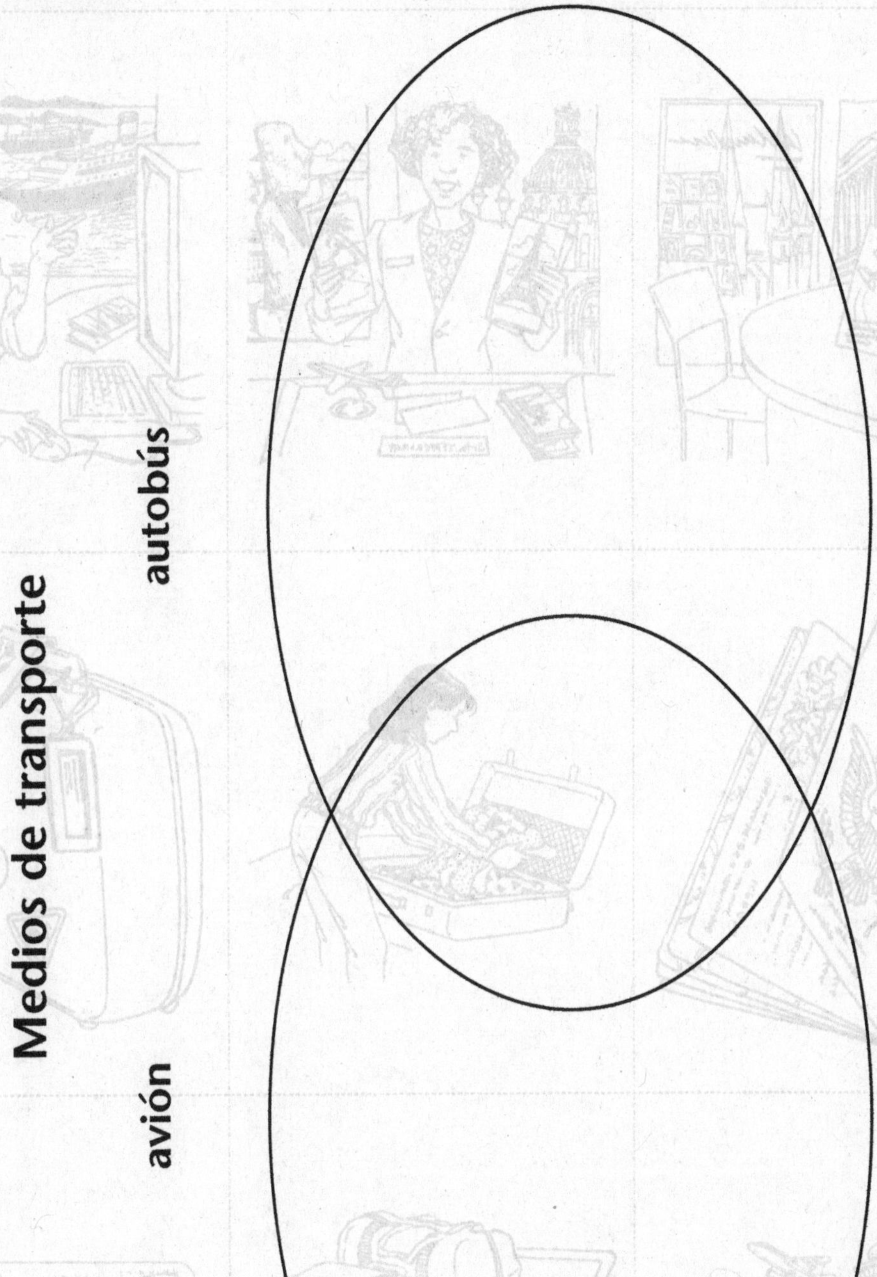

Vocabulary Clip Art

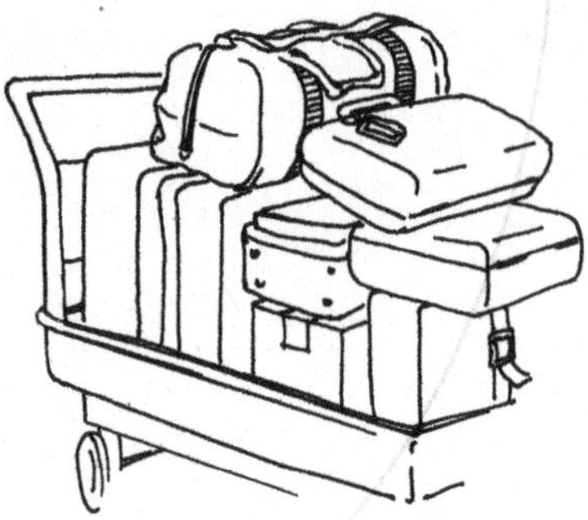

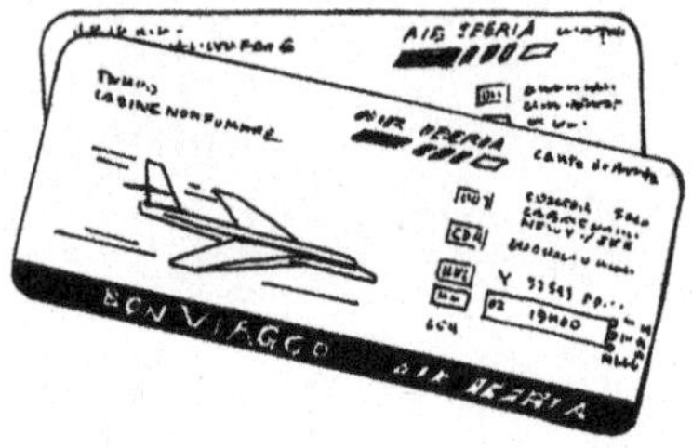

Vocabulary Clip Art

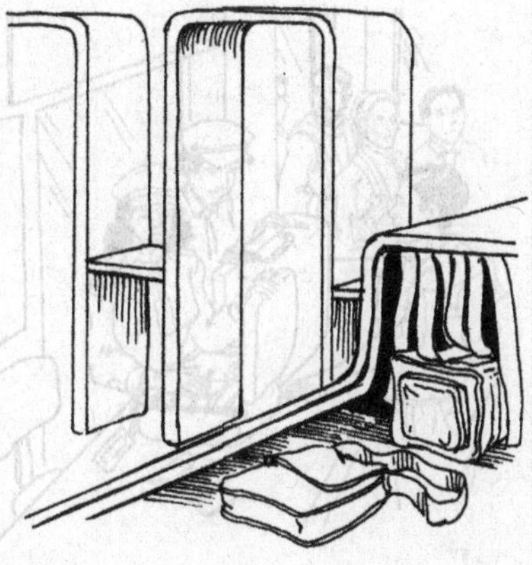

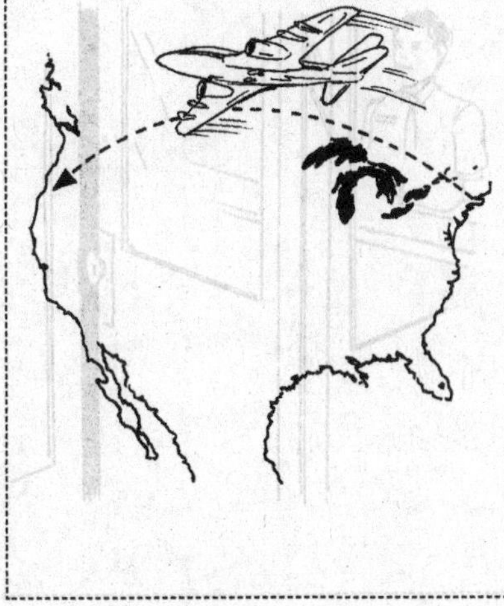

Vocabulary Clip Art

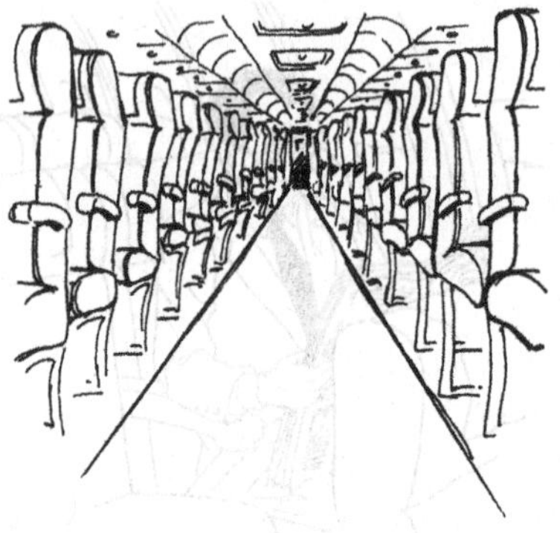

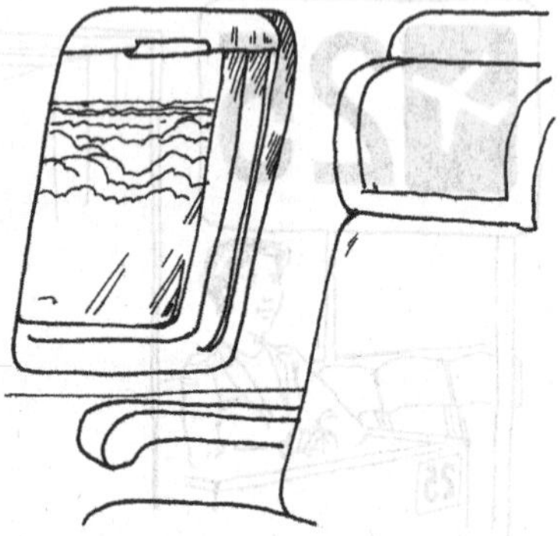

Realidades 2

Capítulo 8A

Vocabulary Clip Art

Core Practice Answers

8A-A
1. mercado
2. piscina
3. partido
4. ciudades
5. estadio
6. playa
7. campo, lago
8. vacaciones
9. lugar
10. obra, teatro
11. parques, diversiones
12. parque nacional

8A-B
1. Te encanta visitar los monumentos.
2. Voy a montar a caballo.
3. Alejandro y Laura prefieren dar una caminata.
4. Ud. desea pasear en bote.
5. A Uds. les gusta esquiar en las montañas.
6. Federico quiere ir de cámping.
7. Debemos comprar recuerdos.
8. Irene piensa tomar el sol.

8A-1
1. auxiliar de vuelo, pasajeros
2. aduanera, maletas
3. inspecciones, seguridad
4. tarjeta, embarque
5. facturar, equipaje
6. la ventanilla
7. abordar

8A-2
1. vuelo directo
2. de embarque
3. retraso
4. línea aérea
5. destino
6. anuncio
7. registrándo

8A-3
1. No hay agentes porque la agencia está cerrada.
2. El tren llegó con un retraso de más o menos veinte minutos.
3. El viaje dura once horas en tren.
4. Los pasajeros esperan abordar el avión con destino a Lima, Perú.
5. Los pilotos y los auxiliares de vuelo abordan primero.
6. El pasajero no puede pasar por la aduana porque no tiene su pasaporte.
7. Sí, hay muchos turistas en el aeropuerto. Sí, parecen extranjeros porque llevan ropa diferente y parecen estudiantes.

8A-4
1. Ella es la piloto.
2. Debe comprar un boleto de ida y vuelta.
3. Eres un pasajero.
4. Hizo escala.
5. Su amigo tiene que pasar por la aduana después.
6. Está lista para viajar a otro país.
7. Este pasajero necesita tener paciencia.

8A-5
1. Les sugiero que facturen el equipaje.
2. Les digo que hagan reservaciones en un vuelo directo.
3. Quiero que planees el viaje conmigo.
4. Le sugiero que use mi teléfono.
5. Me recomienda que llegue temprano en la salida del vuelo.
6. Les digo que no lleven tanto equipaje.
7. Insiste en que le digamos lo que nos interesa.
8. Les recomiendo que vengan temprano por la mañana.

8A-6
1. vayan en avión
2. sepan el horario de los aviones
3. me des tu dirección en Madrid
4. estén en el aeropuerto dos horas antes de la salida del vuelo
5. me des tu pasaporte para verlo
6. sepan lo que van a hacer todos los días
7. vayan a Toledo
8. sean buenos turistas

8A-7
1. seas paciente
2. vayan a casa de tu amiga ahora
3. sepas los números de nuestros vuelos
4. busque tu maleta ahora
5. estén listos ahora
6. le des tu pasaporte a papá
7. saques más juguetes ahora
8. empieces a apagar las luces

Crucigrama (8A-8)
Horizontal:
2. auxiliares
3. facturar
5. lleguen
6. retraso
9. duró
11. planeó
13. vuelo
15. tendremos
18. haga
20. tengas
22. abramos

Vertical:
1. pasillo
4. aérea
7. anuncio
8. Bienvenidos
10. pasaporte
11. puerta
12. destino
14. pasajeros
16. escala
17. seguridad
19. aduana
21. embarque

Organizer (8A-9)
I. Vocabulary Answers will vary.
II. Grammar
1. The subjunctive mood is used to say that one person influences the actions of another.
2. **Ud./Uds.**
3. **ir:**

vaya	vayamos
vayas	vayáis
vaya	vayan
dar:	
dé	demos
des	deis
dé	den
ser:	
sea	seamos
seas	seáis
sea	sean
saber:	
sepa	sepamos
sepas	sepáis
sepa	sepan

A ver si recuerdas: The infinitive in verbal expressions (p. 399)

- Many verbal expressions contain infinitives. These include:
  Expressing plans, desires, and wishes:
  Mi hermana *piensa nadar* pero yo *quiero pasear* en bote.
  My sister is thinking of swimming but I want to take a boat ride.
  Expressing obligation:
  ***¿Tienes que descansar* ahora?**
  Do you have to rest now?
- In these expressions, only the first verb is conjugated. The second verb remains in the infinitive. Consider these sentences:
  Mi hermana nada y pasea en bote.
  My sister swims and takes boat rides.
  Mi hermana *piensa nadar* y *quiere pasear* en bote también.
  My sister is thinking of swimming and wants to take a boat ride, too.

A. Read the following sentences. Circle the correct verb from the parentheses. Follow the models.

Modelo 1 Julia y Ramón (**van** / **ir**) de pesca a menudo.

Modelo 2 Mi tía y yo queremos (**vamos** / **ir**) al cine.

1. A nosotros nos gustaría (**tomamos** / **tomar**) el sol.
2. Mi padre prefiere (**esquiar** / **esquía**).
3. Todas las tardes, yo (**monto** / **montar**) a caballo.
4. ¿Piensas tú (**vas** / **ir**) de cámping?
5. Yo debo (**comprar** / **compro**) recuerdos para mi familia.
6. Mis amigos (**toman** / **tomar**) muchas fotos.
7. ¿Quieres (**ir** / **vas**) a las montañas con nosotros?
8. Juan y yo tenemos que (**regresar** / **regresamos**) al hotel ahora.

realidades.com
• Web Code: jdd-0801

Realidades 2 | Nombre ____ | Hora ____

Capítulo 8A | Fecha ____ | **AVSR 8A-2**

A ver si recuerdas: The infinitive in verbal expressions (*continued*)

- The infinitive is also used after impersonal verbal expressions:

  ***Es necesario tener* mucho cuidado cuando buceas.**
  It is necessary to be very careful when you scuba dive.

  ***Hay que regresar* antes de las cinco y media.**
  One must (You should) return before 5:30.

B. Circle the most appropriate impersonal expression from the parentheses to complete the sentences below. The first one is done for you.

1. **(Hay que / Es divertido)** montar a caballo en la playa.
2. **(Es interesante / Es necesario)** hacer planes antes de salir de vacaciones.
3. **(Es malo / Es interesante)** visitar el zoológico.
4. **(Hay que / Es divertido)** hacer las reservaciones del hotel un mes antes de salir.
5. **(Es necesario / Es malo)** descansar mucho durante las vacaciones.

C. Using the words given as clues, write full sentences. Remember to use the infinitive after the verbs expressing plans, desires, wishes, and obligations.

Modelo Ramiro / querer / viajar al campo
Ramiro quiere viajar al campo

1. Jorge y Sara / necesitar / regresar a casa
   Jorge y Sara necesitan regresar a casa
2. A Marieli / le / encantar / bucear
   A Marieli le encanta bucear
3. Hay que / calentar el caldo
   Hay que calentar el caldo
4. Luz y yo / pensar / pasear en bote
   Luz y yo pensamos pasear en bote
5. Yo / tener que / pasar tiempo con mis tíos
   Yo tengo que pasar tiempo con mis tíos
6. Es divertido / hacer una fogata
   Es divertido hacer una fogata
7. Tú y Bruni / desear / montar en bicicleta
   Tú y Bruni desean montar en bicicleta

Realidades 2 | Nombre ____ | Hora ____

Capítulo 8A | Fecha ____ | **Vocabulary Flash Cards, Sheet 1**

Write the Spanish vocabulary word or phrase below each picture. Be sure to include the article for each noun.

la agencia de viajes

la agente de viajes

el agente de viajes

el pasaporte

hacer la maleta

la maleta

el aeropuerto

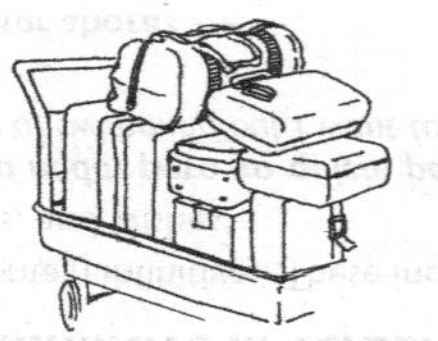

el equipaje

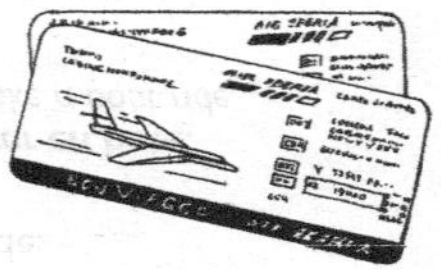

la tarjeta de embarque

Realidades 2 — Capítulo 8A

Nombre ______ Hora ______

Fecha ______

Vocabulary Flash Cards, Sheet 2

Write the Spanish vocabulary word or phrase below each picture. Be sure to include the article for each noun.

 **el** / **pasajero**	 **la** / **pasajera**	 **la** / **turista**
 **el** / **turista**	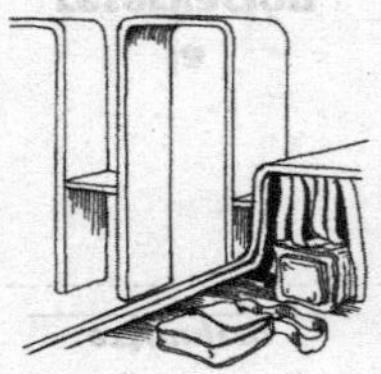 **la inspección** / **de seguridad**	 **la puerta** / **de embarque**
 **el** / **vuelo**	 **la auxiliar** / **de vuelo**	 **el auxiliar** / **de vuelo**

Realidades 2 — Capítulo 8A

Nombre ______ Hora ______

Fecha ______

Vocabulary Flash Cards, Sheet 3

Write the Spanish vocabulary word below each picture. If there is a word or phrase, copy it in the space provided. Be sure to include the article for each noun.

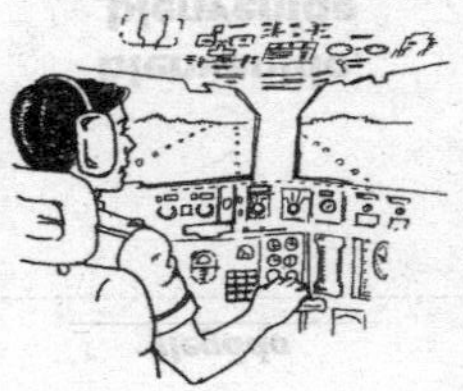 **la** / **piloto**	 **el** / **piloto**	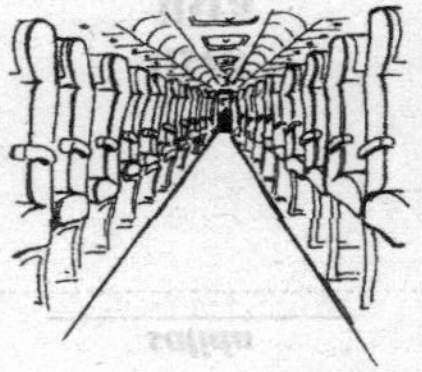 **el** / **pasillo**
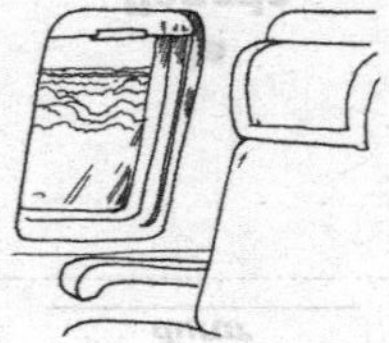 **la** / **ventanilla**	 **el** / **aduanero**	 **la** / **aduanera**
 **registrar**	 **el** / **anuncio**	**abierto, abierta** / **abierto**, / **abierta**

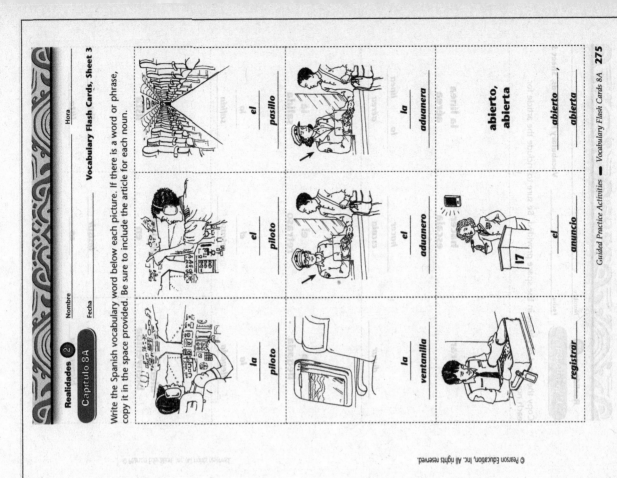

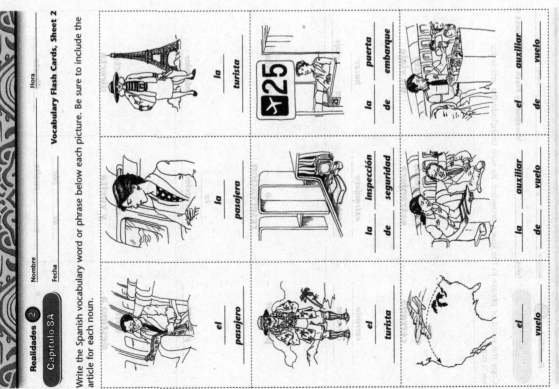

Realidades 2 | Capítulo 8A

Nombre ______ Hora ______

Fecha ______ **Vocabulary Flash Cards, Sheet 4**

Copy the word or phrase in the space provided. Be sure to include the article for each noun.

cerrado, cerrada — *cerrado*, *cerrada*	**extranjero, extranjera** — *extranjero*, *extranjera*	**hacer un viaje** — *hacer* *un* *viaje*
planear — *planear*	**la reservación** — *la* *reservación*	**abordar** — *abordar*
con destino a — *con* *destino* *a*	**de ida y vuelta** — *de* *ida* *y* *vuelta*	**directo, directa** — *directo*, *directa*

Realidades 2 | Capítulo 8A

Nombre ______ Hora ______

Fecha ______ **Vocabulary Flash Cards, Sheet 5**

Copy the word or phrase in the space provided. Be sure to include the article for each noun.

durar — *durar*	**hacer escala** — *hacer* *escala*	**la línea aérea** — *la* *línea* *aérea*
la llegada — *la* *llegada*	**el retraso** — *el* *retraso*	**la salida** — *la* *salida*
bienvenido, bienvenida — *bienvenido*, *bienvenida*	**insistir en** — *insistir* *en*	**listo, lista** — *listo*, *lista*

Realidades 2 | Nombre ____ Hora ____

Capítulo 8A | Fecha ____ **Vocabulary Flash Cards, Sheet 6**

Copy the word or phrase in the space provided. Be sure to include the article for each noun. The blank cards can be used to write and practice other Spanish vocabulary in the chapter.

sugerir *sugerir*	**tendremos** *tendremos*	**tener paciencia** *tener* *paciencia*
la aduana *la* *aduana*	**el empleado, la empleada** *el* *empleado*, *la* *empleada*	**facturar** *facturar*

Realidades 2 | Nombre ____ Hora ____

Capítulo 8A | Fecha ____ **Vocabulary Check, Sheet 1**

Tear out this page. Write the English words on the lines. Fold the paper along the dotted line to see the correct answers so you can check your work.

la agencia de viajes	*travel agency*
el equipaje	*luggage*
extranjero, extranjera	*foreign*
hacer un viaje	*to take a trip*
la maleta	*suitcase*
planear	*to plan*
abordar	*to board*
la aduana	*customs*
el aeropuerto	*airport*
el anuncio	*announcement*
de ida y vuelta	*round-trip*
la salida	*departure*
el vuelo	*flight*
abierto, abierta	*open*

Fold In ←

Tear out this page. Write the Spanish words on the lines. Fold the paper along the dotted line to see the correct answers so you can check your work.

travel agency	***la agencia de viajes***
luggage	***el equipaje***
foreign	***extranjero, extranjera***
to take a trip	***hacer un viaje***
suitcase	***la maleta***
to plan	***planear***
to board	***abordar***
customs	***la aduana***
airport	***el aeropuerto***
announcement	***el anuncio***
round-trip	***de ida y vuelta***
departure	***la salida***
flight	***el vuelo***
open	***abierto, abierta***

Fold In ←

Tear out this page. Write the English words on the lines. Fold the paper along the dotted line to see the correct answers so you can check your work.

el pasaporte	***passport***
la reservación	***reservation***
el turista, la turista	***tourist***
directo, directa	***direct***
durar	***to last***
el empleado, la empleada	***employee***
la línea aérea	***airline***
el pasajero, la pasajera	***passenger***
registrar	***to inspect, to search (luggage)***
bienvenido, bienvenida	***welcome***
necesitar	***to need***
permitir	***to allow, to permit***
preferir	***to prefer***
cerrado, cerrada	***closed***

Fold In ←

Realidades 2 | Nombre | Hora

Capítulo 8A | Fecha | **Vocabulary Check, Sheet 4**

Tear out this page. Write the Spanish words on the lines. Fold the paper along the dotted line to see the correct answers so you can check your work.

passport	***el pasaporte***
reservation	***la reservación***
tourist	***el turista, la turista***
direct	***directo, directa***
to last	***durar***
employee	***el empleado, la empleada***
airline	***la línea aérea***
passenger	***el pasajero, la pasajera***
to inspect, to search *(luggage)*	***registrar***
welcome	***bienvenido, bienvenida***
to need	***necesitar***
to allow, to permit	***permitir***
to prefer	***preferir***
closed	***cerrado, cerrada***

Fold In ←

To hear a complete list of the vocabulary for this chapter, go to www.realidades.com and type in the Web Code jdd-0889. Then click on **Repaso del capítulo.**

Realidades 2 | Nombre | Hora

Capítulo 8A | Fecha | **Guided Practice Activities 8A-1**

The present subjunctive (p. 410)

- You form the present subjunctive in the same way that you form negative **tú** commands and **usted/ustedes** commands. You drop the **-o** of the present-tense indicative **yo** form and add the present subjunctive endings. See the chart below:

hablar		**aprender**		**escribir**	
hable	hablemos	aprenda	aprendamos	escriba	escribamos
hables	habléis	aprendas	aprendáis	escribas	escribáis
hable	hablen	aprenda	aprendan	escriba	escriban

A. Write the subjunctive ending for each of the verbs below. Follow the model.

Modelo yo / asistir — asist *a*

1. los pasajeros / abordar — abord ***en***
2. tú / beber — beb ***as***
3. nosotros / viajar — viaj ***emos***
4. el vuelo / durar — dur ***e***
5. tú / desear — dese ***es***
6. yo / vivir — viv ***a***
7. la familia / planear — plane ***e***
8. nosotros / llevar — llev ***emos***

- The present subjunctive has the same spelling changes that you used with the negative **tú** commands and **usted/ustedes** commands.
- Here are the present subjunctive forms of **llegar** and **sacar:**

llegar		**sacar**	
llegue	lleguemos	saque	saquemos
llegues	lleguéis	saques	saquéis
llegue	lleguen	saque	saquen

realidades.com • Web Code: jdd-0804

The present subjunctive (*continued*)

B. Look at the sentences using the present subjunctive below. Underline the second verb in each and then circle the spelling change in each verb that you underlined. The first one has been done for you.

1. La profesora recomienda que nosotros saquemos más libros de la biblioteca.
2. Yo necesito que ustedes paguen por los boletos hoy.
3. Se recomienda que los empleados busquen cosas prohibidas.
4. El niño desea que la mamá no apague la luz.
5. Prefiero que tú llegues a tiempo.
6. El entrenador quiere que los jugadores jueguen todos los días de esta semana.
7. El Sr. Vega prohíbe que nosotros toquemos las exposiciones.
8. Papá recomienda que yo me seque las manos.

- The same verbs that have irregular **yo** forms in the present indicative are also irregular in the present subjunctive.
- Here are the conjugations of two verbs that have this irregular pattern:

tener		conocer	
tenga	tengamos	conozca	conozcamos
tengas	tengáis	conozcas	conozcáis
tenga	tengan	conozca	conozcan

C. Write the irregular **yo** form of the present indicative for the first part of each example below. Then, write the correct present subjunctive form using the cues given in the second part. The first one is done for you.

	Present Indicative	Present Subjunctive
1. traer	yo *traigo*	Andrés y Toni *traigan*
2. decir	yo ***digo***	tú ***digas***
3. conducir	yo ***conduzco***	Diego ***conduzca***
4. salir	yo ***salgo***	yo ***salga***
5. ofrecer	yo ***ofrezco***	Ana y Javier ***ofrezcan***
6. venir	yo ***vengo***	tú ***vengas***
7. hacer	yo ***hago***	María y yo ***hagamos***
8. oír	yo ***oigo***	Ud. ***oiga***

The present subjunctive (*continued*)

D. Write the correct present subjunctive forms of the verbs given. The first one is done for you.

El agente de viajes sugiere que...

1. ...nosotros *hablemos* (**hablar**) con el piloto antes de salir.
2. ...yo ***busque*** (**buscar**) un asiento cerca de la ventanilla.
3. ...mis padres ***lleguen*** (**llegar**) temprano al aeropuerto.
4. ...nosotros ***hagamos*** (**hacer**) las reservaciones con el hotel.
5. ...tú ***traigas*** (**traer**) el bloqueador solar.
6. ...yo no ***salga*** (**salir**) sin mi pasaporte.
7. ...mis hermanos y yo ***obedezcamos*** (**obedecer**) las reglas del viajero.
8. ...Pedro ***pase*** (**pasar**) a la salida.

- The present subjunctive is used when one person is influencing the actions of another, by advising, prohibiting, or suggesting. Some verbs that often introduce the subjunctive mood are:

decir *to say; to tell*	**preferir** *to prefer*	**querer** *to want*
insistir en *to insist upon*	**permitir** *to permit*	**prohibir** *to prohibit*
necesitar *to need*	**recomendar** *to recommend*	**sugerir** *to suggest*

- These verbs are used in the indicative, but the verbs that follow them are used in the subjunctive. The word **que** connects the two parts of the sentence.

Indicative **Subjunctive**

Su madre le prohibe *que* Agustina salga de la casa después de las nueve.
El profesor recomienda *que* nosotros visitemos el zoológico.

Realidades 2 Nombre ______ Hora ______

Capítulo 8A Fecha ______ **Guided Practice Activities 8A-3a**

The present subjunctive (*continued*)

- Subjunctive sentences have two parts, each part with its own subject. Notice that the first part uses the present indicative to recommend, suggest, prohibit, and so on:

  El agente de viajes quiere...

- The second part uses the present subjunctive to say what the other subject should or should not do:

  ...nosotros visitemos el zoológico.

  El agente de viajes quiere que nosotros visitemos el zoológico.
  The travel agent wants us to visit the zoo.

E. Read the following sentences. In each sentence, underline the verb that shows that one person is trying to influence the action of another (present indicative) and circle the verb that indicates what the other person should do (present subjunctive). Follow the model.

Modelo Mi maestro permite que nosotros trabajemos en grupos.

1. La agente de viajes sugiere que ellos visiten La Paz.
2. El aduanero insiste en que tú tengas el pasaporte en la mano.
3. Los hermanos necesitan que los padres aborden con ellos.
4. El piloto les dice a los pasajeros que apaguen los teléfonos celulares.
5. El tío recomienda que nosotros facturemos el equipaje temprano.

F. In each sentence below, underline the verb that shows that one person is trying to influence the action of another. Then, write the subjunctive form of the verb in parentheses. Follow the model.

Modelo Carlos sugiere que nosotros ***pasemos*** a la casa de cambios. (**pasar**)

1. Pancho sugiere que Julián y Lolis ***traigan*** los pasaportes a la aduana. (**traer**)
2. Los auxiliares de vuelo recomiendan que yo ***beba*** jugo de manzana. (**beber**)
3. Yo quiero que los auxiliares de vuelo me ***ayuden*** (**ayudar**)
4. La profesora le dice a Sofía que ella ***aprenda*** sobre los lugares que visita. (**aprender**)
5. La aduanera permite que tú ***hagas*** la maleta ahora. (**hacer**)

realidades.com • Web Code: jdd-0804

Realidades 2 Nombre ______ Hora ______

Capítulo 8A Fecha ______ **Guided Practice Activities 8A-3b**

The present subjunctive (*continued*)

G. Fill in the blank in the first part of each sentence below with the present indicative form of the verb to show that someone wants to influence another person's actions. In the second part of the sentence, fill in the blanks with the subjunctive form of the verb to say what someone should do. The first one is done for you.

1. Óscar (**sugerir**) ***sugiere*** que nosotros (**visitar**) ***visitemos*** la casa de cambio antes de salir.
2. Nosotros (**recomendar**) ***recomendamas*** que Uds. (**comprar**) ***compren*** una guía de la ciudad.
3. La empleada (**necesitar**) ***necesita*** que tú le ***escribas*** (**escribir**) tu número de pasaporte.
4. Esa agente de vuelos (**prohibir**) ***prohíbe*** que los pasajeros (**llegar**) ***lleguen*** tarde.
5. Mis padres (**preferir**) ***prefieren*** que yo (**comer**) ***coma*** con ellos.
6. Los auxiliares de vuelo (**insistir**) ***insisten*** en que nosotros (**obedecer**) ***obedezcamos*** a los señales (*signs*).

H. Use the words given to write complete sentences in the order in which the words appear. Follow the model.

Remember: The verb that shows that one person is trying to influence the action of another uses the present indicative while the verb that tells what the other person should do uses the present subjunctive.

Modelo Felipe / insistir en / que / Amelia / tener paciencia
Felipe insiste en que Amelia tenga paciencia

1. Los profesores / sugerir / que / los estudiantes / estudiar más horas
   Los profesores sugieren que los estudiantes estudien más horas
2. Nosotros / recomendar / que / Uds. / llegar temprano a los exámenes
   Nosotros recomendamos que Uds. lleguen temprano a los exámenes
3. Mis padres / querer / que / yo / asistir a una buena universidad
   Mis padres quieren que yo asista a una buena universidad
4. Mamá / necesitar / que / nosotros / poner la mesa
   Mamá necesita que nosotros pongamos la mesa
5. Yo / preferir / que / tú / buscar otro trabajo
   Yo prefiero que tú busques otro trabajo

realidades.com • Web Code: jdd-0804

Irregular verbs in the subjunctive (p. 413)

- Verbs with irregular **tú** and **usted/ustedes** commands also have irregular subjunctive forms.

dar		estar		ir		saber		ser	
dé	demos	esté	estemos	vaya	vayamos	sepa	sepamos	sea	seamos
des	deis	estés	estéis	vayas	vayáis	sepas	sepáis	seas	seáis
dé	den	esté	estén	vaya	vayan	sepa	sepan	sea	sean

A. Read each sentence below and circle the verb in its subjunctive form. Then, write the infinitive of the circled verb in the blank. Follow the model.

Modelo Recomiendo que Ana te (dé) la tarjeta de embarque. ***dar***

1. Sugiero que el pasajero (esté) aquí a las cuatro. ***estar***
2. Quiero que (vayas) a la agencia de viajes. ***ir***
3. Deseo que (sepas) la hora de llegada. ***saber***
4. Insisto en que (sean) responsables. ***ser***
5. Necesito que el vuelo (sea) de ida y vuelta. ***ser***

B. Circle the second subject in each sentence. Then, write the correct form of the verb in parentheses using the present subjunctive. The first one is done for you.

1. Deseo que (ustedes) ***estén*** en el aeropuerto muy temprano. (estar)
2. Recomiendo que (ustedes) ***den*** sus maletas a los empleados. (dar)
3. Sugiero que (tú) ***vayas*** a la agencia de viajes. (ir)
4. Quiero que (ella) ***sepa*** dónde está la puerta de embarque. (saber)
5. Necesito que (la maleta) ***sea*** grande. (ser)
6. La empleada de la aerolínea quiere que (yo) le ***dé*** mi tarjeta de embarque. (dar)

realidades.com
• Web Code: jdd-0804

Lectura: Ecuador, país de maravillas (pp. 418–419)

A. The reading in your textbook is about the South American country of Ecuador. Write three things that you would expect to find in your reading about its tourist attractions.

1. ***Answers will vary.***
2. ______
3. ______

B. You can often predict what a reading is about by looking at the title, subheads, and photo captions. Look at the photos and read the captions on pages 418–419 of your textbook. Place an *X* next to the attractions you can find in Ecuador.

Las atracciones turísticas del Ecuador

X woven cloth	***X*** la Mitad del Mundo
___ the island of Puerto Rico	***X*** snow-covered mountains
X the Galapagos Islands	***X*** the church of La Compañía de Jesús

C. Read the excerpt from your reading and circle the letter of the answers to the questions that follow.

> *Es un país pequeño, pero tiene paisajes para todos los gustos* (tastes)*: desde playas tropicales hasta montañas nevadas, desde ciudades coloniales hasta parques naturales. Ecuador es una joya.*

1. ¿Qué clase de país es Ecuador?
   (a.) Es un país pequeño.
   b. Es un país grande.
2. ¿Dónde nieva en Ecuador?
   a. Nieva en las playas tropicales.
   (b.) Nieva en las montañas.
3. ¿Hay ciudades coloniales en Ecuador?
   (a.) Sí, hay ciudades coloniales en Ecuador.
   b. No, no hay ciudades coloniales en Ecuador.
4. ¿Qué clase de parques hay en Ecuador?
   a. Hay parques artificiales en Ecuador.
   (b.) Hay parques naturales en Ecuador.

realidades.com
• Web Code: jdd-0806

Realidades 2 Nombre ______ Hora ______

Capítulo 8A Fecha ______ **Guided Practice Activities 8A-6**

Presentación oral (p. 421)

Task: Imagine that you work at a travel agency. You need to provide travel information to a client who would like to travel to a Spanish-speaking country.

A. Choose one of the following Spanish-speaking countries: Mexico or Ecuador.

B. Read the following travel information about each country. Then, circle one or two recommendations you would offer based on what you read. ***Answers will vary.***

1. La ciudad de Quito en Ecuador está en las montañas y hace mucho frío. Hay una iglesia muy importante.
   - **a.** Recomiendo que lleven poca ropa.
   - **b.** Sugiero que vayan a la iglesia La Compañía de Jesús.
   - **c.** Recomiendo que lleven suéteres o chaquetas.
2. Cancún está en México. En Cancún hay una playa tropical de 14 millas y muchos hoteles elegantes.
   - **a.** Si desean ir a una playa grande, yo recomiendo que vayan a Cancún.
   - **b.** Si buscan un hotel elegante, vayan a Cancún.
   - **c.** Recomiendo que lleven trajes de baño.

C. Use your recommendations in **part B** as a model for your oral presentation. You may use the sentence starters below. Don't forget to use the subjunctive when you are advising, prohibiting, or suggesting something to your client. ***Answers will vary.***

Recomiendo que Uds. viajen a ______ *Allí pueden ver* ______ *Deben llevar* ______

porque ______

D. Now, practice your presentation using the information you have gathered. Try to present the information in a logical sequence and speak clearly.

E. Present the trip you have planned to your partner. Your teacher will grade you on the following:

- how much information you communicate
- how easy it is to understand you

Left page

Antes de ver el video

Actividad 1

There are many ways to travel: by plane, boat, bus, train, or car. Mark with an **X** the method of transportation you think would be best for each situation.

situaciones	avión	barco	autobús	coche	tren
Tengo sólo una semana de vacaciones y está lejos.	X				
Estamos planeando ir a Aruba, la isla en el mar Caribe.	X	X			
Somos estudiantes y no tenemos mucho dinero.			X	X	X
Sólo puedo ir al acto de graduación por el fin de semana.	X				
No me gusta manejar, pero me encanta ver el paisaje.			X		X
Quiero llegar rápido para estar más tiempo con mis primos.	X				
No está tan lejos, somos muchos y tenemos mucho equipaje.			X	X	
Lo más divertido es conocer todas las islas.		X			
Está lejos pero hay varios pueblos interesantes por el camino.				X	X

Right page

¿Comprendes?

Actividad 2

Ana is writing to a friend about her upcoming trip. Some of her statements are true and some are false. If the statement is true, write **cierto.** If the statement is false, rewrite it to make it true.

1. Elena y yo estamos planeando un viaje a Rusia para estudiar ruso.
   Falso, Elena y Ana están planeando un viaje a Londres para estudiar inglés.
2. Esta mañana fuimos a la agencia de viajes para comprar el billete.
   Cierto.
3. Un vuelo directo a Londres en avión cuesta cincuenta euros ida y vuelta.
   Falso, un vuelo directo cuesta más; doscientos dos con ochenta y seis euros ida y vuelta.
4. Decidimos viajar en tren y viajamos en el "eurostar" para ir de Barcelona a Londres.
   Falso, el "eurostar" va de París a Londres.
5. Compramos el billete para estudiantes. La agente nos dijo que muchos niños viajan así.
   Falso, la agente nos dijo que muchos estudiantes extranjeros viajan así.
6. El viaje dura como catorce horas y quince minutos.
   Cierto.
7. Ya hicimos la reserva.
   Cierto.

Actividad 3

Answer the following questions based on what happened in the video.

1. 
   ¿Por qué está Ana tan impaciente en la agencia de viajes?
   Ella está esperando a Elena.
2. ¿Para qué van Ana y Elena a Londres y por cuánto tiempo?
   Ellas van a estudiar inglés; van por dos semanas.

Realidades 2 | Nombre ______ Hora ______

Capítulo 8A | Fecha ______ **VIDEO**

3. ¿Cómo quieren ir a Londres? **Ellas quieren viajar en avión.**
4. ¿Qué sugerencia les hace la agente de viajes? **Viajar en tren hasta París y después ir a Londres en el "eurostar".**
5. ¿Qué tipo más barato de billete pueden comprar? **El billete para estudiantes.**
6. 
¿Por qué Elena no está muy segura de viajar en tren?
Porque es un viaje muy largo.
7. 
¿Cómo deciden finalmente viajar a Londres las muchachas?
Ellas deciden ir a Londres en tren.
8. 
¿Por qué Elena y Ana tienen que regresar a la agencia?
Ellas olvidaron los billetes en la agencia.

Y, ¿qué más?

Actividad 4

Think about a trip you would like to take one day with a friend or family member. Answer the following questions to help create your itinerary.

¿Qué sitio te gustaría conocer en estas vacaciones?

Answers will vary.

¿Cómo quieres viajar?

¿Con quién te gustaría ir?

¿Cuánto tiempo tienes para hacer el viaje?

¿Qué documentos necesitas para el viaje?

Realidades 2 | Nombre ______ Hora ______

Capítulo 8A | Fecha ______ **AUDIO**

Actividad 5

Listen to the messages recorded by different airlines for customers to listen to as they wait for the next available agent to take their phone call. As you listen to each announcement, identify which picture best matches each taped message. Write the number of the conversation in the blank under the corresponding picture. You will hear each message twice.

2

4

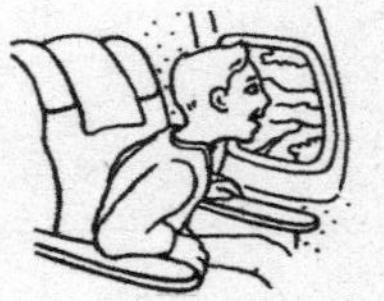
1

3

6

5

Actividad 6

Several Spanish club members just got back from a summer trip to Europe with their teacher. On the way home from the airport, two girls talk about what happened on the trip and how their classmates acted. As you listen, decide whether the student they are talking about was a **buen(a) turista** or **mal(a) turista** and mark the grid below with your answer. You will hear each conversation twice.

	1	2	3	4	5	6
Buen(a) turista			X		X	
Mal(a) turista	X	X		X		X

Realidades 2 Nombre Hora

Capítulo 8A Fecha AUDIO

Actividad 7

When her friends and family find out that Elisa is going on a school trip to Europe, they all have advice for her about her initial plane trip to Madrid. As you listen to each person's advice, match his or her suggestion to the corresponding picture below. Write the number of the conversation underneath the correct drawing. You will hear each suggestion twice.

2

4

5

3

1

Actividad 8

Listen to a panel of seasoned travelers and school officials as they give suggestions to students who are taking a trip next month. As you listen to each suggestion, decide whether it is a: **a) sugerencia para planear el viaje; b) sugerencia para el aeropuerto y durante el vuelo; c) sugerencia para cuando viajan por las ciudades que visitan;** or **d) sugerencia sobre qué comprar como recuerdo del viaje.** Write the correct letter in each space below. You will hear each suggestion twice.

1. b 3. b 5. c 7. d 9. b

2. d 4. a 6. c 8. a 10. c

Realidades 2 Nombre Hora

Capítulo 8A Fecha AUDIO

Actividad 9

People sometimes encounter difficulties while traveling. As you listen to each of these three people discuss his or her problem, determine what the problem is and circle the appropriate answer. You will hear each discussion twice.

Viajero(a)	Problema
Sr. Machado	**a.** Necesita ir a Chile para una reunión importante por la tarde. **b.** No tiene su pasaporte para pasar por la aduana. (**c.** Su vuelo directo a Buenos Aires llega demasiado tarde.)
Sra. Manizales	**a.** Perdió a su mejor amigo en el aeropuerto. (**b.** Olvidó el oso de peluche de su hija en el avión.) **c.** Olvidó una maleta en el avión.
Luis	(**a.** Él es muy impaciente.) **b.** Tiene miedo de las inspecciones de seguridad. **c.** Llegó tarde al avión.

Realidades 2 — Nombre ________ Hora ________

Capítulo 8A — Fecha ________ **WRITING**

Actividad 10

You are showing your friend Ricardo your pictures from a recent trip to Guatemala. Because Ricardo has never traveled by plane, he is curious about what it was like. Describe your trip to him, using the photos below to help you.

1. **Answer should include *tarjeta de embarque***

2. **Answer should include *abordar***

3. **Answer should include *el aduanero***

4. **Answer should include *de ida y vuelta***

5. **Answer should include *facturar***

6. **Answer should include *el retraso***

7. **Answer should include *la ventanilla***

8. **Answer should include *el auxiliar de vuelo***

Realidades 2 — Nombre ________ Hora ________

Capítulo 8A — Fecha ________ **WRITING**

Actividad 11

Two new students at your school are asking you how to succeed in Spanish class. Answer their questions below in complete sentences.

BERTO: Nos gustaría saber más de la clase de español. Por ejemplo, ¿cuántas horas recomiendas que nosotros estudiemos todas las noches?

TÚ: **Answers will vary but will likely include verbs given in questions.**

TITO: ¿Sugieres que nosotros tomemos la clase del profesor Álvarez?

TÚ: ________

BERTO: ¿El profesor Álvarez permite que los estudiantes usen los libros en los exámenes?

TÚ: ________

TITO: ¿Qué más prefiere él que los estudiantes hagan?

TÚ: ________

BERTO: ¿Qué prohíbe que su clase haga?

TÚ: ________

TITO: Otra pregunta: ¿La escuela insiste en que yo tome tres años de español?

TÚ: ________

BERTO: Muchas gracias por tu ayuda. ¿Tienes más recomendaciones para nosotros?

TÚ: ________

Actividad 12

A. Some students and teachers are having an informal discussion in the cafeteria about some issues at school. Combine a subject and verb from **Columna A** with a logical subject and verb from **Columna B** to write complete sentences telling what some of the issues are. You may need to add some information to complete the sentences. Follow the model.

Columna A	Columna B
Nosotros/querer	yo/saber el vocabulario
Los profesores/preferir	tú/ser malo
El principal/prohibir	los profesores/no dar exámenes
La profesora de francés/insistir en	nosotros/ir a clase
Yo/recomendar	tú/estar despierto

Modelo *Nosotros queremos que los profesores no den exámenes los lunes.*

1. Answers will vary.
2. ____
3. ____
4. ____

B. Now, write three recommendations to your own school's administration using the verbs **ser, estar, ir, saber,** or **dar**.

1. Answers will vary.
2. ____
3. ____

Actividad 13

Your friend Rosario is coming to visit you from Ecuador next week. She is a bit nervous about traveling by plane alone, so you write her an e-mail reminding her of what to do while traveling. Complete the e-mail below with advice for Rosario.

Fecha: 9/4/12
Sujeto: Algunas recomendaciones
Recipiente: rosario@xyz.xyz
De: ____
Mensaje: Hola, Rosario. No puedo esperar hasta tu llegada. Antes de ir al aeropuerto, quiero que des el número de tu vuelo a tus padres.

Answers will vary.

¡Buena suerte y te veo pronto!

Test Preparation Answers

Reading Skills
p. 274 2. **C**
p. 275 2. **B**

Integrated Performance Assessment
p. 276
Answers will vary.

School-to-Home Connection

Dear Parent or Guardian,

The theme of our current unit is *Cómo ser un buen turista* (How to be a good tourist). This chapter is called *Quiero que disfrutes de tu viaje* (I want you to enjoy your trip).

Upon completion of this chapter students will be able to:

- discuss recreational activities while traveling in a foreign city
- talk about staying in a hotel
- explain how to be a good tourist
- make recommendations about travel and sightseeing
- understand cultural perspectives on traveling

Students will also explore:

- the use of the suffix *–ero(a)*

Our textbook, *Realidades,* helps with the development of reading, writing, and speaking skills through the use of strategies, process speaking, and process writing. In this chapter, students will:

- read about the historic city of Antigua, Guatemala
- prepare an illustrated brochure about a Spanish-speaking country

To reinforce and enhance learning, students can access a wide range of online resources on **realidades.com,** the personalized learning management system that accompanies the print and online Student Edition. Resources include the eText, textbook and workbook activities, audio files, videos, animations, songs, self-study tools, interactive maps, voice recording (RealTalk!), assessments, and other digital resources. Many learning tools can be accessed through the student Home Page on **realidades.com.** Other activities, specifically those that require grading, are assigned by the teacher and linked on the student Home Page within the calendar or the Assignments tab.

You will find specifications and guidelines for accessing **realidades.com** on home computers and mobile devices on MyPearsonTraining.com under the SuccessNet Plus tab.

realidades.com

For: Tips to Parents
Visit: www.realidades.com
Web Code: jce-0010

Check it out! At the end of the chapter, have your child name four appropriate tourist behaviors. Then have your child name three tourist activities he or she would enjoy on a trip.

Sincerely,

Videocultura Script

Viajar en Centroamérica

Spanish version:

América Central se sitúa justo al sur de México. En este istmo estrecho, se encuentran siete países de abundante belleza natural, historia, cultura y gente acogedora.

Un buen plan de viaje debe incluir una visita a la ciudad capital de uno de estos países, para conocer personas y lugares interesantes.

La influencia indígena se ve en la vida cotidiana. En Guatemala, el 40 por ciento de la población es de ascendencia maya.

Aparte de la gente y los sitios turísticos, puedes probar comida deliciosa. *Casamiento*, una combinación de arroz y frijoles, *plátanos* o *pupusas*, es la versión salvadoreña de la tortilla.

La verdadera belleza de estos países está en su naturaleza, lejos de las ciudades grandes.

Las islas de Roatán en Honduras reciben visitantes de todo el mundo que llegan para ver la impresionante vida marina.

En Nicaragua, hay muchísimos volcanes, como Concepción y Maderas.

Costa Rica es uno de los países con mayor biodiversidad del mundo. Hay selvas tropicales en las que puedes observar muchísimos animales y plantas.

América Central es sin duda una región perfecta para explorar e ir de vacaciones.

English version:

Central America is located just south of Mexico. The narrow isthmus contains seven countries that are known for their history, culture, natural beauty, and welcoming people.

A trip to any country in Central America offers an amazing opportunity. You can start in the capital city of one of these countries.

You can also see the history of the region in its people. In Guatemala, 40% of the population are of Mayan descent, and you may encounter the indigenous influence in everyday life.

In addition to the people and places, you can try authentic dishes such as *casamiento*, the combination of black beans and rice popular in El Salvador, fried bananas called *plátanos*, or *pupusas*, a version of the tortilla.

In any of the countries in Central America, you'll want to leave the big city to discover its diverse natural beauty.

In the Roatán islands in Honduras, visitors come from around the world for snorkeling and diving. The blue waters are teeming with marine life and stunning coral reefs.

In Nicaragua you can climb the impressive volcanoes such as Concepción and Maderas.

Costa Rica offers some of the greatest biodiversity in the world. You can visit dense tropical rain forests and misty cloud forests, observing the many plants and animals.

If you are looking for a vacation that combines history, culture, great food, and a variety of activities, add Central America as a future destination!

Input Script

Presentation

Input Vocabulary 1: Bring to class books about Spain that have vivid photos of the tourist sites in the *A primera vista* itinerary. Use adhesive notes to mark the pages of the photos. Present the itinerary by telling students that this is the schedule you followed on your latest trip to Madrid. Unfortunately, your film did not turn out and you have no pictures of your trip. Ask students to help you by drawing pictures of all the places you visited and the fun activities you did on your trip.

Distribute paper and color pencils or markers to students and tell students to draw one tourist site or activity per sheet of paper. Begin describing each place on the itinerary. Show students the photo of each place you describe.

After you have finished and students have completed their drawings, tell them that next time, you are going to do your trip in a different order. Tell them your new itinerary and have them arrange their drawings of tourist sites and activities in the order you mention them.

Input Vocabulary 2: Present the rules for tourists by describing each rule out of order. Have students point in their books to the rules you describe and read the text aloud. Then act out each rule to show what tourists should and should not do. Students will identify the rule involved in the situation you acted out and then show with a "thumbs-up" or "thumbs-down" sign if it is good or bad behavior.

For *ser cortés*, invite a student to play the role of a shopkeeper in a Spanish-speaking city. Walk in the store and request an item politely. For *no debes hacer ruido*, have a student pretend to be asleep in a hotel room. You enter the room next to him and turn on a radio playing loud music and begin to "rock out" to the music. For *darle una propina*, pretend to be dining at a fancy restaurant with a student playing the server. Leave him or her a big tip. For *estar muy atento*, have a student pretend to be a guide discussing a tourist site. You and another student are tourists talking loudly together while the guide lectures. For *ser puntual*, have a student pretend to be a tour bus driver. Run after the student as he or she drives away. For *cambiar dinero*, go back to the shopkeeper student and ask if you can buy something with American dollars. He or she will tell you "no."

Comprehension Check

- Have students scramble their drawings. Call out the tourist sites and activities and have students separate their drawings into Madrid sites, Toledo sites, and Valencia sites and activities, placing them in the order you mention them.
- Have students act out a skit about two friends on vacation in Valencia. One of the friends invites the other one to do different water activities. The other one declines and suggests a land activity. He or she does not want his or her friend to know that he or she cannot swim.
- Pair students, then call out different rules for tourists and have them act out the behaviors.

Audio Script

Audio DVD, Capítulo 8B

Track 01: *A primera vista, Quiero que disfrutes de tu viaje,* Student Book, p. 426, (5:12)

Vocabulario y gramática en contexto

Lee en tu libro mientras escuchas el diálogo.

ADULT FEMALE: Aquí tienen nuestro itinerario. Vamos a pasar diez días visitando Madrid, la capital de España, la ciudad histórica de Toledo y la ciudad de Valencia.

Vas a escuchar cada palabra o frase dos veces. Después de la primera vez hay una pausa para que puedas pronunciar la palabra o frase. Luego vas a escuchar de nuevo la palabra o frase.

itinerario	en punto
histórica	excursión
hacer una gira de	famoso
siguientes	La Catedral
palacio	estupendas
bello	

Lee en tu libro mientras escuchas el itinerario.

Itinerario para el grupo de la señora Guzmán

Día uno: Llegada al Aeropuerto de Barajas en Madrid. Transporte en autobús al hotel en Madrid.

Días dos a cuatro: Primero vamos a hacer una gira de la capital y en los días siguientes vamos a regresar a los lugares más famosos de la ciudad.

- La Plaza Mayor: un lugar histórico con tiendas y cafés al aire libre
- El Palacio Real: palacio ceremonial de los reyes
- El Parque del Retiro: un parque bello, originalmente lugar privado de los reyes
- El Museo del Prado: uno de los museos de arte más grandes y famosos del mundo

Día cinco: Lugares cerca de Madrid. El autobús sale a las ocho en punto: no vamos a salir tarde.

- El Escorial: palacio impresionante de Felipe II, el rey de España entre los años 1556–1598
- El Valle de los Caídos: monumento a los españoles que murieron en la Guerra Civil (entre 1936–1939)

Día seis: Excursión a Toledo. El autobús sale a las siete y media de la mañana y regresa a las cinco de la tarde.

- El Alcázar: originalmente un palacio árabe y después palacio del rey Carlos V en 1545
- La Iglesia de Santo Tomé: para ver el famoso cuadro de El Greco, *El entierro del conde de Orgaz* (1586–1588)
- La Catedral: un buen ejemplo de la arquitectura gótica y una de las catedrales más estupendas del mundo

Track 02: *A primera vista,* Student Book, p. 427, (4:53)

Vocabulario y gramática en contexto

Vas a escuchar cada palabra o frase dos veces. Después de la primera vez hay una pausa para que puedas pronunciar la palabra o frase. Luego vas a escuchar de nuevo la palabra o frase.

guía	hacer ruido
navegar	una propina
el surf de vela	observar
el esquí acuático	atento
la moto acuática	puntual
el bote de vela	cambiar
disfrutar de	una casa de cambio
cortés	el cajero automático
la habitación	

Lee en tu libro mientras escuchas el itinerario.

Días siete y ocho: Viaje en tren a Valencia. Dos días de excursiones en Valencia.

- Ciudad de las Artes y las Ciencias: un lugar con un poco de todo
- Museo Nacional de Cerámica: una colección de cerámica en un edificio histórico

Día nueve: Descansar en la playa cerca de Valencia. Con el permiso de sus padres, pueden hacer surf de vela, esquí acuático y moto acuática. También podemos ir con nuestro guía a navegar en un bote de vela.

Día diez: Regresamos a los Estados Unidos en el vuelo 519.

Para disfrutar de este viaje a España, tenemos que ser buenos turistas. Por eso necesitamos prestar atención a las siguientes reglas.

Durante el viaje hay que…

- Ser cortés. Los buenos modales siempre son importantes.
- Estar en la habitación a las once en punto. No debes hacer ruido en las habitaciones.
- Darle una propina al hombre que lleva el equipaje. Es una costumbre que debes observar.
- Estar muy atento—prestar atención a los guías cuando hacemos excursiones y giras.
- Quedarse en grupos y ser puntual. Es necesario llegar a tiempo.
- Usar el tiempo libre para cambiar dinero. Se puede ir a una casa de cambio, al banco o se puede usar el cajero automático.

Track 03: *A primera vista,* Act. 1, Student Book, p. 427, (2:43)

¿Madrid, Toledo o Valencia?

Vas a escuchar varias descripciones de lugares en España. En una hoja de papel, escribe el nombre de la ciudad (Madrid, Toledo o Valencia) donde se encuentra cada lugar. Vas a escuchar las descripciones dos veces.

1. En este lugar hay muchas tiendas y cafés afuera.
2. Los turistas vienen de todas partes del mundo para ver esta catedral estupenda.

3. Vamos a la playa para navegar en un bote de vela o hacer el esquí acuático.
4. Vamos a ver un cuadro muy famoso del artista El Greco en esta iglesia.
5. Vamos a hacer una gira en este museo enorme, que es famoso por sus colecciones importantes de arte.
6. En una de nuestras excursiones, vamos a este parque grande y bello.
7. Hay una bella colección de cerámica en este lugar.

Track 04: *A primera vista*, Act. 2, Student Book, p. 427, (2:44)

¿Es buena idea o no?

Imagina que eres turista en España con tu clase de español. Escucha lo que dicen tus compañeros y si es buena idea, señala con el pulgar hacia arriba. Si es mala idea, señala con el pulgar hacia abajo. Vas a escuchar las frases dos veces.

1. Se puede hacer mucho ruido en la habitación a la una de la mañana.
2. Hay que dejar una propina después de comer en un restaurante.
3. Hay que estar atento a lo que dice el guía.
4. Se pueden cambiar cheques o dinero en una casa de cambio.
5. Ser cortés y puntual no será tan importante en este viaje.
6. Se puede salir solo para hacer una gira en la ciudad.
7. No es necesario observar las horas de salida en el itinerario.
8. Se puede sacar dinero del banco usando el cajero automático.

Track 05: *A primera vista, Videohistoria*, Student Book, pp. 428–429, (2:45)

Un día en Toledo

¡Acompaña a Ignacio y a Javier durante su visita a Toledo! Lee en tu libro mientras escuchas la *Videohistoria*.

See Student Book pages 428–429 for script.

Track 06: *Manos a la obra*, Act. 6, Student Book, p. 431, (2:26)

Escucha y escribe

Vas a escuchar lo que puede hacer un turista en un país extranjero. En una hoja de papel, haz dos columnas. Sobre una columna, escribe *cortés*. Sobre la otra columna, escribe *descortés*. Escribe en cada columna las acciones apropiadas que escuchas. Vas a escuchar las frases dos veces.

1. Hacer mucho ruido en la habitación del hotel.
2. Regatear en un almacén grande.
3. Estar atento cuando el guía está hablando.
4. Observar las costumbres del país extranjero.
5. Darle una propina a la persona que lleva tu maleta a tu habitación.
6. Decir "Buenos días," "por favor" y "gracias."
7. Reírse de la artesanía que tienen los vendedores.

Track 07: *Manos a la obra*, Act. 9, Student Book, p. 433, (3:36)

Los mejores hoteles

Imagina que eres agente de viajes y puedes recomendarles a tus clientes uno de los hoteles en estos anuncios. Lee los anuncios. Después escucha las preferencias de las personas y escribe *Hotel Real, Hotel Canarias* o *los dos hoteles* según la información en los anuncios. Vas a escuchar las frases dos veces.

1. **Adult Female:** A nosotros nos encanta nadar, tomar el sol y hacer deportes acuáticos.
2. **Adult Male:** Vamos a viajar al hotel en un avión privado pequeño.
3. **Adult Female:** No puedo pasar una semana sin ver mis telenovelas favoritas.
4. **Adult Male:** Mi esposa tiene que llamar por teléfono cada día a la tienda en Nueva York donde trabaja.
5. **Adult Female:** Tenemos cuatro hijos de 10 a 19 años; por eso necesitamos una pequeña casa privada.
6. **Adult Female:** Mi esposo va a trabajar durante el viaje. Tiene que reunirse con otros empleados de su compañía.
7. **Adult Male:** Siempre compramos recuerdos para nuestros amigos cuando vamos de vacaciones.
8. **Adult Male:** A mis hijos les gusta jugar al golf, pero mi esposa y yo preferimos el tenis.
9. **Adult Female:** A mis hijos les importa mucho bañarse y arreglarse el pelo antes de salir por la noche.

Track 08: Audio Act. 5, Writing, Audio & Video Workbook, p. 159, (3:50)

Listen as several tourists in Spain call the front desk of the hotel for assistance. Then write the number of the phone call under the corresponding picture. You will hear each phone call twice.

1. Perdón. Necesito un mapa para saber dónde está el Palacio Real. Es mi primera visita a Madrid y quiero ir a todos los lugares históricos de la ciudad. Alguien me dijo que el hogar de los reyes es estupendo.
2. Mis amigos y yo queremos saber cuánto cuesta navegar en uno de los botes de vela. Pensamos navegar media hora. Es un día perfecto, ¿no?
3. Hola. ¿Me puede ayudar? Quiero hacer una gira por Madrid. Me gustaría visitar el Parque del Retiro, el Museo del Prado y el Palacio Real. Prefiero ir con el guía que habla español porque necesito practicar un poco.
4. Buenos días. Me gustaría ir a la excursión a Sevilla. Sevilla es una ciudad muy bella. ¿El autobús sale a las ocho en punto de la mañana? ¡Ay, no! Ya son las ocho y cinco de la mañana.
5. Nuestro grupo va a la Plaza Mayor hoy por la tarde. Dicen que es un lugar histórico con tiendas y cafés. Pero necesito sacar dinero en efectivo del cajero automático porque quiero comprar algunos recuerdos de los vendedores. ¿Me puedes ayudar?

6. Bienvenidos al vuelo número 424 con destino a San Juan de Puerto Rico. Les deseamos un vuelo muy bueno en el día de hoy. Hace buen tiempo en San Juan, con una temperatura de noventa y ocho grados. Nuestras auxiliares de vuelo están muy contentas de servirles. Por favor, llámennos si necesitan algo.

Track 09: Audio Act. 6, Writing, Audio & Video Workbook, p. 160, (4:47)

A student tour group is on the train to begin a two-day tour of the historic town of Toledo, Spain. Eager to use the Spanish they have learned, they talk to some of the Spanish-speaking passengers on the train. As you listen to each conversation, place a check mark under the picture of the place they are talking about in the grid below. You will hear each conversation twice.

1. **Adult Male 1:** Hace muchos años que vivo en Toledo. En una ciudad estupenda.
   Teen Male 1: ¿Conoce el Hotel Marqués?
   Adult Male 1: Claro que sí. Es un hotel bien conocido. Muchos de los reyes de España se quedaron allí. Las habitaciones son muy bellas y tienen muebles históricos.
2. **Adult Female 1:** Toledo es una ciudad muy bella.
   Teen Female 1: ¿Que recomienda Ud. que compre de recuerdo?
   Adult Female 1: En las tiendas de artesanías hay muchas cosas para comprar. Yo recomiendo que compres joyas típicas de Toledo… unos aretes o un anillo. Puedes regatear con los vendedores.
3. **Adult Male 2:** ¿Sabías que Toledo fue la capital de España antes de Madrid?
   Teen Female 2: No, no lo sabía.
   Adult Male 2: ¿Sí. Es una ciudad muy importante en la historia de España. La catedral es muy famosa y una de las más grandes del mundo. Recomiendo que no hagan ruido ni saquen fotos cuando la visiten.
4. **Adult Female 2:** La ciudad de Toledo es rica en cultura. Es mi ciudad favorita en España.
   Teen Male 2: Hay muchos lugares que puedo ver en Toledo, pero no sé cuáles.
   Adult Female 2: Te sugiero que compres una guía de Toledo en el quiosco de la estación del tren. La guía tiene mucha información y puedes decidir qué lugares visitar.
5. **Adult Male 3:** ¿Llevas algunos recuerdos para tu familia?
   Teen Female 3: No, todavía no los he comprado.
   Adult Male 3: ¿Toledo tiene muchas tiendas de recuerdos. Puedes comprar una estatua de Don Quijote o una réplica de la famosa Catedral de Toledo.

Track 10: Audio Act. 7, Writing, Audio & Video Workbook, p. 160, (3:56)

Although Señora Milano wants her Spanish students to enjoy their first trip to Spain, she also wants to be sure that they behave appropriately while they are there. Listen as she gives them advice at their last meeting before they leave on their trip. Categorize her advice as suggestions for how to: a) act in the hotel; b) dress while touring; c) stay safe on the trip; and d) interact with the people who live there. Mark with an *X* in the appropriate box as you listen to each recommendation. You will hear each recommendation twice.

1. Es importante que Uds. no lleven pantalones cortos cuando visitemos los catedrales. Para demostrar respeto, es mejor que las chicas lleven falda y los chicos lleven pantalones largos.
2. Es mejor que estén en sus habitaciones después de las diez de la noche. Y es importante que no hagan mucho ruido en las habitaciones después de las once.
3. Es mejor que no caminen por las calles de la ciudad cuando esté oscuro. Los ladrones les roban el dinero y las joyas a los turistas que no tienen cuidado.
4. Es bueno que tengan paciencia con los camareros cuando vayan a los restaurantes españoles. En España no todos los restaurantes son rápidos como los restaurantes en los Estados Unidos.
5. Es necesario que no lleven camiseta y jeans cuando vayan a la Catedral. Los españoles se visten muy elegantes para ir a la iglesia los domingos.
6. Es mejor que no tengan mucho dinero en efectivo en sus bolsos. Les recomiendo que lleven tarjetas de crédito. Pueden usarlas en las tiendas y restaurantes sin problema.
7. Es bueno que sean atentos con los empleados de la recepción del hotel. Si tienen problemas, ellos les ayudarán con mucho gusto.

Track 11: Audio Act. 8, Writing, Audio & Video Workbook, p. 161, (4:09)

A few graduating seniors have recorded messages with advice for the underclassmen in their schools. Match each senior with the topics of his or her advice by placing a check mark in the corresponding box. You will hear each message twice.

1. **Teen Female 1:** Hola, amigos, les habla Isabel Aguilar. Les envío este mensaje: Es importante que se diviertan cuando estén en la escuela. Los estudios son importantes, pero los amigos son para toda la vida. Es mejor sentirse contentos que sacar una "A" en todas las clases.
2. **Teen Male 1:** Hola, soy Jorge Santos. Quiero que sepan que es importante que se acuerden de sus buenos amigos de la escuela secundaria. Visiten a sus amigos cuando vengan de vacaciones a su ciudad o escríbanles cartas si no pueden verlos. Es bueno que les pidan ayuda a sus amigos, porque ellos los quieren mucho.
3. **Teen Female 2:** Me llamo Lisa Hernández. Les dejo este mensaje: Es importante reír. Ser serio todo el tiempo hace que la vida sea muy aburrida. Es necesario ponerle energía a la vida. Un consejo más: es mejor que no mientan, para que la gente los quiera más y los ayuden cuando lo necesiten.

4. **Teen Male 2:** Hola, me llamo Beto. Ahora que piensan ir a la universidad les digo que es muy importante que no pierdan el tiempo en la escuela. Lo que aprenden en la escuela les ayuda a tener mejores notas en la universidad. Es bueno que sigan sus sueños. Por eso tenemos que trabajar fuerte en la escuela.

Track 12: Audio Act. 9, Writing, Audio & Video Workbook, p. 161, (5:43)

Listen as teenagers use their international calling cards to talk to their parents while they travel in Spain. Based on what each says, match a picture below to the main idea of his or her conversation. You will hear each conversation twice.

1. **Adult Male 1:** ¿Cómo te va, hija?
   Teen Female 1: Muy bien. Me encanta este hotel. Estoy en una habitación doble con Elena. Ella es muy graciosa y nos divertimos mucho en el viaje. Cada noche nos reímos de lo que pasó durante el día. Quiero que nuestra familia viaje a España el verano que viene.
2. **Adult Female 1:** Hola, ¿quién habla? ¿Eres tú, María?
   Teen Female 2: Hola, sí, soy yo, María. Te hablo de España. Hoy visité el Palacio Real. Es muy grande e impresionante. Es el palacio ceremonial del rey y la reina. Los reyes no viven en ese palacio, pero es muy famoso.
3. **Adult Female 2:** ¡Hola, mi amor! ¿Cómo estás?
   Teen Female 3: Estoy muy contenta. Fui a varias tiendas de artesanías y compré varios recuerdos para la familia. Hice una gira por Toledo. Es una ciudad muy bella y estupenda. Es mejor que sepas que gasté un poco más de dinero de lo que había pensado. No puedo regatear bien.
4. **Adult Male 2:** ¡Qué bueno que llamas! Pensamos mucho en ti.
   Teen Male 1: Yo pienso en Uds. también. Por eso fui a un quiosco y les compré varias tarjetas postales de los lugares históricos de España. Les envié tarjetas postales del Escorial, el Alcázar y de la Catedral de Toledo. Todos esos edificios son estupendos. Les sugiero que visiten este país tan bello.
5. **Adult Female 3:** ¿Cómo estás, mi vida? Ya quiero que estés aquí con nosotros.
   Teen Male 2: Ayer disfruté mucho. Fui a un lago muy bonito cerca de Madrid. Y navegué en una moto acuática. Las muchachas españolas creen que soy muy impresionante. A ver… Quiero decirte que… pues,… es mejor que sepas que quiero casarme con una española.
   Adult Female 3: ¡¿Cómo?!

Track 13: *Repaso del capítulo,* Student Book, p. 446, (4:59)

Vocabulario y gramática

Escucha las palabras y expresiones que has aprendido en este capítulo.

See Student Book page 446 for vocabulary list.

Track 14: *Preparación para el examen,* Student Book, p. 447, (0:47)

Escuchar

Practice task

You need some advice for your trip to Mexico. Listen to these recommendations and determine what is the most important thing to do when you get there. What is the best thing to do there?

Adult Female: Para ser un buen turista, es importante que Uds. aprendan español antes de salir y que practiquen cada día.

Adult Male: Así es. Si hablan con la gente del lugar, pueden disfrutar más de su visita al país.

Video Script

A primera vista: *Un día en Toledo*, (7:46)

Javier: A ver si llegamos bien…

Ignacio: Sí, hombre. Me dijeron que el hotel está muy cerca de aquí. Dejamos nuestras cosas y luego vamos a caminar por la ciudad.

Javier: Vamos a parecer como típicos turistas.

Ignacio: Pues sí. La verdad es que ésta es la primera vez que vengo aquí sin mis padres.

Javier: Quiero comprar algunas cosas. Quizás alguna artesanía.

Ignacio: Para eso podemos ir a una tienda. Mira, allí está el hotel.

Ignacio: Buenos días, señor.

Desk clerk: Buenos días, ¿en qué os puedo ayudar?

Ignacio: Soy Ignacio Blanco y mi amigo, Javier Puyol. Somos miembros del equipo de fútbol que juega mañana para el campeonato de la ciudad.

Desk clerk: A ver… Sí, aquí están vuestros nombres. ¿Queréis dos habitaciones individuales?

Ignacio: No, mejor una habitación doble.

Desk clerk: Aquí está la llave. Vuestra habitación está en el tercer piso. Podéis usar las escaleras o el ascensor.

Ignacio and Javier: Gracias.

Ignacio: Tenemos tres horas. Vamos a hacer una pequeña gira por la ciudad.

Javier: ¿Qué vamos a ver primero?

Ignacio: No sé… Necesitamos una guía. Mira, allí hay un quiosco. Vamos a comprar una.

Ignacio: Aquí tienes. Cuatro con ochenta euros. Gracias.

Ignacio: Es que Toledo tiene tanto que ver… Podemos empezar por la Catedral. Luego vamos al Alcázar y al final, si tenemos tiempo, al museo de El Greco.

Javier: Oye, pero no te olvides de que yo quiero comprar algo típico de aquí.

Ignacio: Sí, sí. Tenemos tiempo suficiente. Podemos hacerlo todo. Vamos por esa calle.

Ignacio: Y esto es el museo de El Greco.

Javier: Pero está cerrado.

Ignacio: Mejor vamos a una tienda.

Javier: Sí, ya estoy cansado.

Ignacio: Oye, ¿no es muy grande?

Javier: Sí, y seguro que es cara también. ¿Cuánto cuesta? ¡Uy! Noventa euros. Oye, ¿se puede regatear aquí?

Ignacio: No, esto no es un mercado. Vas a ofender al vendedor.

Javier: Vaya. Pues, mejor compro unas tarjetas. Perfecto. Ahora vamos a regresar al hotel. Estoy un poco cansado, pero he disfrutado. Toledo es una ciudad muy interesante.

Ignacio: Tienes razón. Hemos conocido Toledo y hemos visto muchas cosas interesantes. Pero ahora debemos descansar un poco. Mañana tenemos un partido muy importante.

Javier: Ah sí, pero vamos a ganar.

***GramActiva* Videos, (6:58)**

Present subjunctive with impersonal expressions

Luisa: *Hola,* world travelers. Look at these phrases: *es importante que, es necesario que,* and *es mejor que.* We call these phrases impersonal expressions because we don't really know who thinks something is important or necessary, and we don't really care either. What we DO care about, is that if you see these expressions, then it's a pretty safe bet you'll see the subjunctive coming right after them.

V.O.: *Es importante que se duche.*
Es mejor que Ud. tire esos zapatos.
Es necesario que Ud. vaya a la escuela.

Luisa: Today, on Travel Radio, I have a special guest with me—the Ugly American.

Ugly: *Hola.*

Luisa: *¿Cuál es su pregunta?*

Ugly: *Quiero ir de vacaciones a otro país. ¿Qué debo hacer?*

Luisa: *Hmm… es necesario que Ud. tenga buenos modales y sea cortés.*

Ugly: *Bien. ¿Qué más?*

Luisa: *A ver… es importante que Ud. salga del hotel, haga alguna gira.*

Ugly: *¿Puedo llevar esta camiseta estupenda?*

Luisa: *Es mejor que no la lleve.*

Ugly: *¿Puedo comer hamburguesas?*

Luisa: *Es mejor que no las coma.*

Ugly: *¿Verdad?*

Luisa: *Sí. Y es importante que Uds. tengan la prueba.*

Quiz

V.O.: Complete the sentences with the correct form of the subjunctive.
(trabajar) Es importante que ustedes ______ mucho.
Es importante que trabajen mucho.
(parar) Es mejor que nosotros ______ el coche ahora.
Es mejor que paremos el coche ahora.

Present subjunctive of stem-changing verbs

Luisa: Wherever you go in your Spanish-learning adventures, you'll run into stem-changing verbs. And the subjunctive is no exception.

V.O.: *-ar* and *-er* verbs change their stems like this: *o* to *ue*… and *e* to *ie*.
Notice, they have a stem change in all forms except *nosotros* and *vosotros*.

LUISA: The endings for *-ar* verbs and *-er* verbs in the subjunctive flipflop.
-ar verb endings are *-e, -es, -e, -emos, -éis,* and *-en.*
So, *recordar* becomes *yo recuerde.*
-er verb endings are *-a, -as, -a, -amos, -áis,* and *-an.*
So, *perder* becomes *yo pierda.*
Flipflop.

V.O.: She prefers that they eat at the table.
Ella prefiere que coman en la mesa.
I suggest that you come home now.
Sugiero que volváis a casa ahora.

V.O.: *-ir* stem-changing verbs have the same endings as *-er* stem-changing verbs: *-a, -as, -a, -amos, -áis,* and *-an.*
There are three types of *-ir* stem-changing verbs:
e to *ie*
o to *ue*
and *e* to *i.*

LUISA: *-ir* stem-changing verbs are tricky, tricky verbs. Take my advice. Watch out or they'll fool you. And then there'll be nothing to cheer about.

CHEERLEADER: All right team! *E* to *ie* verbs do a double stem change. Yeah! They change inside the boot and outside the boot! Inside the boot changes to *ie* and outside the boot goes to an *i*. Inside *ie* and outside *i*… Ready team? Let's do *divertir!*

CHEERLEADERS: *¡Divierta, diviertas, divierta, divirtamos, divirtáis, diviertan!*

ROAD WORKER: *O* to *ue* verbs like *dormir*. We've got that inside the boot/outside the boot thing working again here. Inside the boot changes to *ue*, outside the boot changes to *u*. Take a look at *dormir*.

ROAD WORKERS: *¡Duerma, duermas, duerma, durmamos, durmáis, duerman!*

LUISA: In the subjunctive, *-ir* verbs that change from *e* to *i* are even trickier, so be careful. We can take our trusty old boot verb concept and throw it out the window.

V.O.: Look at *pedir* in the subjunctive.
E changes to *i* in all forms of the verb, even in the *nosotros* and *vosotros* forms. *Pida, pidas, pida, pidamos, pidáis, pidan.*

V.O.: It's the same with *servir*, another *-ir* verb.
Sirva, sirvas, sirva, sirvamos, sirváis, sirvan.
All the *es* change to *is*.
Goodbye boot. Hello snowshoe.

V.O.: *Es malo que tú no duermas.*
[It's bad for you to not sleep.]

V.O.: *Prefiero que pidamos ahora.*
[I prefer that we order now.]

V.O.: *Prefiere que Ud. cierre la puerta.*
[She prefers that you close the door.]

V.O.: *Es importante que nosotros empecemos la prueba.*
[It's important that we begin the quiz.]

Quiz

V.O.: Complete the sentences with the correct subjunctive form of the verb.
(dormir) Es importante que tú ______ por la noche.
Es importante que duermas por la noche.
(pedir) Quieren que nosotros ______ la cena ahora.
Quieren que pidamos la cena ahora.
(preferir) Es bueno que ellos ______ la artesanía.
Es bueno que prefieran la artesanía.

Talk!

Realidades 2

Capítulo 8B

Nombre ____________________

Fecha ____________________

Communicative Pair Activity **8B-1**

Estudiante **A**

In this activity, you and your partner take turns. You are **O** and your partner is **X.** Your partner will begin the activity by choosing a number. Read the sentence in that box and wait for his or her answer. For each sentence, your partner must supply the correct tense of the verb. If your partner responds correctly, mark an **X** in the box. If the response is incorrect, make no mark and and do not tell the answer. Your partner may choose that number again later. During your turn, your partner will mark an **O** in the appropriate box if your answer is correct. The first person to have three correct answers in a row is the winner.

1 Es mejor que *(llevar)* dinero para el viaje. (lleves)	**2** Es bueno que *(comprar)* un sombrero si vas a estar en el sol. (compres)	**3** Es importante que *(traer)* todos los documentos para tu viaje. (traigas)
4 Es posible que *(poder)* cambiar dinero cuando llegas. (puedas)	**5** Es preferible que tú *(regresar)* la semana siguiente. (regreses)	**6** Es necesario que *(tener)* tu pasaporte válido. (tengas)
7 Es seguro que tú *(comer)* muy bien en ese restaurante. (comerás)	**8** Es imposible que tú *(hacer)* una reservación en ese hotel. (hagas)	**9** Es bueno que *(nadar)* en la piscina. (nades)

Realidades 2

Nombre

Capítulo 8B

Communicative Pair Activity **8B-1**

Fecha

Estudiante **B**

In this activity, you and your partner take turns. You are **O** and your partner is **X.** Your partner will begin the activity by choosing a number. Read the sentence in that box and wait for his or her answer. For each sentence, your partner must supply the correct suffix, *-ero* or *-era*, to make the sentence right. If your partner responds correctly, mark an **X** in the box. If the response is incorrect, make no mark and and do not tell the answer. Your partner may choose that number again later. During your turn, your partner will mark an **O** in the appropriate box if your answer is correct. The first person to have three correct answers in a row is the winner.

1 El *(maletas)* del hotel lleva el equipaje hasta la habitación. (maletero)	**2** El *(viaje)* compró un boleto en la estación del tren. (viajero)	**3** Fuimos a la corrida a ver a un buen *(toro)*. (torero)
4 La *(cocina)* del hotel cocina delicioso. (cocinera)	**5** El *(aduana)* tiene que abrir las maletas de los viajeros. (aduanero)	**6** ¿Por qué no hablas con la *(banco)* para cambiar el dinero? (banquera)
7 Muy pronto el *(mesa)* va a traer el almuerzo. (mesero)	**8** Es importante que leamos los *(letra)* para conocer los lugares en la ciudad. (letrero)	**9** Mira como el *(jardín)* cuida las flores de este hotel. (jardinero)

You will play the role of a customer at a travel agency who is planning a camping trip in Spain. Your partner will play the travel agent who has found the perfect campground for you. Ask the following questions about the campground. Record the answers on the lines provided. Be prepared to say if you would or would not like to visit this campground and why.

1. ¿Cómo se llama el campamento? ______________________

2. ¿Por qué tiene ese nombre? ______________________

3. ¿Dónde está y cuándo está abierto? ______________________

4. ¿Qué puedo hacer en la playa? ______________________

5. ¿Qué servicios hay en el campamento? ______________________

6. (No) Me gustaría acampar allí porque ______________________

You will play the role of a travel agent. You think you have found the perfect campground for your customer who is going to Mexico. Use the information below to answer your partner's questions. You will also need to provide some information that is not given here.

Campamento Yucatán

¡Surf de vela! ¡Buceo!

¡Tiendas de acampar! ¡Piscina con trampolines!

¡Esquí acuático! ¡Moto acuática!

¡Natación! ¡Tenis! ¡Restaurantes!

Situado a 20 minutos de Cancún. Tiene playa privada, donde se pueden practicar toda clase de deportes acuáticos. Ofrecemos excursiones para explorar las ruinas mayas de Chichén Itzá o para ir de compras en Cancún. En el campamento se pueden estudiar las plantas, ver los pájaros en la selva, dar una caminata por los senderos cercanos, buscar fósiles, jugar al tenis o apreciar la tarde en el mar. Traiga su propia tienda de acampar o alquile una de nuestras cabañas modernas. Nuestro campamento tiene servicios sanitarios y duchas, luz eléctrica, teléfono, restaurante, supermercado y piscina. Está a dos kilómetros de una clínica. Abierto todo el año.

Nombre ______________________________

Fecha ______________________________

Communicative Pair Activity **8B-2**

Estudiante **B**

You will play the role of a travel agent. You think you have found the perfect campground for your customer who is going to Spain. Use the information below to answer your partner's questions. You will also need to provide some information that is not given here.

Campamento Dos Mundos

- Esquiar en las montañas
- Dar caminatas
- Hacer esquí acuático
- Nadar
- Hacer moto acuática
- Bucear

¡Somos el mejor de las montañas y de la playa!

Nuestro campamento está al sudeste de Granada, a 45 kilómetros de Almería. En las montañas de la Sierra Nevada es posible hacer muchas actividades. En la Costa del Sol se puede nadar en bellas playas mediterráneas y practicar deportes acuáticos, como el surf de vela. Nuestro campamento tiene luz eléctrica, teléfono, restaurante, supermercado, servicios sanitarios, agua caliente en las duchas, piscinas y minigolf. Abierto casi todo el año; cerrado el mes de octubre.

You will play the role of a customer at a travel agency who is planning a camping trip in Mexico. Your partner will play the travel agent who has found the perfect campground for you. Ask the following questions about the campground. Record the answers on the lines provided. Be prepared to say if you would or would not like to visit this campground and why.

1. ¿Cómo se llama el campamento? ______________________________

____

2. ¿Dónde está? ______________________________

____

3. ¿Cuándo está abierto? ______________________________

____

4. ¿Es posible hacer excursiones? ¿Adónde? ¿Qué más puedo hacer? ______________________________

____

5. ¿Hay una playa cerca del campamento? ¿Qué deportes acuáticos debo practicar?

____

6. (No) Me gustaría acampar allí porque ______________________________

______________________________.

Situation Cards

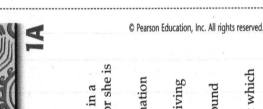

1A

Capítulo 8B — Realidades 2

Talking about traveling in a foreign city

With a friend, you are planning a trip to a city in a foreign country. You ask your friend what he or she is going to do upon arrival.

— Ask your friend if he or she can find information about that city before traveling.

— Ask what he or she is going to do when arriving at the destination airport.

— Ask your friend if he or she plans to get around in the city by taxi, bus, or renting a car.

— Ask your friend how he or she can find out which places to visit.

1B

Capítulo 8B — Realidades 2

Talking about traveling in a foreign city

You are planning a trip to a foreign country with a friend, and he or she will ask you some questions about what you are going to do when arriving in an unknown city.

— Respond to your friend's questions.

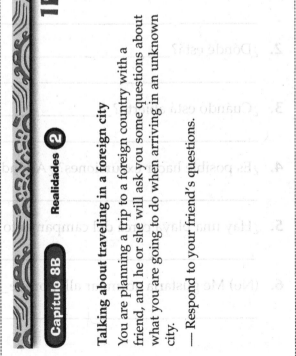

2A

Capítulo 8B — Realidades 2

Talking about being a good tourist

You are talking with a friend about being a good tourist.

— Ask your friend if he or she observes first what the people who live in the place he or she is visiting do.

— Respond to your friend's question.

— Ask your friend what he or she would do when invited to eat typical food.

— Respond to your friend's question.

2B

Capítulo 8B — Realidades 2

Talking about being a good tourist

You are talking with a friend about being a good tourist.

— Respond to your friend's question. Then ask him or her if he or she does the same.

— Respond to your friend's question.

— Ask your friend if he or she should behave the same as he or she does at home.

GramActiva

Quiero que disfrutes de tu viaje

Escucha y escribe, p. 431

Cortés	Descortés

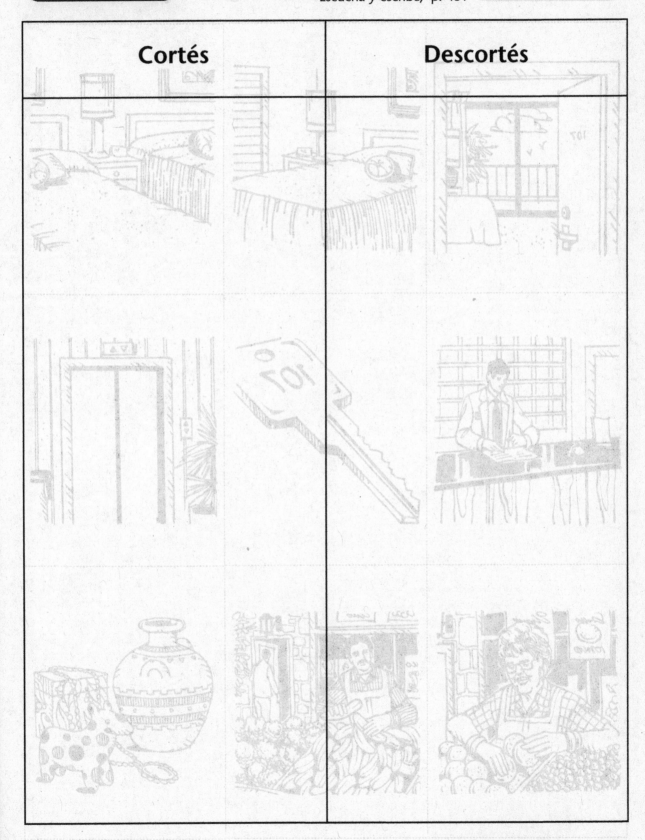

Realidades 2

Capítulo 8B

Vocabulary Clip Art

Realidades 2

Capítulo 8B

Vocabulary Clip Art

Vocabulary Clip Art

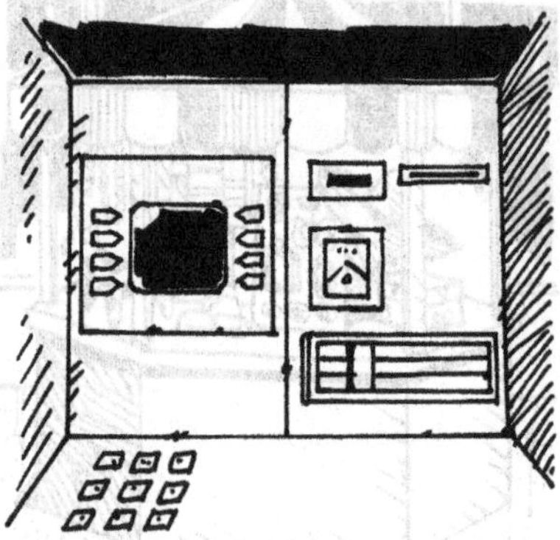

Vocabulary Clip Art

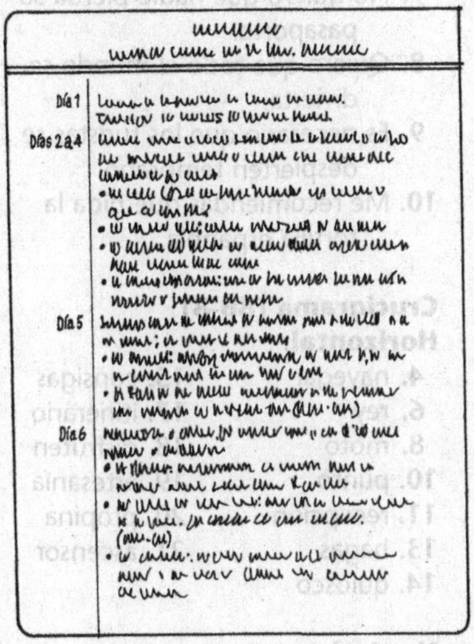

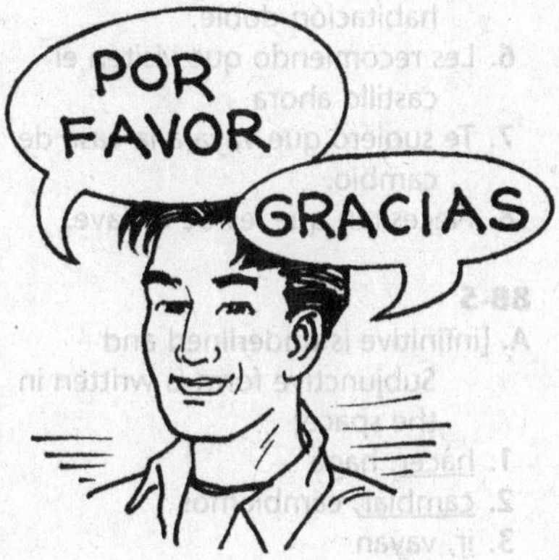

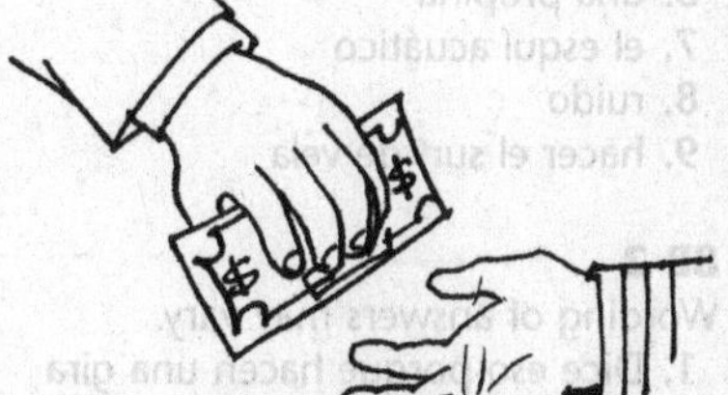

Core Practice Answers

8B-1
1. palacio, reyes
2. cajero automático
3. bote de vela
4. catedral
5. guía
6. una propina
7. el esquí acuático
8. ruido
9. hacer el surf de vela

8B-2
Wording of answers may vary.
1. Dice eso porque hacen una gira de toda la ciudad.
2. El Rey está en el Palacio Real. Lola dice que quiere conocer al Rey en el Palacio Real.
3. Van a ver tres lugares, según el itinerario.
4. Sí, a Lola le gusta el arte español. Dice que quiere ir más de una vez al Prado para ver los cuadros bellos.
5. Sí, las muchachas pueden disfrutar de la comida española en un restaurante famoso en la Plaza Mayor de Madrid.
6. Van a aprender sobre el rey Felipe II en el Escorial.
7. Según el itinerario, sólo un día pasa entre la excursión a Toledo y la al Escorial.
8. La catedral más grande de España está en Toledo.

8B-3
1. tal vez
2. vendedor
3. cortés
4. en punto
5. bella
6. cambiar dinero
7. habitación individual
8. recepción
9. ascensor
10. disfrutar de
11. atenta
12. una gira

8B-4
1. Les recomiendo que la consigan en un quiosco.
2. Te sugiero que regatees en los mercados.
3. Te recomiendo que compre artesanías.
4. Te sugiero que les envíe tarjetas postales.
5. Les sugiero que pidan una habitación doble.
6. Les recomiendo que visiten el castillo ahora.
7. Te sugiero que vaya a la casa de cambio.
8. Necesitan que les dé la llave.

8B-5
A. [infinitive is underlined and Subjunctive form is written in the space]
1. <u>hacer</u>, haga
2. <u>cambiar</u>, cambiemos
3. <u>ir</u>, vayan
4. <u>llegar</u>, llegue
5. <u>conocer</u>, conozcas
6. <u>estar</u>, esté

B. Impersonal expressions will vary.
1. Es mejor que los turistas no hagan ruido en la catedral.
2. Es importante que yo salga a las ocho en punto.
3. Es necesario que hagas la gira por la mañana.
4. Es bueno que el profesor dusfrute del tiempo libre.
5. Es necesario que consigamos un pasaporte.

8B-6
1. pidas más agua
2. duerman un poco
3. no pierdan la llave
4. se sienten unos minutos
5. se vistan ahora mismo
6. cierren las ventanas
7. recuerden la dirección del hotel
8. jueguen al fútbol en el parque
9. entiendan un poco de español

8B-7
1. Es mejor que siempre vuelvan temprano.
2. Preferimos que todos almuercen aquí.
3. Es importante que todo el mundo recuerde la hora de la cena.
4. Es bueno que quieran ver la catedral.
5. Insistimos en que se despidan de sus amigos.
6. Es importante que sigan las instrucciones del guía.
7. No quiero que nadie pierda su pasaporte.
8. Quiero que todo el mundo se divierta.
9. Es necesario que los turistas se despierten temprano.
10. Me recomiendas que pida la tortilla española.

Crucigrama (8B-8)
Horizontal:

4. navegar	15. consigas
6. rey	17. itinerario
8. moto	18. disfruten
10. punto	19. artesanía
11. recepción	20. propina
13. hagas	21. ascensor
14. quiosco	

Vertical:

1. regateen	10. postales
2. guía	11. ruido
3. cajero	12. puntual
5. habitación	15. catedral
7. palacio	16. atentos
9. ofendas	

Organizer (8B-9)
I. Vocabulary Answers will vary.
II. Grammar
1. es necesario, es importante, es bueno, es mejor
2. Stem-changing **-ar** and **-er** verbs have the same stem changes in the subjunctive as in the indicative. Stem-changing **-ir** verbs have changes in all forms of the present subjunctive.
3. **recordar:**

recuerde	recordemos
recuerdes	recordéis
recuerde	recuerden
pedir:	
pida	pidamos
pidas	pidáis
pida	pidan
perder:	
pierda	perdamos
pierdas	perdáis
pierda	pierdan
dormir:	
duerma	durmamos
duermas	durmáis
duerma	duerman

Realidades 2

Capítulo 8B

Nombre ______ Hora ______

Fecha ______

Vocabulary Flash Cards, Sheet 1

Write the Spanish vocabulary word or phrase below each picture. Be sure to include the article for each noun.

 ***la*** ***habitación***	 ***la habitación*** ***individual***	 ***la habitación*** ***doble***
 ***la*** ***recepción***	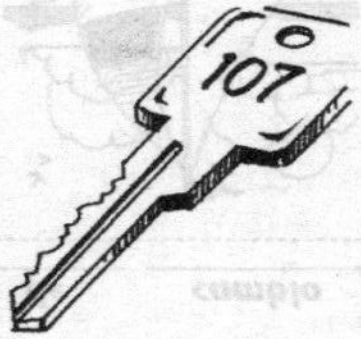 ***la*** ***llave***	 ***el*** ***ascensor***
 ***la*** ***vendedora***	 ***el*** ***vendedor***	 ***la*** ***artesanía***

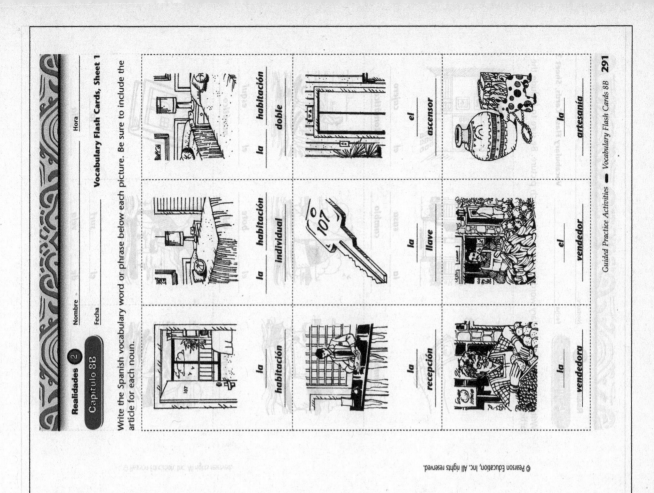

Realidades 2 Nombre ______ Hora ______

Capítulo 8B Fecha ______ **Vocabulary Flash Cards, Sheet 2**

Write the Spanish vocabulary word or phrase below each picture. Be sure to include the article for each noun.

el quiosco

la tarjeta postal

hacer una gira

la guía

el guía

el palacio

el castillo

la catedral

el rey

Realidades 2 Nombre ______ Hora ______

Capítulo 8B Fecha ______ **Vocabulary Flash Cards, Sheet 3**

Write the Spanish vocabulary word or phrase below each picture. Be sure to include the article for each noun.

cambiar

la casa de cambio

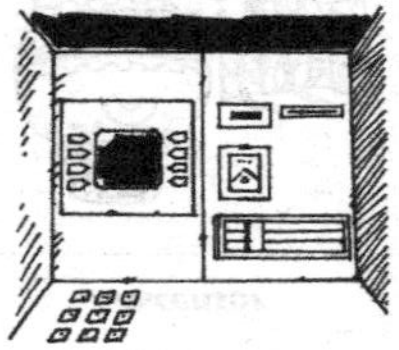

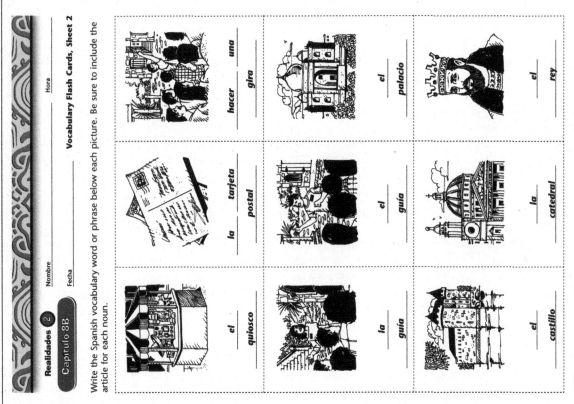

el cajero automático

navegar

el bote de vela

el esquí acuático

la moto acuática

el surf de vela

la guía

Realidades 2 Nombre Hora

Capítulo 8B Fecha **Vocabulary Flash Cards, Sheet 4**

Write the Spanish vocabulary word below each picture. If there is a word or phrase, copy it in the space provided. Be sure to include the article for each noun.

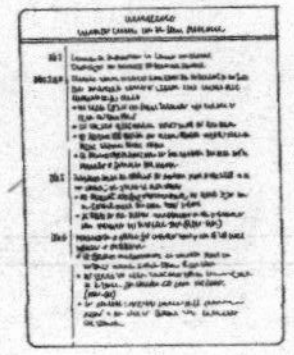 *el* *itinerario*	 *cortés*	 *la* *propina*
histórico, histórica *histórico* , *histórica*	**atento, atenta** *atento* , *atenta*	**ofender** *ofender*
puntual *puntual*	**disfrutar de** *disfrutar* *de*	**la excursión** *la* *excursión*

Realidades 2 Nombre Hora

Capítulo 8B Fecha **Vocabulary Flash Cards, Sheet 5**

Copy the word or phrase in the space provided.

regatear *regatear*	**bello, bella** *bello* , *bella*	**en punto** *en* *punto*
estupendo, estupenda *estupendo* , *estupenda*	**famoso, famosa** *famoso* , *famosa*	**siguiente** *siguiente*
tal vez *tal* *vez*	**típico, típica** *típico* , *típica*	**hacer ruido** *hacer* *ruido*

Realidades 2 Nombre ____ Hora ____

Capítulo 8B Fecha ____ **Vocabulary Flash Cards, Sheet 6**

Copy the word or phrase in the space provided. Be sure to include the article for each noun. The blank cards can be used to write and practice other Spanish vocabulary in the chapter.

conseguir ***conseguir***	**observar** ***observar***	____
____	____	____
____	____	____

Realidades 2 Nombre ____ Hora ____

Capítulo 8B Fecha ____ **Vocabulary Check, Sheet 1**

Tear out this page. Write the English words on the lines. Fold the paper along the dotted line to see the correct answers so you can check your work.

la casa de cambio	***currency exchange***
el palacio	***palace***
el quiosco	***newsstand***
el ascensor	***elevator***
la llave	***key***
la recepción	***reception desk***
la artesanía	***handicrafts***
el bote de vela	***sailboat***
el guía, la guía	***guide***
bello, bella	***beautiful***
en punto	***exactly (time)***
famoso, famosa	***famous***
siguiente	***next, following***
tal vez	***maybe, perhaps***

Fold In

Realidades 2 | Nombre | Hora

Capítulo 8B | Fecha

Vocabulary Check, Sheet 2

Tear out this page. Write the Spanish words on the lines. Fold the paper along the dotted line to see the correct answers so you can check your work.

currency exchange	***la casa de cambio***
palace	***el palacio***
newsstand	***el quiosco***
elevator	***el ascensor***
key	***la llave***
reception desk	***la recepción***
handicrafts	***la artesanía***
sailboat	***el bote de vela***
guide	***el guía, la guía***
beautiful	***bello, bella***
exactly (time)	***en punto***
famous	***famoso, famosa***
next, following	***siguiente***
maybe, perhaps	***tal vez***

Fold In

Realidades 2 | Nombre | Hora

Capítulo 8B | Fecha

Vocabulary Check, Sheet 3

Tear out this page. Write the English words on the lines. Fold the paper along the dotted line to see the correct answers so you can check your work.

el cajero automático	***ATM***
la catedral	***cathedral***
histórico, histórica	***historical***
conseguir	***to obtain***
la habitación	***room***
cortés	***polite***
hacer ruido	***to make noise***
ofender	***to offend***
la propina	***tip***
cambiar	***to change, to exchange***
disfrutar de	***to enjoy***
navegar	***to sail, to navigate***
el vendedor, la vendedora	***vendor***
típico, típica	***typical***

Fold In

Tear out this page. Write the Spanish words on the lines. Fold the paper along the dotted line to see the correct answers so you can check your work.

ATM	***el cajero automático***
cathedral	***la catedral***
historical	***histórico, histórica***
to obtain	***conseguir***
room	***la habitación***
polite	***cortés***
to make noise	***hacer ruido***
to offend	***ofender***
tip	***la propina***
to change, to exchange	***cambiar***
to enjoy	***disfrutar de***
to sail, to navigate	***navegar***
vendor	***el vendedor, la vendedora***
typical	***típico, típica***

Fold In ↓

To hear a complete list of the vocabulary for this chapter, go to www.realidades.com and type in the Web Code jdd-0899. Then click on **Repaso del capítulo**.

Present subjunctive with impersonal expressions (p. 434)

- You can use impersonal expressions, such as **es importante, es necesario, es mejor,** and **es bueno,** to tell people what they should do. Sentences with these impersonal expressions are often followed by **que** + subjunctive:

  Es necesario que nosotros le demos una propina al empleado.
  It's necessary that we give a tip to the employee.

  Es mejor que tú observes las reglas para el viaje.
  It's better that you observe the rules for the trip.

A. Choose the correct verb form in parentheses to complete each sentence. Follow the model.

Modelo Es importante que nosotros (**llevemos** / **llevamos**) la llave. (circled: llevemos)

1. Es mejor que nosotros (**visitamos** / **visitemos**) la catedral. (circled: visitemos)
2. Es necesario que ustedes (**van** / **vayan**) a la recepción. (circled: vayan)
3. Es bueno que tú (**tomas** / **tomes**) el ascensor. (circled: tomes)
4. Es importante que yo (**cambie** / **cambia**) dinero. (circled: cambie)
5. Es mejor que el grupo (**haga** / **hace**) una gira de la capital. (circled: haga)

B. Read the sentences below. Fill in the blanks with the correct form of the verbs in parentheses. The first one is done for you.

1. Es importante que ustedes _*visiten*_ el castillo. (**visitar**)
2. Es necesario que tú _***lleves***_ la guía. (**llevar**)
3. Es bueno que nosotros _***naveguemos***_ en un bote de vela. (**navegar**)
4. Es mejor que yo _***haga***_ una gira. (**hacer**)
5. Es importante que Mateo _***conozca***_ los lugares históricos. (**conocer**)
6. Es necesario que usted _***cambie***_ dinero en la casa de cambio. (**cambiar**)
7. Es mejor que nosotros _***busquemos***_ un lugar para comer ahora. (**buscar**)
8. Es bueno que Ignacio y Javier _***vayan***_ con nosotros. (**ir**)

realidades.com
• Web Code: jdd-0813

Realidades 2 Nombre ______ Hora ______

Capítulo 8B Fecha ______ **Guided Practice Activities 8B-2**

Present subjunctive with impersonal expressions (*continued*)

- To speak generally about things that should or should not be done, use an impersonal expression plus an infinitive. Note that **que** is not used. Compare the following sentences:

  Subjunctive
  Es importante que tú *seas* cortés. *It is important that you be polite.* (specific)

  Infinitive
  Es importante *ser* cortés. *It is important to be polite.* (general)

C. Read the following sentences. Write **S** (for specific) if the sentence mentions specific people. Write **G** (for general) if it does not mention specific people. Follow the models.

Modelo 1 _G_ Es necesario ser puntual.
Modelo 2 _S_ Es necesario que ustedes sean puntuales.

1. _G_ Es necesario estar atento en el bote de vela.
2. _S_ No es bueno que nosotros hagamos ruido en las habitaciones.
3. _S_ Es importante que tú observes al guía.
4. _G_ Es mejor no ofender a los reyes.
5. _G_ Es bueno dar propinas.
6. _S_ Es importante que usted sea cortés con los vendedores.

D. Read each sentence and decide if it needs the subjunctive (*specific*) or the infinitive (*general*). Then, fill in the blank with the correct form of the verb given. Follow the models.

Modelo 1 Es esencial _dar_ (dar) propinas.
Modelo 2 Es necesario que la abuela _suba_ (subir) en el ascensor.

1. Es necesario _cambiar_ (cambiar) dinero en el banco.
2. Es importante _llevar_ (llevar) las llaves del hotel.
3. Es bueno que tú _saques_ (sacar) muchas fotos en la ciudad.
4. Es mejor _llegar_ (llegar) temprano al aeropuerto.
5. Es importante que nosotros _seamos_ (ser) corteses.

realidades.com • Web Code: jdd-0813

Realidades 2 Nombre ______ Hora ______

Capítulo 8B Fecha ______ **Guided Practice Activities 8B-3**

Present subjunctive of stem-changing verbs (p. 437)

- Stem-changing verbs ending in **-ar** and **-er** have the same stem changes in the subjunctive as in the indicative. Just like the present indicative, the **nosotros** and **vosotros** forms do not have a stem change.
- Here are the conjugations for **cerrar** and **volver:**

cerrar (e → ie)		volver (o → ue)	
cierre	cerremos	vuelva	volvamos
cierres	cerréis	vuelvas	volváis
cierre	cierren	vuelva	vuelvan

A. Read each sentence and complete the verb with the correct stem-changing vowels. Follow the model.

Modelo **(recordar)** Es necesario que usted rec_ue_rde la dirección.

1. **(encender)** Es importante que tú enc_ie_ndas las luces antes de entrar.
2. **(empezar)** La profesora quiere que Simón emp_ie_ce con el examen ahora.
3. **(contar)** Es mejor que tú c_ue_ntes el dinero fuera de la tienda.
4. **(poder)** Es bueno que ustedes p_ue_dan visitar tantos lugares.
5. **(llover)** Hace mal tiempo, pero es mejor que no ll_ue_va durante el partido de béisbol.

B. Complete the following sentences with the subjunctive form of the verb in parentheses. The first one is done for you.

1. Es mejor que nosotros _almorcemos_ bien antes de ir de excursión. **(almorzar)**
2. Es importante que tú _entiendas_ lo que el guía dice. **(entender)**
3. Rosa no tiene dinero. Es necesario que ella _encuentre_ un cajero automático. **(encontrar)**
4. Es bueno que ustedes se _despierten_ temprano para visitar el castillo. **(despertar)**
5. Marta no conoce la ciudad. Es mejor que yo le _recomiende_ un buen hotel. **(recomendar)**
6. Antes de salir del hotel, es importante que ellos _devuelvan_ la llave. **(devolver)**
7. El camarero sugiere que nosotros _comencemos_ la cena ahora. **(comenzar)**

realidades.com • Web Code: jdd-0814

Present subjunctive of stem-changing verbs (*continued*)

- Stem-changing verbs ending in **-ir** have changes in all forms of the present subjunctive.
- Here are the conjugations for **pedir, dormir,** and **divertirse:**

pedir (e → i)		dormir (o → ue), (o → u)		divertirse (e → ie), (e → i)	
pida	pidamos	duerma	durmamos	me divierta	nos divirtamos
pidas	pidáis	duermas	durmáis	te diviertas	os divirtáis
pida	pidan	duerma	duerman	se divierta	se diviertan

C. Complete the following sentences using the present subjunctive of the **-ir** stem-changing verbs in parentheses. Follow the model.

Modelo (**pedir**) Es necesario que ustedes ***pidan*** ayuda.

1. (**repetir**) Los turistas quieren que la guía ***repita*** la explicación.
2. (**sentirse**) Deseamos que nuestros parientes ***se*** ***sientan*** bien.
3. (**divertirse**) Nuestros padres quieren que nosotros ***nos*** ***divirtamos*** mucho.
4. (**seguir**) Es importante que nosotros ***sigamos*** las instrucciones.
5. (**dormir**) Es mejor que Felipe y Ana ***duerman*** en el avión.

D. Use the words given to write complete sentences in the order in which the words appear. Follow the model.

Modelo Es bueno / que / ustedes / divertirse / en las vacaciones
Es bueno que ustedes se diviertan en las vacaciones.

1. Es necesario / que / tú / conseguir / una llave para la habitación
   Es necesario que tú consigas una llave para la habitación.
2. Yo no / querer / que / mi hermano / reírse / de mí
   Yo no quiero que mi hermano se ría de mí.
3. Es importante / que / yo / hervir / los huevos primero
   Es importante que yo hierva los huevos primero.
4. Es mejor / que / el camarero / servir / la comida ahora
   Es mejor que el camarero sirva la comida ahora.
5. El jefe / recomendar / que / nosotros / pedir / una propina
   El jefe recomienda que nosotros pidamos una propina.

Lectura: Antigua, una ciudad colonial (pp. 442–443)

A. The reading in your textbook is a travel brochure about Antigua, Guatemala. Look at the photos, the heads, and the subheads in this brochure to get an idea of what the reading will be about. What are three things this brochure might mention?

1. ______, 2. ______, 3. ______

B. Read the following excerpt from the reading in your textbook and complete the sentences below.

> ***¿Qué hay que ver en la ciudad de Antigua?***
> *La ciudad de Antigua tiene muchos sitios de interés. Se puede apreciar toda la historia de esta ciudad mirando sus casas y monumentos coloniales. En el centro de la ciudad está la Plaza Mayor. Los edificios principales son el Ayuntamiento (City Hall), la Catedral y el Palacio de los Capitanes.*

1. In the city of Antigua, you can see ***a***.
   a. interesting places **b.** hotels
2. The Plaza Mayor is in ***a***.
   a. the center of the city **b.** Tikal
3. The Palacio de los Capitanes is ***b***.
   a. a sailboat **b.** one of the important buildings

C. The name **Antigua** means *antique*, or *old* in Spanish. Read this introduction from the reading. Then, write some of the words or phrases that indicate the city is old. One example is provided for you.

> *Situada a 45 minutos de la Ciudad de Guatemala, Antigua le fascina al turista por sus calles de piedras, su arquitectura colonial y sus ruinas de iglesias y monasterios. El español Francisco de la Cueva fundó la ciudad el 10 de marzo de 1543. La "Ciudad de las Perpetuas Rosas," nombrada así por sus jardines con flores, tiene un clima muy agradable y preserva un sabor colonial único. Caminar por sus calles es como visitar el pasado y descubrir una ciudad típica española del siglo (century) XVII.*

calle de piedras

Presentación escrita (p. 445)

Task: Imagine you are going to visit a Spanish-speaking country with a group. Prepare an illustrated brochure so you can share your experience with others.

A. Think about the preparations you must make before you go on your trip. Answer the questions below to help you organize your brochure. ***Answers will vary.***

1. ¿Qué país vas a visitar? ____________
2. ¿Cómo vas a viajar? ____________
3. ¿Qué vas a llevar? ____________
4. ¿Qué lugares vas a visitar? ____________
   ____
5. ¿Qué actividades vas a hacer? ____________
   ____

B. Use the information from **part A** to complete the sentences below. You can use the following paragraph as a model.

> *Voy a viajar a México. Voy a viajar por avión. Es importante que yo lleve una guía porque voy a visitar el centro histórico y el famoso castillo. También es bueno que yo haga excursiones y navegue en el océano.*

Voy a viajar a ____________. Voy a viajar por ____________. Es importante que yo lleve ____________ porque voy a visitar ____________ y ____________. También es bueno que yo ____________ y ____________.

C. Choose some illustrations for your brochure. You can use photos from home or from magazines, or you can draw pictures to illustrate what you will see and do on your trip.

D. Reread your draft and check the spelling, vocabulary, and verb usage. Share your draft with a classmate, who will check for clarity, organization, and errors.

E. Make a new version of the brochure with changes and corrections. Don't forget to attach your illustrations for the brochure where they will be most appropriate.

Realidades 2 Nombre ____ Hora ____

Capítulo 8B Fecha ____ VIDEO

Antes de ver el video

Actividad 1

What are the first things you want to do when you arrive in a new city? Make a list of five activities you would do upon arriving in a foreign city. Follow the model.

Modelo *Caminar*

1. Answers will vary.
2. ____
3. ____
4. ____
5. ____

¿Comprendes?

Actividad 2

Read each of the following descriptions and decide whether it describes Ignacio, Javier, or both (**los dos**). Circle the correct answer for each. (In this answer key, the circled answer is shown in bold.)

1. Tiene un partido de fútbol mañana.	Ignacio	Javier	**Los dos**
2. Quiere comprar alguna artesanía.	Ignacio	**Javier**	Los dos
3. Compra una guía.	**Ignacio**	Javier	Los dos
4. Es la primera vez que visita Toledo sin sus padres.	**Ignacio**	Javier	Los dos
5. Quiere regatear por la espada (*sword*).	Ignacio	**Javier**	Los dos
6. Le gusta la ciudad de Toledo.	Ignacio	Javier	**Los dos**
7. Compra unas tarjetas postales.	Ignacio	**Javier**	Los dos
8. Dice que está cansado.	Ignacio	**Javier**	Los dos

Realidades 2 Nombre ____ Hora ____

Capítulo 8B Fecha ____ VIDEO

Actividad 3

Next to each video scene, write a sentence describing what was happening at that moment in the video. Follow the model.

Answers may vary.

Modelo  *Ignacio y Javier van a dejar sus cosas en el hotel.*

1.  Ignacio y Javier quieren una habitación doble.
2.  Hacen una gira por la ciudad.
3.  Compran una guía.
4.  Van al Museo de El Greco pero está cerrado.
5.  Javier quiere comprar algo típico de la ciudad.
6.  Javier quiere saber si se puede regatear aquí.
7.  Javier va a comprar unas tarjetas postales.

Realidades 2 Nombre Hora

Capítulo 8B Fecha VIDEO

Y, ¿qué más?

Actividad 4

Your friend is going on her first plane trip out of the country. Write five sentences of advice for her. Follow the model.

Modelo *Te aconsejo que tengas siempre buenos modales con la gente.*

Answers will vary.

Realidades 2 Nombre Hora

Capítulo 8B Fecha AUDIO

Actividad 5

Listen as several tourists in Spain call the front desk of the hotel for assistance. Then, write the number of the phone call under the corresponding picture. You will hear each phone call twice.

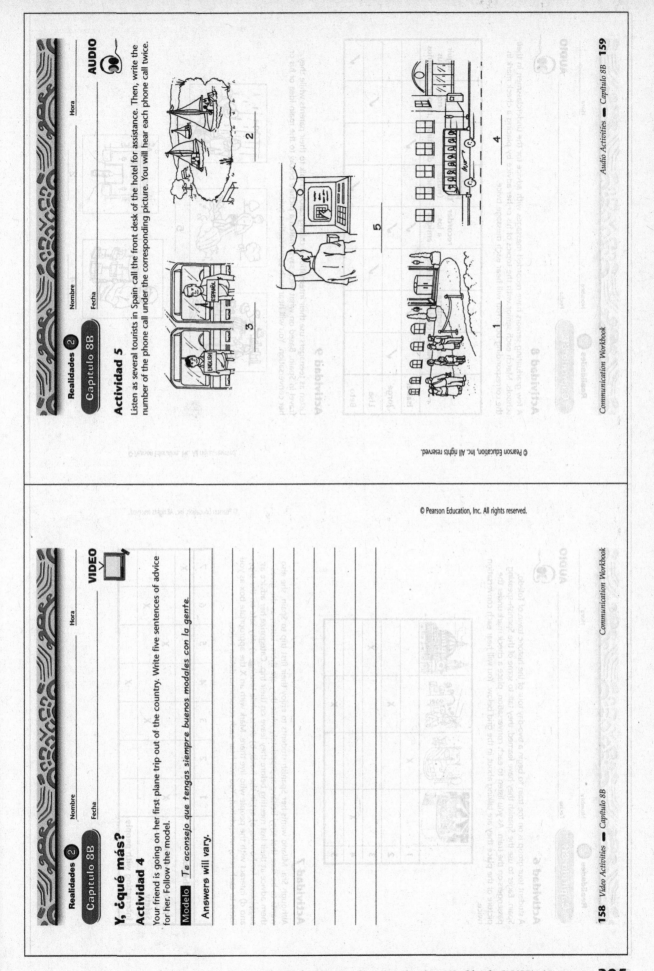

3

2

5

1

4

Realidades 2 | Nombre | Hora

Capítulo 8B | Fecha | AUDIO

Actividad 6

A student tour group is on the train to begin a two-day tour of the historic town of Toledo, Spain. Eager to use the Spanish they have learned, they talk to some of the Spanish-speaking passengers on the train. As you listen to each conversation, place a check mark under the picture of the place they are talking about in the grid below. You will hear each conversation twice.

		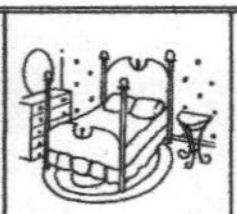		
1		X		
2			X	
3				X
4	X			
5			X	

Actividad 7

Although Sra. Milano wants her Spanish students to enjoy their first trip to Spain, she also wants to be sure that they behave appropriately while they are there. Listen as she gives them advice at their last meeting before they leave on their trip. Categorize her advice as suggestions for how to: a) act in the hotel; b) dress while touring; c) stay safe on the trip; and d) interact with the people who live there. Mark with an X the appropriate box as you listen to each recommendation. You will hear each recommendation twice.

	1	2	3	4	5	6	7
Hotel behavior		X					X
Appropriate dress	X				X		
Safety			X			X	
Interacting with people				X			

Realidades 2 | Nombre | Hora

Capítulo 8B | Fecha | AUDIO

Actividad 8

A few graduating seniors have recorded messages with advice for the underclassmen in their schools. Match each senior with the topics of his or her advice by placing a check mark in the corresponding box. You will hear each message twice.

	pedir ayuda	sentirse contento	reírse	recordar a los amigos	no perder tiempo (*waste time*)	divertirse	no mentir	seguir sus sueños
Isabel		✓		✓		✓		
Jorge	✓			✓				
Lisa			✓				✓	
Beto					✓			✓

Actividad 9

Listen as teenagers use their international calling cards to talk to their parents while they travel in Spain. Based on what each says, match a picture below to the main idea of his or her conversation. You will hear each conversation twice.

3

5

1

4

2

Realidades 2 Nombre Hora

Capítulo 8B Fecha **WRITING**

Actividad 10

You are working at a travel agency answering e-mails from travelers who have questions. Read their questions below and answer them in complete sentences.

1. Mi esposo y yo queremos hacer una reservación en un hotel. ¿Qué tipo de habitación debemos conseguir?
   Deben conseguir una habitación doble.
2. ¿Cómo es un buen turista? ¿Qué cosa no hace?
   Un buen turista es cortés y paciente. No ofende y no es descortés.
3. ¿Qué actividades puedo hacer en el lago Ontario?
   Se puede pasear en bote y usar una moto acuática.
4. Voy a Madrid y no sé qué lugares debo visitar. ¿Dónde busco esta información?
   Se busca esta información en una guía o debes preguntarle a un guía profesional.
5. En los mercados de México, ¿debemos aceptar el precio que el vendedor nos dice?
   No, se puede regatear en México.
6. ¿A quiénes les doy una propina en los Estados Unidos?
   En los Estados Unidos se les da una propina a los camareros y a los taxistas.
7. Cuando llego al hotel, ¿adónde voy?
   Cuando se llega al hotel, se va a la recepción.
8. ¿Adónde voy para cambiar dinero al llegar a Argentina?
   Para cambiar dinero se va a una casa de cambio.

Realidades 2 Nombre Hora

Capítulo 8B Fecha **WRITING**

Actividad 11

Your school has handed out a survey to students in order find out their opinions on different topics related to school life. Write two opinions for each category below, using complete sentences. The first one has been done for you.

1. la comida
   Es importante que sirvan pizza todos los días.
   Quiero que preparen galletas de chocolate.
2. los autobuses
   Answers will vary.
3. las horas de la escuela
4. las clases
5. los deportes
6. los profesores
7. los estudiantes

Actividad 12

You are helping your Health teacher make fliers for Health Awareness Week. Using the phrases below, write six recommendations on the flier to the people indicated in the parentheses. Then, write six recommendations about what they should avoid. Use complete sentences. The first one has been done for you.

jugar a los deportes (los jóvenes)	seguir las sugerencias del médico (nosotros)
perder peso (los estadounidenses)	pedir comida saludable (la gente)
acostarse temprano (tú)	~~dormir ocho horas (nosotros)~~
comenzar un programa de ejercicio (los estudiantes)	

LA SEMANA DE LA SALUD

- *Nos recomienda que durmamos ocho horas cada noche.*
- *Es mejor que no comamos muchas galletas.*
- Answers will vary.
-
-
-
-

Actividad 13

Your younger brother and sister are going on a trip to Spain with their class and have asked you to help them get ready.

A. First, organize your thoughts by writing appropriate responses to their questions below.

¿Qué debemos traer al aeropuerto?

Answers will vary.

¿Qué/A quiénes vamos a encontrar en el aeropuerto?

Answers will vary.

B. Now, give your siblings advice about their trip using the ideas you wrote above. Follow the model.

Modelo A tu hermano:
Es necesario que traigas tu carnet de identificación al aeropuerto.

A tu hermana:

Answers will vary.

A los dos:

Test Preparation Answers

Reading Skills
p. 277 2. **D**
p. 278 2. **A**

Integrated Performance Assessment
p. 279
Answers will vary.

Practice Test: Dos atracciones turísticas de América Latina
p. 281

1. B
2. F
3. C
4. H
5. Las respuestas variarán pero pueden incluir: Antes no se limitó el número de turistas al parque y por eso fue difícil conservar el ecosistema del parque. Tampoco se usó el dinero del turismo para conservar el ecosistema y proteger las diferentes especies en las Islas.
6. Las respuestas variarán pero pueden incluir: Es bueno porque hay más dinero para proteger el ecosistema del parque y porque la gente tiene más interés en saber cómo proteger las especies que viven allí; es malo porque los turistas pueden destruir los hábitats de las especies que viven allí y también hacer cambios peligrosos en el ecosistema.

Table of Contents

Tema 9: ¿Cómo será el futuro?

Capítulo 9A: ¿Qué profesión tendrás?

Capítulo 9B: ¿Qué haremos para mejorar el mundo?

Theme Project

¿Cómo será el futuro?
La exposición de carreras

Overview:

You are in charge of planning a job fair for high school students. You will make and present a poster advertising five different jobs and the responsibilities that each job will entail. You must use the future tense. At least one of the jobs must deal with the environment. Pictures or drawings on the poster should serve as visual aids.

Resources:

Digital or print photos, page layout/word processing software and/or poster board, markers, glue or tape, scissors, photos

Sequence:

STEP 1. Review instructions with your teacher.

STEP 2. Submit a rough draft of your list of jobs and their requirements. Work with a partner and present your drafts to each other.

STEP 3. Create layouts, leaving room for photos and descriptions.

STEP 4. Submit a draft of your poster.

STEP 5. Present your poster to the class, explaining each job description and describing selected pictures.

Assessment:

Your teacher will provide you with a rubric to assess this project.

Theme 9 Project: La exposición de carreras

Project Assessment Rubric

RUBRIC	Score 1	Score 3	Score 5
Evidence of Planning	No written draft or sketch layout provided.	Draft was written and layout created, but not corrected.	Evidence of corrected draft and layout.
Use of Illustrations	No photos/ visuals included.	Very few photos/visuals included.	Several photos/ visuals included.
Presentation	Contains details that develop ideas about jobs.	Contains two or three jobs and descriptions.	Contains five or more jobs and descriptions.

21st Century Skills Rubric: Encourage Critical Thinking and Problem Solving

RUBRIC	Score 1	Score 3	Score 5
Seeking information on Internet	Does not seek sources for information on Internet	Seeks information from up to three sources	Seeks information from four or more sources
Local sources	Does not discuss or use information about local economy	Discusses local economy but does not generate ideas for using information in project	Discusses local economy and generates ideas for using information in project
Synthesis of ideas	Does not incorporate information from Internet or local sources in project	Incorporates some ideas from Internet and local sources in project	Incorporates many ideas from Internet and local sources in project

School-to-Home Connection

Dear Parent or Guardian,

The theme of our current unit is *¿Cómo será el futuro?* (What will the future be like?). This chapter is called *¿Qué profesión tendrás?* (What will your profession be?).

Upon completion of this chapter students will be able to:

- discuss professions and make plans for the future
- talk about future events
- understand cultural perspectives on folk art

Students will also explore:

- the correct pronunciation of letters with the *diéresis (ü)*

Our textbook, *Realidades,* helps with the development of reading, writing, and speaking skills through the use of strategies, process speaking, and process writing. In this chapter, students will:

- read about languages and careers
- speak about the jobs they expect to have in the future based on their current hobbies and pursuits

To reinforce and enhance learning, students can access a wide range of online resources on **realidades.com,** the personalized learning management system that accompanies the print and online Student Edition. Resources include the eText, textbook and workbook activities, audio files, videos, animations, songs, self-study tools, interactive maps, voice recording (RealTalk!), assessments, and other digital resources. Many learning tools can be accessed through the student Home Page on **realidades.com.** Other activities, specifically those that require grading, are assigned by the teacher and linked on the student Home Page within the calendar or the Assignments tab.

You will find specifications and guidelines for accessing **realidades.com** on home computers and mobile devices on MyPearsonTraining.com under the SuccessNet Plus tab.

realidades.com

For: Tips to Parents
Visit: www.realidades.com
Web Code: jce-0010

Check it out! At the end of the chapter, have your child name two or three professions or types of work he or she is interested in.

Sincerely,

Videocultura Script

El medio ambiente

Spanish version:

En toda América Latina, hay organizaciones que trabajan en la preservación de diversos sistemas ecológicos.

Grupos privados y públicos se encargan de proteger las bellas costas y la vida marina…

de proteger los bosques tropicales…

de preservar la riqueza de la cuenca del río Amazonas…

y de proteger los bosques que rodean la Cordillera de los Andes.

En Guatemala y Nicaragua, la Alianza Internacional de Reforestación se dedica a plantar árboles para ayudar a las áreas que han sido devastadas por huracanes.

El Centro de Investigación y Extensión Forestal Andino Patagónico estudia los bosques de la región patagónica en el sur de Argentina y Chile.

En América Central, la Comisión Centroamericana de Ambiente y Desarrollo trabaja en el desarrollo de la agenda ambiental.

Con sede en Ecuador, Futuro Latinoamericano es otra organización que participa en la planificación del desarrollo sostenible de América Latina.

Es muy fácil aprender sobre el movimiento ambiental en América Latina.

Todas las organizaciones y fundaciones tienen sitios en Internet que te pueden brindar información sobre sus esfuerzos. Tú te puedes involucrar donando dinero o participando personalmente en actividades de voluntariado.

Tanto los estudiantes como los adultos en toda América Latina trabajan con gran esfuerzo en la preservación del medio ambiente para las futuras generaciones.

English version:

Throughout Latin America, you will find organizations that focus on preserving its diverse ecological systems.

Public and private groups are protecting the beautiful coastlines and sea life...

protecting the tropical rain forests...

preserving the rich Amazon river basin...

and protecting the forests that surround the Andes mountains.

In Guatemala and Nicaragua, the *Alianza Internacional de Reforestación* focuses on planting trees and establishing tree nurseries as they rebuild from the devastation of several hurricanes.

A similar organization called *Centro de Investigación y Extensión Forestal Andino Patagónico* studies the forests in the Patagonia region in southern Argentina and Chile.

In Central America, the *Comisión Centroamericana de Ambiente* y *Desarrollo* draws attention to environmental issues.

Another organization called *Futuro Latinamericano,* based in Ecuador, participates in long-term planning for sustainable development in Latin America.

It is easy to learn more about the environmental movement throughout Latin America.

Organizations and foundations have Web sites that will educate you about their efforts. You can get involved through financial donations or by volunteering to help in person.

Adults and students throughout Latin America are working hard to preserve their beautiful and diverse environment for future generations.

Input Script

Presentation

Input Vocabulary: Distribute the Vocabulary Clip Art of careers to students and have them cut them into individual images. Then announce to students that a "biodome" experiment is going to be conducted in your area. In the experiment, ten people will live in a completely enclosed and totally self-sustaining glass dome for five years. The scientists have asked for help in choosing the ten people who will live in the dome. Since the people must be completely self-sufficient for five years, it is important that the people have a variety of skills to help them survive in the dome.

Point to the different careers and describe them to students. Have students point in their books to each career as you describe it. Tell how the skills involved in each career would be useful to others in the "biodome". Then call out the names of the careers and have students hold up the Clip Art image of each career and give it a number value on a scale of 1–10, 1 being least useful and 10 being most useful.

Next, have students form small groups and select the ten careers they believe are most useful for people in the "biodome" to have. Have them draw pictures of any other careers they learned previously which they feel are vital to "biodome" survival, such as *médico(a)*. Have them arrange their Clip Art images of the ten careers on their desks in order of most useful to least useful. Compare the groups' selections and invite students to argue in favor of or against any careers. As a class, try to come to a consensus on which ten careers will be most useful in the "biodome."

Input Dialogues: Transition to the dialogue on p. 452 by telling students that fortunately we do not live in a "biodome" and we may choose among a wider variety of careers, rather than just those that have to do with physical survival. Ask if they have been to a career fair and what it was like. Then read the introduction to the career fair and have volunteers guess from context the meanings of the boldface words. Have volunteers read the teenagers' thoughts on p. 453. Then have the class vote with a show of hands for their favorite career on that page.

Comprehension Check

- Have students arrange any nine of their Clip Art images showing careers in three rows of three to form a tic-tac-toe grid. Describe careers at random to students. When they hear one of the careers in their grid described, they will turn that Clip Art image over. The first student to get three in a row, horizontally, vertically, or diagonally, wins.
- Choose a student to be the judge of a courtroom. Have another student be a person accused of some small infraction of the law having to do with his or her career. You will be the defense attorney. Give your closing remarks to the judge and jury in which you defend your client. Your remarks should give clues to your client's career, but not state it outright. Have the other students guess what career the person has based on your closing remarks.

Audio Script

Audio DVD, Capítulo 9A

Track 01: ***A primera vista, ¿Qué profesión tendrás?,* Student Book, p. 452, (7:12)**

Vocabulario y gramática en contexto

Vas a escuchar cada palabra o frase dos veces. Después de la primera vez hay una pausa para que puedas pronunciar la palabra o frase. Luego vas a escuchar de nuevo la palabra o frase.

la oficina	la jueza
el secretario	el abogado
la secretaria	la abogada
el contador	seguirán
la contadora	derecho
los negocios	un programa de estudios
bilingües	leyes
el futuro	el agricultor
idiomas	la agricultora
el arquitecto	el cartero
la arquitecta	la cartera
el diseñador	el mecánico
la diseñadora	la mecánica
el técnico	militar
la técnica	el hombre de negocios
habrá	la mujer de negocios
el juez	

Lee en tu libro mientras escuchas la narración.

ADULT FEMALE: Bienvenidos a la Exposición de carreras. Hoy les vamos a hablar sobre las posibilidades que hay para Uds. después de graduarse del colegio. Después de la graduación de la escuela secundaria, algunos de Uds. asistirán a la universidad y estudiarán para una profesión. Otros irán a una escuela técnica, y otros conseguirán un trabajo inmediatamente. Tenemos información para todos.

En el mundo de los negocios es importante tener a personas bilingües, y en el futuro hablar dos idiomas, como el inglés y el español, será aún más importante.

Habrá carreras importantes en la tecnología: arquitectos para la construcción de casas y edificios y diseñadores para sitios Web y juegos de computadoras.

Algunos de Uds. seguirán la carrera de derecho y tendrán un programa de estudios muy interesante. Para ser abogado o juez hay que ir a la universidad y estudiar leyes seis u ocho años.

Hay muchas otras oportunidades de trabajo: carreras de agricultor, mecánico, bombero o cartero, por ejemplo. Tal vez algunos seguirán una carrera militar.

Track 02: ***A primera vista,* Student Book, p. 453, (2:45)**

Vocabulario y gramática en contexto

Vas a escuchar cada palabra o frase dos veces. Después de la primera vez hay una pausa para que puedas pronunciar la palabra o frase. Luego vas a escuchar de nuevo la palabra o frase.

el político	la veterinaria
la política	el ingeniero
el gerente	la ingeniera
la gerente	el científico
el veterinario	la científica

Lee en tu libro mientras escuchas las opiniones.

TEEN MALE 1: Me gusta estudiar las ciencias sociales. Creo que seguiré una carrera en la política.

TEEN MALE 2: Hace dos años que trabajo como dependiente en una tienda de ropa. Quisiera ser gerente de la tienda.

TEEN FEMALE 1: Me interesa el estudio de la medicina, pero también me gustan los animales. Estudiaré para ser veterinaria.

TEEN MALE 3: Las matemáticas siempre han sido fáciles para mí. Me gustaría ser ingeniero.

TEEN FEMALE 1: A mí me encantan las ciencias. Seré científica y trabajaré en un laboratorio.

Track 03: ***A primera vista,* Act. 1, Student Book, p. 453, (2:20)**

Las profesiones

Escucha las descripciones de diferentes profesiones. Mira los dibujos y las fotos y señala la profesión que se describe en cada frase. Vas a escuchar las frases dos veces.

1. El diseñador puede imaginar cómo será algo antes de crearlo.
2. Los carteros son importantes porque nos traen el correo.
3. Mi vecina vende casas. Es una mujer de negocios.
4. Mi hermano siempre ha dibujado bien. Ahora estudia para ser arquitecto.
5. Una jueza tiene que conocer muy bien el derecho.
6. Seguiré un programa de estudios para ser abogado.
7. El gerente en la tienda donde trabajo es muy simpático.

Track 04: ***A primera vista,* Act. 2, Student Book, p. 453, (2:43)**

¿Lógico o no?

¿Qué sabes sobre las profesiones y las carreras? Levanta una mano si lo que escuchas es lógico y levanta las dos manos si no es lógico. Vas a escuchar las frases dos veces.

1. TEEN FEMALE 1: No me gusta trabajar con las manos. Voy a ser mecánica.
2. TEEN MALE 1: Hablo dos idiomas. Puedo ser un hombre de negocios para una compañía norteamericana en España o en México.
3. TEEN MALE 2: Un contador tiene que trabajar mucho con los números.
4. TEEN MALE 3: Me gustaría ser agricultor porque me gusta trabajar en el campo al aire libre.
5. TEEN FEMALE 3: Los científicos hacen experimentos e investigaciones interesantes.
6. TEEN MALE 3: No me gustan los animales. Por eso

quiero ser veterinario.

7. **Teen Female 2:** Es necesario ir a la universidad antes de tener una carrera militar.

Track 05: *A primera vista, Videohistoria,* Student Book, pp. 454–455, (2:10)

Y tú, ¿qué vas a ser?

¿Qué van a ser Angélica, Esteban y Pedro? ¿Qué le pasa a Pedro?

Lee la historia.

Read along as you listen to the dialogues.

See Student Book pages 454–455 for script.

Track 06: *Manos a la obra,* Act. 5, Student Book, p. 456, (4:00)

Así es mi trabajo

Copia la tabla en una hoja de papel. Vas a escuchar a seis personas hablar de su trabajo. Escribe lo que escuchas sobre los estudios de cada persona, lo que hace en su trabajo y cuál es su profesión.

1. **Adult Female:** En la universidad, estudié los negocios. Me gustan mucho las matemáticas y los números. En mi trabajo, uso mucho la computadora y una calculadora.
2. **Adult Male 1:** En mi trabajo les reparo los coches a otras personas. A veces uso una computadora. Asistí a una escuela técnica por dos años para prepararme para este trabajo.
3. **Adult Female 2:** Cuando me gradué del colegio, fui a una escuela técnica. Después de la graduación empecé a trabajar en el correo. Conozco a todas las personas que viven en el barrio donde entrego las cartas a sus casas.
4. **Adult Male 2:** Cada día paso muchas horas dibujando o pintando. A veces estoy en casa y otros días voy al campo o a la playa. Asistí a una escuela para las artes.
5. **Adult Female 3:** En la universidad yo estudié el derecho. Antes era abogada, pero ahora escucho a lo que dicen los abogados y tengo que tomar unas decisiones muy importantes.
6. **Adult Male 3:** Después de graduarme del colegio, asistí a la universidad para estudiar las ciencias. Siempre me han gustado los animales. Ahora trabajo en una clínica médica donde cuido a los animales enfermos o heridos.

Track 07: *Pronunciación, Diéresis,* Student Book, p. 459, (1:54)

As you have seen, when *gu* is used before *e* and *i*, the *u* is silent. To indicate that the *u* is pronounced, it is written with a *diéresis (ü).* Listen to and say the following sentence:

Ramón Guevara es bilingüe. Quiere seguir una carrera como guía para los turistas extranjeros.

¡Compruébalo!

Listen to the sentences as they are read. Complete the spelling of the words by adding *güe* or *güi*. *¡Ojo!* In one case, you will also have to add a written accent mark to the *e* or *i*.

1. Un ave graciosa de la Antártida es el pin___no.
2. Si hablas sólo un idioma, eres monolin___.
3. El estudio del lenguaje se llama la lin___stica.
4. Si haces algo malo debes tener ver___nza.

¡Trabalenguas!

Gárgaras

Gla-gle-gli-glo-glu-güe-güi

¡qué difícil es así!

Güi, güe, glu, glo, gli, gle, gla

¡qué trabajo igual me da!

Track 08: Audio Act. 5, Writing, Audio & Video Workbook, p. 169, (5:18)

Listen to the following students describe their interests and talents, then match each one up with his or her ideal career by writing the number of the statement under the corresponding picture. You will hear each statement twice.

1. **Teen Male 1:** Soy Mauricio. Creo que los animales son muy importantes en la vida. En muchos casos, son nuestros mejores amigos. De pequeño, visitaba a mis abuelos en el campo y cuidaba sus caballos, vacas, perros y gatos. Me interesa mucho una carrera en la que pueda trabajar con animales.
2. **Teen Male 2:** Mi madre siempre me decía que me gustaba discutir cualquier tema cuando era pequeño. Siempre podía defender a mis amigos cuando tenían un problema en la escuela. Después de graduarme, quiero seguir la carrera de derecho para ser abogado.
3. **Teen Female 1:** La clase de matemáticas es mi clase favorita. Siempre voy a la tienda en busca del último modelo en calculadoras. Me encanta jugar con dinero. Es mi actividad favorita. Cuando me gradúe quiero ser contadora de una compañía importante.
4. **Teen Male 3:** Me encantan los coches. Cuando era pequeño, mi papá iba conmigo a las carreras de coches deportivos. Pero mis favoritos son los coches antiguos. Quiero ganarme la vida con un garaje propio para reparar coches antiguos.
5. **Teen Female 2:** Recuerdo que cuando era niña vestía a mis muñecas con ropa diferente. Jugaba con mis amigas a los desfiles de moda. Quiero ir a una escuela técnica para aprender a hacer ropa elegante para las mujeres de negocios.
6. **Teen Female 3:** Yo sé muy bien cómo dar un discurso. Mis profesores me dicen que doy las mejores presentaciones de la clase. Quiero seguir una carrera en ciencias políticas para ser la mejor presidenta del país. No me importa el salario, sólo quiero ayudar a la gente.

Track 09: Audio Act. 6, Writing, Audio & Video Workbook, p. 170, (5:08)

Listen to the latest listings that were recently posted on a job hotline. Match the job qualifications with each of the pictures below by writing the number of each conversation underneath the corresponding picture. You will hear each listing twice.

1. Se busca un técnico en computadoras. Debe tener experiencia militar. Es mejor que pueda trabajar por las noches. Es necesario que sepa usar los programas del gobierno. Es mejor que haya estudiado en una escuela técnica.
2. Se busca una gerente responsable para una nueva tienda de ropa. Ofrecemos un programa de estudios para que siga una carrera como diseñadora de ropa de mujer y de hombre. Nuestra compañía es más grande cada día. Su futuro con nosotros será estupendo.
3. Se busca una secretaria bilingüe para una oficina de negocios internacionales. Es necesario que sepa escribir bien en español e inglés. Con beneficios buenos y con muchas oportunidades de viajar a algunos países de América del Sur. Debe empezar el 5 de junio.
4. Se busca un diseñador de ropa para mujeres. Es necesario que no tenga miedo de las nuevas ideas de la moda. Es mejor que se gradúe de una escuela de arte o de una escuela de diseño. Debe haber mucha creatividad en sus diseños. La experiencia no es un requisito.
5. Necesitamos un científico para enseñar ciencias a nuestros nuevos estudiantes. La Universidad del Este ofrece salarios y beneficios muy buenos. Las clases son pequeñas para que los estudiantes aprendan más. El Colegio de Artes y Ciencias de la universidad exige que la persona sea bilingüe.

Track 10: *Manos a la obra,* Act. 12, Student Book, p. 460, (2:28)

Escucha y escribe

Un estudiante va a escribir un artículo para el periódico de su escuela sobre los planes de los estudiantes que se graduarán del colegio este año. Escucha los planes de sus compañeros y escríbelos según el modelo. Vas a escuchar las frases dos veces.

1. Mi mejor amigo va a seguir una carrera militar.
2. Tú vas a trabajar en una tienda de equipo deportivo para ganar dinero.
3. Dos de mis amigos van a asistir a una escuela técnica.
4. Vamos a pasar tiempo con nuestros amigos antes de salir para la universidad.
5. Varios atletas van a participar en una liga de béisbol de verano.
6. Mi amiga y yo vamos a aprender a hacer surf de vela.

Track 11: Audio Act. 7, Writing, Audio & Video Workbook, p. 170, (5:58)

Listen as friends get together and talk about what they would like to do as a career in the future. What seems to motivate each of them the most? Is it: a) the imagined salary; b) the possibility of fame; or c) the possible benefit of his or her work to society? Listen to each person and place an X in the corresponding box in the grid. You will hear each conversation twice.

1. **Teen Female 1:** Iré a la universidad por más de seis años para ser abogada. Es importante que los abogados del futuro piensen en los derechos de los niños. Ellos son inocentes y el beneficio de ser abogada será la satisfacción de saber que ellos estarán seguros y protegidos en mi corte.
2. **Teen Male 1:** Algún día viviré en una casa fabulosa cerca de la playa. Invitaré a todos mis amigos a unas fiestas estupendas. ¡Seré un hombre de negocios con compañías y fábricas por todas partes! ¡Ganaré millones de dólares y seré muy feliz!
3. **Teen Male 2:** Voy a ser un científico de una universidad importante y descubriré la cura para el cáncer. Los otros científicos del mundo me invitarán a sus universidades para conocer mejor mi trabajo. Todo el mundo reconocerá mi nombre y apareceré en la portada de muchas revistas.
4. **Teen Female 2:** Estudiaré para ser la mejor agricultora del mundo. Inventaré algo para que los animales se pongan bien grandes. Crearé verduras bien grandes para que todo el mundo pueda comer y no haya hambre en el mundo.
5. **Teen Male 3:** Después de salir de la universidad, crearé una compañía de ingenieros para hacer los edificios más altos del mundo. Sólo las personas más ricas del mundo los comprarán. Mi compañía será la más rica del mundo.
6. **Teen Female 3:** Asistiré a la mejor escuela técnica para seguir una carrera de diseñadora de ropa de hombre. Vestiré a los hombres más famosos del mundo. Mis diseños pasarán al salón de la fama de los diseñadores modernos.
7. **Teen Male 4:** Cuidaré a los enfermos que no tengan dinero para pagar por el hospital. Crearé nuevas medicinas para que la gente no se ponga vieja y viva para siempre. Trabajaré para ser buen médico.

Track 12: Audio Act. 8, Writing, Audio & Video Workbook, p. 171, (4:37)

The first day on the job can be a challenge for anyone. Listen as these people are shown around their new offices. As you listen to each conversation, determine what kind of job each person has. In the blanks provided, write the letter of the picture that corresponds to each conversation. You will hear each conversation twice.

1. **Adult Female 1:** Bienvenido. Ésta será su oficina y yo soy su secretaria, Ana. Tendrá su primera reunión a las nueve sobre el proyecto del nuevo centro comercial. Habrá más de cien tiendas y oficinas allí. La construcción empezará dentro de dos meses.
2. **Adult Male 1:** Hola. Bienvenidos. Uds. distribuirán el correo a todos los departamentos de estos dos edificios. Habrá doscientas oficinas en total, pero podrán dividir el correo entre Uds. dos.

3. ADULT FEMALE 2: ¡Hola! Espero que no estés muy nervioso. Tu oficina estará en el primer piso y podrás escribir todos los libros que quieras. La oficina tendrá una cocina para que no tengas que salir a comer.
4. ADULT MALE 2: Bienvenido a los Laboratorios Reinoso. Tendrá el mejor y más moderno equipo de laboratorio de la compañía. Creará mejores medicinas para los enfermos y sabrá hacer muchas cosas nuevas.
5. ADULT FEMALE 3: Buenos días, señor. Hoy habrá dos reuniones muy importantes con los presidentes de Francia y España por la mañana. Y luego, tendrá que dar un discurso para la graduación de la Universidad Central.
6. ADULT MALE 3: ¡Buenas tardes! Bienvenida a Diseños Femeninos. Hoy empiezas a trabajar con nosotros. Harás ropa con los materiales más finos del mundo. Tendrás que compartir tu oficina con Marta por ahora, porque no tenemos espacio.

Track 13: Audio Act. 9, Writing, Audio & Video Workbook, p. 171, (3:38)

There are advantages and disadvantages to choosing a career in art. As you listen to each statement, check off whether it describes an advantage or disadvantage of being in the art industry. You will hear each statement twice.

1. Tendrás muchas oportunidades de trabajar, y no sólo como pintor o escritor.
2. Verás las cosas más bellas del mundo y algunas serán tu propia creación.
3. Siempre tendrás que vender tu arte, y a veces no habrá a nadie que le guste.
4. Podrás tener mucha fama y mucho dinero.
5. Sabrás que muchos quieren tener dinero y fama, pero pocos lo consiguen.
6. Habrá mucha competencia para el trabajo que quieres. Siempre estarás trabajando.
7. No tendrás que trabajar de las nueve hasta las cinco todos los días. Tendrás un horario más libre.
8. A veces tendrás que buscar otro trabajo que te guste menos para ganar dinero y tener la vida que prefieres.
9. A veces no tendrás inspiración alguna. Eso podrá durar un mes, un año o más.
10. Tendrás lo que quieres: una vida como artista.

Track 14: *Repaso del capítulo*, Student Book, p. 472, (6:02)

Vocabulario y gramática

See Student Book page 472 for vocabulary list.

Track 15: *Preparación para el examen*, Student Book, p. 473, (1:06)

Escuchar

Practice task

At the Senior Send-off Assembly, some graduating seniors are asked what they will do after they graduate. Listen and identify: a) what each will do next year; b) what profession they will pursue; and c) what they think their salary will be.

1. Después de la graduación, iré a la universidad. Quiero seguir una carrera de arquitecto. Creo que el salario de un buen arquitecto es más de cien mil dólares.
2. No sé cuanto es el salario ni me importa, pero estudiaré para ser veterinaria en la universidad. Me gustan mucho los animales y quiero ayudarlos.

Video Script

A primera vista: *Y tú, ¿qué vas a ser?*, (5:34)

Angélica: Ya voy, ya voy… Hola, Pedro, ¿qué tal?

Pedro: Hola. Muy bien, ¿y tú? ¿Está Esteban?

Angélica: Ah, sí. Te está esperando.

Pedro: Hola, Esteban. Vamos. Ya es tarde.

Esteban: Sí, sí. Vamos.

Angélica: ¿Adónde van?

Esteban: A la escuela. No tenemos mucho tiempo.

Angélica: ¿A la escuela? Pero si hoy es domingo.

Esteban: Sí, pero hoy hay un concurso de arte, de dibujos. Y Pedro va a participar.

Pedro: Y bien, ¿qué les parece?

Esteban: ¡Genial!

Angélica: A mí no me gustan.

Esteban: Es porque tú no comprendes el mundo de las artes.

Angélica: Sí lo comprendo, pero me gustan más otras cosas.

Pedro: Pues a mí me gusta todo tipo de arte. Y me encanta dibujar.

Angélica: A mí también me gusta dibujar, pero algún día prefiero ganarme la vida como mujer de negocios. Tendré un horario bueno, un salario decente y también beneficios.

Angélica: Sí, Señor Rodríguez. El negocio es muy bueno. No hay problema. Todo está listo. ¿Hola? Buenos días, Señor Martínez. ¿Cómo va todo? Un momento, por favor. ¿Señor Rodríguez? Oh, perdón, Señor Martínez. ¿Señor Rodríguez? ¿Señor Martínez? ¿Señor Martínez?

Esteban: Sí, claro. Y algún día querrás ser dueña de tu negocio…

Angélica: ¿Y por qué no? Tú podrás ser el gerente y Pedro, el contador.

Esteban: No, gracias. El mundo de los negocios no es para mí. Prefiero seguir una carrera técnica.

Pedro: ¡Ay! Tenemos tres años hasta graduarnos y entrar a la universidad. ¿No creen que es un poco temprano para discutir sobre nuestras profesiones? Mejor vamos o llegaremos tarde al concurso.

Esteban: Sí. ¿Vienes con nosotros?

Angélica: Cuando no hay clases, ¡ay no!

Esteban and Pedro: Vamos.

Esteban: Sí, más bien.

Esteban: Oye, creo que eres muy talentoso. Algún día podrás ser pintor.

Pedro: No sé. Es difícil ganarse la vida como artista. Quizás podré ser escritor. Sabes que también me gusta mucho escribir.

Pedro: Y tú, ¿qué piensas hacer?

Esteban: Pues a mí me gustan las profesiones técnicas. Quiero estudiar para ingeniero o arquitecto.

School Principal: Silencio. Por favor, silencio. Y este concurso es un gran éxito para nuestra escuela. Todos los trabajos que vemos aquí son excelentes, pero uno de ellos es el mejor. A ver… ¡Pedro Salazar! ¡Felicidades!

Pedro: Muchas gracias. Gracias.

School Principal: ¡Buena suerte! Y, como saben, el año que viene Pedro podrá estudiar en la Escuela de Artes Visuales de Nueva York.

Lisa: ¡Felicidades, Pedro!

Pedro: Muchas gracias, Lisa. Éste es un momento muy importante para mí.

Esteban: ¿Un autógrafo, por favor?

Pedro: ¿Cómo? Ah, sí, por supuesto. Voy a ser un pintor muy famoso.

***GramActiva* Videos, (6:00)**

The future tense

King: You will learn the future tense! The future tense is much easier than other tenses because you use the same set of endings for all verbs. I say so, because I am king! And I say the endings are *-é, -ás, -á, -emos, -éis,* and *-án.* My word is law.

V.O.: Here's an example: "will buy."
Compraré, comprarás, comprará, compraremos, compraréis, comprarán.

King: The best part of the future tense is: the endings are the same for *-ar, -er,* and *-ir* verbs. Why? Because I say so! It's good to be king.

Grand Vizier: Also, all the endings except *nosotros* and *nosotras* have an accent mark on the vowel. Keep an eye out for the accent marks. Now, let's look at some more examples.

King: That's my line! Guards! Throw him in the dungeon! Now let's look at some more examples, starring my favorite person—me.
I'm sick of having peasants for subjects. I want a high-tech kingdom.
You there. *Será el veterinario. Salga.*
You two. *Seréis las contadoras. Salgan.*
Serás el juez.
¡Y yo seré rey del mundo!

Quiz

V.O.: Fill in the blank with the correct verb form in the future.
(comprar) Yo ______ un secador.
Yo compraré un secador.
(jugar) Ella ______ al hockey.
Ella jugará al hockey.
(comer) Nosotros ______ chuletas de cerdo.
Nosotros comeremos chuletas de cerdo.
(escribir) Ellos ______ una carta.
Ellos escribirán una carta.

The future tense: irregular verbs

Host: In the future, skyscrapers may touch the clouds. Wealth may be abundant. Or we may be overrun by the mole people. While we can't predict the future, we can tell you about irregular verbs in the future tense.
You already know your future endings, right? *-é, -ás, -á, -emos, -éis,* and *-án.*
To form irregular verbs in the future, take your irregular stem and add on your endings. Like *tener.* The stem changes to *tendr-.* And add your endings.

Mexican Hat Dancer: And now we dance!
Tendré, tendrás, tendrá, tendremos, tendréis, tendrán.

V.O.: Besides *tener,* here are some more irregular verbs and their stems: *poder—podr-. Saber—sabr-. Haber—habr.* And *hacer—har-.*

Mexican Hat Dancer: *¡Poder!*
Podré, podrás, podrá, podremos, podréis, podrán.
¡Saber!
Sabré, sabrás, sabrá, sabremos, sabréis, sabrán.
¡Haber!
Habré, habrás, habrá, habremos, habréis, habrán.
¡Hacer!
Haré, harás, hará, haremos, haréis, harán.

Host: Examples! Get your red-hot examples!

V.O.: *¿Qué clase de trabajo tendrán ellos… EN EL FUTURO?*
[What kind of work will she do… IN THE FUTURE?]
¿Podremos ganarnos la vida… EN EL FUTURO?
[Will we be able to make a living… IN THE FUTURE?]
¿Sabrás hablar más de dos idiomas… EN EL FUTURO?
[Will you know how to speak more than two languages…IN THE FUTURE?]

Quiz

V.O.: Fill in the blank with the correct future-tense form of the irregular verb.
(saber) ¿ ______ nosotros hablar tres idiomas en el futuro?
¿Sabremos nosotros hablar tres idiomas en el futuro?
(poder) Él ______ cocinar.
Él podrá cocinar.
(tener) Algún día yo ______ un buen trabajo con un excelente salario.
Algún día tendré un buen trabajo con un excelente salario.

Realidades 2 — Nombre ______________________

Capítulo 9A — Fecha ______________________

Communicative Pair Activity **9A-1**

Estudiante **A**

You are interested in knowing what careers your classmates are choosing for their future. Ask your partner the following questions. Record your partner's answers on the lines provided.

1. ¿Qué estudiará Fernando? ______________________
2. ¿Quiénes estudiarán español? ______________________
3. ¿Quién quiere ser actriz? ______________________
4. ¿Qué estudiará Teresa? ______________________
5. ¿Quiénes estudiarán matemáticas? ______________________
6. ¿Quién estudiará computadoras? ______________________
7. ¿Quién practicará deportes? ______________________
8. ¿Quiénes quieren estudiar cine? ______________________
9. ¿Quiénes estudiarán arquitectura? ______________________
10. Y tú, ¿qué quieres ser? ______________________

Use the following information to answer your partner's questions.

Lalo

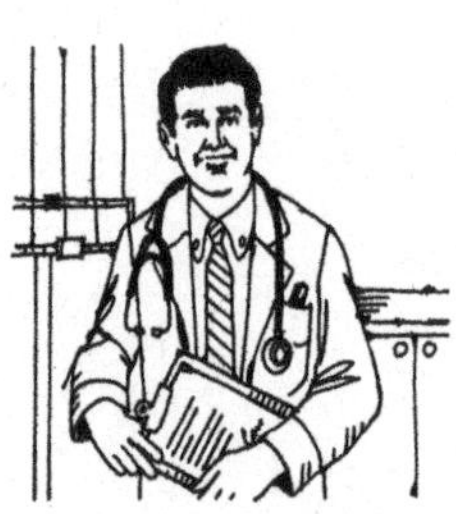

Samuel

Alejandro y Natalia

Álvaro

Rosa y Mateo

Martín

Mario

yo

Josefina

Jaime y Vicente

Realidades 2

Capítulo 9A

Nombre ______________________

Fecha ______________________

Communicative Pair Activity **9A-1**

Estudiante **B**

Use the following information to answer your partner's questions.

Pedro y Emma

Julián

Elizabeth

yo

Adelaida y Ramiro

Andrés y Juanita

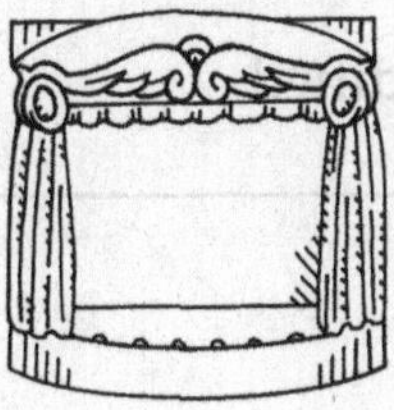

Maritza

Luis y Daniel

Fernando

Teresa

You are interested in knowing what careers your classmates are choosing for their future. Ask your partner the following questions. Record your partner's answers on the lines provided.

1. ¿Qué estudiará Mario? ______________________
2. ¿Quiénes estudiarán para ser jardineros? ______________________
3. ¿Quién quiere ser médico? ______________________
4. ¿Qué estudiará Josefina? ______________________
5. ¿Quién estudiará computadoras? ______________________
6. ¿Quiénes estudiarán cine? ______________________
7. ¿Quién estudiará mecánica? ______________________
8. ¿Quiénes quieren estudiar leyes? ______________________
9. ¿Quién quiere ser cartero? ______________________
10. Y tú, ¿qué quieres ser? ______________________

Nombre ______________________

Fecha ______________________

What do you think about the following professions? Look at the opinions listed at the bottom of the page. Fill in your answers in the column marked *Yo*. Then ask your partner what he or she thinks and write those answers in the column marked *Mi compañero(a)*. Example: *—¿Qué piensas del club de español?—¡Es fantástico!* How do Diego and Graciela feel about the same activities? First ask your partner a question about Diego or Graciela to fill in one of the missing answers on your chart. *(¿Qué piensa Graciela de ser cantante?)* Next, answer your partner's question. Take turns asking and answering questions about Diego and Graciela until both charts are completely filled in.

	Yo	Mi compañero(a)	Diego	Graciela
			divertido	
			difícil	
				peligroso
				no me gusta
las computadoras			aburridas	
la arquitectura				
las matemáticas				interesantes

OPINIONES:

- aburrido, -a
- bueno, -a
- difícil
- divertido, -a
- estupendo, -a
- fabuloso, -a
- interesante
- maravilloso, -a
- no me gusta
- no sé
- peligroso, -a
- tonto, -a

Realidades 2

Nombre ____________________

Capítulo 9A

Fecha ____________________

Communicative Pair Activity **9A-2**

Estudiante **B**

What do you think about the following professions? Look at the opinions listed at the bottom of the page. Fill in your answers in the column marked *Yo*. Then ask your partner what he or she thinks and write those answers in the column marked *Mi compañero(a)*. Example: *—¿Qué piensas del club de español?—¡Es fantástico!* How do Diego and Graciela feel about the same activities? First ask your partner a question about Diego or Graciela to fill in one of the missing answers on your chart. *(¿Qué piensa Graciela de ser cantante?)* Next, answer your partner's question. Take turns asking and answering questions about Diego and Graciela until both charts are completely filled in.

	Yo	Mi compañero(a)	Diego	Graciela
				estupendo
				bueno
			peligroso	
			no sé	
las computadoras				no me gustan
la arquitectura			fabulosa	
las matemáticas			difíciles	

OPINIONES:

- aburrido, -a
- bueno, -a
- difícil
- divertido, -a
- estupendo, -a
- fabuloso, -a
- interesante
- maravilloso, -a
- no me gusta(n)
- no sé
- peligroso, -a
- tonto, -a

Situation Cards

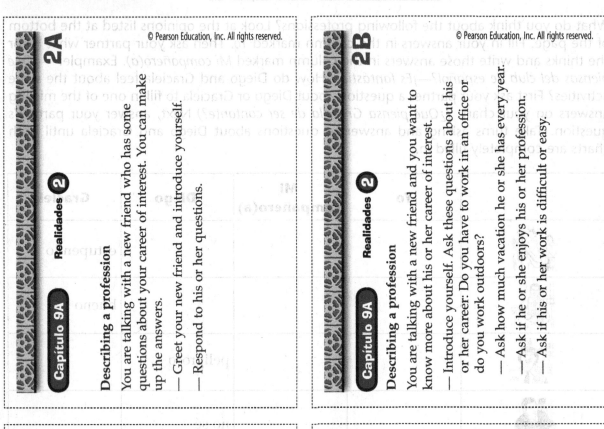

1A

Capítulo 9A Realidades 2

Talking about careers and work

You are talking with a friend about careers.

— Greet your friend. Ask what career he or she would like in the future.

— Respond to your friend's question. Then ask which other career he or she would like as a second option.

— Respond to your friend's question.

1B

Capítulo 9A Realidades 2

Talking about careers and work

You are talking with a friend about careers.

— Respond to your friend's question. Then, ask what career he or she would like to study.

— Respond to your friend's question.

— Ask your friend if he or she knows other people working in those two careers.

2A

Capítulo 9A Realidades 2

Describing a profession

You are talking with a new friend who has some questions about your career of interest. You can make up the answers.

— Greet your new friend and introduce yourself.

— Respond to his or her questions.

2B

Capítulo 9A Realidades 2

Describing a profession

You are talking with a new friend and you want to know more about his or her career of interest.

— Introduce yourself. Ask these questions about his or her career: Do you have to work in an office or do you work outdoors?

— Ask how much vacation he or she has every year.

— Ask if he or she enjoys his or her profession.

— Ask if his or her work is difficult or easy.

GramActiva

¿Qué profesión tendrás?

¿Qué harás en el futuro?, p. 466

la educación	lo que hace	su profesión

Vocabulary Clip Art

Vocabulary Clip Art

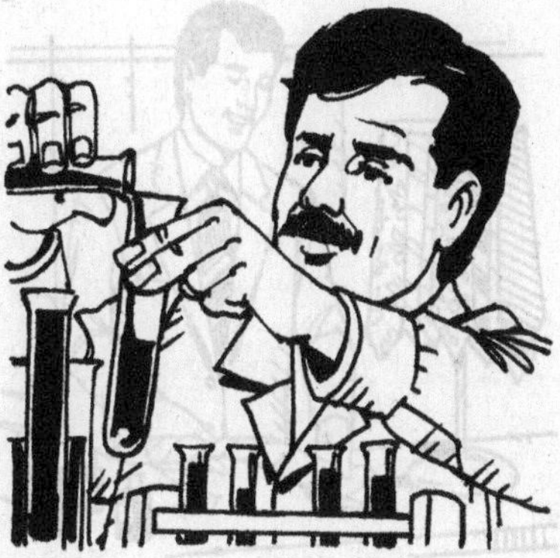

Vocabulary Clip Art

Vocabulary Clip Art

Vocabulary Clip Art

Capítulo 9A

Core Practice Answers

9A-A
1. árboles, flores
2. botellas, plástico
3. montañas
4. cajas de cartón
5. botellas, latas
6. pájaros
7. centro de reciclaje
8. vidrio
9. el lago

9A-B
1. Yo recojo periódicos en casa.
2. Tú consigues botellas de plástico en el parque.
3. Ellos envían cartas a los políticos en el club.
4. Marta sigue estudiando las ciencias naturales en la universidad.
5. Raúl y Bárbara no destruyen el papel en casa.
6. Yo escojo lugares para tirar el vidrio roto en la comunidad.
7. Los trabajadores separan el plástico y el vidrio en el centro de reciclaje.
8. Trabajamos como voluntarios en la comunidad.
9. Inés recoge la ropa usada de la comunidad.
10. Reciclo las botellas en casa.

9A-1
1. mujer de negocios
2. arquitecto
3. agricultor
4. cartera
5. ingenieros
6. jueza
7. mecánico
8. secretaria
9. científica
10. abogado, juez
11. técnica
12. gerente

9A-2
programa de estudios / la universidad / graduarme / abogada / jueza / ingeniero / técnico / científico / veterinario / política

9A-3
A.
la vida / dueño / oficina / salario / beneficios / idiomas / carrera / universidad / negocios / profesión

B.
Después de graduarse de la universidad.

9A-4
A.
1. Falso. Jorge quiere seguir una carrera de derecho.
2. Falso. Linda quiere seguir una carrera política.
3. Cierto.
4. Falso. Catrina no quiere estudiar las ciencias para su profesión.
5. Cierto.
6. Falso. Teresa quiere seguir una carrera de artes.

B.
1. el derecho
2. la veterinaria
3. la oficina
4. un artista
5. el dueño

9A-5
1. seguirá una carrera de negocios
2. trabajará de cartero
3. habrá muchas oportunidades para usar el español
4. se graduarán este año
5. escogeremos un programa de estudios
6. dibujaré en la computadora
7. comprenderás el mundo de las artes
8. se casarán
9. asistiremos a la universidad

9A-6
1. sabrás qué quieres estudiar
2. habrá trabajos interesantes
3. tendrán que asistir a una escuela técnica
4. haremos un picnic
5. podrán venir a vernos
6. tendremos tiempo para todo
7. sabré todo el vocabulario
8. habrá más profesores
9. podrás ir a la universidad
10. haré el papel del galán

9A-7
te perderás / será / tomaré / Tendrás / sabrá / estaré / gustará / podré / habrá / haré / conocerás / te divertirás / presentaré / iremos / tendrás

Crucigrama (9A-8)
Horizontal:

2. técnicos	15. pintor
3. científico	16. beneficios
7. arquitecta	17. veterinaria
8. juez	21. salario
9. ganas	22. cartero
11. contador	23. carrera
14. escuela	24. derecho

Vertical:

1. bilingüe	12. oficina
4. graduaré	13. negocios
5. programa	18. escritora
6. dueño	19. agricultor
10. futuro	20. idioma

Organizer (9A-9)
I. Vocabulary Answers will vary.
II. Grammar
1. **trabajar:**

trabajaré	trabajaremos
trabajarás	trabajaréis
trabajará	trabajarán

seguir:

seguiré	seguiremos
seguirás	seguiréis
seguirá	seguirán

2. Row 1: sabré, haré
Row 2: podré, tendré

Realidades 2 Nombre ________________ Hora ________

Capítulo 9A Fecha ________________ **AVSR 9A-1**

A ver si recuerdas: Verbs with spelling changes in the present tense (p. 449)

- As you know, some verbs have spelling changes in the present tense for reasons of pronunciation. Some verbs, such as **escoger, recoger, seguir,** and **conseguir,** change spelling only in the *yo* form.

  Mi hermano *escoge* unas vacaciones en las montañas mientras que yo *escojo* la playa.
  My brother chooses a vacation in the mountains while I choose the beach.

  Los turistas no siempre *siguen* las reglas; yo sí las *sigo*.
  The tourists do not always follow the rules; I do follow them.

- Other verbs, such as **enviar** and **esquiar,** simply add accent marks on the **i** in all persons except **nosotros** and **vosotros.**

  Mi hermano *esquía* mucho. Nosotros *esquiamos* juntos a veces.
  My brother skis a lot. We ski together sometimes.

A. Write the present tense **yo** form of the infinitives below. Then write the second form in the present tense using the cue provided. Follow the model.

Modelo	escoger	yo	*escojo*	usted	*escoge*
1.	conseguir	yo	***consigo***	tú	***consigues***
2.	enviar	yo	***envío***	nosotros	***enviamos***
3.	recoger	yo	***recojo***	ellas	***recogen***
4.	seguir	yo	***sigo***	ella	***sigue***
5.	escoger	yo	***escojo***	nosotras	***escogemos***
6.	esquiar	yo	***esquío***	tú	***esquías***

realidades.com
• Web Code: jdd-0901

Realidades 2 Nombre ____ Hora ____

Capítulo 9A Fecha ____ **AVSR 9A-2**

A ver si recuerdas: Verbs with spelling changes in the present tense (*continued*)

B. Pablo is working at a summer camp. Complete his letter home by writing the **yo** form of the verbs given. The first one is done for you.

Queridos padres:

¿Cómo están? Yo estoy muy bien aquí en las montañas, y estoy trabajando mucho. Todos los días yo **sigo** *(**seguir**) las instrucciones de mi jefe. Siempre* **recojo** *(**recoger**) la basura de la cafetería y* **envío** *(**enviar**) las cartas de los niños. Después, yo* **consigo** *(**conseguir**) el horario del día del director del campamento. Lo* **sigo** *(**seguir**) con cuidado, y por la tarde tengo dos horas libres. A veces* **esquío** *(**esquiar**) en agua—¡mi actividad favorita! Por la noche, yo* **escojo** *(**escoger**) un juego para jugar con los niños. Siempre me acuesto muy cansado.*

Un abrazo,

Pablo

C. Complete the following answers, paying special attention to the verbs with spelling changes. Follow the model.

Modelo ¿Les envías muchas cartas a tus parientes?

Sí, yo siempre les *envío cartas*

1. ¿Quién recoge la basura en tu casa?
   Yo **recojo la basura** en mi casa.
2. ¿Esquías todos los inviernos?
   Sí, yo **esquío todos los inviernos**
3. ¿Siempre sigues las reglas de tus padres?
   Sí, yo siempre **sigo las reglas de mis padres**.
4. ¿Dónde consigues regalos para tus parientes?
   Yo **consigo regalos para mis parientes en una tienda**.

Realidades 2 Nombre ____ Hora ____

Capítulo 9A Fecha ____ **Vocabulary Flash Cards, Sheet 1**

Write the Spanish vocabulary word below each picture. Be sure to include the article for each noun.

el colegio

la graduación

graduarse

la universidad

el agricultor

la agricultora

el mecánico

la mecánica

la cartera

Realidades 2 Nombre ______ Hora ______

Capítulo 9A Fecha ______ **Vocabulary Flash Cards, Sheet 2**

Write the Spanish vocabulary word below each picture. Be sure to include the article for each noun.

el cartero

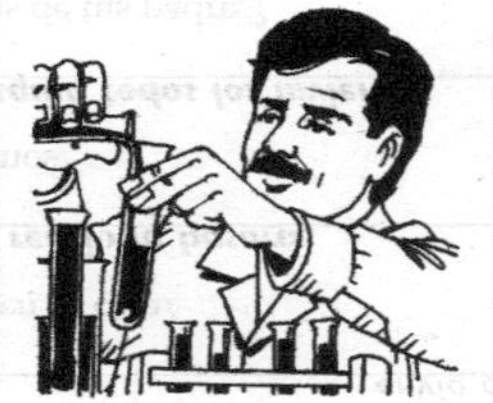

el científico

la científica

el veterinario

la veterinaria

el hombre de negocios

la mujer de negocios

la secretaria

el secretario

Realidades 2 Nombre ______ Hora ______

Capítulo 9A Fecha ______ **Vocabulary Flash Cards, Sheet 3**

Write the Spanish vocabulary word below each picture. Be sure to include the article for each noun.

la contadora

el contador

la arquitecta

el arquitecto

la ingeniera

el ingeniero

la diseñadora

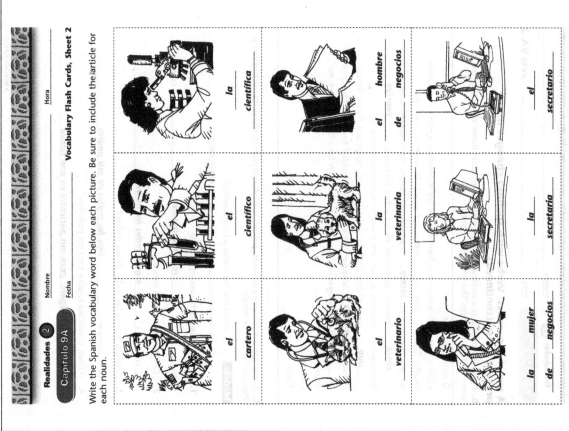

el diseñador

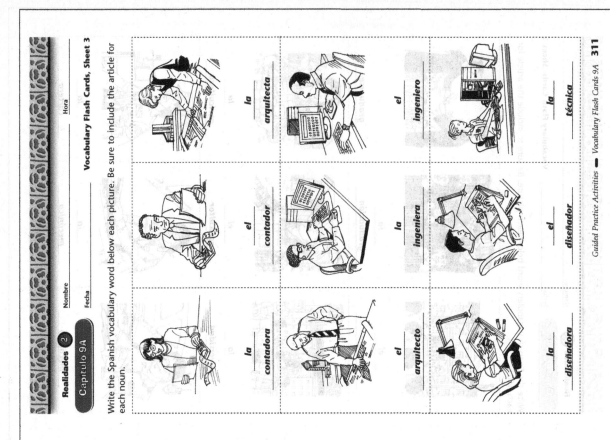

la técnica

Realidades 2 Nombre ______ Hora ______

Capítulo 9A Fecha ______ **Vocabulary Flash Cards, Sheet 4**

Write the Spanish vocabulary word below each picture. Be sure to include the article for each noun.

el

técnico

la

escritora

el

escritor

la

artista

el

artista

la

pintora

el

pintor

el

político

la

política

Realidades 2 Nombre ______ Hora ______

Capítulo 9A Fecha ______ **Vocabulary Flash Cards, Sheet 5**

Write the Spanish vocabulary word below each picture. If there is a word or phrase, copy it in the space provided. Be sure to include the article for each noun.

el

abogado

la

abogada

el

juez

la

jueza

la

oficina

la ley

la

ley

la política

la

política

algún día

algún

día

los beneficios

los

beneficios

Realidades 2 Nombre Hora

Capítulo 9A Fecha **Vocabulary Flash Cards, Sheet 6**

Copy the word or phrase in the space provided. Be sure to include the article for each noun.

bilingüe *bilingüe*	**la carrera** *la* *carrera*	**la escuela técnica** *la escuela* *técnica*
el futuro *el* *futuro*	**ganarse la vida** *ganarse* *la vida*	**habrá** *habrá*
el idioma *el* *idioma*	**militar** *militar*	**el programa de estudios** *el programa* *de estudios*

Realidades 2 Nombre Hora

Capítulo 9A Fecha **Vocabulary Flash Cards, Sheet 7**

Copy the word or phrase in the space provided. Be sure to include the article for each noun. The blank cards can be used to write and practice other Spanish vocabulary for the chapter.

el salario *el* *salario*	**seguir (una carrera)** *seguir* *(una carrera)*	**el dueño, la dueña** *el dueño,* *la dueña*
el gerente, la gerente *el gerente,* *la gerente*	**las artes** *las* *artes*	**el derecho** *el* *derecho*
la profesión *la* *profesión*		

Realidades 2 | Nombre ____ Hora ____

Capítulo 9A | Fecha ____

Vocabulary Flash Cards, Sheet 8

These blank cards can be used to write and practice other Spanish vocabulary for the chapter.

Realidades 2 | Nombre ____ Hora ____

Capítulo 9A | Fecha ____

Vocabulary Check, Sheet 1

Tear out this page. Write the English words on the lines. Fold the paper along the dotted line to see the correct answers so you can check your work.

el científico, la científica	***scientist***
el ingeniero, la ingeniera	***engineer***
el veterinario, la veterinaria	***veterinarian***
el contador, la contadora	***accountant***
el dueño, la dueña	***owner***
el gerente, la gerente	***manager***
los negocios	***business***
el hombre de negocios, la mujer de negocios	***businessman, businesswoman***
el secretario, la secretaria	***secretary***
el artista, la artista	***artist***
el abogado, la abogada	***lawyer***
el derecho	***(study of) law***
el colegio	***high school***
la universidad	***university***

Fold In ←

Realidades 2 — Capítulo 9A

Nombre ______ Hora ______

Fecha ______

Vocabulary Check, Sheet 2

Tear out this page. Write the Spanish words on the lines. Fold the paper along the dotted line to see the correct answers so you can check your work.

scientist	***el científico, la científica***
engineer	***el ingeniero, la ingeniera***
veterinarian	***el veterinario, la veterinaria***
accountant	***el contador, la contadora***
owner	***el dueño, la dueña***
manager	***el gerente, la gerente***
business	***los negocios***
businessman, businesswoman	***el hombre de negocios, la mujer de negocios***
secretary	***el secretario, la secretaria***
artist	***el artista, la artista***
lawyer	***el abogado, la abogada***
(study of) law	***el derecho***
high school	***el colegio***
university	***la universidad***

Fold In ←

Realidades 2 — Capítulo 9A

Nombre ______ Hora ______

Fecha ______

Vocabulary Check, Sheet 3

Tear out this page. Write the English words on the lines. Fold the paper along the dotted line to see the correct answers so you can check your work.

el agricultor, la agricultora	***farmer***
el arquitecto, la arquitecta	***architect***
el diseñador, la diseñadora	***designer***
el mecánico, la mecánica	***mechanic***
el cartero, la cartera	***mail carrier***
el escritor, la escritora	***writer***
el pintor, la pintora	***painter***
la ley	***law***
la política	***politics***
el político, la política	***politician***
bilingüe	***bilingual***
la carrera	***career***
el salario	***salary***
la profesión	***profession***

Fold In ←

Realidades 2 — Capítulo 9A

Nombre ______ Hora ______

Fecha ______

Vocabulary Check, Sheet 4

Tear out this page. Write the Spanish words on the lines. Fold the paper along the dotted line to see the correct answers so you can check your work.

farmer	***el agricultor, la agricultora***
architect	***el arquitecto, la arquitecta***
designer	***el diseñador, la diseñadora***
mechanic	***el mecánico, la mecánica***
mail carrier	***el cartero, la cartera***
writer	***el escritor, la escritora***
painter	***el pintor, la pintora***
law	***la ley***
politics	***la política***
politician	***el político, la política***
bilingual	***bilingüe***
career	***la carrera***
salary	***el salario***
profession	***la profesión***

Fold In

To hear a complete list of the vocabulary for this chapter, go to www.realidades.com and type in the Web Code jdd-0989. Then click on **Repaso del capítulo.**

Realidades 2 — Capítulo 9A

Nombre ______ Hora ______

Fecha ______

Guided Practice Activities 9A-1

The future tense (p. 460)

- The future tense tells what will happen. To form the future tense of regular verbs ending in **-ar**, **-er**, and **-ir**, add these endings to the infinitive: **-é, -ás, -á, -emos, -éis, -án.**

  En unos años *seré* un abogado.

  In a few years, I will be a lawyer.

- Here are the future forms for **trabajar, ser,** and **vivir:**

yo	trabajaré seré viviré	nosotros/nosotras	trabajaremos seremos viviremos
tú	trabajarás serás vivirás	vosotros/vosotras	trabajaréis seréis viviréis
usted/él/ella	trabajará será vivirá	ustedes/ellos/ellas	trabajarán serán vivirán

A. Fill in the blanks with the correct future tense ending of each verb using the cues provided. Follow the model.

Modelo los estudiantes conseguir *án*

1. yo viajar ***é***
2. nosotros vivir ***emos***
3. Beto se graduar ***á***
4. tú ir ***ás***
5. ustedes ser ***án***
6. Lisa pintar ***á***
7. yo trabajar ***é***
8. nosotros comer ***emos***

B. Write the future tense of the verbs in parentheses. Follow the model.

Modelo (trabajar) Tú *trabajarás* como gerente en una tienda grande.

1. (asistir) Uds. ***asistirán*** a la universidad del estado.
2. (ser) Yo ***seré*** el mejor científico de esta región.
3. (hablar) Nosotros ***hablaremos*** con gente famosa.
4. (esquiar) Pablo ***esquiará*** en las montañas altas del mundo.
5. (graduarse) Tú te ***graduarás*** el año que viene.

realidades.com • Web Code: jdd-0904

The future tense (*continued*)

C. Look at the underlined verbs in the sentences. Complete each sentence by using the future tense to tell what people will do, according to the picture. The first one is done for you.

1. Jaime y Victoria son abogados, pero algún día ***serán*** jueces.

2. Mario trabaja de cartero, pero el año que viene él ***trabajará*** de mecánico.

3. La familia Pérez vive en un apartamento, pero algún día la familia ***vivirá*** en una casa.

4. Generalmente Pilar y Mateo no ven videos, pero mañana ellos ***verán*** la tele.

5. Isabel es estudiante, pero algún día ella ***será*** política.

6. Yo no escribo muchas cartas, pero más tarde le ***escribiré*** a mi primo.

The future tense: irregular verbs (p. 462)

- Some verb stems are irregular in the future tense: **hacer → har-; poder → podr-; saber → sabr-; tener → tendr-; haber → habr-**.
- Though the stems are irregular, the endings for these verbs are the same as regular future tense verbs. Look at the verb **hacer**.

HACER			
yo	**haré**	nosotros/nosotras	**haremos**
tú	**harás**	vosotros/vosotras	**haréis**
usted/él/ella	**hará**	ustedes/ellos/ellas	**harán**

A. Write the correct future tense ending of the verb in parentheses for each sentence. Follow the model.

Modelo **(hacer)** Yo har***é*** la tarea esta tarde.

1. **(poder)** Ricardo podr***á*** contarnos unos chistes.
2. **(tener)** Mis primos tendr***án*** muchas oportunidades en ese trabajo.
3. **(saber)** Nosotros sabr***emos*** la verdad después de unos minutos.
4. **(haber)** Habr***á*** mucha gente en las tiendas.

B. Read what these people will do in the future. Write the irregular future tense stem to complete the verb in each sentence. Follow the model.

Modelo **(poder)** Mis primos no ***podr***án venir a la fiesta.

1. **(hacer)** Nosotros ***har***emos ejercicio este fin de semana.
2. **(poder)** Yo ***podr***é ayudarte con la tarea.
3. **(Saber)** ¿***Sabr***á Juan llegar a tu casa?
4. **(Haber)** ***Habr***á una graduación el fin de semana.
5. **(tener)** Tú ***tendr***ás tiempo el viernes por la tarde.
6. **(poder)** Ustedes ***podr***án terminar con la tarea esta noche.
7. **(tener)** Nosotros ***tendr***emos que ir a la escuela temprano.

The future tense: irregular verbs (*continued*)

C. Complete each sentence in the future tense with the correct form of the verb in parentheses. The first one is done for you.

1. **(poder)** Francisco ***podrá*** usar la computadora.
2. **(saber)** Tú ***sabrás*** de ciencias.
3. **(hacer)** La veterinaria le ***hará*** un examen a mi perro.
4. **(poder)** Marta ***podrá*** ser contadora.
5. **(tener)** Mis amigos y yo ***tendremos*** clases en la universidad.
6. **(haber)** En junio ***habrá*** una graduación.

D. Follow Isidro's list of things that he wants to do after graduation. Use the future tense of the verbs in parentheses. The first one is done for you.

Después de graduarme...

1. ...yo ***podré*** hacer un viaje con mis amigos. **(poder)**
2. ...nosotros ***iremos*** a Europa. **(ir)**
3. ...mis amigos y yo ***gastaremos*** mucho dinero. **(gastar)**
4. ...mis padres no ***sabrán*** qué hago cada minuto de cada día. **(saber)**
5. ...mi hermano ***buscará*** un trabajo, pero yo no. **(buscar)**
6. ...yo ***asistiré*** a una universidad. **(asistir)**
7. ...***habrá*** muchas oportunidades para mí. **(haber)**

realidades.com • Web Code: jdd-0905

Lectura: ¡Descubre tu futuro! (pp. 468–469)

A. The reading in your textbook is about a career center. Read the heads and subheads to find out some basic information. Then, place an *X* next to the information you may find in this reading.

X an aptitude test ***X*** career choices

______ movie listings ***X*** a personal information record

B. Read the following selection from the reading and the questions below. Circle the letter of the correct answer for each question.

> *Los estudiantes que vienen al centro, pueden...*
> - *investigar diferentes carreras*
> - *buscar información sobre cientos de universidades*
> - *asistir a presentaciones sobre cómo financiar los estudios*

1. What can a student do at the Career Center?
   (**a.**) find out about careers and universities
   b. find out about restaurants
2. About how many universities can students find information?
   a. less than 100 universities
   (**b.**) more than 100 universities
3. What can students learn at the presentations offered by the Career Center?
   (**a.**) how to finance their education
   b. how to become involved in sports or clubs

C. Fill out the following **portafolio personal** by using either your own information or made-up information. ***Answers will vary.***

Nombre: ______
Dirección: ______
Grado: ______ Intereses extracurriculares: ______
______
Universidades que me interesan: ______
______

realidades.com • Web Code: jdd-0907

Realidades 2 | Nombre ____ Hora ____

Capítulo 9A | Fecha ____ **Guided Practice Activities 9A-6**

Presentación oral (p. 471) *Answers will vary.*

Task: Prepare a presentation to a partner about a job you might expect to have in the future. Explain why you would choose that job.

A. Charts can help you organize information for a presentation. Think about classes you like and, in the first column, fill in the two subjects you prefer. In the second column, list two activities that you enjoy doing. The first line is done for you as an example.

Cursos favoritos	Diversiones
la literatura	*leer libros*

B. Use your answers from **part A** and the list of professions below, or choose another profession you have learned about in this chapter to complete the sentences.

contador, -a	veterinario, -a	abogado, -a	gerente
arquitecto, -a	ingeniero, -a	profesor, -a	pintor, -a

Mis clases favoritas son ____ y ____.

Las actividades que más me gustan son ____ y ____.

Estudiaré para ser ____ porque me gusta ____.

C. Read your statements from **part B** to practice for the oral presentation. Practice your presentation several times. Try to:

- provide as much information as you can
- speak clearly

D. Tell your partner about your interests and what you plan to do in the future.

Realidades 2 — Capítulo 9A

Nombre ______ Hora ______

Fecha ______ VIDEO

Antes de ver el video

Actividad 1

There are many different professions and careers you might choose to pursue. In the first column below, write five professions or careers that interest you. In the second column, write something with which each career or profession is associated. The first one is done for you.

Carrera o profesión	Cosas
Profesor(a)	*la educación*
Answers will vary.	

¿Comprendes?

Actividad 2

Each of the following sentences is false. Rewrite each one to make it true.

1. 
Angélica prefiere el mundo de las artes.
Angélica prefiere el mundo de los negocios.

2. 
Pedro dijo: "A mí me gusta todo tipo de arte. Y me encanta correr."
Pedro dijo: "A mí me gusta todo tipo de arte. Y me encanta dibujar."

3. 
Pedro podría ser médico; le gusta mucho escribir.
Pedro podría ser escritor; le gusta mucho escribir.

Realidades 2 — Capítulo 9A

Nombre ______ Hora ______

Fecha ______ VIDEO

4. 
Esteban quiere estudiar para ingeniero o contador.
Le gustan las profesiones técnicas.
Esteban quiere estudiar para ingeniero o arquitecto.
Le gustan las profesiones técnicas.

5. 
Esteban pide la dirección electrónica de Pedro.
Esteban pide el autógrafo de Pedro.

Actividad 3

Answer each of the following questions in complete sentences based on what you saw in the video.

1. ¿Por qué quieren ir los amigos al colegio un domingo?
Quieren ir al colegio porque hay un concurso de arte.

2. ¿Qué dice Angélica cuando ve el dibujo de Pedro?
Dice: "A mí no me gusta."

3. ¿Cómo prefiere Angélica ganarse la vida algún día?
Angélica prefiere ganarse la vida como mujer de negocios.

4. ¿Cómo prefiere Esteban ganarse la vida algún día?
Esteban quiere ser ingeniero o arquitecto.

5. ¿Cuándo van a graduarse los amigos?
Van a graduarse en dos años.

6. ¿Por qué dice Pedro: "Gracias, es un momento muy importante para mí"?
Pedro lo dice porque él gana el concurso.

Realidades 2 — Capítulo 9A

Nombre ______ Hora ______

Fecha ______ VIDEO

Y, ¿qué más?

Actividad 4

The friends from the video seem to know what they want to be when they are older. Think about the five professions you wrote about in **Actividad 1** and how you can work towards achieving each goal. Use the model to guide you.

Modelo *Para ser profesora yo necesito ir a la universidad y estudiar educación. También necesito aprender a enseñar la clase.*

1. Answers will vary.
2. ______
3. ______
4. ______
5. ______

Realidades 2 — Capítulo 9A

Nombre ______ Hora ______

Fecha ______ AUDIO

Actividad 5

Listen to the following students describe their interests and talents, then match each one up with his or her ideal career by writing the number of the statement under the corresponding picture. You will hear each statement twice.

4

1

6

5

2

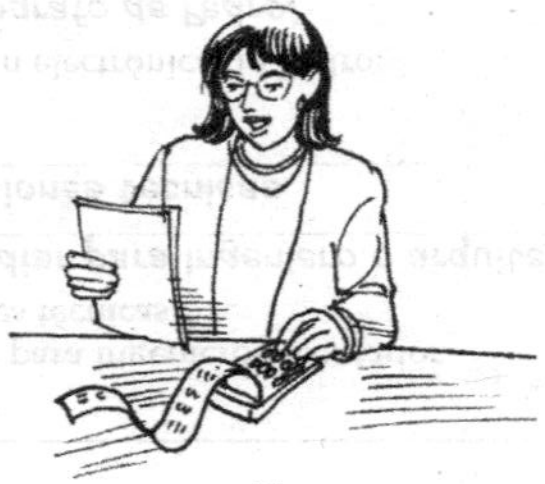

3

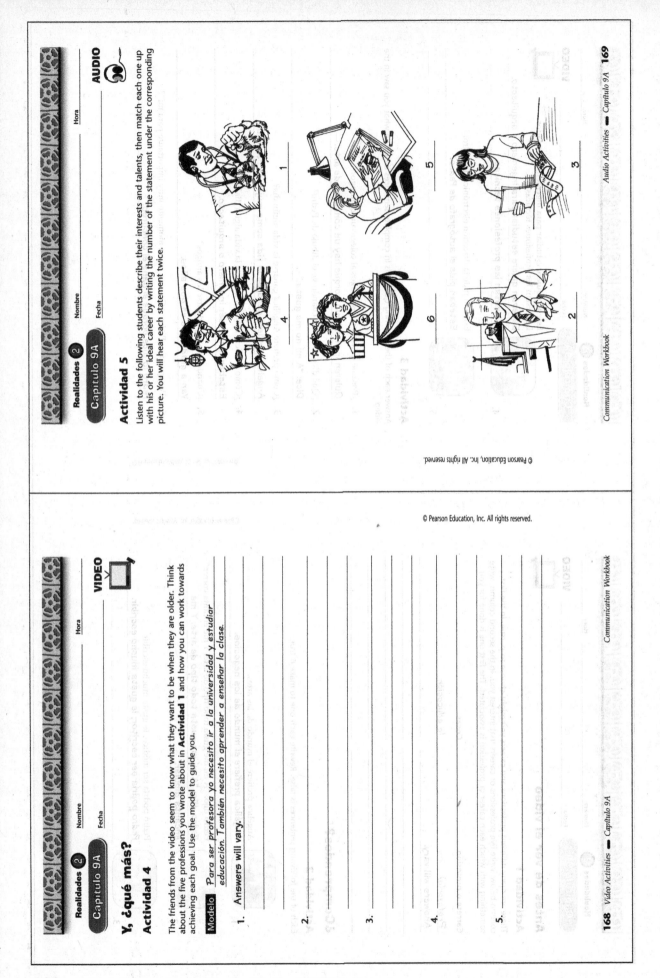

Realidades 2 Nombre ____ Hora ____

Capítulo 9A Fecha ____ AUDIO

Actividad 6

Listen to the latest listings that were recently posted on a job hotline. Match the job qualifications with each of the pictures below by writing the number of each conversation underneath the corresponding picture. You will hear each listing twice.

2

4

5

1

3

Actividad 7

Listen as friends get together and talk about what they would like to do as a career in the future. What seems to motivate each of them the most? Is it: a) the imagined salary; b) the possibility of fame; or c) the possible benefit of his or her work to society? Listen to each person and place an X in the corresponding box in the grid. You will hear each conversation twice.

	1	2	3	4	5	6	7
¿El salario?		X			X		
¿La fama?			X			X	
¿Los beneficios a la sociedad?	X			X			X

Realidades 2 Nombre ____ Hora ____

Capítulo 9A Fecha ____ AUDIO

Actividad 8

The first day on the job can be a challenge for anyone. Listen as these people are shown around their new offices. As you listen to each conversation, determine what kind of job each person has. In the blanks provided, write the letter of the picture that corresponds to each conversation. You will hear each conversation twice.

A

B

C

D

E

F

1. A 2. D 3. E 4. C 5. F 6. B

Actividad 9

There are advantages and disadvantages to choosing a career in art. As you listen to each statement, check off whether it describes an advantage (**ventaja**) or disadvantage (**desventaja**) of being in the art industry. You will hear each statement twice.

	1	2	3	4	5	6	7	8	9	10
Ventaja	✓	✓		✓			✓			✓
Desventaja			✓		✓	✓		✓	✓	

Actividad 10

Your friend Carolina is visiting from Ecuador, and you have taken her to your neighborhood's annual summer party. Using the picture below, write complete sentences to tell her what each person at the party does for a living and what the job entails. Follow the model.

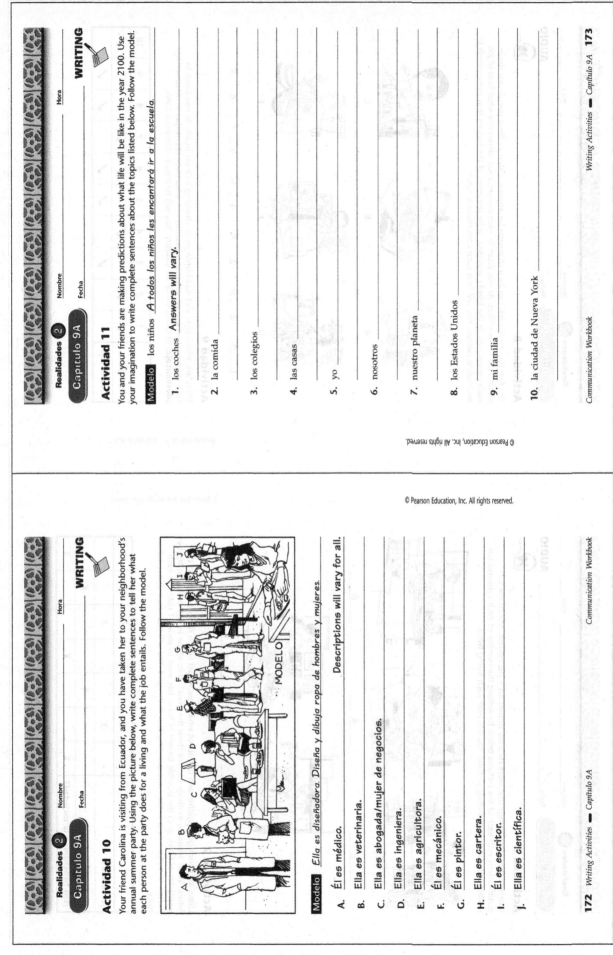

Modelo *Ella es diseñadora. Diseña y dibuja ropa de hombres y mujeres.*

A. *Él es médico.* *Descriptions will vary for all.*

B. *Ella es veterinaria.*

C. *Ella es abogada/mujer de negocios.*

D. *Ella es ingeniera.*

E. *Ella es agricultora.*

F. *Él es mecánico.*

G. *Él es pintor.*

H. *Ella es cartera.*

I. *Él es escritor.*

J. *Ella es científica.*

Actividad 11

You and your friends are making predictions about what life will be like in the year 2100. Use your imagination to write complete sentences about the topics listed below. Follow the model.

Modelo los niños *A todos los niños les encantará ir a la escuela.*

1. los coches *Answers will vary.*
2. la comida
3. los colegios
4. las casas
5. yo
6. nosotros
7. nuestro planeta
8. los Estados Unidos
9. mi familia
10. la ciudad de Nueva York

Actividad 12

Juanito is running for class president. Help him write his campaign promises about each topic by using the following verbs: **hacer, poder, saber, tener,** and **haber.** You may use each verb twice. Follow the model.

Modelo La escuela *tendrá tres cafeterías.*

1. Yo Answers will vary.
2. Los profesores ______.
3. El baile de la escuela ______.
4. Los estudiantes ______.
5. Mis mejores amigos y yo ______.
6. El día escolar ______.
7. La administración ______.
8. Nosotros ______.
9. La cafetería ______.
10. Los deportes ______.

Actividad 13

You are playing the fortune-teller at your school's winter carnival. Some of your friends want to find out what is going to happen to them in the future. Write at least three predictions for each of the people listed below. The first one has been started for you.

1. Nombre de un(a) amigo(a) Name will vary.
   Predicciones:
   Mi amigo tendrá una casa grande. Answers will vary.
2. Nombre de dos amigos(as): Names will vary. y ______
   Predicciones:
3. (Yo) Predicciones:
4. (Nosotros) Predicciones:

Realidades 2

Capítulo 9A

Test Preparation Answers

Reading Skills
p. 283 2. **B**
p. 284 2. **A**

Integrated Performance Assessment
p. 285
Answers will vary.

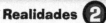

Capítulo 9B School-to-Home Connection

Dear Parent or Guardian,

The theme of our current unit is *¿Cómo será el futuro?* (What will the future be like?). This chapter is called *¿Qué haremos para mejorar el mundo?* (How can we make the world a better place?).

Upon completion of this chapter students will be able to:

- make predictions about what the world will be like in the future
- express doubt about ecological issues
- discuss environmental problems and possible solutions
- understand cultural perspectives on worldwide ecological problems and their solutions

Students will also explore:

- antonyms

Our textbook, *Realidades,* helps with the development of reading, writing, and speaking skills through the use of strategies, process speaking, and process writing. In this chapter, students will:

- read about the Antarctic and Tierra del Fuego
- write an article for your community to organize other young people for a volunteer project

To reinforce and enhance learning, students can access a wide range of online resources on **realidades.com,** the personalized learning management system that accompanies the print and online Student Edition. Resources include the eText, textbook and workbook activities, audio files, videos, animations, songs, self-study tools, interactive maps, voice recording (RealTalk!), assessments, and other digital resources. Many learning tools can be accessed through the student Home Page on **realidades.com.** Other activities, specifically those that require grading, are assigned by the teacher and linked on the student Home Page within the calendar or the Assignments tab.

You will find specifications and guidelines for accessing **realidades.com** on home computers and mobile devices on MyPearsonTraining.com under the SuccessNet Plus tab.

realidades.com

For: Tips to Parents
Visit: www.realidades.com
Web Code: jce-0010

Check it out! At the end of the chapter, have your child name three ways in which he or she would like to get involved in helping to protect Earth.

Sincerely,

Capítulo 9B

Videocultura Script

El medio ambiente

Spanish version:

En toda América Latina, hay organizaciones que trabajan en la preservación de diversos sistemas ecológicos.

Grupos privados y públicos se encargan de proteger las bellas costas y la vida marina…

de proteger los bosques tropicales…

de preservar la riqueza de la cuenca del río Amazonas…

y de proteger los bosques que rodean la Cordillera de los Andes.

En Guatemala y Nicaragua, la Alianza Internacional de Reforestación se dedica a plantar árboles para ayudar a las áreas que han sido devastadas por huracanes.

El Centro de Investigación y Extensión Forestal Andino Patagónico estudia los bosques de la región patagónica en el sur de Argentina y Chile.

En América Central, la Comisión Centroamericana de Ambiente y Desarrollo trabaja en el desarrollo de la agenda ambiental.

Con sede en Ecuador, Futuro Latinoamericano es otra organización que participa en la planificación del desarrollo sostenible de América Latina.

Es muy fácil aprender sobre el movimiento ambiental en América Latina.

Todas las organizaciones y fundaciones tienen sitios en Internet que te pueden brindar información sobre sus esfuerzos. Tú te puedes involucrar donando dinero o participando personalmente en actividades de voluntariado.

Tanto los estudiantes como los adultos en toda América Latina trabajan con gran esfuerzo en la preservación del medio ambiente para las futuras generaciones.

English version:

Throughout Latin America, you will find organizations that focus on preserving its diverse ecological systems.

Public and private groups are protecting the beautiful coastlines and sea life...

protecting the tropical rain forests...

preserving the rich Amazon river basin...

and protecting the forests that surround the Andes mountains.

In Guatemala and Nicaragua, the *Alianza Internacional de Reforestación* focuses on planting trees and establishing tree nurseries as they rebuild from the devastation of several hurricanes.

A similar organization called *Centro de Investigación y Extensión Forestal Andino Patagónico* studies the forests in the Patagonia region in southern Argentina and Chile.

In Central America, the *Comisión Centroamericana de Ambiente* y *Desarrollo* draws attention to environmental issues.

Another organization called *Futuro Latinamericano,* based in Ecuador, participates in long-term planning for sustainable development in Latin America.

It is easy to learn more about the environmental movement throughout Latin America.

Organizations and foundations have Web sites that will educate you about their efforts. You can get involved through financial donations or by volunteering to help in person.

Adults and students throughout Latin America are working hard to preserve their beautiful and diverse environment for future generations.

Input Script

Presentation

Input Vocabulary 1 and Dialogue 1: Come to class dressed as Mother Nature. Wear a long, flowing wig with flowers and leaves intertwined in it, a long dress, and sandles. Enter the classroom as if you are very agitated. Distribute copies of the Vocabulary Clip Art and have students cut them into individual images. Place the transparency showing types of environmental pollution on the screen. Introduce yourself as Mother Nature and say how angry you are at the way people have been destroying the earth's environment. Point to the types of environmental problems and describe how outraged you are about each one. Have students point to the problems in their books.

Then use the dialogue as a script to propose the solutions to the problems. Read the solutions out of order and have students hold up the Clip Art images of the problem each solution you mention addresses. Next, ask students to arrange their Clip Art images on their desks from most pressing problem to least pressing problem. Discuss how they ranked the problems.

Input Vocabulary 2: Act reassured that they appear to be taking the problems of environmental pollution seriously. Place the transparency showing different aspects of the environment on the screen. Present the vocabulary as an impasssioned speech in favor of protecting the environment. Summarize by reviewing each aspect of the environment that needs protection. Have students arrange their Clip Art images in the order you discuss them.

Then enlist volunteers to the Mother Nature's Environmental Protection Club. Have potential members read the text as convincingly as they can to the rest of the class. Critique their performance and coach them in making their speeches more emotional and stirring.

Finally give students index cards, tongue depressor sticks, and glue sticks. Write the sentence starters *Tenemos que…, Debemos…,* and *Es importante que haya…,* and have students create protest signs with sentences about what people should do to help the environment.

Comprehension Check

- Make logical and illogical statements about protecting the different parts of the earth's environment. Have students give a "thumbs-up" sign for logical statements and a "thumbs-down" sign for illogical statements.
- Describe the different regions of an imaginary country and have students draw a map showing the country's forests, jungles, valleys, hills, and deserts according to your description.

Audio Script

Audio DVD, Capítulo 9B

Track 01: *A primera vista, ¿Qué haremos para mejorar el mundo?*, Student Book, p. 476, (2:44)

Vocabulario y gramática en contexto

Lee en tu libro mientras escuchas la narración.

TEEN MALE: La destrucción de nuestro medio ambiente afecta a cada persona. Tenemos que luchar contra este problema grave.

Para la salud de la gente de nuestro pueblo, hay que eliminar la contaminación del aire y del agua.

Tenemos que reducir el uso de la electricidad y usar otras fuentes de energía.

Debemos proteger a los animales que están en peligro de extinción.

Para mejorar la situación del mundo es necesario resolver los problemas entre los países. Es importante que haya paz y no haya guerra.

Vas a escuchar cada palabra o frase dos veces. Después de la primera vez hay una pausa para que puedas pronunciar la palabra o frase. Luego vas a escuchar de nuevo la palabra o frase.

la contaminación	el agua contaminada
el aire contaminado	la calefacción solar
el pueblo	la paz

Track 02: *A primera vista*, Student Book, p. 477, (1:38)

Vocabulario y gramática en contexto

Lee en tu libro mientras escuchas la narración.

¡Hay muchas maneras en que ustedes pueden ayudar a proteger la belleza de nuestra naturaleza… en el espacio… en las selvas tropicales… en los desiertos… en los bosques! Júntense con amigos y participen en uno de los grupos ecológicos de nuestra comunidad hoy.

Vas a escuchar cada palabra o frase dos veces. Después de la primera vez hay una pausa para que puedas pronunciar la palabra o frase. Luego vas a escuchar de nuevo la palabra o frase.

la Luna	la planta
la Tierra	el valle
la colina	

Track 03: *A primera vista*, Act. 1, Student Book, p. 477, (2:12)

En las noticias

Escucha lo que dice el señor del grupo ecológico en la página 476. Señala con el dedo qué parte de la escena se describe en cada frase. Vas a escuchar las frases dos veces.

1. Los coches producen mucha de esta contaminación.
2. Si continuamos la destrucción del medio ambiente, habrá más animales en peligro de extinción.
3. Usar la calefacción solar es buena idea para reducir el uso de la electricidad.
4. Un pueblo es más pequeño que una ciudad.
5. Las naciones deben luchar por la paz.
6. Hay que eliminar las fuentes de contaminación del agua.

Track 04: *A primera vista*, Act. 2, Student Book, p. 477, (2:07)

¿Cierta o falsa?

En una hoja de papel, escribe los números del 1 al 7. Si la frase que escuchas es cierta, escribe *C*. Si es falsa, escribe *F*. Vas a escuchar las frases dos veces.

1. Nosotros vivimos en la Luna.
2. Hay muchos lagos y océanos en el desierto.
3. Hace mucho calor en la selva tropical.
4. Hay muchos árboles diferentes en el bosque.
5. Una colina es más alta que una montaña.
6. La naturaleza de la Tierra está en peligro.
7. Los valles se encuentran entre las montañas.

Track 05: *A primera vista, Videohistoria*, Student Book, pp. 478–479, (2:27)

¡Caramba, qué calor!

Hoy hace mucho calor en San Antonio. Lee la historia para saber qué hacen Esteban y Pedro.

See Student Book pages 478–479 for script.

Track 6: *Manos a la obra*, Act. 4, Student Book, p. 480, (2:38)

Descripciones del medio ambiente

Escucha las descripciones del medio ambiente. En una hoja de papel, escribe los números del 1 al 8. Escribe el nombre de lo que está describiendo. Vas a escuchar las frases dos veces.

1. Es un lugar donde hay muchos árboles y donde viven los osos.
2. Es algo que vemos en el cielo de noche.
3. Es similar a un árbol pero más pequeño.
4. Es el lugar en el espacio donde vivimos.
5. Es un lugar entre dos montañas.
6. Es similar a una montaña, pero no es tan alta.
7. Es el lugar donde están el Sol, los planetas y las estrellas.
8. Es un lugar donde hay poca lluvia.

Track 07: Audio Act. 5, Writing, Audio & Video Workbook, p. 179, (4:30)

Listen to the following people talk about the future. As you hear each statement, determine whether the speaker is an optimist or a pessimist and place a check mark in the corresponding box in the grid. You will hear each statement twice.

1. Yo creo que en el futuro habrá bastante comida para todos en nuestro planeta porque los científicos descubrirán mejores métodos para cultivar las plantas.

2. Yo creo que habrá una guerra que terminará con nuestra civilización. Siempre existirán personas agresivas y malas.
3. Yo creo que habrá ríos más contaminados por las fábricas. Desafortunadamente, siempre habrá personas que piensen que el dinero es más importante que el medio ambiente.
4. Yo creo que habrá paz si hay cooperación entre todos los líderes mundiales.
5. Yo creo que habrá una enfermedad horrible y, desafortunadamente, los científicos no podrán encontrar una cura a tiempo. Millones de personas morirán.
6. Yo creo que las familias viajarán a la Luna de vacaciones en el verano y no costará mucho dinero hacerlo.
7. Yo creo que la contaminación del aire será un problema muy grave en los Estados Unidos. Habrá muchos coches que usarán demasiada gasolina dentro de cinco años. Nadie podrá vivir en las ciudades grandes.
8. Yo creo que la gente se juntará para usar otras fuentes de energía, como la energía solar. No usaremos tanta electricidad para la calefacción de las casas durante el invierno. Así reduciremos el uso de los recursos de la naturaleza.

Track 08: Audio Act. 6, Writing, Audio & Video Workbook, p. 179, (4:16)

Listen as students in Señor Naranjo's science class make predictions about the year 2020. As you hear each one, mark the number of the description underneath the picture it describes. Then mark an X in the grid below to tell whether you agree with the prediction or doubt it will come true. Be prepared to tell why you answered the way you did. You will hear each prediction twice.

1. En el año 2020, el aire y el agua serán puros a causa de la eliminación de los coches.
2. Sí. Estoy de acuerdo. Todos montarán en bicicleta en vez de manejar en coche. Las bicicletas serán más económicas que los coches.
3. Yo creo que en el año 2020 todos los líderes de los países se juntarán para resolver los conflictos mundiales. No habrá ni guerra ni armas de destrucción masiva.
4. Creo que los científicos encontrarán más curas para las enfermedades graves al estudiar las plantas de la selva tropical. Podrán usarlas para hacer medicinas nuevas.
5. Creo que en el año 2020 habrá nuevas medicinas que nos permitan vivir doscientos años. La gente tendrá más músculos y nada de pelo.
6. Ni la calefacción ni el aire acondicionado del año 2020 necesitarán energía o electricidad. Ahorraremos mucho dinero y seremos millonarios todos.
7. Todos los coches del año 2020 serán eléctricos y no habrá contaminación. La Tierra será un mejor lugar para vivir porque no estará contaminada.

Track 09: *Manos a la obra*, Act. 12, Student Book, p. 484, (2:04)

Escucha y escribe

Unos jóvenes hablan de sus experiencias como voluntarios en un centro de reciclaje. Hablan de lo que ocurre siempre y de lo que ocurrirá en el futuro. Escucha las seis frases y escríbelas. Después escribe *presente* si ocurre ahora o futuro si ocurrirá en el *futuro*. Vas a escuchar las frases dos veces.

1. ¿A qué hora saldremos para el centro de reciclaje?
2. Mis hermanos vendrán conmigo esta vez.
3. ¿Qué haremos para ayudarlos?
4. Siempre nos dicen que somos muy trabajadores.
5. Pondré el plástico y el vidrio en cajas diferentes.
6. Generalmente quieren darnos refrescos.

Track 10: Audio Act. 7, Writing, Audio & Video Workbook, p. 180, (4:13)

Listen as Julia and Elena plan Julia's campaign for class president. Some of the campaign promises they come up with are A) silly and not possible, while others are B) serious and possible. As you listen to each idea, write *A* or *B* in the blanks provided. You will hear each statement twice.

1. **Julia:** Haremos una lista de ideas. Vamos a ver… ¡Ya sé! Como presidenta, lucharé por un almuerzo de dos horas y unas clases de treinta minutos.
2. **Elena:** Yo tengo otra. Como presidenta, los estudiantes nuevos tendrán una guía escrita cada año.
3. **Julia:** ¿Qué más? Como presidenta, pondré refrescos en cada sala de clases. Y galletas también.
4. **Elena:** Y como presidenta, siempre nos dirás la verdad. Es muy importante.
5. **Julia:** Sí, de acuerdo. Y como presidenta, querré eliminar todos los exámenes finales. Saldremos de cada semestre con notas buenas por nuestra participación, nada más.
6. **Elena:** ¡Qué bueno! Aquí va una nueva… como presidenta podrás hacer un nuevo horario. Los estudiantes llegarán a la escuela a las doce y saldrán a las dos de la tarde.
7. **Julia:** ¡Fantástico! Ya sé… como presidenta querré que los almuerzos sean mejores para la salud y que tengan más cosas en el menú.
8. **Elena:** ¡Muy bien! Y como presidenta de la clase querré que estemos en clases solo un día a la semana.

Track 11: Audio Act. 8, Writing, Audio & Video Workbook, p. 180, (5:35)

The debate coach is observing a mock debate in order to determine whom she will select as partners for an upcoming debate on *"El futuro para nosotros."* Listen as the debaters answer the coach's questions. Fill in the chart below by circling each debater's opinion on the three issues. Which two people share the most opinions? You will hear each conversation twice.

1. **Adult Female:** Bueno. Para empezar..., ¿es posible que tengamos escuelas sin profesores en el futuro, Ramón?
Ramón: Hay mucha información para navegar la Web, pero no creo que sea posible que eliminemos a los profesores de las escuelas.
Adult Female: ¿Sandra?
Sandra: Es posible que no vayamos a la escuela en el futuro porque podremos aprender todo en nuestras casas por la Web. No necesitaremos ni los profesores ni los libros.
Adult Female: ¿Lucas?
Lucas: No estoy seguro de que aprendamos tanto por la Web. Con una profesora en la clase, podemos pedir ayuda si no entendemos algo. Creo que necesitamos los profesores y los compañeros de la clase para aprender mejor.
2. **Adult Female:** ¿Es posible que tengamos paz en el mundo en el futuro?
Ramón: La gente nunca estará contenta con los demás. Siempre nos pelearemos porque queremos lo que otros tienen. Sería muy bonito pero no creo que sea posible.
Adult Female: ¿Sandra?
Sandra: La gente dejará de pelearse cuando no haya hambre. El hambre es nuestro peor problema. Cuando no exista el hambre, habrá paz.
Adult Female: ¿Lucas?
Lucas: Olvídalo, siempre habrá gente con hambre. Siempre habrá gente rica y gente pobre. Dudo que un día haya paz mundial.
3. **Adult Female:** ¿Es posible vivir en la Luna en el futuro?
Ramón: No creo que sea posible, porque sería muy caro tener edificios en la Luna. Necesitaremos un medio ambiente artificial. ¿Qué pasará si no funciona? Todos se morirán.
Sandra: La Tierra estará tan contaminada que tendremos que vivir en la Luna. Nuestra situación es muy grave; no vamos a tener otra opción.
Lucas: La gente necesita ver árboles. En la Luna no hay árboles. Además, la gente tendrá que estar en su casa o en un edificio todo el tiempo. ¡Qué aburrido! No creo que vayamos a vivir en la Luna.

Track 12: Audio Act. 9, Writing, Audio & Video Workbook, p. 180, (5:40)

Listen to this class discussion about the problems in the world and solutions for a better world in the future. As you hear each comment, decide if the person is describing a problem or offering a solution. Place a check mark in the appropriate column in the grid below. You will hear each comment twice.

1. Hay muchos animales en peligro de extinción. Es cierto que necesitamos protegerlos. Quiero que los niños del futuro conozcan los tigres y los osos.
2. Tendremos que reducir el uso de la electricidad. No dudamos que hay otras fuentes de energía. Es importante que las investiguemos.
3. Nuestros abuelos no tenían aire acondicionado ni en sus casas ni en sus coches. Es cierto que podemos existir sin ello en el mes de junio. La Tierra saldrá mejor si apagamos el aire acondicionado más.
4. Además de preocuparse por el medio ambiente, es cierto que los gobiernos del mundo necesitan juntarse para eliminar los conflictos entre los grupos políticos y religiosos por el mundo. Es posible que nuestros niños dirán que esto sigue siendo un problema.
5. Los árboles de las selvas tropicales de América del Sur se están muriendo porque no los cuidamos. Los animales no podrán vivir sin las plantas.
6. Tenemos que poner más árboles en las selvas tropicales de América del Sur. También tendremos que hablar con la gente para que cuiden de las selvas tropicales. Las medicinas para el futuro vendrán de plantas en las selvas de América.
7. Es cierto que el balance ecológico se rompe cuando ponemos basura cerca de los ríos y lagos. Muchos animales se mueren porque hay tanta basura. Nosotros necesitamos muchas cosas de esos animales.
8. Es cierto que podemos proteger a nuestros animales y plantas si reciclamos la basura que creamos. Querremos reciclar los periódicos para hacer nuevos cuadernos que los niños podrán usar para escribir. Así tendremos un medio ambiente puro y sin contaminación.

Track 13: *Repaso del capítulo,* Student Book, p. 496, (5:15)

Vocabulario y gramática

Escucha las palabras y expresiones que has aprendido en este capítulo.

See Student Book page 496 for vocabulary list.

Track 14: *Preparación para el examen,* Student Book, p. 497, (0:52)

Escuchar

Practice task

In honor of *Día de la Tierra,* a class is discussing what people currently do or will do to improve the environment. Listen to their comments, and write *presente* if their statements deal with the present or *futuro* if they deal with the future.

Teen Male 1: Mi familia usa el aire acondicionado solar para conservar la electricidad.
Teen Female: Viviremos en el espacio.
Teen Male 2: Limpiamos los lagos contaminados.

Video Script

A primera vista: *¡Caramba, qué calor!*, (5:21)

ESTEBAN: ¿Qué pasa?

PEDRO: No sé, pero creo que no tenemos aire acondicionado.

ESTEBAN: ¿Qué? ¿Con este calor? Imposible. Mamá, ¿qué pasa con el aire acondicionado?

ANGÉLICA: ¿Qué necesitas, Esteban? Mamá no está. Ella y Cristina fueron al almacén, ¿recuerdas?

ESTEBAN: Creo que el aire acondicionado está mal. No lo oigo. ¿Puedes ir a ver qué pasa?

ANGÉLICA: ¡Por supuesto que no! Hazlo tú. ¡Además, no hace tanto calor!

PEDRO: ¡Silencio! Yo mismo voy a ver lo que pasa.

PEDRO: Esteban, me parece que el aire acondicionado no funciona…

PEDRO: Dudo que sea la electricidad.

ESTEBAN: Bueno, no podemos quedarnos aquí. Tenemos que ir a algún lugar que tenga aire acondicionado.

ESTEBAN: ¿Por qué no vamos a ver una película? Allí vamos a estar bien. Angélica, hermanita, ¿no nos puedes llevar en el coche?

ANGÉLICA: Bueno, pero tendrán que esperar media hora. Tengo que terminar algo.

ESTEBAN: ¿Media hora? Pero, ¿qué dices?

PEDRO: ¿Por qué no caminamos? El cine Alameda no está demasiado lejos.

ESTEBAN: Bueno. Vamos.

PEDRO: ¿No te gustaría tener aire acondicionado solar?

ESTEBAN: ¿Por qué?

PEDRO: Pues, conserva energía, reduce el uso de la electricidad y siempre funciona.

ESTEBAN: ¿De veras? ¿Siempre funciona?

PEDRO: Debemos mejorar nuestras formas de energía. Usar mejor lo que tenemos. ¿Ves? El autobús, por ejemplo, es muy eficiente.

ESTEBAN: Sí, y es bastante económico.

PEDRO: Debemos montar más en bicicleta para reducir la contaminación. Necesitamos aire puro.

ESTEBAN: Sí, pero con tanto calor. El coche es más cómodo y más rápido.

PEDRO: Ay, Esteban, pero podemos ahorrar energía y dinero al mismo tiempo.

ESTEBAN: Sí, Pedro, debemos conservar y proteger el medio ambiente, pero ahora vamos al cine. Hace un calor terrible.

ESTEBAN: Perdón, ¿no tienen aire acondicionado?

PERSON AT TICKET COUNTER: No, y dudo que lo tengamos mañana.

ESTEBAN: Sí, Angélica. Aquí, Esteban. Oye, ¿nos puedes venir a recoger en tu coche?

ANGÉLICA: ¡Esteban…!

***GramActiva* Videos, (7:41)**

The future tense: other irregular verbs

HOST: Let's take a look at some more verbs with irregular stems.

V.O.: *Poner, salir,* and *venir* have similar conjugations. They all have *-dr-* at the end of their stems. *Pondr-, saldr-, vendr-*.

HOST: *Poner.*

Pondré, pondrás, pondrá, pondremos, pondréis, pondrán.
Salir.
Saldré, saldrás, saldrá, saldremos, saldréis, saldrán.
Venir.
Vendré, vendrás, vendrá, vendremos, vendréis, vendrán.
Decir.
Diré, dirás, dirá, diremos, diréis, dirán.
Querer.
Querré, querrás, querrá, querremos, querréis, querrán.

V.O.: *Pondremos más globos en nuestro cuarto.*
En el futuro querremos vivir en Marte.
En el futuro dirán que la destrucción de las selvas tropicales causó muchos problemas ecológicos.

HOST: Think you're an irregular verb whiz? Then check out this quiz.

Quiz

V.O.: Fill in the blank with the correct future tense form of the verb.
(salir) Yo ______ temprano mañana.
Yo saldré temprano mañana.
(venir) Tú ______ conmigo a la playa.
Tú vendrás conmigo a la playa.
(querer) Ellas ______ paz.
Ellas querrán paz.

The present subjunctive with expressions of doubt

HOST: We've come to the final episode of *GramActiva.* Number 72 out of 72 grammar topics that you've studied. We thought we'd take a look back and remember the good times we've had and not actually study any grammar. Ah, who are we kidding? Bring on the expressions of doubt!

V.O.: Do you remember the subjunctive? It's baaaaack!

COACH: *Necesito que lave el coche.* And make it snappy!

HOST: Since the subjunctive usually deals with things like wishes and opinions, it's not a far stretch to use it for wishes and opinions that you're *[loses balance a bit]* not totally sure about. If you hear any of the following expressions of doubt, you need to use the subjunctive after these expressions. Woah!

V.O.: *Dudar que.* [to doubt]
No creer que. [to not believe]
No estar seguro(a) de que. [to be unsure]
Es posible que. [it's possible]
Es imposible que. [it's impossible]
No es cierto que. [it's not certain]

SCRATCHY HOST: If you've been itching to use the verb *hay* in the subjunctive, you're in luck. The subjunctive of *hay* is *haya*.

HANDYMAN: Is it really almost the end of *GramActiva?*

OLD MAN: *No creo que sea el final.*

FOREMAN: *Es posible que sea un chiste.*

FORTUNE TELLER: *Yo dudo que haya más* GramActiva.

EXCLAMATION MAN: *¡Es imposible que no haya más* GramActiva!

COWBOY: *Oh, es posible.*

PRODUCER: Psst! Cowboy! I know we're trying to build up to this dramatic ending and all, but I still need you to do an example sentence in the subjunctive.

COWBOY: Oh, right! Jolly good!
No es cierto que haya más trabajo para nosotros.

GUITAR GUY: Well, if that's the case, then there's just one thing left to do.

GAL: You're right. Let's have a quiz.

Quiz

V.O.: Complete the sentences with the appropriate form of the subjunctive:
(ahorrar) Es posible que ellos ______ mucha energía.
Es posible que ellos ahorren mucha energía.
(haber) Dudo que ______ un valle allí.
Dudo que haya un valle allí.
(tener) No estoy seguro de que Ud. no ______ más preguntas.
No estoy seguro de que Ud. no tenga más preguntas.

EVERYONE: *¡Hasta luego y buena suerte de sus amigos de* GramActiva!

Nombre ______________________

Fecha ______________________

Communicative Pair Activity **9B-1**

Estudiante **A**

Entrevista con ______________________

Interview a classmate. Ask your partner the following questions about his or her ideas regarding nature and the environment. Record your partner's answers on the lines provided.

1. ¿Cuál es tu animal favorito?

____

____

2. ¿Qué te gustan más, las selvas o los desiertos? ¿Por qué?

____

____

3. ¿Sabes qué es reciclar? ¿Reciclas tú?

____

____

4. ¿Te gusta el ecoturismo? ¿Por qué?

____

____

5. ¿Hay contaminación de aire en tu ciudad?

____

____

Nombre ____________________

Fecha ____________________

Communicative Pair Activity **9B-1**
Estudiante **B**

Entrevista con ____________________

Interview a classmate. Ask your partner the following questions about his or her ideas regarding nature and the environment. Record your partner's answers on the lines provided.

1. ¿Sabes cómo ahorrar agua?

   ____

   ____

2. ¿Por qué hay animales en peligro de extinción?

   ____

   ____

3. ¿Conoces una fuente natural de energía?

   ____

   ____

4. ¿Qué cosas se pueden reciclar?

   ____

   ____

5. ¿En tu ciudad cómo se junta la gente para mejorar el medio ambiente?

   ____

   ____

Realidades 2

Capítulo 9B

Nombre ______________________

Fecha ______________________

Communicative Pair Activity **9B-2**

Estudiante **A**

You and your friends go outdoors for an ecology class. Your teacher splits the class into groups so each group can explore a different environment. Ask your partner who went where by using the cues below. Example: *¿Quiénes están en la selva?* Record his or her answers on the lines provided.

1.

____

3.

____

5.

____

2.

____

4.

____

6.

____

Use the following information to answer your partner's questions.

Silvia y Carlos

Mauricio, Helena, Rafael y María

Alberto y Juana

Pedro y Luisa

Sofía, Jorge y Rosa

Realidades 2

Capítulo 9B

Nombre ______________________________

Fecha ______________________________

Communicative Pair Activity **9B-2**

Estudiante **B**

Use the following information to answer your partner's questions.

Raul, Juanita, Susana y Ramón

Juan, Benito, Lina y Melisa

Paula, Carmen, Jaime y Camilo

José, Daniela, Pablo y Carolina

Silvia, David, Adriana y Eduardo

Luis, Gabriela, Ana y Gustavo

You and your friends went outdoors to enjoy the environment. All of you like different activities. Ask your partner who did what activity by using the cues below. Example: *¿Quiénes hicieron moto acuática?* Record his or her answers on the lines provided.

1.

____

2.

____

3.

____

4.

____

5.

____

Realidades 2

Capítulo 9B

Situation Cards

Capítulo 9B — Realidades 2 — 1A

Describing the natural environment

You are talking with a friend about places you enjoy. Think about a place outdoors that you think is beautiful.

— Mention this place to your friend.

— Respond to your friend's questions.

— Then ask your friend about his or her favorite outdoor destination and about why he or she likes it so much.

Capítulo 9B — Realidades 2 — 1B

Describing the natural environment

You are talking with a friend about places you enjoy. Think about a place outdoors that you think is beautiful.

— Respond to your friend's choice of a favorite place by asking why he or she likes it so much and what he or she likes to do there.

— Respond to your friend's question. Then, ask what must be done to protect the place.

Capítulo 9B — Realidades 2 — 2A

Discussing outdoor activities

You and a friend are planning a weekend camping trip, but you've never been camping before. Think of three activities you would like to do on the trip.

— Suggest one of the activities and ask your friend what you would need to bring in order to do it.

— Suggest the second activity and ask what he or she thinks of it.

— Mention the third activity and ask if he or she would like to do it also.

Capítulo 9B — Realidades 2 — 2B

Discussing outdoor activities

Your friend is accompanying you on a camping trip. He or she has never been camping before and has some questions for you (an experienced camper).

— Respond to your friend's questions offering suggestions and advice as needed, including items he or she should bring along.

GramActiva

¿Qué haremos para mejorar el mundo?
En el presente y en el futuro, p. 486

	yo (ahora)	yo (futuro)	mi compañero(a) (ahora)	mi compañero(a) (futuro)
vivir				
salir con				
tener que				
querer				
saber (+ *infinitivo*)				
¡Respuesta personal!				

Vocabulary Clip Art

Vocabulary Clip Art

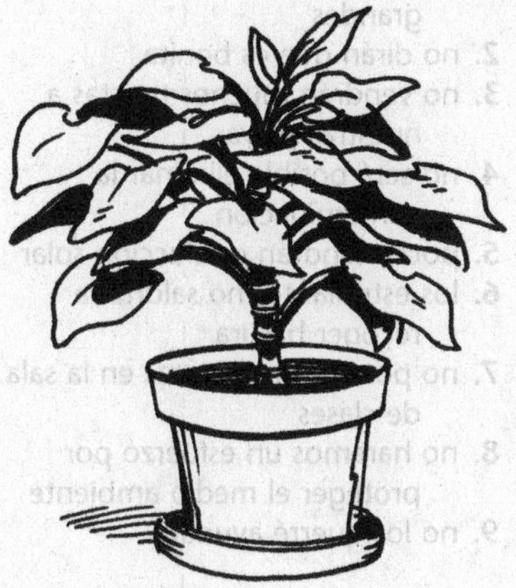

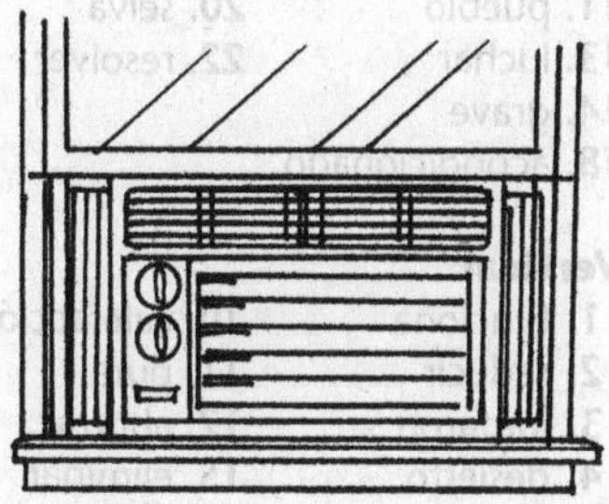

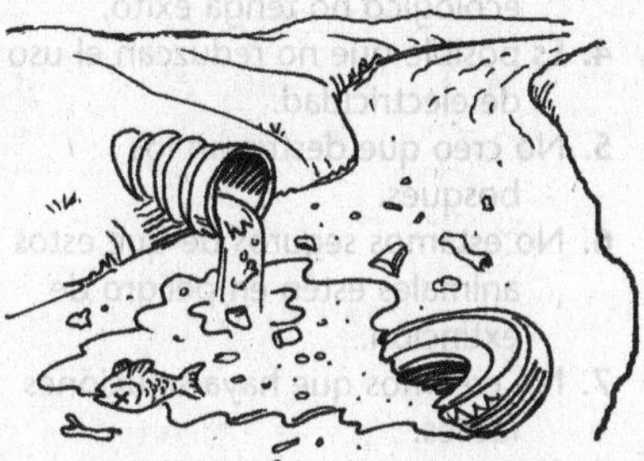

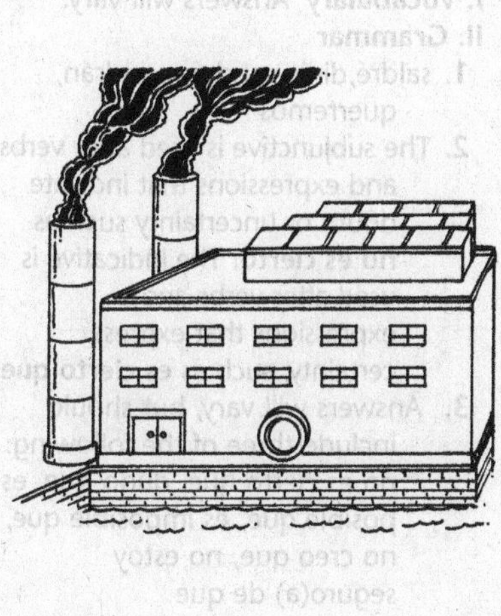

Core Practice Answers

9B-1
1. contaminada
2. peligro, extinción
3. la electricidad
4. ambiente
5. selvas tropicales
6. la naturaleza
7. ecológico
8. la Tierra

9B-2
A.

1. protejamos	5. eliminar
2. mejorar	6. reducir
3. se junten	7. destruyendo
4. luchan	8. resuelve

B.
nos juntamos / ecológico / resolver / luchar / medio ambiente / grave / contaminación / fuentes

9B-3
1. económico
2. el aire acondicionado
3. conservar
4. pura
5. ahorrar
6. fuente
7. la Luna
8. la calefacción
9. selvas tropicales
10. pueblo
11. guerras
12. paz

9B-4
1. Una de las causas más graves es la destrucción de los árboles.
2. Podemos reciclar el papel para conservar los bosques.
3. Una manera de ahorrar la energía y reducir el aire contaminado es montar en bicicleta en vez de manejar en coche.
4. La paz es necesario para resolver los problemas políticos del mundo.
5. Si la Tierra se contamine demasiado, podemos ir al espacio.
6. El desierto es un lugar perfecto para usar la calefacción solar.
7. Es necesario reducir el petróleo porque causa el aire contaminado.

9B-5
1. no habrá muchos bosques grandes
2. no dirán que es bonita
3. no vendrán muchos turistas a nuestras playas
4. no será posible eliminar la contaminación
5. pocos tendrán calefacción solar
6. los estudiantes no saldrán a recoger basura
7. no pondremos plantas en la sala de clases
8. no haremos un esfuerzo por proteger el medio ambiente
9. no los querré ayudar

9B-6
1. Dudamos que resuelvan estos problemas ecológicos.
2. No creo que los estudiantes se junten para conservar la naturaleza.
3. Es imposible que el grupo ecológico no tenga éxito.
4. Es posible que no reduzcan el uso de electricidad.
5. No creo que destruyan los bosques.
6. No estamos seguros de que estos animales estén en peligro de extinción.
7. No creemos que haya soluciones fáciles.
8. No es cierto que sea difícil mejorar la situación del agua.
9. Dudo que se pueda eliminar toda la contaminación.

9B-7
1. Yo digo que salvarán los animales en el futuro.
   Yo dudo que salven los animales en el futuro.
2. Yo digo que reducirán la contaminación en el futuro.
   Yo dudo que reduzcan la contaminación en el futuro.
3. Yo digo que mejorarán el agua en el futuro.
   Yo dudo que mejoren el agua en el futuro.
4. Yo digo que habrá pocos problemas con el medio ambiente en el futuro.
   Yo dudo que haya pocos problemas con el medio ambiente en el futuro.
5. Yo digo que pasarán leyes estrictas sobre la contaminación en el futuro.
   Yo dudo que pasen leyes estrictas sobre la contaminación en el futuro.
6. Yo digo que protegerán los bosques en el futuro.
   Yo dudo que protejan los bosques en el futuro.
7. Yo digo que habrá menos contaminación del aire en el futuro.
   Yo dudo que haya menos contaminación del aire en el futuro.
8. Yo digo que usarán otras fuentes de energía en el futuro.
   Yo dudo que usen otras fuentes de energía en el futuro.

Crucigrama (9B-8)
Horizontal:

8. contaminación	19. peligro
11. pueblo	20. selva
13. luchar	22. resolver
14. grave	
18. acondicionado	

Vertical:

1. funciona	10. calefacción
2. reducir	11. pura
3. juntaron	12. ahorrar
4. desierto	15. eliminar
5. fuentes	16. manera
6. luna	17. contaminada
7. ecológico	19. proteger
9. medio	21. valle

Organizer (1A-9)
I. Vocabulary Answers will vary.
II. Grammar
1. saldré,dirás,vendrá, pondrán, querremos
2. The subjunctive is used after verbs and expressions that indicate doubt or uncertainty such as **no es cierto**. The indicative is used after verbs and expressions that express certainty, such as **es cierto que**.
3. Answers will vary, but should include three of the following: no es cierto que, dudo que, es posible que, es imposible que, no creo que, no estoy seguro(a) de que

Nombre ______ Hora ______

Fecha ______

Vocabulary Flash Cards, Sheet 1

Write the Spanish vocabulary word below each picture. Be sure to include the article for each noun.

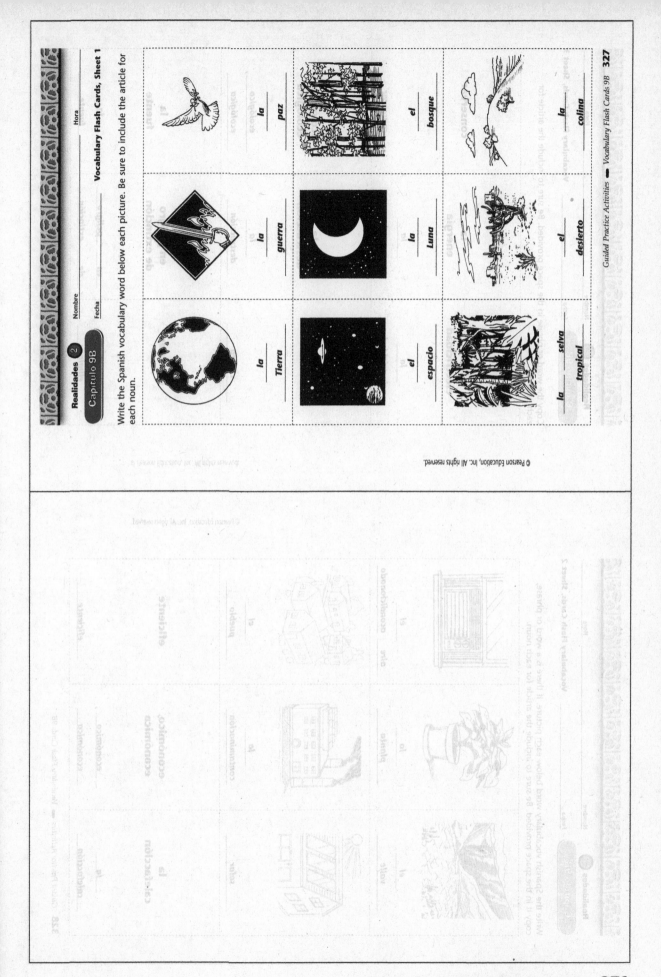

la *Tierra*

la *guerra*

la *paz*

el *espacio*

la *Luna*

el *bosque*

la *selva* *tropical*

el *desierto*

la *colina*

Vocabulary Flash Cards, Sheet 2

Write the Spanish vocabulary word below each picture. If there is a word or phrase, copy it in the space provided. Be sure to include the article for each noun.

el
valle

la
planta

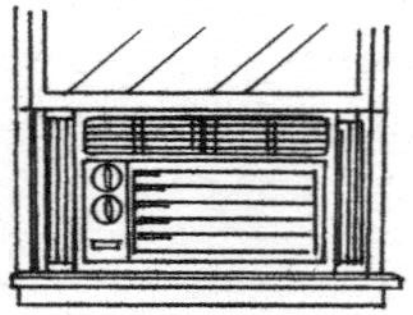

el
aire acondicionado

solar

la
contaminación

el
pueblo

la calefacción

la
calefacción

económico, económica

económico ,
económica

eficiente

eficiente

Vocabulary Flash Cards, Sheet 3

Copy the word or phrase in the space provided. Be sure to include the article for each noun.

la electricidad

la
electricidad

la energía

la
energía

conservar

conservar

contra

contra

la destrucción

la
destrucción

ecológico, ecológica

ecológico ,
ecológica

eliminar

eliminar

en peligro de extinción

en *peligro*
de *extinción*

la fuente

la
fuente

Realidades 2 | Nombre ____ Hora ____

Capítulo 9B | Fecha ____

Vocabulary Flash Cards, Sheet 4

Copy the word or phrase in the space provided. Be sure to include the article for each noun.

funcionar *funcionar*	**grave** *grave*	**juntarse** *juntarse*
luchar *luchar*	**la manera** *la* *manera*	**el medio ambiente** *el* *medio* *ambiente*
mejorar *mejorar*	**proteger** *proteger*	**puro, pura** *puro*, *pura*

Realidades 2 | Nombre ____ Hora ____

Capítulo 9B | Fecha ____

Vocabulary Flash Cards, Sheet 5

Copy the word or phrase in the space provided. Be sure to include the article for each noun.

reducir *reducir*	**resolver** *resolver*	**además (de)** *además* *(de)*
dudar *dudar*	**es cierto** *es* *cierto*	**haya** *haya*
ahorrar *ahorrar*	**la naturaleza** *la* *naturaleza*	**contaminado, contaminada** *contaminado*, *contaminada*

Realidades 2 | Nombre | Hora

Capítulo 9B | Fecha

Vocabulary Flash Cards, Sheet 6

These blank cards can be used to write and practice other Spanish vocabulary for the chapter.

Realidades 2 | Nombre | Hora

Capítulo 9B | Fecha

Vocabulary Check, Sheet 1

Tear out this page. Write the English words on the lines. Fold the paper along the dotted line to see the correct answers so you can check your work.

la naturaleza	***nature***
el bosque	***forest***
el desierto	***desert***
la selva tropical	***rain forest***
el aire acondicionado	***air conditioning***
la calefacción	***heat***
la electricidad	***electricity***
la energía	***energy***
conservar	***to conserve***
la contaminación	***pollution***
contaminado, contaminada	***polluted***
la destrucción	***destruction***
ecológico, ecológica	***ecological***
el medio ambiente	***environment***

Fold In ←

Realidades 2 | Nombre | Hora

Capítulo 9B | Fecha

Vocabulary Check, Sheet 2

Tear out this page. Write the Spanish words on the lines. Fold the paper along the dotted line to see the correct answers so you can check your work.

nature	***la naturaleza***
forest	***el bosque***
desert	***el desierto***
rain forest	***la selva tropical***
air conditioning	***el aire acondicionado***
heat	***la calefacción***
electricity	***la electricidad***
energy	***la energía***
to conserve	***conservar***
pollution	***la contaminación***
polluted	***contaminado, contaminada***
destruction	***la destrucción***
ecological	***ecológico, ecológica***
environment	***el medio ambiente***

Fold In ←

Realidades 2 | Nombre | Hora

Capítulo 9B | Fecha

Vocabulary Check, Sheet 3

Tear out this page. Write the English words on the lines. Fold the paper along the dotted line to see the correct answers so you can check your work.

el espacio	***(outer) space***
la Luna	***the moon***
la Tierra	***Earth***
económico, económica	***economical***
eficiente	***efficient***
contra	***against***
en peligro de extinción	***endangered, in danger of extinction***
funcionar	***to function, to work***
luchar	***to fight***
mejorar	***to improve***
reducir	***to reduce***
además (de)	***in addition (to), besides***
dudar	***to doubt***
proteger	***to protect***

Fold In ←

Realidades 2 Nombre ______ Hora ______

Capítulo 9B Fecha ______ **Vocabulary Check, Sheet 4**

Tear out this page. Write the Spanish words on the lines. Fold the paper along the dotted line to see the correct answers so you can check your work.

(outer) space	***el espacio***
the moon	***la Luna***
Earth	***la Tierra***
economical	***económico, económica***
efficient	***eficiente***
against	***contra***
endangered, in danger of extinction	***en peligro de extinción***
to function, to work	***funcionar***
to fight	***luchar***
to improve	***mejorar***
to reduce	***reducir***
in addition (to), besides	***además (de)***
to doubt	***dudar***
to protect	***proteger***

Fold In

To hear a complete list of the vocabulary for this chapter, go to www.realidades.com and type in the Web Code jdd-0999. Then click on **Repaso del capítulo.**

Realidades 2 Nombre ______ Hora ______

Capítulo 9B Fecha ______ **Guided Practice Activities 9B-1**

The future tense: other irregular verbs (p. 484)

- Other verbs that have irregular stems in the future tense are:
  decir → dir- **querer → querr-** **salir → saldr-**
  poner → pondr- **venir → vendr-**
- Here is the future tense of the verb **querer:**

QUERER			
yo	**querré**	nosotros/nosotras	**querremos**
tú	**querrás**	vosotros/vosotras	**querréis**
usted/él/ella	**querrá**	ustedes/ellos/ellas	**querrán**

A. Look at each sentence and write the infinitive form of the underlined verb.

Modelo Ellos dirán que nuestro valle es bonito. *Infinitive:* ***decir***

1. Nosotros pondremos plantas en las salas de clases. *Infinitive:* ***poner***
2. Yo querré conservar la naturaleza. *Infinitive:* ***querer***
3. Los turistas no vendrán a nuestro pueblo. *Infinitive:* ***venir***
4. Tú saldrás a luchar contra la contaminación. *Infinitive:* ***salir***
5. Ustedes dirán que el agua está contaminada. *Infinitive:* ***decir***

B. Complete the following exchanges by writing the correct future form of the verb in parentheses. Follow the model.

Modelo PEDRO: ¿Qué ***dirán*** ustedes del medio ambiente? **(decir)**
ILIANA: Nosotros ***diremos*** que está muy contaminado. **(decir)**

1. PEDRO: ¿Cuándo ***saldrán*** ustedes al bosque? **(salir)**
   ILIANA: Nosotros ***saldremos*** por la mañana. **(salir)**
2. PEDRO: ¿Qué ***querrás*** hacer tú para proteger el medio ambiente? **(querer)**
   ILIANA: Yo ***querré*** usar la energía solar. **(querer)**
3. PEDRO: ¿Tu hermana ***pondrá*** más plantas en la casa? **(poner)**
   ILIANA: Sí, y ella también ***pondrá*** flores. **(poner)**
4. PEDRO: ¿Ella ***vendrá*** con nosotros a proteger la selva tropical? **(venir)**
   ILIANA: Sí, ella y mis hermanos ***vendrán***. **(venir)**

realidades.com
• Web Code: jdd-0913

The future tense: other irregular verbs (*continued*)

C. Look at the pictures and read the sentences. Then, look at the verb choices in parentheses and complete each sentence with the appropriate future form of the verb you choose. Follow the model.

Modelo Tú ***querrás*** reducir la contaminación. (querer / salir)

1. Ellos no ***querrán*** destruir el bosque. (querer / venir)

2. Nosotros ***diremos*** que debemos conservar energía en nuestra casa. (querer / decir)

3. Todos los estudiantes ***vendrán*** en bicicleta para reducir la contaminación del aire. (venir / poner)

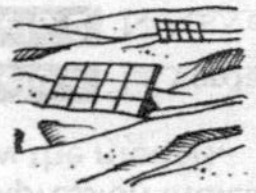

4. Nosotros ***pondremos*** energía solar en nuestras casas. (salir / poner)

5. Si hay demasiada contaminación en la Tierra, Federico ***saldrá*** al espacio. (salir / venir)

The present subjunctive with expressions of doubt (p. 487)

- In the same way that the subjunctive is used with impersonal expressions and to communicate a desire to influence someone else's actions, it is also used after verbs and expressions of doubt or uncertainty. Some expressions of doubt or uncertainty are:

dudar que	*to doubt that*
no es cierto que	*it is not certain that*
no creer que	*to not believe that*
no estar seguro, -a de que	*to be unsure that*
es imposible que	*it is impossible that*
es posible que	*it is possible that*

No es cierto que puedan proteger el medio ambiente.
It is not certain that they can protect the environment.

A. In the sentences below, underline the expressions that indicate uncertainty or doubt. Then, circle the verbs in the subjunctive form. The first one is done for you.

1. Es imposible que nosotros no cuidemos la Tierra.
2. Dudo que nosotros no luchemos contra la contaminación.
3. Es posible que muchos animales estén en peligro de extinción.
4. No es cierto que en nuestra casa usemos mucha energía.
5. Nosotros no creemos que ellos no cuiden la colina.
6. No estoy seguro de que los bosques se conserven bien.
7. Es imposible que nosotros no protejamos la naturaleza.

Realidades 2 | Nombre ____ | Hora ____

Capítulo 9B | Fecha ____ | **Guided Practice Activities 9B-4**

The present subjunctive with expressions of doubt (*continued*)

- While the subjunctive is used to show uncertainty, the indicative is used to show certainty. Compare these sentences:
  No es cierto que ellas ahorren energía. *It is not certain that they will save energy.*
  Es cierto que ellos ahorran energía. *It is certain that they are saving energy.*

B. Read the following sentences and underline the expressions of doubt or certainty. If the expression indicates certainty, write **C.** If it indicates doubt or uncertainty, write **D.** Follow the models.

Modelo 1 Es verdad que tenemos que reducir la contaminación. C

Modelo 2 No es verdad que tengamos que reciclar. D

1. No creemos que el aire esté contaminado. D
2. Estamos seguros de que muchos animales están en peligro de extinción. C
3. Creo que la energía solar es muy eficiente. C
4. No estoy seguro de que sea económico usar la calefacción. D
5. Es cierto que los problemas ecológicos se resuelven. C
6. Creo que debemos conservar energía. C

C. Circle the correct form of the verbs in parentheses to complete each sentence. Use the expression of doubt or certainty in each sentence to choose whether you circle the present subjunctive or the present indicative.

1. Yo estoy seguro de que nosotros (**podamos** / **podemos**) cuidar la Tierra.
2. Mis profesores creen que los niños de hoy (**trabajan** / **trabajen**) mucho para conservar energía.
3. Es imposible que los Estados Unidos (**usa** / **use**) menos energía que otros países.
4. Dudamos que tú (**estés** / **estás**) preocupado por la conservación de los bosques.
5. Es cierto que Uds. (**quieren** / **quieran**) resolver los problemas ecológicos.
6. No es cierto que los norteamericanos (**destruyan** / **destruyen**) los bosques.

Realidades 2 | Nombre ____ | Hora ____

Capítulo 9B | Fecha ____ | **Guided Practice Activities 9B-4a**

The present subjunctive with expressions of doubt (*continued*)

- The subjunctive form of **hay** is **haya**, from the verb **haber**:
  Es posible que haya suficiente electricidad.
  *It is possible that **there is** enough electricity.*

D. Complete the sentences by writing either the indicative form **hay** or the subjunctive form **haya**. Follow the model.

Modelo ¿No crees que *haya* un problema grave?

1. Dudamos que **haya** una fuente de energía nueva.
2. Es cierto que **hay** mucha destrucción en las selvas tropicales.
3. Él está seguro de que **hay** una manera de reducir la contaminación.
4. Es imposible que **haya** vida en el espacio.
5. Es posible que **haya** desiertos en la Luna.

E. Complete the following advertisement with the subjunctive or the indicative form of the verbs given. The first one is done for you.

¿Dudas que tu ayuda *sea* (**ser**) importante para la Tierra? ¿No estás seguro de que los humanos **puedan** (**poder**) hacer cambios importantes para la naturaleza? Debes visitar el parque zoológico Las Palmas. Aquí sabrás que ¡es cierto que nosotros **trabajamos** (**trabajar**) para los animales que están en peligro de extinción! ¡Es posible que una corporación grande **conserve** (**conservar**) agua y energía! ¡Es imposible que tú no **ayudes** (**ayudar**) a la causa! En el zoológico Las Palmas, sabemos que tú **vas** (**ir**) a divertirte. Creemos que tú y tu familia **protegen** (**proteger**) la naturaleza mientras observan los animales. Juntos, es posible que nosotros **luchemos** (**luchar**) contra la extinción.

Lectura: Protegemos la Antártida (pp. 492–493)

A. When you read an article, you should be aware that the writer may have strong opinions about the issues. Identify and circle the words below that indicate an opinion.

(Dudo...)	Hay...	Sabemos...
(Es peligroso...)	(Es importante...)	Se llama...

B. Read the following paragraph from the article in your textbook. You may not know some of the words and phrases below from the article. Try to determine the meaning of them from their context in the paragraph and from what you already know about the Antarctic.

> *¡Estamos en peligro!*
> *Las regiones polares son muy importantes para la supervivencia de la Tierra entera. Los casquetes de hielo en las zonas polares reflejan luz solar y así regularizan la temperatura de la Tierra. Cuando se destruyen estos casquetes, hay menos luz solar que se refleja y la Tierra se convierte en un receptor termal. Esto se llama el efecto de invernadero. Es en la Antártida que en 1985 se reportaron por primera vez los hoyos en la capa del ozono y aquí es donde hoy día se trata de encontrar una solución.*

1. casquetes de hielo	a. holes	(b.) ice caps
2. efecto de invernadero	(a.) greenhouse effect	b. point of departure
3. supervivencia	a. abundance	(b.) survival
4. hoyos	(a.) holes	b. scientific teams
5. capa del ozono	a. rules	(b.) ozone layer

C. Determine the author's point of view in the paragraph in **part B** by circling the letter of the correct ending for each sentence.

1. Según el título, el autor cree que ______
   a. todo va bien.
   (b.) todo no va bien.
2. El autor cree que las regiones polares ______
   (a.) son importantes para la Tierra.
   b. no sirven para nada.
3. Es posible que el autor piense que ______
   (a.) es necesario resolver el problema de los hoyos en la capa del ozono.
   b. los hoyos en la capa del ozono son buenos para la Tierra.

realidades.com • Web Code: jdd-0915

Presentación escrita (p. 495) *Answers will vary.*

Task: Write an article for the daily paper explaining your volunteer project to improve your community.

A. Choose a volunteer project from the box or write one that you would like to do in your community.

- recoger basura en un parque
- comenzar un programa para reciclar periódicos viejos
- ahorrar dinero para proteger a los animales en peligro de extinción
- ______

B. Based on the project you chose in **part A,** complete the following sentences by circling one of the options listed.

1. Para este proyecto trabajaré
   a. todos los días. b. los fines de semana.
2. Pueden participar
   a. personas mayores. b. todas las personas.
3. Es importante porque
   a. protegemos el medio ambiente. b. ayudamos a las personas.

C. Use your answers from **part B** to answer the following questions about your volunteer project. You may use the model to help you.

Modelo

¿Qué ...?	*Me gustaría recoger basura en un parque.*
¿Quién(es)...?	*Mis amigos y yo vamos a trabajar juntos.*
¿Por qué...?	*Queremos tener un medio ambiente limpio y sano.*
¿Dónde...?	*Vamos a trabajar en el parque del centro de la ciudad.*
¿Cuándo...?	*Trabajaremos todos los fines de semana durante el verano.*

1. ¿Qué...? ______
2. ¿Quién(es)...? ______
3. ¿Por qué...? ______
4. ¿Dónde...? ______
5. ¿Cuándo...? ______

D. Use your answers in **part C** to write your article. Check for correct spelling, verb forms, and vocabulary, and rewrite your article if necessary.

Antes de ver el video

Actividad 1

Make a list of five things that can affect the environment or the Earth in general. One has been done for you.

1. *guerra*
2.
3.
4.
5.

¿Comprendes?

Actividad 2

Answer the following questions in order to better understand what happened in the video.

Wording will vary.

1. Pedro está en casa de Esteban. ¿Qué pasa?

Pedro y Esteban están jugando videojuegos.

2. ¿Qué piensa Pedro?

Pedro piensa que el aire acondicionado no funciona.

3. Ellos tienen mucho calor. ¿Adónde deciden ir y por qué?

Ellos quieren ir al cine porque allí hay aire acondicionado.

4. ¿De qué hablan Esteban y Pedro cuando van caminando al cine?

Hablan de conservar energía y reducir la contaminación.

5. ¿A quién llama Esteban por el teléfono celular y para qué?

Esteban llama a Angélica para que los recoja en su coche.

Actividad 3

Pedro and Esteban are talking about the good and bad effects things we use every day have on the environment. Write what each boy says about the following things.

Modelo bicicleta
Pedro: *reduce la contaminación y ahorra dinero*
Esteban: *el coche es más cómodo y más rápido*

Suggested answers below summarize the boys' views.

1. aire acondicionado solar
Pedro: **conserva energía y reduce el uso de electricidad**
Esteban: **nunca se rompe**

2. aire acondicionado
Pedro: **es caro y consume mucha energía (electricidad)**
Esteban: **es importante en los días de mucho calor**

3. coche
Pedro: **contamina el aire y el medio ambiente**
Esteban: **es rápido y cómodo**

4. autobús
Pedro: **es eficiente y económico**
Esteban: **es bastante económico pero no tan rápido como el coche**

Realidades 2 | Nombre ______ | Hora ______

Capítulo 9B | Fecha ______ | VIDEO

Actividad 4

Pedro has some good ideas about how to protect and preserve the environment but he cannot convince Esteban. Think about one way to protect and preserve the environment. Then, write three complete sentences to tell why your idea is important.

1. Answers will vary.
2. ______
3. ______

Realidades 2 | Nombre ______ | Hora ______

Capítulo 9B | Fecha ______ | AUDIO

Actividad 5

Listen to the following people talk about the future. As you hear each statement, determine whether the speaker is an optimist or a pessimist and place a check mark in the corresponding box in the grid. You will hear each statement twice.

	1	2	3	4	5	6	7	8
Optimista	✓			✓		✓		✓
Pesimista		✓	✓		✓		✓	

Actividad 6

Listen as students in Sr. Naranjo's science class make predictions about the year 2020. As you hear each one, mark the number of the description underneath the picture it describes. Then, mark an X in the grid below to tell whether you agree with the prediction or doubt it will come true. Be prepared to tell why you answered the way you did. You will hear each prediction twice.

6   1   4   7

5   3   2

Answers will vary since these are opinions. Suggested answers below.

	1	2	3	4	5	6	7
Lo dudo	X	X			X	X	
Estoy de acuerdo			X	X			X

Realidades 2 Nombre ____ Hora ____

Capítulo 9B Fecha ____ **AUDIO**

Actividad 7

Listen as Julia and Elena plan Julia's campaign for class president. Some of the campaign promises they come up with are a) silly and not possible, while others are b) serious and possible. As you listen to each idea, write **a** or **b** in the blanks provided. You will hear each statement twice.

1. a 2. b 3. a 4. b 5. a 6. a 7. b 8. a

Actividad 8

The debate coach is observing a mock debate in order to determine whom she will select as partners (**compañeros**) for an upcoming debate on **"El futuro para nosotros."** Listen as the debaters answer the coach's questions. Fill in the chart below by circling each debater's opinion on the three issues. Which two people share the most opinions? You will hear each conversation twice.

	Las escuelas sin profesores	La paz mundial (*world peace*)	Vivir en la Luna
Ramón	Es posible **Es imposible**	Es posible **Es imposible**	Es posible **Es imposible**
Sandra	**Es posible** Es imposible	**Es posible** Es imposible	**Es posible** Es imposible
Lucas	Es posible **Es imposible**	Es posible **Es imposible**	Es posible **Es imposible**

¿Quiénes deben ser compañeros? Ramón y Lucas

Actividad 9

Listen to this class discussion about the problems in the world and solutions for a better *world in the future. As you hear each comment, decide if the person is describing a problem* or offering a solution. Place a check mark in the appropriate column in the grid below. You will hear each comment twice.

	1	2	3	4	5	6	7	8
Problema	✓			✓	✓		✓	
Solución		✓	✓			✓		✓

Realidades 2 Nombre ____ Hora ____

Capítulo 9B Fecha ____ **WRITING**

Actividad 10

Look at the drawings below of environmental problems and their solutions. Describe how each one affects the environment. Write two complete sentences for each. Follow the model.

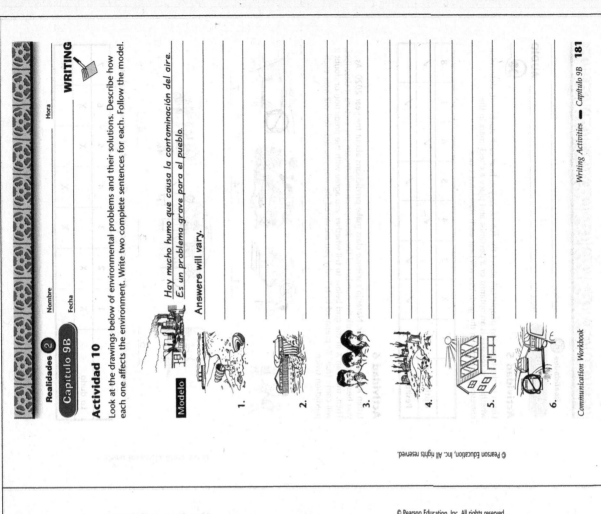

Modelo 
Hay mucho humo que causa la contaminación del aire.
Es un problema grave para el pueblo.

1. Answers will vary.

2.

3.

4.

5.

6.

Realidades 2 | Capítulo 9B

Nombre ____ Hora ____

Fecha ____ **WRITING**

Actividad 11

The Valencia family is making plans to move to a new house. Look at the pictures below and tell what each person is planning, using the future tense of the verbs provided.

Answers will vary. Possible answers:

1. yo (poner)
Yo pondré la cama cerca de la ventana de mi cuarto nuevo.

2. Marisa (querer)
Marisa querrá un espejo nuevo en su cuarto.

3. nosotros (salir)
Nosotros saldremos de la casa el quince de mayo.

4. mis amigos (venir)
Mis amigos vendrán a la fiesta en mi casa nueva.

5. yo (hacer)
Yo haré cortinas nuevas para las ventanas.

6. tú (decir)
Tú dirás que la casa es....

Realidades 2 | Capítulo 9B

Nombre ____ Hora ____

Fecha ____ **WRITING**

Actividad 12

Humberto is listening to the president's speech on the radio and is skeptical about what he hears. Read the excerpts below from the speech and write Humberto's reactions using phrases to express doubt. The first one has been done for you.

Los Estados Unidos deben ahorrar sus recursos naturales. Tendremos que conservar energía y reciclar para poder disfrutar una buena vida. Yo quiero reducir la contaminación del medio ambiente en los años que vienen...

También, quiero hacer planes para resolver nuestros conflictos internacionales. No podemos vivir si seguimos luchando entre países...

... Tenemos un problema con la economía. Les sugiero que los mejores economistas trabajen para mejorarla... Todos tienen que juntarse para proteger la Tierra... Mi plan puede funcionar si todos trabajamos juntos.

1. *Dudo que conservemos energía.* **Answers will vary. Suggestions below.**
2. **Es posible que los Estados Unidos ahorren sus recursos naturales.**
3. **Es imposible que Ud. reduzca la contaminación del medio ambiente.**
4. **Es imposible que protejamos a todos los animales en peligro de extinción.**
5. **No estoy seguro de que Ud. vaya a resolver nuestros conflictos internacionales.**
6. **Es imposible que los economistas mejoren la economía.**
7. **Dudo que nos juntemos para proteger la Tierra.**
8. **Es imposible que su plan funcione.**

Actividad 13

You and your friends are proposing a plan to help preserve the environment, starting right in your own school.

A. Write a proposal to your school to launch your plan by listing five things you, your friends, and your school can do to make a difference. Use the future tense of some of the following verbs: **haber, hacer, poner, saber, decir, tener, venir, querer.** The first one has been done for you.

Tenemos que proteger nuestra Tierra. Por eso, nosotros haremos muchos cambios en nuestros hábitos:

- *Reciclaremos las latas y las botellas.*
- **Answers will vary.**
-
-
-
-

B. Next, persuade the administration to accept your proposal by describing the environmental consequences of your plan. The description has been started for you.

Si seguimos este plan, veremos muchos cambios importantes. Es seguro que la Tierra mejorará. Dudamos que la destrucción continúe.

Answers will vary.

Test Preparation Answers

Reading Skills
p. 286 2. **C**
p. 287 2. **B**

Integrated Performance Assessment
p. 288
Answers will vary.

Practice Test: Español, el idioma del futuro
p. 290

1. C
2. G
3. D
4. G
5. Las respuestas variarán, pero los estudiantes pueden citar la importancia del creciente mercado de hipanohablantes en los Estados Unidos y la importancia de los mercados en España y América Latina.
6. Las respuestas variarán, pero los estudiantes pueden citar lo siguiente: el español es el tercer o cuarto idioma que más se habla en el mundo; se habla el español en los cinco continentes; hay una gran población hispana en los Estados Unidos; en Brasil es obligatorio estudiarlo en las escuelas secundarias.

Notes

Notes

Notes

Notes

Notes

Notes

Notes